TOKYO
World Travel Guide

Author: **Patrick Duval**
Translation: **Tom Kessler**
Editor: **Lisa Davidson-Petty**
Photo credits:
Pix: J.-P. Abrial & Y. Seki, pp. 69, 123, 158, 263 — J.-P. Abrial, pp. 10, 53, 76, 115, 135, 171, 177 — Y. Seki, p. 101 — M. Trigalou, p. 45. **Patrick Duval:** pp. 40, 84, 93, 97, 105, 112, 127, 150-151, 185, 189, 196, 201, 208, 213, 244.

This edition published in Great Britain by **Bartholomew**, Duncan Street, Edinburgh, EH9, 1TA.
Bartholomew is a Division of HarperCollins *Publishers*.
This guide is adapted from *à Tokyo-Kyoto*, published by Hachette Guides de voyage, 1988.
© Hachette Guides de voyage, Paris, 1991. First edition.
English translation © Hachette Guides de voyage, Paris, 1991.
Maps © Hachette Guides de voyage, Paris, 1991.

British Library Cataloguing in Publication Data

Duval, Patrick

Tokyo.
1. Japan. Tokyo - Visitors' guides
I. Title II. [A Tokyo-Kyoto. English)
915.21350449

ISBN 0-7028-1285-4

Printed in France by AUBIN Imprimeur Liguré, Poitiers

·Bartholomew·

TOKYO
World Travel Guide

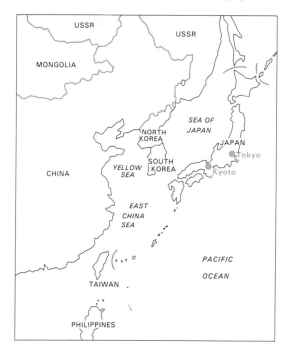

Bartholomew
A Division of HarperCollins*Publishers*

HOW TO USE YOUR GUIDE

● Before you leave home, read the sections **Planning Your Trip** p. 33, **Practical Information** p. 41, **Tokyo in the Past** p. 77 and **Tokyo Today** p. 85.

● The rest of the guide is for use once you arrive. It is divided into chapters discussing **cities** (Tokyo, Kyoto, Osaka). These chapters contain practical information (accommodation, useful addresses and so on) and include sections pointing out what to see in the particular city.

● Practical advice and information on people, places and events can be located quickly by referring to the **Index** p. 264. A **Glossary** p. 245 provides helpful definitions of Japanese terms and a **Useful Vocabulary** section p. 252 will help you with specific words and phrases you may hear or wish to use. For further information about Japan, consult the **Suggested Reading** section at the back of the book p. 262.

● To easily locate recommended sites, hotels and restaurants on the maps, refer to the map coordinates printed in blue in the text (example: II, C3, n° 3). The number or letter following the grid reference refers to a hotel or restaurant indicated on the map.

SYMBOLS USED

Sites, monuments, museums and points of interest

★★★ Exceptional
★★ Very interesting
★ Interesting

Hotels and Restaurants
See p. 217 (Tokyo Addresses)

MAPS

▬ CONTENTS

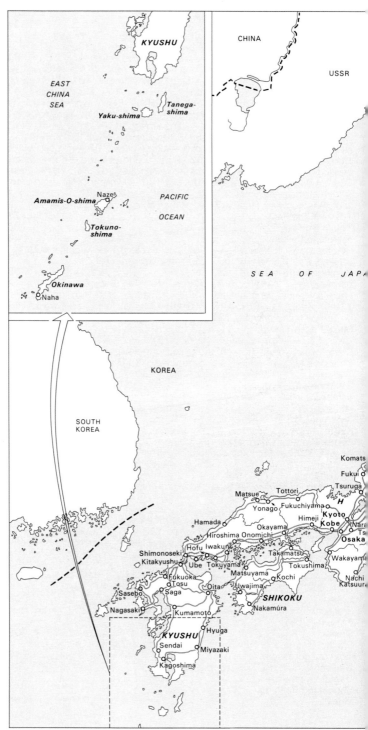

JAPAN

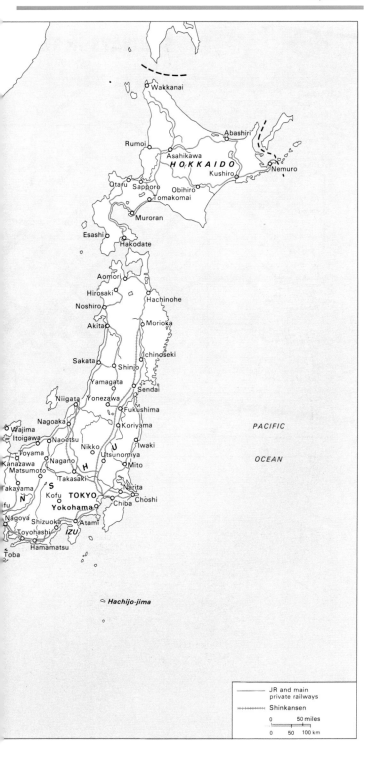

SUBWAYS IN TŌKYŌ

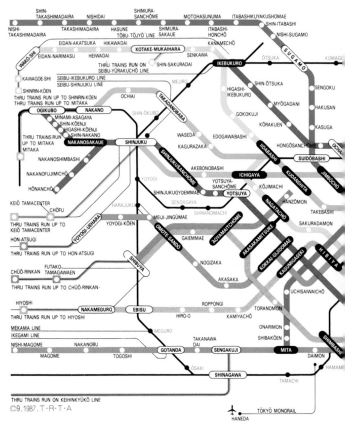

TEITO RAPID TRANSIT AUTHORITY

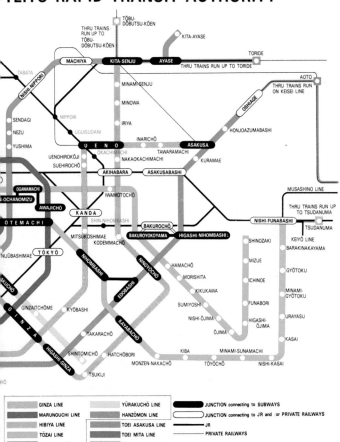

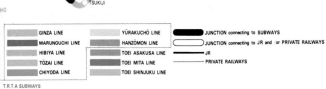

	GINZA LINE		YŪRAKUCHŌ LINE		JUNCTION connecting to SUBWAYS
	MARUNOUCHI LINE		HANZŌMON LINE		JUNCTION connecting to JR and / or PRIVATE RAILWAYS
	HIBIYA LINE		TOEI ASAKUSA LINE		JR
	TŌZAI LINE		TOEI MITA LINE		PRIVATE RAILWAYS
	CHIYODA LINE		TOEI SHINJUKU LINE		

T.R.T.A SUBWAYS

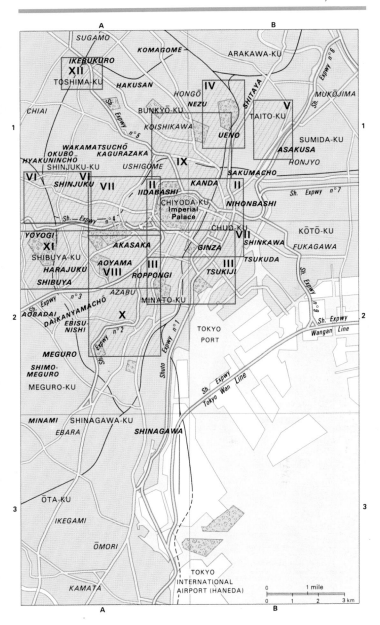

TOKYO I: GENERAL MAP

Raised pedestrian walkways facilitate the flow of traffic around the Shibuya station.

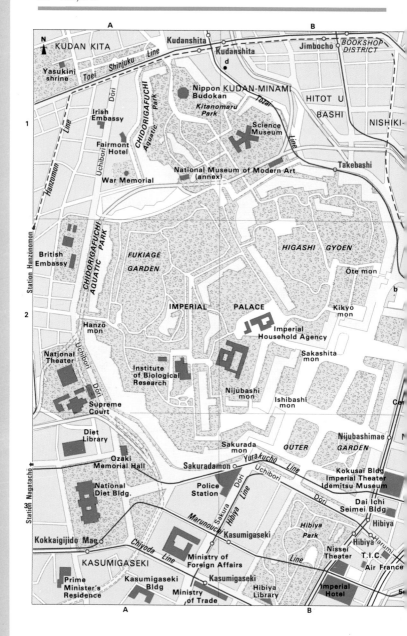

TOKYO II: IMPERIAL PALACE - NIHONBASHI

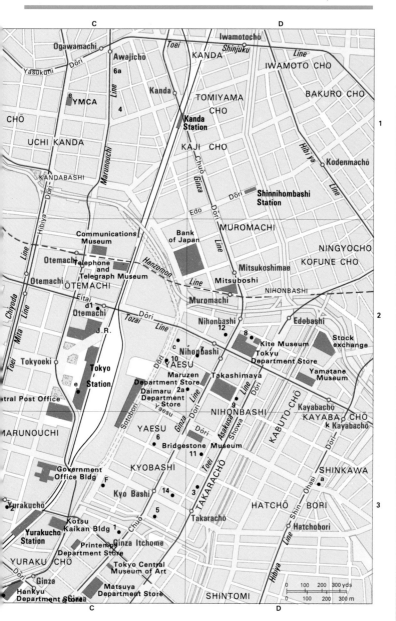

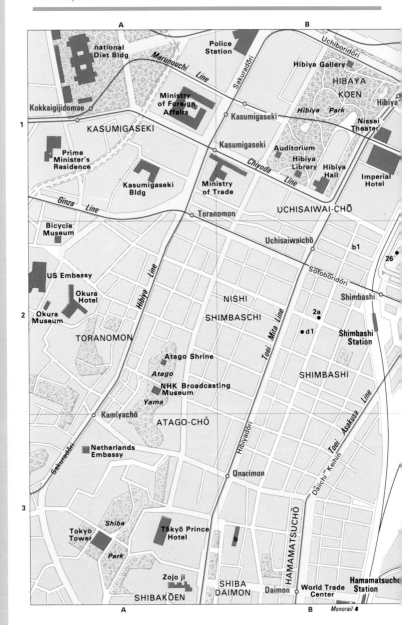

TOKYO III: MINATO-KU - GINZA

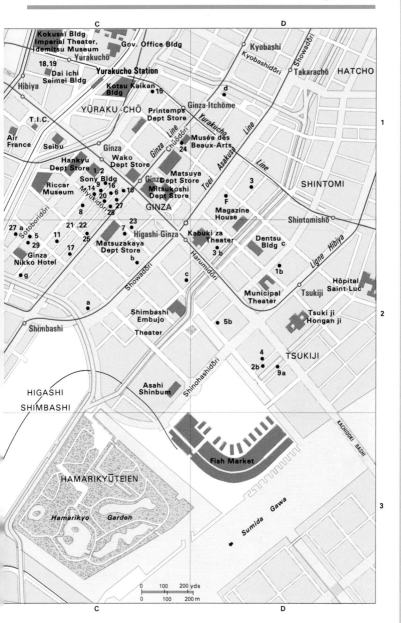

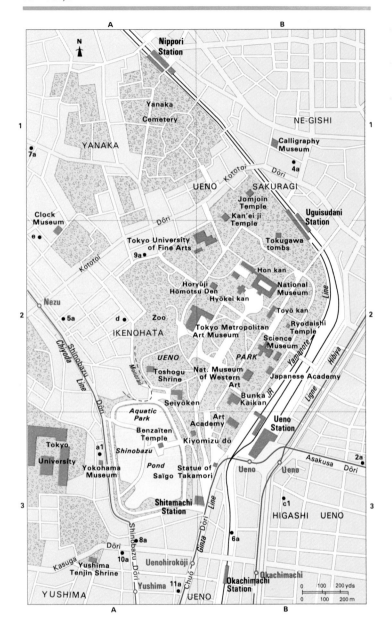

TOKYO IV: UENO

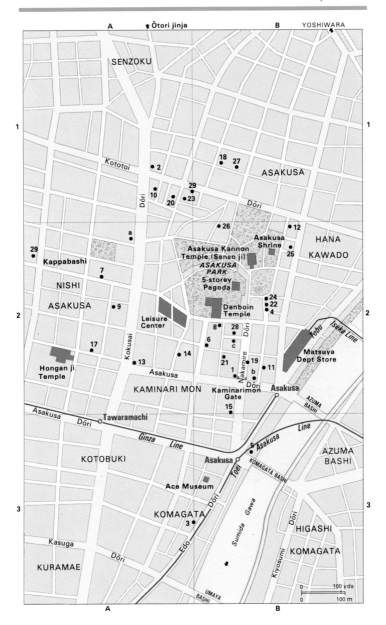

TOKYO V: ASAKUSA

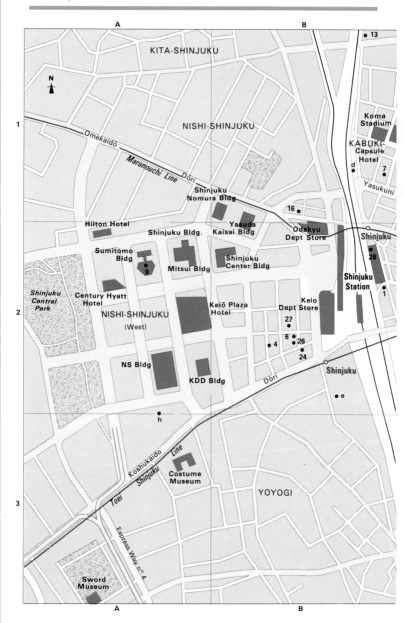

TOKYO VI: SHINJUKU-KU

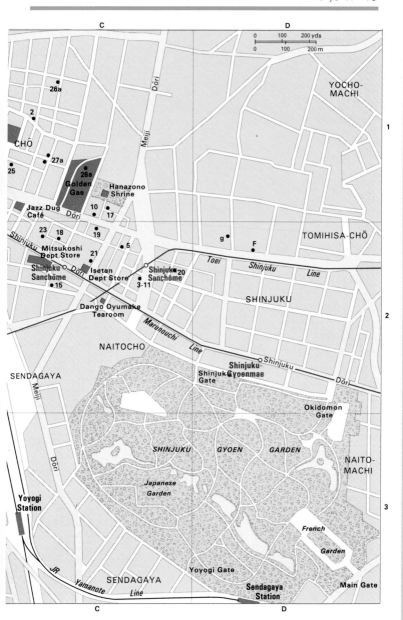

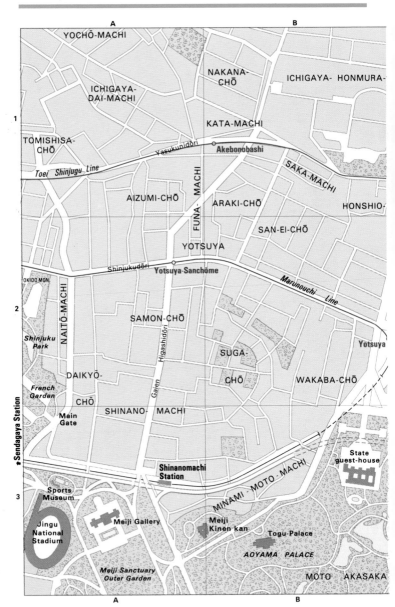

TOKYO VII: YOTSUYA

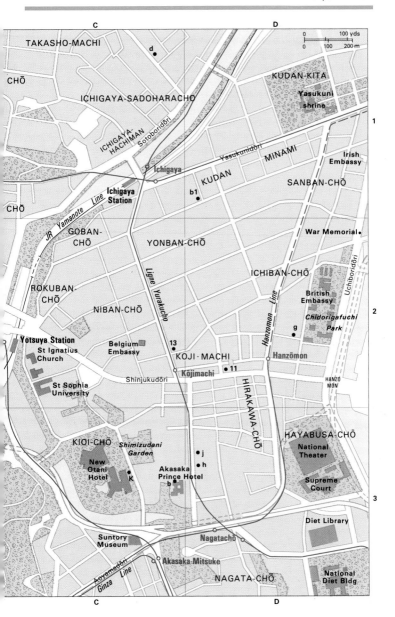

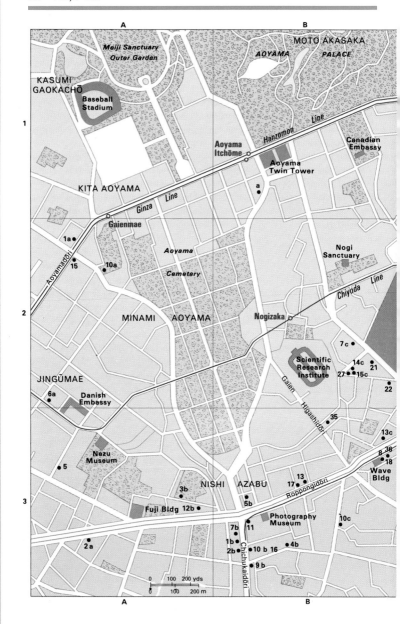

TOKYO VIII: AOYAMA-ROPPONGI

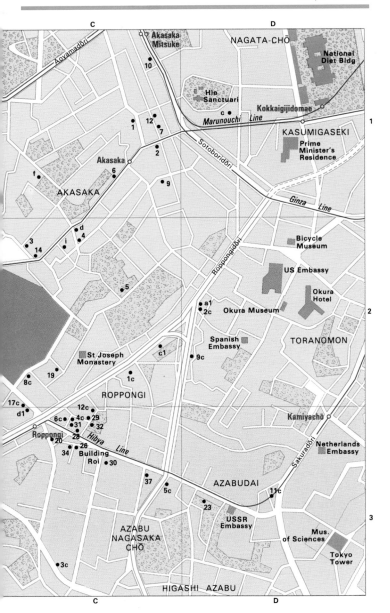

C

Aovamadōri

Akasaka
Mitsuke

10

NAGATA-CHŌ

National
Diet Bldg

D

Hie
Sanctuari

c

Kokkaigijidomae

Marunouchi Line

1

12

7

Akasaka

Sotoboridōri

KASUMIGASEKI

Prime
Minister's
Residence

2

6

Ginza   Line

f

9

AKASAKA

Bicycle
Museum

d

4

i

Roppongidōri

US Embassy

3

14

Okura
Hotel

5

a1

2c

Okura Museum

2

Spanish
Embassy

TORANOMON

c1

9c

St Joseph
Monastery

19

1c

8c

ROPPONGI

17c

Kamiyachō

d1

12c

6c   4c   29

31   32

26

28

Hibya   Line

Roppongi

20

Netherlands
Embassy

34

Building
Roi   30

Sakuradōri

37

5c

AZABUDAI

11c

23

USSR
Embassy

3

AZABU
NAGASAKA
CHŌ

Mus.
of Sciences

Tokyo
Tower

3c

HIGASHI AZABU

C

D

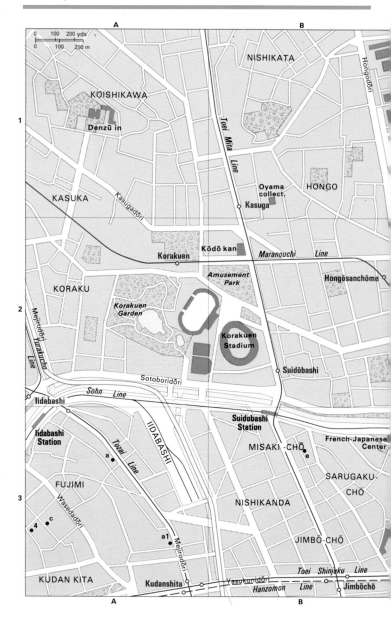

TOKYO IX: IDABASHI-AKIHABARA

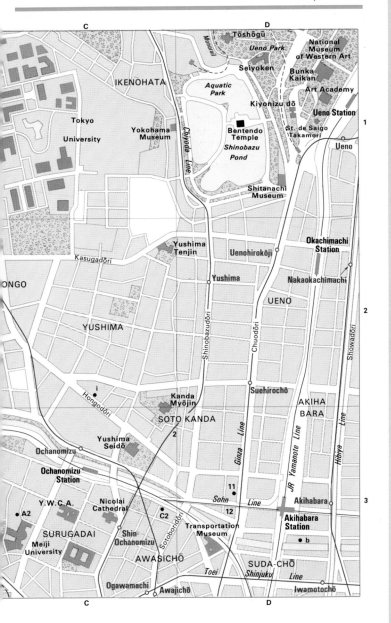

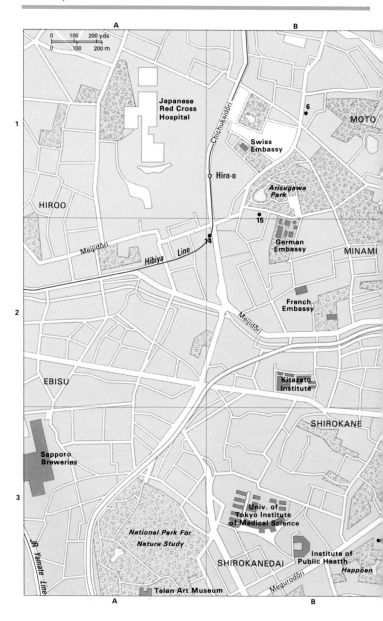

TOKYO X: AZABU-TAKANAWA

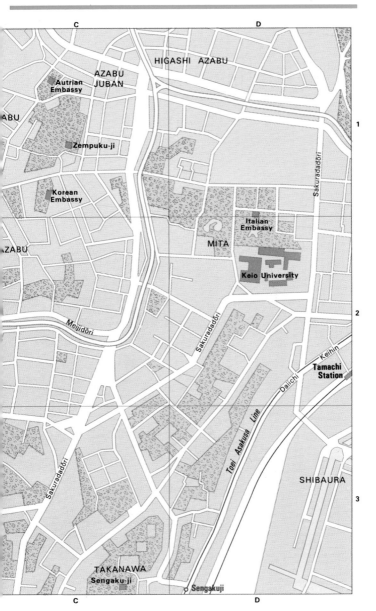

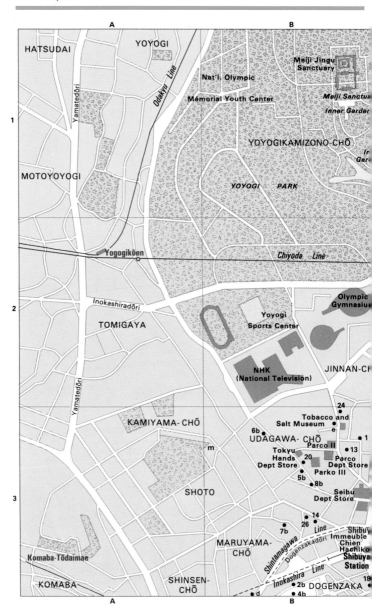

TOKYO XI: SHIBUYA-KU

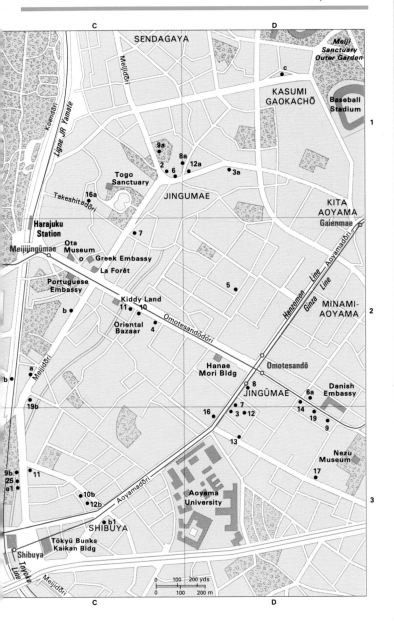

SENDAGAYA

Meiji Sanctuary Outer Garden

c

KASUMI GAOKACHŌ

Baseball Stadium

1

Meijidōri

Ligne JR Yamate

Koendōri

9a

2   8a   12a

6   3a

Togo Sanctuary

16a

Takeshitadōri

JINGUMAE

KITA AOYAMA

Gaienmae

7

Harajuku Station

Ota Museum

Meijijingūmae

o   Greek Embassy

La Forêt

Portuguese Embassy

b

Kiddy Land

11   10

Oriental Bazaar   4

Ōmotesandōdōri

5

Hanzōmon Line   Aoyamadōri

Ginza Line

MINAMI-AOYAMA

2

a

Meijidōri

b

19b

Hanae Mori Bldg

Ōmotesandō

8

JINGŪMAE

16   7   3   12

6a   Danish Embassy

14   19   9

13

Nezu Museum

17

9b   11

25

a1

10b   12b

Aoyamadōri

Aoyama University

b1

SHIBUYA

Tōkyū Bunks Kaikan Bldg

Shibuya

Toyoko Line

Meijidōri

3

0   100   200 yds

0   100   200 m

C   D

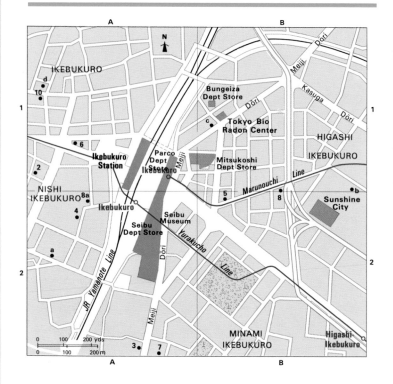

TOKYO XII: IKEBUKURO

INTRODUCTION TO TOKYO AND KYOTO

New York City... only worse! This is what many tourists think when they arrive in Tokyo. The bustle of crowded, unnamed streets and the mysterious confusion of train lines and highways can at first be intimidating, but you will soon discover that this enormous conurbation is really a string of peaceful villages, with each part as complementary to the others as rice grains are in a lacquered bowl.

The complex image that is Tokyo would take a lifetime to discover; even taxi drivers are obliged to consult their street plans many times a day. These directories are of dubious help, however, because streets in Tokyo do not have names! But try not to worry — if you can get yourself to roughly the right neighbourhood, a local housewife or policeman will always be able to give you directions to your destination from there. Once you conquer your fear of being a 'stranger in a stange land' you will discover that one of the great pleasures of Tokyo is to wander at random through the small streets. It is here you will sense the real Japan, where the exotic quickly becomes familiar.

The Japanese are a hospitable people who will be flattered when you say 'I like Japan' (or better *'Nihon ga suki desu'*). Even a complete stranger may invite you to a restaurant that serves the best *sashimi* (raw fish) in Tokyo, or he may ask you to come along and 'do the rounds' in the little bars in Shinjuku — in which case you should be able to hold your sake!

You will notice often during your visit that Tokyo, despite its size (824 sq mi/2135 sq km), maintains signs of its village origins. Under the shadows of the skyscrapers in Aoyama or Ikebukuro hides a smaller town on a human scale, where buildings rarely exceed a single storey.

It is in Kyoto, however, that you will discover traditional Japan. The ancient Imperial capital has changed little since the days of the shoguns. Lovers of temples and gardens will be delighted; the tea ceremony, flower arranging and Kabuki theatre — all of ancient Japanese culture — flourish here under the shadow of the former Imperial Palace.

In order to develop a comprehensive vision of Japan, you must visit both Tokyo and Kyoto. Formerly great rival cities, between which the seat of power vacillated throughout history, Tokyo and Kyoto represent modern and ancient Japan, respectively.

Tokyo in brief

Name: Edo (Door of the Bay) was renamed Tokyo (Eastern Capital) when it became the Imperial capital in 1868.

Location: Tokyo is on the eastern coast of Japan at the head of Tokyo Bay. It is halfway between Wakkani in northern Hokkaido and Kagoshima in southern Kyushu. Located at 140° E and 35° N (roughly the same latitude as Baghdad and Memphis, Tennessee), Tokyo is 6740 mi/10,840 km from New York City and 5910 mi/9510 km from London.

Total area: 824 sq mi/2135 sq km (New York City is 300 sq mi/777 sq km).

Government: The City of Tokyo is administered by an elected governor who is directly responsible to the Prime Minister. In addition, each *ku* (ward) elects a mayor who sits on the town council.

Administrative division: The city is officially divided into 23 *ku* (wards), 7 *machi* (towns) and 8 *mura* (villages).

Population: 8.3 million in the city itself. About 12 million people live in Greater Tokyo (more than in Sweden or Hungary), and nearly 30 million people (25% of Japan's total population) live within less than 30 mi/50 km of the Imperial Palace.

Language: Standard Japanese, the dialect of educated Tokyo, is the official language of the nation. English is spoken in the business world.

Shipping activity: Tokyo Bay (the agglomeration of Tokyo, Kawasaki and Yokohama) is the world's largest concentration of industrial ports. Continually expanding, it is one of the most important ports in the Pacific Ocean. The Port of Tokyo concentrates mainly on domestic traffic, while Kawasaki and Yokohama are more international.

Religion: Most of the Japanese are both Shintoist and Buddhist as these two religions are not contradictory. Shintoism (see p. 125), the oldest religion of Japan, is closely linked to nature and is based on the cult of *kami* (gods). Buddhism (see p. 125) was introduced from continental Asia in the 6th century AD and is based on the idea of enlightenment through meditation. There are also 560,000 Christians in Tokyo today.

PLANNING YOUR TRIP

Tokyo is the destination most frequently chosen by tourists visiting Japan. If you are planning on visiting only the Kansai region (Kyoto, Nara, Kobe and Osaka), there are also direct international flights to Osaka.

▬ WHEN TO GO

The best time to visit Japan is in the spring or the autumn. Spring is pleasant (average temperature 55° F/13° C) and coincides with the *ume* (apricot) and *sakura* (cherry) blossoming season — an event widely celebrated in Japan. Autumn is warm (average temperature 63° F/17° C) and the forests are ablaze with colour.

Summer, on the other hand, begins with a rainy season that lasts from mid-June to mid-July, then grows hot and disagreeably muggy (average temperature 77° F/25° C). Between June and September, the relative humidity is around 80%. In the area around Tokyo, winter is cool to cold (average temperature 39° F/4° C) but short and sunny.

Peak seasons occur during the New Year holiday (December 27 to January 4) and Golden Week (April 29 to May 5). The annual school vacations occur from the end of March to the beginning of April as well as from the end of July to the end of August. If you are planning to go to Japan during any of these periods, it is wise to reserve well in advance. Furthermore, Tokyo is full of students taking university matriculation exams in February, March, September and November. Kyoto is particularly crowded during the autumnal *koyo* season.

Mid-October to mid-November is the ideal time to visit Japan, the month of May the next best.

Temperatures (°F/°C)

	Winter (Jan)	Spring (Apr)	Summer (July)	Autumn (Dec)
Tokyo	39.4/4.1	56.3/13.4	77.4/25.0	62.4/16.7
Kyoto	38.3/3.4	55.6/13.0	79.0/25.5	62.1/16.6

Humidity (Relative humidity %/no. of rainy days)

	Winter (Jan)	Spring (Apr)	Summer (July)	Autumn (Dec)
Tokyo	57/7	66/10	79/10	74/11
Kyoto	72/5	67/7	76/8	74/5

GETTING THERE

Plane

There are daily flights to Tokyo from most cities in the world. Frequent and regular services are offered by over 30 airlines including: Aeroflot Soviet Airlines, Air New Zealand, British Airways, Canadian Airlines, Cathay Pacific, Japan Air Lines, Northwest Airlines, Qantas and United Airlines.

Japan Air Lines (JAL) flies from Europe and North America as well as from major Asian cities — Bangkok, Beijing, Delhi, Hong Kong, Jakarta, Karachi, Kuala Lumpur, Manila, Pusan, Seoul, Shanghai and Singapore. It also offers inexpensive plane-plus-hotel package tours.

From Australia and New Zealand

Japan Air Lines, in combination with Qantas and Air New Zealand, offers nonstop flights from Brisbane, Cairns, Christchurch, Melbourne, Perth and Sydney as well as direct flights from Auckland.

Qantas has daily nonstop flights from Sydney, daily flights from Melbourne and five flights a week from Brisbane.

Air New Zealand has four direct flights a week, three of which are nonstop.

From Canada

Japan Air Lines offers two nonstop flights a week from Vancouver and three nonstop flights a week from Toronto.

Canadian Airlines has daily direct flights from Toronto via Vancouver.

From Great Britain

Japan Air Lines offers two flights a day from London Heathrow. The Polar route, via Anchorage, takes 18 hours while the nonstop Siberian route takes 12 hours.

British Airways has 12 direct flights a week from London to Tokyo, six of which are nonstop. The other flights follow the Polar or Siberian routes via Anchorage (four times a week) and Moscow (twice a week) respectively.

Cathay Pacific offers 10 direct flights a week including a daily flight via Bangkok and Hong Kong. Aeroflot Soviet Airlines has three flights a week via Moscow.

From the United States

Japan Air Lines offer daily nonstop flights from New York, Los Angeles, San Francisco, Honolulu and Anchorage as well as five nonstop flights a week from Chicago and two flights a week from Atlanta via Seattle.

Northwest Airlines has nonstop flights from New York, Chicago, Detroit, Honolulu, Seattle, San Francisco and Los Angeles as well as direct flights from Boston, Washington, Philadelphia, Minneapolis/St Paul and Memphis to Tokyo.

United Airlines combines its extensive US network with daily flights to Tokyo via Portland, Seattle, San Francisco, San Diego, Washington, New York, Chicago, Denver and Honolulu.

Flight times to Tokyo are roughly 15 hours from New York, 12 hours from Los Angeles, 9 hours from San Francisco and 7 hours from Honolulu.

Boat

Air travel has eliminated the month-long sea crossings to Japan which were once the only way of getting there. Today, apart from luxury cruises and the occasional tramp freighter, the only regular shipping lines to Japan are ferry services from the Soviet Union, Korea, China and Taiwan.

From the Soviet Union

The **Far East Shipping Company** connects Nakhodka (the Pacific terminal of the Trans-Siberian Railway) to Yokohama. The voyage takes 51 hours. Sailing times vary according to the season. For full information contact Intourist or the Japan National Tourist Organization (see p. 71) in any major city or, in Tokyo, the **Japan-Soviet Tourist Bureau,** Kamiyacho Building, 5-2-21 Toranomon, Minato-ku, III, A2 ☎ 3432 6161. The line's agent in Japan is the United Orient Shipping and Agency Company, ☎ 3475 2841.

From Korea

A ferry service connects the Korean port of Pusan to Shimonoseki in western Honshu every day except Saturday. The voyage across the Tsushima Straits takes only a few hours. For up-to-date information contact the **Tourist Information Center** in Tokyo (see p. 71) or the **Kampu Ferry Company,** Ginza Asahi Building, 3-8-10 Ginza, Chou-ku, ☎ 3567 0971. There is also a service that operates twice a week between Pusan and Osaka. This route is much longer and takes 22 hours. For more information contact the **Kuk Jae Ferry Company Ltd.** in Osaka, ☎ (06) 263 0200.

From Taiwan

A regular weekly service sails between Taiwan and Japan. For more information contact the **Tourist Information Center** in Tokyo (see p. 71) or the **Arimura Sangyo Company,** Echo Kyobashi Building, 3-12-1 Kyobashi, Chou-ku, ☎ 3562 2091.

From China

There is a weekly service between Shanghai and Japan, alternating every other trip between Osaka and Kobe. The journey takes two days. For more information, contact the **Japan-China International Ferry Company** in Kobe, ☎ (078) 392 1021.

Train

From Europe, taking the Trans-Siberian Railway is a possible alternative to flying. The route crosses the entire continent of Eurasia and can take anything from 10 days to two weeks. Neither the most economical nor the most luxurious means of transport, it is nevertheless comfortable. The journey can be shortened by flying over certain sections of Siberia. Stop-overs in Moscow and Lake Baikal (in summer) more than compensate for the monotonous stretches of the trip. It is best to take the Trans-Siberian to — rather than from — Japan.

The procedure is simple. Take the train from Paris to Moscow, change to the Trans-Siberian and then take the boat from Nakhodka to Japan. Contact **Intourist** for details. Do not forget to apply for a Soviet visa before leaving.

Japan Rail Pass

This pass offers the bearer economical and unlimited travel on any service in Japan operated by Japan Railways (JR). It is valid on the *kyuko* (rapid), the *tokkyu* (limited express) and the *Shinkansen* (Bullet Train) as well as on buses and ferries. There are no surcharges except on night trains. Since the cost of the pass is about the same as the cost of the return fare between Tokyo and Kyoto on the *Shinkansen,* the advantage of the pass is obvious. The pass is not valid on other private railway lines.

The Japan Rail Pass (JRP) must be applied for outside Japan through an office or an authorized agent of Japan Air Lines, the Japan Travel Bureau, the Nippon Travel Agency, the Kinki Nippon Tourist or the Tokyu Tourist Corporation. Any local travel agency should be able to arrange this for you. The pass itself is delivered to the applicant at any major station in Japan in exchange for an Exchange Order purchased at any of the above.

Sold for periods of 7, 14 or 21 days, the pass is open-dated. On request, it may be validated to start on any date within three months after the date of issue of the Exchange Order. Foreign residents living in Japan are not entitled to use this pass, however, and travelers may be asked to show their passports as proof of recent entry.

For prices and full information contact **Japan Air Lines** or the nearest **Japan Travel Bureau** agency (see p. 36).

Organized tours

Many travel agencies organize tours to Japan. Some tours are combined with visits to China, Korea, Hong Kong or Siberia. Most of these tours last from 10 to 25 days and almost all include Tokyo and Kyoto, Japan's two major centers of interest. Other towns visited are Nara, Osaka and — more occasionally — Fukuoka, Hiroshima and Nagasaki.

The tours range from completely organized groups with permanent guides to individualized, independant travel schemes.

Tour organizers in the United States

American Express, American Express Plaza, New York, New York 10004, ☎ (212) 640 5130.

Japan Travel Bureau, 787 Seventh Ave., New York, New York 10019, ☎ (212) 246 8030.

Maupintour, 408 East 50th St., New York, New York 10022, ☎ (212) 688 4106.

Tour organizers in Great Britain

Bales Tours, Bales House, Barrington Rd, Dorking, Surrey.
Kuoni Travel Ltd., Kuoni House, Dorking, Surrey.
Swan, 237 Tottenham Court Rd., London, W1P OA1.

Tour organizers in Japan

There are also many tour organizers in Japan, but these services tend to function like military squads complete with uniformed guides using coloured flags and whistles. If you're still interested, most of the tours of the large cities are conducted in English.

Japan Travel Bureau, 1-6-4 Marunouchi, Chiyoda-ku, ☎ 3284 7026.
Nippon Express, 3-12-9 Soto-Kanda, Chiyoda-ku, ☎ 3253 1111.
Nippon Travel Agency, 2-20-15 Shimbashi, Minato-ku, ☎ 3572 8181.
Tokyo Tourist Corporation, 1-16-14 Shibuya-ku, ☎ 3407 0121.

▬ *ENTRY FORMALITIES*

Passport and visa

A valid passport or an internationally recognized travel document is required to enter Japan. Citizens of English-speaking countries (except Australia and South Africa) do not need visas if they enter as tourists and stay for less than 90 days. This period is extended to 180 days for nationals of Ireland and Great Britain (except colonial territories).

A commercial visa is required, however, for anyone entering Japan for any purpose other than tourism, even for less than 90 days.

If you wish to stay for more than the maximum period, even as a tourist, you must register with the authorities and obtain an Alien Registration Card (ARC), which you must carry with you at all times. For complete details contact the **Tokyo Immigration Office,** 3-3-20 Konan, Minato-ku, Tokyo, ☎ 3471 5111. Diplomats and US military personnel are exempt from this regulation.

Vaccinations

At the present time, vaccinations are required only for people coming from infected areas. The Japanese authorities, however, are seriously considering asking foreigners planning to visit Japan to obtain a certificate stating that they are not carriers of the AIDS virus. For possible developments contact the nearest Japanese embassy or consulate (see p. 38).

Customs

There are no restrictions on the importation of currency into Japan. Gifts and souvenirs should not exceed ¥200,000. The allowances on alcohol (three 760 cc bottles), tobacco (400 cigarettes or 500 gr), perfume

(2 oz) and jewelry are similar to those of most other countries. Contact the nearest embassy or consulate for information concerning any recent changes. Cars and motorcycles may be temporarily imported after obtaining a Transit Voucher validated by the Japan Automobile Federation (see below).

It is forbidden to import pornography or food products; they will be confiscated. Illegal drugs, anti-Japanese propaganda, firearms or ammunition will land you in jail.

There are no restrictions on exporting foreign currency, but sums of more than ¥5 million must be declared.

Driver's License

To drive in Japan as a tourist, you will need an International Driver's License. It is valid for up to six months. For more information contact the **Japanese Automobile Federation (JAF)**, 3-5-8 Shiba Park, Minato-ku, Tokyo, ☎ 3436 2811.

MONEY

The monetary unit of Japan is the yen *(endaka)*, symbolized by both ¥ and 円. Banknotes are printed in denominations of ¥1000, ¥5000 and ¥10,000 and coins are minted in values of ¥1, ¥5, ¥10, ¥50, ¥100 and, recently, ¥500.

Credit Cards

Visa, American Express, MasterCard and Diner's Club are accepted by the larger hotels and restaurants as well as by most souvenir shops. Such establishments, usually expensive and geared towards the wealthy traveler, have prominently placed signs outside clearly stating which credit cards they will accept.

Traveler's Checks

Traveler's checks are not very practical in Japan. The Japanese are in the habit of paying — and being paid — in cash. As the risk of theft is minimal in Japan, it is advisable to take currency with you or to change at least part of your money into cash on your arrival at the airport.

Budget

As a result of the strong rise of the yen, the cost of living is high in Japan. A double room in a hotel will cost about ¥15,000 per night.

Eating out is also relatively expensive. Evening meals can be particularly costly; a bill of ¥4000 or ¥5000 per person is in no way exceptional. At noon, however, it is possible to eat a good meal for less than ¥1500 by ordering a *teishoku* (fixed-priced lunch menu).

In hotels and restaurants, there is an additional 3% tax imposed if the bill is less than ¥10,000 per person per night or per meal and an additional 6% if over ¥10,000. The deluxe hotels add a 10% service charge, and the *ryokan* (traditional Japanese hotels) charge 15% extra.

A subway ticket costs a minimum of ¥120, while a coffee costs ¥350 or more if you sit down in a café. All imports are exceedingly expensive, particularly foreign newspapers.

It is difficult to visit Japan for less than $100 per day. This estimate is a minimum and does not include out-of-town transportation costs or personal purchases.

WHAT TO TAKE

Between June 15 and July 15, a light raincoat is indispensable. Footwear requires special attention: no matter what time of year you go, bring shoes that are easy to take off as you will have to remove them before entering temples, private homes, *ryokans* (Japanese-style hotels) and even many restaurants.

If you are planning to visit a Japanese family (the Tourist Information Center can arrange this for you) bring a small gift from your own country. This is more personal than buying something in Japan and far better than arriving empty-handed.

USEFUL ADDRESSES

Australia

Embassy
Canberra: 112 Empire Circuit, Yarralumla, ACT 2600, ☎ (062) 733244.

Consulates General
Brisbane: 12 Creek St., Queensland 4000, ☎ (07) 2215188.
Melbourne: 492 Saint Kilda Rd., Victoria 3004, ☎ (03) 2673244.
Perth: 221 Saint George's Terrace, WA 6000, ☎ (09) 3217816.
Sydney: 52 Martin Place, NSW 2000, ☎ (02) 2313455.

Japan National Tourist Organization
Sydney: 115 Pitt St., NSW 2000, ☎ (02) 2324522.

Canada

Embassy
Ottawa: 255 Sussex Drive, Ontario KIN 9E6, ☎ (613) 2368541.

Consulates General
Edmonton: 2480 Manulife Place, 10180-101 St., Alberta T5J 3S4,☎ (403) 4223752.
Montreal: 600 rue de la Gauchetière Ouest, Suite 1785, Québec H3B 4L8, ☎ (514) 8663429.
Toronto: Toronto-Dominion Centre, Suite 2702, PO Box 10, Ontario M5K 1A1, ☎ (416) 3637038.
Vancouver: 900 Board of Trade Tower, 1177 West Hastings St., British Columbia V6E 2K9, ☎ (604) 6845868.
Winnipeg: 730-215 Garry St., Credit Union Central Plaza, Manitoba R3C 3P3, ☎ (204) 9435554.

Japan National Tourist Organization
Toronto: 165 University Ave., Ontario M5H 3B8, ☎ (416) 3667140.

Great Britain

Embassy and Consulate General
London: 43-46 Grosvenor St., W1X OBA, ☎ (71) 4936030.

Japan National Tourist Organization
London: 167 Regent St., W1, ☎ (71) 7349638.

New Zealand

Embassy
Wellington: 3-11 Hunter St., Wellington 1, ☎ 731540.

Consulate General
Auckland: 37-45 Shortland St., Auckland 1, ☎ 34106.

United States

Embassy
Washington DC: 2520 Massachusetts Ave., NW, 20008-2869, ☎ (202) 9396700.

Consulates General

Anchorage: 909 West Ninth Ave., Alaska 99501, ☎ (907) 279 8428.
Atlanta: 1201 Peachtree St., Georgia 30361, ☎ (404) 892 2700.
Boston: 600 Atlantic Ave., Massachusetts 02210, ☎ (617) 973 9772.
Chicago: 737 North Michigan Ave., Illinois 60611, ☎ (312) 280 0400.
Honolulu: 1742 Nuuanu Ave., Hawaii 96817-3294, ☎ (808) 536 2226.
Houston: 1000 Louisiana St., Texas 77002, ☎ (713) 652 2977.
Kansas City: 911 Main St., Missouri 64105-2076, ☎ (816) 471 0111.
Los Angeles: 250 East First St., California 90012, ☎ (213) 624 8305.
New Orleans: 639 Loyola Ave., Louisiana 70113, ☎ (504) 529 2101.
New York: 299 Park Ave., New York 10171, ☎ (212) 371 8222.
Portland: 1300 South-West Fifth Ave., Oregon 97201, ☎ (503) 221 1811.
San Francisco: 50 Fremont St., California 94105, ☎ (415) 777 3533.
Seattle: 1301 Fifth Ave., Washington 98101, ☎ (206) 682 9107.

Japan National Tourist Organization

Chicago: 401 North Michigan Ave., Illinois 60611, ☎ (312) 222 0874.
Dallas: 2121 San Jacinto St., Texas 75201, ☎ (214) 754 1820.
Los Angeles: 624 South Grand Ave., California 90017, ☎ (213) 623 1952.
New York: 630 Fifth Ave., New York 10111, ☎ (212) 757 5640.
San Francisco: 360 Post St., California 94108, ☎ (415) 989 7140.

The Japan National Tourist Organization can supply you with a list of local Japan Travel Bureau offices in your home country.

PRACTICAL INFORMATION

▬ ACCOMMODATION

If you are planning to stay only a short time in Tokyo, choose a hotel in one of the city's centres: Shinjuku, Roppongi, Ueno or Shibuya. You will avoid traveling long distances in and out of town and also be able to stay out late without having to worry about the last train (at midnight) or the 20% taxi supplement after 11pm.

Even though Tokyo has a large number of hotels, it is wise to reserve in advance. Mid-February is particularly crowded as the city is full of students taking university matriculation examinations.

Unlike European hotels, Japanese hotels do not charge by the room but by the number of occupants. With the exception of the large Western-style hotels, where the price is degressive, the cost is double for two people and triple for three. In first class and deluxe hotels, a 10% service charge (15% in *ryokan*) is normally added to the bill which eliminates tipping, a practice virtually unknown in Japan. There is no service charge in business hotels, capsule hotels, *minshuku,* youth hostels and YMCAs. In all hotels there is a 6% excise tax on rooms costing more than ¥10,000 per night per person and a 3% excise tax on rooms costing less than ¥10,000.

There are basically six types of hotels in Japan, each described briefly below. A detailed list of hotels by district is given at the end of this guide (see 'Tokyo Addresses' p. 217).

International-style hotels

These luxurious establishments are equivalent to four- or five-star hotels (rated ▲▲▲ to ▲▲▲▲ in this guide) and offer all the corresponding comforts. English is generally spoken. A 10% service charge is added to the bill.

The three best-known luxury hotels in Tokyo are the **Okura**, III, A2, the **New Otani**, VII, C3 and the **Imperial**, II, B3 (see p. 217).

Business hotels

Also Western in style (▲ and ▲▲ in this guide), business hotels are the type of establishment most often used by tourists and Japanese businessmen.The rooms are not particularly large but are generally comfortable.The prices vary between ¥7000 and ¥10,000 per person per night. Room service is not provided and there are no additional hotel charges.

Youth hostels and YMCAs

Youth hostels usually demand proof of valid membership in an association affiliated to the International Youth Hostel Federation. The YMCAs, on the other hand, are open to everyone. The YMCAs are concentrated in the Iidabashi district between the Imperial Palace and the University of Tokyo. In Tokyo, both youth hostels and YMCAs cost about ¥5000 per day, including two meals.

On a sunny festival day in Harajuku, Tokyo, these young girls are awaiting their friends to go to the Meiji shrine.

Capsule hotels

These establishments hardly deserve the name 'hotel'. The Japanese use them only when they have missed the last train or are too drunk to go home. Located near important stations, capsule hotels rent small, spartan boxes — miniature rooms. Although relatively comfortable, they are not recommended to anyone suffering from claustrophobia. The average cost is about ¥4000 per night.

Love hotels *(abec hoteru)*

As their name indicates, love hotels are for amorous couples. The rooms, extravagantly decorated, are equipped to meet the most eccentric needs. The most famous love hotel *(abec hoteru,* pronounced 'labou-hoterou') is the **Meguro Emperor**, 2-1 Shimo-Meguro, Meguro-ku, I, A2, ☎ 3494 1211. A sort of pasteboard castle, it caters to the most bizarre fantasies. The price varies from ¥5000 for an hour to ¥15,000 for the night. Champagne is extra — very much so!

Ryokan

Ryokan are Japanese-style hotels. The floors are covered with *tatami* (see p. 46) and the guests sleep on *futon* — Japanese mattresses that are put away every morning and unfolded every night. The service is impeccable, and the meals, always included in the price, are of high quality.

Unfortunately, all the *ryokan* in Tokyo are expensive. They cost a minimum of ¥15,000 per night, including two meals and a 15% service charge. Evening meals are not served after 6pm.

The least expensive *ryokan* in Tokyo are **Sawanoya**, 2-3-11 Yanaka, Taito-ku, II, A2, d, ☎ 3822 2251, in Ueno; **Inabaso**, 4-6-13 Shinjuku, Shinjuku-ku, IV, A2, e, ☎ 3341 9581, in Shinjuku; and **Mikawaya Bekkan**, 1-31-11 Asakusa, Taito-ku, VI, D2, 9, ☎ 3843 2345, on the Nakamise Dori in Asakusa. The *ryokan* in the Hongo district, near the University of Tokyo, are also excellent. They are always packed in February, March, September and November because of university matriculation examinations, but they generally have vacancies during the summer. Try **Hongokan,** 1-28-10 Hongo, Bunkyo-ku (off map), ☎ 3811 6236; or **Chomei-Kan**, 4-4-8 Hongo, Bunkyo-ku (off map), ☎ 3811 7205. The nearest subway stations are Kasuga and Hongo-sanchome.

Private home lodging *(minshuku)*

Although uncommon in Tokyo, *minshuku* (lodgings in a private home) are a common practice in the rest of Japan. These establishments are usually farmhouses or fishermen's homes that occasionally take in paying guests. For the moderate sum of about ¥5000 you can have a room and two well-prepared meals a day. If you are moving around a great deal, even relatively close to Tokyo, this type of accommodation is particularly attractive. Without being any more expensive than a hotel, a *minshuku* provides a glimpse into everyday Japanese life that would be difficult to find otherwise. It is possible to obtain a complete list of *minshuku* in Japan from the **Japan National Tourist Office** in Tokyo (see p. 71). You can also write to or telephone the **Japan Minshuku Association,** New Pearl Building, 2-10-8 Hyakunincho, Shinjuku-ku, ☎ 3367 0155.

Sleeping Japanese Style (Futon)

Beds are found only in Western-style hotels. Japanese-style hotels and inns are equipped with *futon,* thin mattresses that are stored in cupboards during the day. In good weather, the Japanese hang their *futon* in front of windows on bamboo supports to air them and to restore their shape.

ARRIVAL

With the exception of China Airlines flights, all international flights to Tokyo land at **Narita International Airport,** about 41 mi/65 km to the east of the city. Neither customs nor passport control normally pose any major problems. For customs regulations, see p. 36.

On arrival, pets must be presented to the quarantine service for examination. Controls are severe and several certificates issued by competent governmental authorities of the exporting countries are necessary in order to import an animal. Before bringing your pet to Japan, contact the nearest Japanese embassy or consulate (see p. 38). In Japan, all inquiries are dealt with by the **Ministry of Agriculture,** 2 Kasumigaseki 1-chome, Chiyoda-ku, Tokyo, ☎ 3502 8111.

Money can be changed 24 hours a day inside the customs zone. There is another exchange office on the 4th floor of the airport terminal. If you are carrying any currency other than US dollars, it is best to change it at the airport, particularly if you are not going to stay in Tokyo.

Transportation to the city

There are several ways to get to Tokyo from the airport — the one you choose depends as much on your destination as on your budget.

Taxis

Taxis are not recommended, considering the distance. Without really being any quicker than the bus, a cab will cost seven to eight times as much and take 60 to 90 minutes. Moreover, Japanese taxis have very little room for luggage.

Bus

The bus, although a little more expensive than the train, is much more convenient for getting to the center of Tokyo. There are departures every 10 minutes to various destinations in the city.

The **Airport Limousine Bus** offers a non-stop service to the Tokyo City Air Terminal (TCAT) near Ginza. The trip from the airport to the TCAT takes about 70 minutes and costs about ¥2500. The hotel district in Ginza is another 15 minutes away by taxi (about ¥3000 more). For travelers with heavy suitcases, this system allows airport-bound passengers to preregister their baggage before leaving Tokyo. The Airport Limousine Buses also serve the hotel districts of Ikebukuro, Shinjuku, Akasaka, Ginza, Shiba, Shinagawa and Haneda. The journey takes 80 to 110 minutes and costs ¥2600 to ¥3000 depending on the destination.

The **Airport Shuttle Bus** is another non-stop service to many of the large hotels in various parts of town. This service is often the most practical way of getting to your hotel. Ask at the airport information desk for details and departure times. The journey takes 80 to 110 minutes depending on the traffic and costs ¥2600-3000.

Train

There are several different local and express trains that you can take from the airport to the city center. The most practical is the *Skyliner.* The journey is comfortable and gives you a glimpse of Tokyo's suburbs. Trains leave from Keisei Narita station every 30 minutes and arrive at Ueno station about an hour later. The *Skyliner* costs about ¥1600. Alternatively, there is the Limited Express that takes 75 minutes and costs about ¥900.

Helicopter

The **City Airlink Corporation** operates a helicopter transfer service to Haneda Airport for ¥18,000. There are eight 30-minute flights a day.

Luggage

If you have a lot of luggage, take advantage of the *haitatsu* (baggage delivery) service, which will deliver anywhere in Tokyo within 48 hours for a standard fee. This service also functions from Tokyo to the airport.

There are several *haitatsu* companies on the first floor of the airport terminal.

On leaving Narita — whether by bus, train or car — you will undoubtedly notice an impressive police force deployed around the perimeter of the airport. Since the beginning of the airport's construction about 15 years ago, the local farmers (who had been evicted) have continued to demand its closure. Their often violent protests have forced the authorities to transform the entire area into an entrenched camp behind barbed wire fences. Although this does not create a very good first impression, you must remember that in Japan security comes first.

▬ BANKS (GINKO)

Banks are open Monday to Friday 9am-3pm and Saturday 9am-noon. They are closed on Sunday, public holidays and the second Saturday of every month.

Bank of Japan, 2-4 Nihombashi-Hongokucho 2-chome, Chuo-ku, ☎ 3279 1111.

Bank of Tokyo, 6-3 Nihombashi-Hongokucho 1-chome, Chuo-ku, ☎ 3245 1111.

First National, 2-1 Otemachi 2-chome, Chiyoda-ku, ☎ 3279 5411.

▬ COURTESY

Calling cards *(meishi)*

Even if you plan to stay in Japan only for a short time, the occasion to exchange your *meishi* (calling card) with someone will undoubtedly arise, for in Japan, it is customary to exchange cards even after talking to someone for just a few minutes. The *meishi* is the only acceptable form of identification, and driver's licenses or passports are never carried for this purpose. In the business world, a *meishi* states its owner's rank. It influences the ensuing protocol and regulates the language (the verbs and forms of address) used in conversation.

It is best to have double-sided, bilingual calling cards made before you arrive in Japan. Japan Air Lines can arrange this for a fee. Otherwise, you can have them printed at the **Imperial Hotel,** II, B3, ☎ 3591 5733 or at **Itoya,** II, C3, ☎ 3561 8311. Both offer 100 cards for about $40/£22. Allow a week for delivery.

Photography

A nation of camera fanatics, the Japanese are generally very willing to be photographed as long as you ask politely beforehand. Say *'Sumimasen, Shashin o torasete kudasi'* ('Please, may I photograph you?'), and you will most likely have a more-than-willing model (see Useful vocabulary p. 252).

It is forbidden to take photographs in certain temples and museums. Check beforehand.

Shoes

Choose good, heavy shoes because you will do a great deal of walking in Japan. Make sure that they are easy to slip off and on as you will frequently have to remove them before entering temples, restaurants, fitting rooms and even private homes. Remember that the state of your socks or hosiery will be a secret to no one!

Slippers *(surippa)*

Traditionally, only *surippa* (slippers) were worn inside Japanese buildings. Even today they are usually found at the entrance of temples and shrines, as well as in certain museums and all private homes. Whenever you see

For the Japanese, whose photographic equipment is considered the best in the world, the art of taking pictures is learned young.

Honne and tatemae

As you will undoubtedly notice during your stay in Japan, the Japanese are horrified by open confrontation, even for the simplest of matters. They have conceived a philosophy that permits them to hold their own without offending others. This consists of splitting your thoughts into *honne* (that which is thought but never said) and *tatemae* (that which is said but not thought). The former is a private reality, while the latter is a façade that pleases others. Thus, while a Japanese acquaintance may be in total agreement with a Frenchman as to the superiority of French cooking, he will, nevertheless, insist on taking the Frenchman to a Japanese restaurant. What foreigners see as hypocrisy, the Japanese deem an astute manner of avoiding unpleasant confrontation.

Furthermore, the Japanese will rarely say 'no'. This is often simply a matter of language. In Japanese, a query is answered by the affirmative contained in the question. If, for example, you ask, 'Are there no toilets here?' a 'yes' will mean 'no' (that is, 'Yes, there are no toilets here').

The Japanese sometimes find Westerners too direct and are too embarrassed *(komatta, ne!)* to answer. Be sensitive and do not torment them with questions that require direct answers.

In Japan, an important distinction is made between *uchi* (the house, the inside, Japan and so on) and *soto* (the outside, foreigners, other nations and so on). The Japanese react according to the group to which they belong. Their attitude may range from extreme deference (to the family or the Emperor) to total indifference (to a road accident or a foreign catastrophe).

According to sociologist Takeo Doi, the Japanese are guided by the concept of *amae* (sphere of dependence), a complex notion that starts with the mother and extends to the Emperor. Each of these concentric spheres of dependence (including the family, the company and the nation) corresponds to a certain number of reciprocal obligations. Whatever is outside an inner circle of dependence is no longer held in obligation and is not governed by the code of conduct.

them, it is imperative that you remove your shoes before going any farther.

Tatami

Tatami are floor mats made of rice straw. The floors of traditional Japanese houses are covered by these mats and are walked on only in socks or stockings. Never walk on *tatami* with shoes or even slippers.

CURRENCY EXCHANGE

Money can be changed at Narita International Airport. The airport banks are open from 6am until after the arrival of the last plane.

In Japan, money can be changed only at authorized banks, large hotels and a few stores. These banks always have an 'Authorized Foreign Exchange Bank' sign prominently displayed. In Tokyo and other large cities, changing money is easy but in small towns it can be difficult. US dollars are the easiest currency to change. Note that in Japan it is illegal to use any currency other than yen.

EARTHQUAKES (JISHIN)

Earthquakes are frequent in Japan. About 1500 are recorded every year in Tokyo alone. Fortunately, large tremors are rare. Most seismic movement is detected only by the use of sensitive instruments. The last major destructive shock wave hit the city on September 1, 1923, and claimed about 100,000 lives. This disaster occurred at lunch time when the *hibachi* (traditional portable stoves) were lit, and the devastating fires that resulted claimed far more victims than the earthquake itself.

Today, precautionary measures and building codes are rigorously enforced. The Japanese regularly hold practice drills and every inhabitant knows exactly what to do in the advent of danger. All neighbourhoods are provided with shelters, generally located in the parks.

As a tourist, you ought to be aware of the measures that should be taken in the case of an earthquake. Above all, do not panic if you feel a tremor. First, turn off anything that could start a fire (gas, radiators and lights) and open the door to the room you are in. In the event that you are forced to leave, the door will not be jammed in the frame. Get outside if you can. If you cannot, stay near a solid wall and avoid the center of the room at all costs. Hide under a table or a bed if no other protection is available. In a traditional Japanese house, go to the toilet. Due to the narrowness of the room, it always collapses last. Absolutely avoid elevators!

If you are in the street at the time of the tremor, move away from anything that might fall, collapse or give in. Large buildings in Japan are designed to withstand strong shock waves, but the windows are likely to shatter and fall out onto the street below.

Trains, particularly high-speed trains, are equipped with security systems that cut the current as soon as the seismic vibrations exceed a certain threshold.

EMBASSIES

American Embassy, 1-10-15 Akasaka, Minato-ku, VIII, D2 ☎ 3583 7141. Roppongi station.
Australian Embassy, 1-12 Shiba-Koen 1-chome, Minato-ku, III, A3 ☎ 3453 0251. Shiba-Koen station.
British Embassy, 1 Ichibancho, Chiyoda-ku, VII, D2, ☎ 3265 5511.
Canadian Embassy, 3-38 Akasaka 7-chome, Minato-ku, Aoyama-itchome station, VIII, B1, ☎ 3408 2101.
New Zealand Embassy, 20-40 Kamiyamacho, Shibuya-ku, VIII, A2 ☎ 3467 2271. Yoyogi-Koen, Shibuya or Komaba-Todaimae stations.

EMERGENCIES

Ambulance: 119.
Fire: 119.
Police: 110.

You will be answered in Japanese. These calls are toll-free, and you do not have to insert any money; you must, however, press the red button before dialing.

EMPEROR (TENNO)

The emperor is both the most sacred and the most forbidden subject in Japan. For many Japanese, he is a living god who is directly descended from Amaterasu, the sun goddess. His birthday (December 23) is a national holiday.

The present emperor of Japan is Akihito, but only foreigners refer to him by this name. Akihito is his first name (emperors do not have family names) and it would be a sign of disrespectful familiarity for the Japanese to use it. The Japanese generally call him by his reign-name, Heisei (Peace), or, more commonly, by the term *tenno* ('he who comes from the sky').

A reign-name is also used in reference to a past reign, as well as to an emperor in person: the Showa (Radiating Peace) period from 1926-89, the Taisho (Great Justice) period from 1912-26 or the Meiji (Enlightened Rule) period from 1868-1912.

When an emperor dies he assumes the reign-name of the historical period during which he ruled: Mutsuhito (1852-1912) is thus known as the emperor Meiji after the Meiji period, and Hirohito (who died in 1989 and was the father of the present emperor) is known as the emperor Showa after the Showa period.

After World War II, Hirohito assumed full responsibility for Japan's involvement in the war and asked to be executed in order to exonerate his people. On the condition that he publicly renounce his divine origins, he not only was spared execution but also was allowed to remain emperor. To protest against this moral capitulation, considered humiliating to the nation, the writer Yukio Mishima committed *seppuku* (ritual suicide by disembowelment) in 1970.

Today, the emperor holds no political power. He appears publicly at the window of the palace only twice a year, once on January 2 to wish the people a good New Year and again on December 23, his birthday. The gardens of the Imperial Palace are opened to the public on only these two special occasions.

ENTERTAINMENT

Nightlife

Nightlife is essentially concentrated around Shinjuku (see 'Shinjuku' p. 107).

Sumo

Sumo is a Japanese form of wrestling. The Shintoist religious ritual on which the sport is based is considered as important as the match itself. Before the confrontation begins, the huge *sumotori* (wrestlers) purify themselves several times with salt. When the umpire (whose costume resembles that of a Shinto priest) lowers his fan, the contestants rush at one another with all their brute force. A wrestler wins by forcing his opponent out of the earthen circle of combat or by throwing him to the ground. If any part of the body other than the feet touches the ground, the match is over and the loser unceremoniously leaves the ring.

If you are in Tokyo in January, May or September, you may be able to watch a *hinoshita kaisan* (universal champion) in action. These peerless wrestlers are idolized in Japan and are permitted to wear the much-coveted *yokozuna,* a rope belt made of bleached hemp. Even at ordinary matches the atmosphere often becomes very heated, and you may find yourself shouting the name of your favourite *sumotori* along with the rest of the crowd.

Tickets go on sale one month before the date of the tournament. You can reserve either at the box office or in some of the large department stores: **Matsuya** (Ginza), III, C1; **Isetan**, VI, C2; **Keio** (Shinjuku), VI, B2; **Seibu** (Shibuya), XI, B3; **Seibu** (Ikebukuro), XII, A1-2. The reservation office is called *Playguide.* You can also try to buy tickets on the day of the match as there are always a few left. Admission costs between ¥1000 and ¥9000.

The matches are held at **Kokujikan Sumo Stadium,** 1-3-28 Yokohami, Sumida-ku, I, B1, ☎ 36235111. This new center, near Ryogoku station, also contains a small museum devoted to the sport. All the *heya* (teams) as well as many *chanko-nabe* restaurants are located in this district.

Theatre

Emerging around the 14th century as an independent art from, Japanese theater is based on older, traditional religious dances that evolved over the centuries into various theatrical genres, each with its own rules and rhythms.

Bunraku

Bunraku is a form of Japanese musical narrative puppetry. It developed in Osaka during the 16th century and was heavily influenced by the religious elements of both Noh drama and Kabuki theatre.

The exquisite marionettes are about two-thirds life size and art operated by puppeteers dressed in black who, without making any attempt to hide, skilfully manage to remain 'unseen'. A narrator sits on a dais and recites the story to the music of a *samisen,* a traditional three-stringed instrument.

The repertoire is similar to that of *Kabuki* theatre, consisting of ballads and stories as well as moral and historical dramas. *Bunraku* is perhaps the most 'Japanese' of these theatrical genres and is widely considered to be the highest form of Japanese theatre.

You can see *Bunraku* any time of the year in Osaka but only once or twice a year in Tokyo. In the capital, performances invariably take place at the **National Theater** (Kokuritsu Gekijo), 4-1, Hayabusacho, Chiyoda-ku, Hanzomon station, II, A2, ☎ 32657411.

Kabuki

Kabuki is the most popular and best-known form of Japanese theatre. First performed in Kyoto in the late 16th century, Kabuki was heavily influenced by Noh drama. The plays were generally social and romantic dramas catering to the tastes of the common people.

Originally, the men's roles were played by women and the women's roles were played by men. In an attempt to suppress the popularity of this erotically tainted entertainment and the havoc that reigned in the theatres, the authorities banned women from appearing on stage in 1629. This gave rise to *onnagata* (female impersonators) who, ironically, only increased the popularity of the form!

Today, Kabuki is considered a serious form of theatre with eccentric costumes, and dramatic decor (forest fires, raging seas, etc.). Generically, it can be placed somewhere between the Comedia Dell'Arte and the Grand Guignol. Composed of a succession of self-contained moments rather than a continuous action, Kabuki is spectacular and has developed a high degree of stagecraft. Dance plays an important role, and the inclusion of many ancient ritual dances in the theatre's repertoire has saved them from being permanently lost.

The actors enter on the left by the *hanamichi* (flower-path). This pathway, which runs transversally through the audience from the back of the theatre to the stage, functions both as a means of entering and exiting and as a way of focusing the action amid the spectators. As a theatrical device, it also serves to evoke a sense of voyaging through mountains, tempests or forest fires. The *hanamichi* has often been copied and used in contemporary Western theatre.

On the right of the stage, the *gidayu* (narrator) chants the adventures of the heroes in an ancient dialect. He is accompanied by music played on a *samisen*, a three-stringed instrument with a resonance chamber covered with cat skin.

There are about 350 different plays in the Kabuki repertoire, all drawn from the more spectacular episodes of Japanese history and mythology. As soon as the actors appear — particularly if they are portraying the characters Tamasaburo and Ennosuke — they are greeted by uproarious shouts and applause. At times, it is difficult to imagine that you are in a theatre and not in a sports arena.

In Tokyo, two theatres perform Kabuki throughout the year:

Kabuki-za, 4-12 Ginza, Chuo-ku, III, D2, ☎ 3541 3131 (English spoken).
Shimbashi Embujo, 6-18-2 Ginza, Chuo-ku, III, C2, ☎ 3541 2211.

The programs are announced in the *Tokyo Tour Companion,* obtained free of charge at the Tourist Information Center (see p. 71) or in the large hotels.

Ordinarily, performances start at 11am and 4:30pm and can last up to five hours. Tickets cost between ¥3000 and ¥12,000. It is usually possible to buy tickets on the same day.

Noh drama

Noh drama is the oldest form of Japanese theater, originating during the 14th century (when Japan was heavily influenced by Zen philosophy) as a means by which Buddhist monks could propagate their doctrine. The performance is a mixture of mime and dance, accompanied by chanting. The texts, inspired by Zen, are recited alternately by the chorus and the two principal actors in archaic Japanese. The actors, masked and dressed in 14th-century costumes, move by dancing in extremely stylized fashion to the relatively monotonous sound of three drums, a flute and a voice.

Noh drama is nonrealistic. Having no plot in the conventional sense, it is a particular moment of a story that is expounded and analyzed. Overall, Noh drama is a scholarly, aristocratic form of theatre with a moralistic purpose. A special form of Noh drama for the common people, called subscription Noh, greatly influenced the development of *Kabuki* and *Bunraku*. The Noh repertoire consists of about 240 plays and 300 *kyogen* (comic interludes between the main plays).

Unlike Kabuki which is lively and loud, Noh is slow and sombre. To be perfectly honest, it is rare that foreigners (and for that matter, a majority of the Japanese) do not soon become bored by a Noh drama performance. Even the fascinating transformation of the expressions on the masks (as the actors move under the lights) is usually not enough to awaken the audience from the torpor that has set in within the first few minutes. Traditionally, performances last all day long.

If you wish to attend a Noh drama performance, go to the **Kanze Noh Theatre,** 1-16-4 Shoto, Shibuya-ku, Shibuya station, XI, A3, ☎ 3469 5241. It is the oldest in Tokyo. Performances are also given at the **National Noh Theatre,** XI, CD1, 4-18-1 Sendagaya, Shibuya-ku, Sendagaya station, ☎ 3423 1331. This theatre first opened its doors in 1983. Tickets cost between ¥2500 and ¥10,000.

Music in Japan

The presence of music in prehistoric times is demonstrated by abundant archaeological material, including stone whistles and *dotaku* (metal bells), as well as figurines of dancers and musicians with various stringed instruments.

Native Japanese music was influenced by Korean, Chinese and Indian music in the 5th, 7th and 8th centuries, respectively. By the Heian period the range of instruments included: *oteki* (bamboo flutes); *hichiriki* (bamboo reed instruments); *sho* (mouth organs), *shoko, kakko,* and *taiko* (all percussion instruments); *koto* and *biwa* (two-stringed instruments producing a drone).

The Kamakura and Muromachi periods saw the development of Zen-based Noh drama music and the rise of itinerant musical guilds who wandered the country spreading political propaganda. During the 16th century the *samisen* (a long-necked, three-stringed instrument played with a plectrum) was introduced from China via Okinawa. It quickly became associated with Kabuki theatre and is one of the most popular traditional Japanese instruments today.

During the Edo period, Western concepts of melody merged with the folk music of the period. Bugles were adopted by some *daimyo* for their armies.

In 1870, after the Imperial Restoration, the Imperial Court pressed for the introduction of Western music. In 1877, Japanese musicians gave the first all-Western concert, under the direction of an Englishman, and in 1903, the first Western opera was performed. The Japanese quickly became great performers and conductors. By the 1960s, most cities in Japan had at least one modern orchestra.

Today traditional Japanese music exists only in closed guilds and Buddhist monasteries.

▬ FESTIVALS

For additional information concerning the events listed below, contact the **Tourist Information Center** (see p. 71) or your local **Japan National Tourist Organization** (see p. 38) before leaving. Details of weekly events in Tokyo can also be found in the *Tokyo Tour Companion,* a publication that appears every Sunday and is distributed free of charge at the TIC or in the large hotels.

January

Ganjitsu (New Year) is one of the most important Shinto festivals of the year and is celebrated for three days. It is mainly a family celebration. Throughout Japan, houses are decorated with pine branches and bamboo stalks. Traditionally, *mochi* (rice cakes) are eaten. If you are with Japanese friends, wish them *'Akemashite omedeto gozaimasu'* — roughly equivalent to 'Happy New Year'. On New Year's Eve, trains run all night long so that travelers may attend the various religious ceremonies that take place at different Shinto shrines throughout the country. The Meiji Jingu shrine in Tokyo attracts by far the greatest number of people and offers one of the most colourful celebrations of the year.

Ippan sanga, when the Emperor presents his greetings to the Japanese people, takes place on January 2. The grounds of the Imperial Palace are opened to the public and thousands of loyal subjects come and wave small flags under the monarch's window.

Dezomeshiki (Fireman's Parade), a tradition dating back to the 17th century, is held on January 6. Spectacular acrobatic demonstrations are performed on tall bamboo ladders by firemen dressed in traditional uniforms of the Edo period. The event takes place at Harumi, only 15 minutes by bus from Yurakucho.

Coming of Age Day, a national holiday, is celebrated on January 15. It honours those who have reached the age of 20 within the year. Young women go either to their local neighbourhood temple or to the Meiji shrine dressed in their best traditional kimonos.

Japanese poetry: haiku and tanka

Haiku is the form of Japanese poetry best known in the West. A short text composed of three lines of 5, 7 and 5 syllables, it developed during the 15th century from *renga* (*tanka* linked verse). Without giving an explanation or a description, *haiku* evokes an incident or a fleeting sensation. According to Barthes: 'It is this, it is thus, says the *haiku*, it is so'.

Basho Matsuo (1644-94) is considered the greatest master of *haiku*. Here are two examples of his art:

> An old pond —
> A frog leaping in —
> The sound of water.

> A cloud of cherry blossoms —
> A bell. That of Ueno?
> Or that of Asakusa?

Tanka, a form of poetry less well known in the West, is much older. It developed during the Nara period and became one of the standard forms of Japanese poetry for over a thousand years. Longer than *haiku*, these poems are composed of 31 syllables in lines of 5-7, 5-7 and 7 syllables. Every year since 1948, the Imperial Household (Poetry Bureau) has invited amateur poets throughout the country to compose a *tanka* on a given theme. Between 30,000 and 40,000 poems are examined each year by the palace jury. About 30 of them receive the honour of being read to the Emperor and his family. The *tanka* composed by the Empress is then read three times, while that written by the Emperor is read five times in a row. This ceremony, which takes place on January 15, is broadcast on television.

Kagami biraki is held at Nippon Budokan on the same day. Here, the great masters of the martial arts give public demonstrations. The crowd is offered *shiruko* (a sweet soup of red beans and *mochi*).

The **sumo season** opens around the middle of the month and the first matches of the year are held at the Kokugikan Sumo Stadium in Ryogoku. The *yokozuna* (greatest champions) make a pilgrimage to the Meiji shrine and offer ritual sacrifices to Shintoism, on which this sport is based.

February

Setsubun (Changing of the Season or Bean-Throwing Festival), the beginning of spring, according to the Chinese lunar calendar, is celebrated on February 3. The Japanese throw soya beans *(mame maki)* in every corner of the house while shouting *'fuku wa uchi'* ('happiness in the house') and *'oni wa soto'* ('the devil out'). Tradition has it that by eating a bean for every year of his or her life, an individual ensures that his or her wishes will be fulfilled. The Zojo ji temple, near the Tokyo Tower, is the best place to watch this ceremony.

Harikuyo is held on February 8. This is a very curious ceremony in honour of the needles that have been used by seamstresses during the year. These needles are first stuck in *tofu* (soya bean curd) and then buried by a Buddhist priest. This ceremony can be seen at the Shojuin temple in Shinjuku or at the Senso ji temple in Asakusa.

Kigensetsu (National Foundation Day), on February 11, is the anniversary of the founding of the Japanese nation by the legendary Emperor Jimmu in 660 BC. It is a public holiday.

Saint Valentine's Day is February 14. Girls offer chocolates to boys.

Shiraume Matsuri (Plum Flower Festival) begins sometime after February 15, depending on the flowering of the trees. The festivities are centered around the Yushima Tenjin shrine in Ueno, where numerous events take place until March 25.

March

Hinamatsuri (Doll Festival) is held on March 3. In private homes, collections of *hina-ningyo* dolls representing the Emperor, the Empress or members of the Imperial court dressed in Heian costume, are displayed, along with miniature household articles, on shelves covered with red cloth. Certain collectors' items also are exhibited in department store windows and in elegant hotels.

Kinryu No Mai (Dance of the Golden Dragon) takes place at the Senso ji temple in Asakusa on March 18. A 50-ft/15-m dragon, skillfully manipulated by young people of the neighbourhood, chases a lotus flower around the temple while geisha perform a traditional dance. This colourful festival celebrates the miraculous netting of a small golden statue of the goddess Kannon by three fishermen in AD 628.

The **spring equinox** occurs on March 20 or 21 and is a public holiday (see p. 62). **Higan week,** in commemoration of the dead, also occurs at this time of the year.

April

Hana Matsuri (Flower Festival), coinciding with Buddha's Birthday, is held on April 8. Throughout Japan, flower blossoms are offered to the sage and *amacha* (sweet tea) is poured over statues of the deity. There is a children's parade at the Senso ji temple in Asakusa.

The **cherry trees** generally flower between April 7 and 10. In Tokyo — as everywhere in Japan — this event gives rise to all sorts of merrymaking. After work and over the weekend, Japanese families flock to their favourite parks to celebrate *o'hanami* (see the flowers). Picnicking under the trees by the thousands, they drink, sing and dance late into the night. Ueno Park, Chidorigafuchi Park and Aoyama Cemetery are the favourite spots in Tokyo to 'see the flowers' (and the Japanese).

The **Yasukuni Jinja** spring shrine festival is held April 21-23. There are free sumo matches and martial arts demonstrations. If you arrive early, you can watch the *sumotori* (wrestlers) preparing for combat. This ritual is a rare event and is not normally performed in public.

Golden Week occurs from April 29 to May 6. Four public holidays (April 29 and May 3-5) fall within this period and many people take the whole week off.

The **spring festival** of the Meiji shrine is held from April 29 to May 3. There are traditional dances, music and performances of Noh drama.

May

Constitution Memorial Day, May 3, is a public holiday. It celebrates the anniversary of the constitution of 1947.

Kodomo No Hi (Children's Day), formerly known as Boys' Day, is on May 5. *Koinobori* (multicoloured kites in the shape of carp) are stuck to doors, windows and on long poles. These kites, swelling proudly in the wind, symbolize longevity and manly strength.

Kanda Matsuri, one of the most important Shinto feasts of the year, is held on the second weekend of the month. This three- to four-day event includes processions of *mikoshi* (portable shrines), geisha dancers, samurai in armour and Shinto priests on horseback. Commemorating the Tokugawa victory at Sekigahara in 1600, this festival takes place every other year (on odd-numbered years) at the Kanda Myojin shrine near Ochanomizu Station.

Sanja Matsuri, another important Shinto shrine festival, takes place on the third weekend of May. It is held at the Asakusa shrine just behind the Senso ji temple. Along with *mikoshi*, costume parades and traditional dances, there is an exceptional exposition of Tokyo's tattooed. This bizarre event should not be missed on any account.

Some of the most beautiful doll collections are exhibited in the major department stores on the occasion of the doll festival (Hinamatsura) on March 3.

The **Yushima Tenjin** shrine festival is held toward the end of May. It features parades of people in traditional Heian period costumes and, every other year, *mikushi* processions.

June

Kappa Matsuri is held on June 6. To ensure a plentiful catch for the coming year, young fishermen carry *mikoshi* from the Ebara Jinja shrine (near Shin-Banba Station) to the sea.

Torigoe Jinga Taisai is a festival dedicated to Yamato Takeru, a legendary hero of Japan. It is held at the Torigoe shrine (not far from Kuramae Station) on the second Sunday of the month. Young bearers carry the heaviest existing *mikoshi*, which weighs four tons. Arrive between 5 and 6pm, if you wish to witness this spectacular event.

Sanno Festival, held at the Hie Jinja shrine in Asakusa from June 10 to 16, is well worth attending. Every other year, always on a Saturday, a gigantic *gyoretsu* (parade) in traditional costume and *mikoshi* processions take place in the streets of Akasaka from 9am-6pm.

The first irises usually appear in Tokyo's parks around June 15. This event gives rise to a mad rush of amateur photographers, whose prime target is the famous Iris Garden of the Meiji Jingu shrine, open 8am to 5pm.

July

Suijo Matsuri (Water Festival) occurs on the first of the month. Decorated boats descend the Sumida River from Yanagi Bridge to Tokyo Bay. At the mouth of the river, Shinto priests launch *katashiro* (paper dolls), which are then carried away by the current and are believed to protect the town from bad luck.

Hozuki-ichi is held on July 9 and 10. From early morning until midnight, a plant market takes place in front of the Sensoji temple in Asakusa.

Mitama Matsuri is celebrated at the Yasukuni Jinja shrine from June 13 to 16. This ceremony honours Japan's war heroes. Among several other events, free performances of Noh drama are held in the evenings.

On the last Saturday of the month, the municipality offers a giant **fireworks display** *(hanabi)* near the Sumida River. The best place to watch this colourful presentation is from one of the bridges.

August

At the beginning of the month, usually from the August 4 to 6, **a pottery fair** is held on Shinohashi Dori near Ningyocho Station. It is a good place to find bargains.

Hashi Kuyo is celebrated on August 4. Similar to Harikuyo (see February above) but honouring chopsticks instead of needles, this ceremony takes place at the Hie Jinja shrine in Asakusa.

Bon *Odori* (traditional Bon dances) are held between August 5 and 9 at the Tsukiji Hongan ji temple (near Tsuki ji Station) in preparation for O-Bon, a Buddhist festival in honour of the dead.

O-Bon (Bon Festival) occurs between August 13 and 15. During this time of year, the dead are thought to revisit the earth. In order to guide them homeward, families light lanterns on which the names of the dead are written.

Fukagawa Hachiman Matsuri, an impressive Shinto festival, takes place at the Tomioka Hachimangu shrine around August 15. The crowd throws water on *mikoshi* as they are carried by in a large procession. Every third year, an important feast, *hommatsuri* (main feast), takes place.

Awa Odori (Folk Dance Festival), held at the Koen ji temple on August 27 and 28, features about 4000 dancers who perform *odori* (dances) from Tokushima in the Awa region.

September

The autumn **Sumo season** opens at the Kokugikan Sumo Stadium in Ryogoku. For two weeks the National Theater hosts performances of *bunraku* puppet theater.

Respect-for-the-Aged Day, on September 15, is a public holiday in honour of the elderly. No special events are held.

The **autumnal equinox,** another public holiday, is celebrated on September 23.

Ningyo Kuyo (Doll Festival) is held on September 25. Couples who have not been able to have children offer dolls to the goddess Kannon. In addition, old dolls that are no longer wanted are given to the Kyomizu temple in Ueno. The Japanese find it repugnant to discard them as ordinary objects and they are incinerated according to strict Buddhist rites.

October

Tomin No Hi (Tokyo Festival) takes place on the first of the month. At 6pm a large parade of floats is held in Ginza on Sotobori Dori and Chuo Dori.

Health-Sports Day, on October 10, is a public holiday. An important archery demonstration is held at the Yasukuni Jinja shrine.

The **autumn festival** of the Yasukuni Jinja shrine is celebrated from October 17 to 19. It includes dances, traditional costume parades and performances of Noh drama.

At the end of October (the dates vary depending on the year), there is an interesting **procession of geisha** in formal costumes. The parade starts at the Matsubaya theatre and proceeds to the Yoshiwara Benzaiten shrine (near Iriya Station), a district formerly reserved for prostitution.

November

Emperor Meiji's birthday is celebrated at the Meiji shrine from November 1 to 7. There are numerous events, including theatrical performances and dances. Young Japanese women come to the shrine dressed in traditional kimonos to admire the flowers in the adjacent garden.

Culture Day, November 3, is a public holiday.

Shichi-go-san (Seven-Five-Three), a celebration honouring children aged three, five and seven, is held on November 15. Children in their best kimonos come with their families to be photographed in the large shrines, particularly at the Meiji and the Asakusa shrines.

Tori-no-ichi (Rake Fair or Cock Festival) is celebrated two or three times during the month (the dates vary according to the year) at certain Shinto shrines. Stalls set up near the shrines sell *kumade* (small ornate bamboo rakes), which symbolize the money to be 'raked in' during the year. The Otori Jinja in Asakusa and the Hanazono Jinja in Shinjuku are the best places to see this event.

November is the season of **chrysanthemums.** Tokyoites come by the thousands to visit the flower expositions at the Yasukuni shrine, the Senjo ji temple and, most importantly, the Yoshima Tenjin shrine.

Labor Thanksgiving Day, on November 23, is a public holiday.

December

On December 14, a celebration is held at the **Sengaku ji temple** in honour of the illustrious 47 *ronin* (see p. 124) who were forced to commit *seppuku* after avenging their master. A procession follows the path they took to murder Kira Kozukenosuke on December 14, 1702.

The **Emperor's Birthday,** on December 23, is a public holiday.

For two weeks during December, *bunraku* puppet theatre is performed at the National Theater in Hayabusacho.

Shogatsu (New Year) is celebrated from December 28 to January 4. Most businesses, museums and parks are closed to the public during this period.

FINDING AN ADDRESS

Apart from a few of the large avenues, streets in Japan do not have names. This peculiarity — unique in the world — is due to the fact that Japanese cities are grouped into sub-units rather than divided by streets. The largest administrative units within a city are the *ku* (wards). These consist of several *cho* (districts) and/or *machi* (towns), which in turn are composed of a number of *chome* (neighbourhoods of a couple of dozen houses). Within a *chome*, each building is allotted a one — or two — digit number according to its position on the block (up until 1955 this number was based on the chronological order of construction) and not in relation to the street. Two houses next to each other on the same street will not have consecutive numbers if they belong to different *chome*.

To adopt a system of streets with numbers would be to ignore the Japanese concept of organizing space into hierarchical cellular units and sub-units — a notion they hold dear. The practical result is that only the police and the post office know how to find the inhabitants of a neighbourhood. Without a map, it is impossible — even for the Japanese — to find an address.

Indeed, giving an address amounts to drawing a map. Every restaurant and shop has a map on the back of its business card. If you visit a private home, the host will probably give you his telephone number and the name of the closest train or subway station. Once in the neighbourhood, you can call and someone will come and meet you. If you have to find an address by yourself, go to the neighbourhood *koban* (police-box) and ask to have a map drawn for you.

FLOORS (KAI)

The first floor in a Japanese building corresponds to the street level (British ground floor/American first floor). In elevators, the first floor is frequently marked L (for lobby) and the basement is marked B (or B1, B2, B3 and so forth).

FOOD AND DRINK

A separate chapter is devoted to Japanese cuisine (see p. 89).

GETTING AROUND

Driving in Japan is not recommended. It is difficult and unpleasant. All the road signs (with a few exceptions in the center of Tokyo) are written in Japanese and every day, monstrous traffic jams paralyze the city for hours on end. Although parking is illegal in most parts of the capital, this does not seem to discourage millions of Tokyoites from taking their cars into the congested centers. If you do decide to drive, please note that the Japanese drive on the left.

In Tokyo — with the streets handed over to drivers — pedestrians face a certain number of dangers. You must be particularly vigilant concerning car traffic. Above all, never cross a street against the light. The Japanese would not dream of it and the drivers would probably not even try to avoid hitting you. The police, equipped with loud speakers, will call offenders to order: 'Will the man with the yellow coat please go back to the kerb.' To be on the safe side (and to avoid pestering the police), use footbridges and underground passages whenever possible.

In Japan, sidewalks are shared with cyclists. Do not grumble if — for the *n*th time that day — a bicycle bell rings behind you. It is simply a cyclist warning you that he is about to pass.

▬ HEALTH AND MEDICAL CARE

As medical care is expensive in Japan, you may want to acquire traveler's medical insurance before leaving. Internationally, Japanese doctors and hospitals have a very good reputation. Language is the only real problem that you may run across when seeking medical care. Listed below are a few addresses where English is spoken.

Hospitals and clinics (byoin)
International Catholic Hospital (Seibo Byoin), 5-1 Naka-Ochiai 2-chome, Shinjuku-ku, ☎ 3951 1111. *Open Mon-Sat 8-11am.*
International Clinic, 1-5 Azabudai, Minato-ku, ☎ 3582 2646. This clinic is staffed by general practitioners who speak several languages.
Japan Red Cross Medical Center (Nihon Sekijujisha Iryo Center), 1-22 Hiro-o 4-chome, Shibuya-ku, A1, ☎ 3400 1311. *Open Mon-Fri 8:30-11am; Sat 8:30-10:30am.*
King's Clinic, Olympia Annex, Fourth Floor, 21 Jingumae 6-chome, Shibuya-ku, ☎ 3400 7917. *Open Mon, Tues, Thur and Fri 9am-1pm, 3-5pm; Wed and Sat 9am-1pm.*
Saint Luke's International Hospital Seiroka Byoin), 10 Akashicho 1-chome, Chuo-ku, ☎ 3541 5151. *Open daily 8:30-11am.*
Tokyo Sanitarium Hospital (Tokyo Eisei Byoin), 17-3 Amanuma 3-chome, Suginami-ku, ☎ 3392 6151. *Open Mon-Fri 8:30-11am.*

Dentists (ha-isha)
Besford Dental Office, Mori Building 32, 3-4-30 Shiba-Koen, Minato-ku, III, B2, ☎ 3431 4225. You will be treated by an English dentist. *Open Mon-Fri.*
Olympia Ohba Dental Clinic, 6-31-21 Jingumae, Shibuya-ku, XI, CD1-2, ☎ 3409 7156.

Pharmacies (kusuriya)
American Pharmacy, Hibiya Park Building, 1-8-1 Yurakucho, Chiyoda-ku, III, C1, ☎ 3271 4034. *Closed Sunday.*
Hibiya Pharmacy, Mitsui Building, 1-1-2 Yurakucho, Chiyoda-ku, III, BC1, ☎ 3501 6377.

Professor Tsunoda's theory

Whereas all other peoples of the world use the left hemisphere of their brain for consonants and the right hemisphere for vowels and non-verbal sounds (natural sounds), the Japanese use the left side for all sounds.

According to Professor Tsunoda, otologist and audiologist at the Tokyo Medical and Dental College and author of the book entitled *The Japanese Brain,* this difference is due to the primordial importance of vowels in the Japanese language.

From infancy, the Japanese are accustomed to using only the left hemisphere. They thus inextricably bind language and nature. This, according to Professor Tsunoda, explains why the Japanese are so emotional and why they have such a difficult time learning foreign languages.

True or false, this theory is based on numerous, serious laboratory experiments and has the merit of considering language as a determinant factor in human comportment rather than as a predisposed biological trait.

JAPANESE CALENDAR

At the moment of printing (1990), Japan is in the second year of the Heisei period (Accomplished Peace). The preceding period, known as the Showa (Radiating Peace), lasted 64 years (1926-1989) and was the longest in the history of Japan.

Since the time of the Emperor Meiji, these socio-historic periods have traditionally commenced with the ascension to the throne of the new emperor and ended with his death. The reign-name of the crown prince of the following period is decided upon by a committee of sages but is kept secret as long as the reigning Emperor is still alive.

In daily life (when sending or addressing bills, receipts, letters and so on), the Japanese use the indigenous imperial system more often than the Christian calendar.

LANGUAGE

(See 'Useful vocabulary' p. 252).

Japanese is reputed to be so difficult that any foreigner who speaks it is considered a superman in Japan. Even if you can mutter only *'sayonara'* ('goodbye'), *'arrigato'* (thank you) or *'gomennasai'* ('excuse me'), compliments will rain down on you: *'Nihongo ga desu ne!'* ('How well you speak Japanese!'). The spoken language, however, is not as difficult as it is made out to be. The real complexities of oral communication in Japan are social and not grammatical.

The origin of the Japanese language is obscure. Some authorities place it within the Ural-Altaic group, while other linguists attribute it to the Malayo-Polynesian. Only Korean belongs to the same family as Japanese, with which it shares a remarkably similar grammar.

Furthermore, Japanese has undergone numerous changes and has been heavily influenced by foreign languages over the centuries. Chinese, several Siberian dialects, Portuguese, Dutch, French and, more recently, English, have all influenced it to various degrees. Although the basic daily vocabulary of modern Japanese is only about 5% Chinese, technical and abstract terms of Chinese origin take up the greater part of a Japanese dictionary.

Foreign words, however, are frequently impossible to distinguish from purely indigenous ones due to Japanese pronunciation: 'coffee' becomes *kohi:* 'milk-tea', *miruku-chi;* and 'butter', *bata.* Furthermore, words are sometimes borrowed in different forms. The word 'strike' becomes *sutoraiku* (as in baseball) and *sutoraiki* (as by workers), while 'glass' becomes *gurasu* (to drink from) and *garasu* (the substance). This is particularly true for earlier Chinese loan words.

The empire of signs

If the Japanese language is beyond your capacities, sign language might be for you. Here are a few rules you will need to know.

To count, fold your fingers instead of unfolding them. Start with the thumb ('one') and cover it with the index finger ('two'), then the middle finger ('three') and so forth. This manner of counting has a symbolic value in Japan. The thumb represents the family, which is protected by the other fingers.

To indicate the number two, the Japanese show the index finger and the middle finger and not the thumb and the index finger, which are considered too unequal in size.

If, in a conversation, you wish to indicate 'me' or 'mine', point not to your chest but to your nose.

Finally, two arms crossed over the chest with the hands held open means that your request is impossible to fulfill or that the service offered is terminated.

Words and expressions borrowed from other languages have often lost their original connotation. For example *arubaito*, from the German *arbeit* (work), is used only for student part-time jobs; the French *avec* (with) becomes *abekku*, meaning 'lovers'; 'mansion' is a small building renting furnished rooms!

Pronunciation

The most common romanization (the transliteration of a non-roman script into roman alphabet) of Japanese into *romaji* (roman characters) is the Hepburn transcription. In this system, the vowels are pronounced as in Italian and the consonants are pronounced as in English.

Literature in Japan

Japanese literature holds a place of honour among Asian literatures. Similar to Arabic, Persian and Sanskrit in quality and quantity, it is like European literature in that the novel, drama and love poem play a more predominant role than do philosophical and historical works. Diaries, travel accounts and collections of random thoughts also exist. The shorter works are frequently considered the best. The longer works tend to lack overall coherency and are merely individual episodes arranged chronologically. In a society dominated by men, some of the greatest works of Japanese literature have been written by women.

The earliest texts in Japan were written in Chinese as a result of the introduction of the Chinese system of writing in the 4th century AD. The oldest surviving complete works are the *Kojiki* (AD 712) and the *Nihongi* (AD 720), both officially commissioned histories of Japan. Along with other minor works, these works quote over 200 folk songs in Japanese, some dating to the 5th century AD.

The Nara period saw the publication of a volume of poetry, the *Manyoshu*, around AD 760. It contains over 4500 poems written (in Japanese) by more than 450 poets in skillfully arranged *waka* verse. Derived from earlier folk songs, this style was to remain the standard form for over 1000 years. Purely Japanese, it avoids words of Chinese origin. It is divided into *tanka* (short poems of 31 syllables: 5-7, 5-7, 7) and *choka* (longer poems of the same metre).

The Heian period (mid-9th century) witnessed the publication of *Taketori Monogatari (The Tale of the Bamboo Cutter)*, the first prose story in Japanese literature. About AD 950, the *Ise Monogatari (Tale of Ise)*, a poem tale in *tanka* and prose, introduced a realistic approach to literature. The *Genji Monogatari (Tale of Genji)*, the world's first important novel, was written about 1010 by Lady Murasaki Shikibu.

During the Muromachi period, Noh drama developed into a noble art form. Strongly influenced by Zen Buddhism, it quickly became associated with the shogunal court. In the 15th century, *renga* (linked *tanka* verse forming indefinite chains) became a popular medium among the leading poets of the times, including the priest Sogi (1421-1502). This somewhat elaborate and structured form of expression eventually gave rise to the simpler *haiku*.

During its resurgence in the Edo period, literature became more lively and humorous and less structured. *Tanka* recovered its original simplicity and *haiku* emerged as an important form of expression — the undisputed master of which was Basho Matsuo (1544-1694). *Kabuki* and *bunraku* also developed, from the older and drier Noh drama, and novels reappeared for the first time since the Classical period of Heian literature.

After the Meiji Restoration, European and American influences were very strong. *Haiku* and *Kabuki* managed to retain their purely Japanese forms, but Western ideas heavily influenced the Japanese novel. Among the writers available in English translation are Natsume Soseki (d. 1916), Nagai Kafu (d. 1959), Tanizaki Junichiro (d. 1965) and Sato Haruo (d. 1964). More recent authors include Akutagawa Ryunosuke (d. 1927), Kikuchi Kan (d. 1948), Kawabata Yasunari (d. 1972), Osaragi Jiro (d. 1973), Dazai Osamu (d. 1970) and Mishima Yukio (d. 1970). Living Japanese writers available in translation include Endo Shusaku, Ooka Shohei, Oe Kanzaburo, Ishihara Shintaro and Kazuo Ishiguro.

Standard Japanese has five vowel sounds: 'a' as in papa, 'i' as in marine, 'u' as in lunar, 'e' as in pepper and 'o' as in go.

Certain sounds do not exist in Japanese. The 'f' (with the exception of 'fu') and the 'v' are unknown. The sounds 'ti' and 'tu' are replaced by 'tchi' and 'tsu', respectively. The 'r' is pronounced almost as 'l', and the 's' is never sounded as a 'z'. The 'g' is always hard, and 'ch' is pronounced as 'tch'. The 'j' is pronounced 'dj' as in the Arabic name *Djamila*, and the 'h' is always aspirated.

A few examples:
Meiji: may'-jee
Sumida: soo-me'-dah
Kobe: koh'-bay
Nagasaki: nang-ah-sah'-key

Writing

This is where Japanese becomes complicated!

Until the 4th century AD, the Japanese had no written language. When they discovered that their powerful neighbour China had one, they were captivated by this novelty and immediately tried to adapt the Chinese system to their own tongue. They retained the original meaning of the Chinese ideogram *(kanji)* but replaced its pronunciation with the corresponding Japanese sound. The Chinese ideogram was, in short, used merely as a picture of the Japanese word. After two centuries, it became evident that it was impossible to use the Japanese sounds *(kun yomi)* in composite words. For these the Chinese sounds *(on yomi)* were retained. All at once, ancient Japanese was enriched with as many words as there were ideograms, which numbered in the thousands.

During the 8th century, the scholars who translated Chinese books into Japanese invented an alphabet ('a', 'i', 'u', 'e', 'o', 'ka', 'ki', 'ku', 'ke', 'ko', 'ma', 'mi', 'mu', 'me', 'mo', and so on to transcribe Chinese ideograms into Japanese sounds. Known as *katakana,* this alphabet contains 48 signs based on simplified Chinese ideograms.

Starting in the 10th century, a second phonetic alphabet *(hiragana)* was used by the ladies of the Imperial court who did not wish to learn Chinese. It was with this alphabet that Lady Murasaki Shikibu wrote her brilliant *Genji Monogatari (Tale of Genji),* considered the world's first novel.

Today, Japanese is written in a mixture of *kanji* (ideograms), *hiragana* and *katakana*. The last is reserved for words of foreign origin.

In 1946, the number of officially recognized ideograms that were obligatory in school was reduced to 1850. Written Japanese is still one of the world's hardest languages to master.

▬ LOST AND FOUND (WASUREMONO)

In Japan, before you can retrieve a lost object, you need to know where you lost it.

In a Japan Railways train: Lost and Found Section in the JR Tokyo Station, II, C2, ☎ 231 1880, or the JR Ueno Station, IV, B2, ☎ 384 8069

In the subway (not municipal lines): Lost and Found Center, Ueno Subway Station, IV, B3, ☎ 3834 5577.

In Tokyo Metropolitan buses, subways and street cars: Lost and Found Section, Tokyo Metropolitan Government, 1-35-15 Hongo, Bunkyo-ku, IX, B2, ☎ 3818 5760.

In other railways and buses: all lost objects are returned to the terminus of the line.

In a taxi: contact the Tokyo Taxi Kindaika Center, 7-3-3 Minami-Suna, Koto-ku (off map), ☎ 3648 0300.

In the street: try the local *koban* (police station) or go to the Central Lost and Found Office, Metropolitan Police Board, 1-9-11 Koraku, Bunkyo-ku, IX, A2, ☎ 3814 4151. All objects not claimed at any of the above addresses are sent here after a period of three to five days.

MUSEUMS *(BIJUTSUKAN* OR *HAKUBUTSUKAN)*

Museums are generally open Tuesday to Sunday 10:30am-5:30pm. Visitors are not permitted entrance after 5pm. All museums are closed from December 29 to January 3 for the New Year holiday, as well as whenever a new exhibition is being installed. It is best to telephone in advance. Admission is invariably charged and ranges from ¥100 to ¥700.

In Japan, museums rarely display their complete collections at any one time, due mainly to lack of space. Instead, the central reserve collections are rotated as temporary exhibitions, generally centered on historical themes.

A separate chapter has been devoted to Tokyo museums (see p. 129).

NEWSPAPERS

Apart from Japanese newspapers, there are four English dailies published in Japan. The *Japan Times* (well known for its classified advertisements) and the *Asahi Evening News* are informative. In addition, the *Tokyo Tour Companion* appears in English every Sunday. Published by the *Asahi Shimbun*, this magazine covers all tourist and cultural events in Tokyo and may be acquired free of charge at the Tourist Information Center (see p. 71) or in any of the large hotels. There is also the *Tokyo Journal,* an excellent magazine that contains theatre and cinema programs, articles on the capital and classified advertisements.

PACHINKO

Often erroneously called Japanese pin-ball, *pachinko* has become a very popular game since the end of the last war. First, a player buys a number of small, heavy, metal playing balls. These cost about ¥500 per 1.1 lb/500 gr. Inserted one by one into the machine, the balls are projected through a vertical circuit of pins and holes. If the ball hits particular pins, it drops into the back of the machine and liberates a certain number of other balls. The balls that fall to the bottom of the circuit are lost. A special hole in the center, called the 'tulip' (which it vaguely resembles), wins the jackpot. The machines are rigged and there is absolutely no skill involved in playing the game.

Players lucky enough to amass a certain number of balls may exchange them for small gifts (cigarettes, biscuits or gadgets). Officially, gambling is illegal in Japan, but professional *pachinko* players usually manage to change their winnings back into yen. It is claimed that a professional player, who can spot a winning machine by the configuration of the pins, can make as much money in a few hours as a toiling worker can make in a day.

Manga

The Japanese are among the world's greatest readers of *manga* (comic strips). These magazines are sold in large volumes printed on cheap paper. They are available on any theme: science fiction, detective, crime thriller and sex.

Manga are read (if the term applies) everywhere: on trains, at the barbers and even in restaurants. Once read they are left on the spot for the benefit of the next reader. So many can be found on trains and in cafés that it is a wonder that anyone ever buys them at all.

Stamp collecting

The Japanese post office issues about 30 special collectors' editions *(kinen kitte)* per year. These stamps are displayed in all post offices a few days before sales begin. It is absolutely necessary to buy them on the day of issue as the post offices are literally taken by siege by Japanese stamp collectors. A second chance, however, is offered to would-be philatelists at the Tokyo Central Post Office, 2-3-3 Otemachi, Chiyoda-ku, II, C2-3, ☎ 3241-4891, where they remain on sale a little longer.

POST OFFICE

Central post offices are open Monday to Friday 9am-7pm, Saturday 9am-3pm and Sunday 9am-noon. Stamps *(kitte)* can be purchased in any post office.

Local post offices are open Monday to Friday 9am-3pm and Saturday 9am-12:30pm. They are closed Sunday and public holidays.

Letters sent to Japan by Poste Restante (General Delivery) should be addressed to the main **Central Post Office,** 2-3-3 Otemachi, Chiyoda-ku, II, C2-3. The counter is open daily from 8am-8pm. In theory, mail can be addressed to any local post office, but as the service is practically unknown in Japan, it is best to use only the central post offices. At the counter ask for *tome oki* or *kyoku dome* and present identification.

American Express, Halifax Building, 16-26 Roppongi 3-chome, Minato-ku, Tokyo 106, also holds mail for clients. Hotels will do the same.

In Japan there are telephones everywhere... except in post offices! Telecommunications were privatized in 1985 (see p. 70).

PUBLIC BATHS (SENTO)

Even though most Japanese homes are now equipped with Western-style bathrooms, traditional *sento* (public baths) are still very popular. Every district has its local communal baths where neighbours can get together socially.

The *sento* offers visitors one of the most welcoming changes of atmosphere that can be experienced in Japan. These baths are not for washing, however, but for relaxation and socializing. In Japan, it is customary to wash before going to a public bath. Enter the water slowly as the temperature oscillates between 104° F/40° C and 122° F/50° C!

Geothermically heated natural hot springs *(onsen)* are found throughout Japan. These springs are reputed to be beneficial to the mind and the body. The most famous *onsen* near Tokyo are at Hakone, less than 2 hours from the capital by train (see p. 149). Other well-known spas are located near Nikko.

PUBLIC HOLIDAYS

There are 13 public holidays a year in Japan. If any of them falls on a Sunday, the following Monday is taken as a holiday. May 1 (May Day) is a semi-holiday. May 4, sandwiched between two public holidays, is also taken as a holiday. The New Year is generally celebrated for three days and many organizations, museums and parks are closed. For more details concerning these holidays, see 'Festivals' p. 50.

January 1:	New Year's Day.
January 15:	Coming of Age Day.
February 11:	National Foundation Day.
March 21 (or 20):	Vernal Equinox Day.

April 29:	Greenery Day.
May 3:	Constitution Memorial Day.
May 5:	Children's Day.
September 15:	Respect-for-the-Aged Day.
September 23 (or 24):	Autumnal Equinox Day.
October 10:	Health-Sports Day.
November 3:	Culture Day.
November 23:	Labour Thanksgiving Day.
December 23:	Emperor's Birthday.

RADIO AND TELEVISION

Radio

Radio broadcasts in English can be received throughout Japan on the Far East Network (FEN) of the American Armed Forces in Japan. There are hourly news reports and an evening news commentary every night except Sunday between 6pm and 7pm. In the Tokyo area, FEN transmits on 810 kHz. Programs are published daily in the *Japan Times*.

Television

Altogether there are over one hundred television channels scattered throughout Japan. Besides the NHK (the national network), each region has a number of private commercial channels where there are constant interruptions by exasperating commercials.

All broadcasts are in Japanese. Some foreign films, however, are transmitted in both Japanese and the original language. They may be seen (and heard) on television sets equipped with special bilingual receptors. Cable networks, which can be found in the large hotels and some luxury apartment complexes, usually keep the original soundtrack.

Late at night (generally around 2am), it is usually possible to pick up CNN, an American news television channel.

SAFETY PRECAUTIONS

Tokyo is a particularly safe place to visit. The Metropolitan Police (one of the largest police forces in the world) are extremely efficient and the city has one of the lowest crime rates in the world.

The successful control of crime is partly credited to the administrative division of the capital into local sub-units. Each *chome* (neighbourhood) is closely watched by means of a *koban* (also called police-box). These are miniature police stations employing three or four police officers. The officers know their neighbourhood intimately and the inhabitants know them. Their main task is to prevent rather than to punish crime.

The system works so well that identity checks are practically unknown. Japan is one of the rare countries where the police have the confidence and sympathy of nearly everyone.

SHOPPING

In Tokyo, stores are frequently grouped together in certain districts according to their speciality: shops selling traditional dolls are found mainly in Asakusabashi, kitchen and restaurant suppliers are concentrated in Kappabashi, book dealers are centered almost exclusively around Kanda and electronic goods are found mostly in Akihabara. This tradition is inherited from the *za* (guilds of artisans) that were grouped in various districts during the Edo period.

Tokyo abounds in shops specializing in absolutely everything from French camembert to the latest obscure Tasmanian rock group and from ancient Noh drama masks to sophisticated computers, as well as traditional Japanese wares. There are very few things that cannot be found in Tokyo.

In general, most stores are open Monday to Saturday 10am-8pm and closed on Sunday. Many supermarkets, however, are open 24 hours a day. Vending machines may be found almost everywhere and sell everything from the usual cigarettes and hot and cold drinks to products such as rice and pornographic magazines!

The following list contains some of the more common items. For others refer to 'Useful addresses' p. 217.

Antiques

In Tokyo, the main center for antiques is located in Aoyama on **Kotto Dori,** VIII, A3. Secondhand goods may also be found in **Kamiyacho,** VIII, D3 (on the road that leads to the Tokyo Tower near Ikura Crossing) and in **Roppongi.**

Apart from these large concentrations of antiquarians, there is also the **Tokyo Komingu Kotto Kan** (Tokyo Center for Artisans and Antiquarians), 1-23-1 Kanda-Jimbocho, Chiyoda-ku, II, B2, ☎ 3295 7115. *Open daily 10am-7pm.* In the middle of the Kanda bookstore area, this center has about 50 antique dealers under one roof.

Books

Isseido, 1-7 Kanda, Jimbocho, Chiyoda-ku, II, BC1, ☎ 3292 0071. *Open Mon-Sat 9:30am-6:30pm.* Incontestably the largest dealer of old books in Tokyo, this specialist offers real treasures at astronomical prices. There is a good selection of English and French titles.

Kanda, in Jimbocho, is the booksellers' district. It is *the* center for old books, both Japanese and European. The addresses given below are all concentrated around **Yasukuni Dori,** II, BC1.

Kitazawa, 2-5 Kanda, Jimbocho, Chiyoda-ku, II, BC1, ☎ 3263 0011. *Open Mon-Sat 10am-6pm.* Specializing in philosophy, ethnology and theology, this is one of the most respected booksellers in Kanda.

Sanseido, 1-1 Kanda, Jimbocho, Chiyoda-ku, II, B1, to the east of Jimbocho Station, ☎ 3233 3312. *Open Wed-Mon 10am-8pm.* This eight-storey shop is packed with videocassettes and books, including English and French titles.

Tuttle, 1-5 Kanda, Jimbocho, Chiyoda-ku, II, BC1, ☎ 3291 7072. Tuttle is both a bookseller and an editor. The second floor of the shop was renovated in 1987 and is entirely devoted to works on Japan in foreign languages, particularly English.

International bookstores in Tokyo

Jena, 5-6-1 Ginza, Chuo-ku, III, D2, ☎ 3571 2980. *Open Mon-Sat 10:30am-7:50pm, Sun 12:30-6:45pm.* This shop is in the center of Ginza.

Kinokuniya, 3-17-7, Shinjuku, Shinjuku-ku, VI, C2, ☎ 3354 0131. *Open daily 10am-7pm. Closed the first and third Wed of every month.* This is the best-known international bookseller in Tokyo. The international department on the seventh floor is well stocked with books in English. There are also Western newspapers and magazines.

Maruzen, 2-3-10 Nihombashi, Chuo-ku, II, D2, ☎ 3272 7211. *Open Mon-Sat 10am-6pm.* On Chuo Dori and not far from Tokyo Station, this shop has numerous books in English on Japan.

Cameras and electronic goods

With the increasing strength of the yen, it is becoming less and less advantageous to buy consumer goods in Japan. Japanese products in Japan are frequently more expensive than in other countries! Furthermore, imported articles over a certain value are taxed when you return home (check customs regulations before you leave). There are also trademark regulations and quotas for certain Japanese products registered with US customs.

Moreover, Japanese domestic models are built to local specifications (voltage and frequency) and may not work in your home country.

Listed below are the shops in Tokyo offering the best prices:

Bic Camera, 1-11-7 Higashi-Ikebukuro, Toshima-ku, XII, B1-2, ☎ 3988 0002. *Open daily 10am-8pm.* Near Ikebukuro Station, this store is claimed to be the cheapest in Tokyo for computers and video equipment.

Camera No Doi, 1-18-27 Nishi-Shinjuku, Shinjuku-ku, VI, B2, ☎ 3348 2241. *Open daily 10am-9pm.* The prices are about the same as those at Yodobashi (see below) — so is the hysterical atmosphere.

Yodobashi Camera, 1-11-1 Nishi-Shinjuku, Shinjuku-ku, VI, B2, ☎ 3346 1010. *Open daily 9:30am-8:30pm.* This is the cheapest and the best stocked camera shop in Tokyo. In order to take advantage of *menzei* (duty-free prices), do not forget to bring your passport. When buying, look hesitant and wait until the salesperson has calculated all possible discounts on a pocket calculator before committing yourself. The store has a smaller but less well stocked outlet in Shinjuku near My City.

The **Akihabara district,** IX, D3, is the center for the latest sound equipment. There is a particularly wide selection of Walkmans, CD players and DATs (digital audio tapes) for sale.

The largest dealers in Akihabara are **Laox** (near the subway exit) and **Yamagiwa.** Both stock the very latest models at interesting prices and both have duty-free departments. Don't forget your passport.

Department stores *(depato)*

There are department stores in all the major centers of Tokyo: **Shibuya** (Seibu, Parco, Tokyu and Tokyu Hands), **Shinjuku** (Isetan, Takano, Mistsukoshi, Odakyu, Marui and My City) and **Ginza** (Mitsukoshi, Matsuzakaya, Matsuya, Wako, Seibu and Le Printemps).

Department stores: directions for use

In Japan, department stores are called *depato* (the Japanization of the words 'department store'). Because most of these thriving concerns are owned by the rail companies and located on train lines, it is understandable that millions of Tokyoites are obliged to walk through seemingly unending miles of temptation every day in order to exit the large stations.

Nevertheless, each store has its own particular character and social standing. A gift from Takashimaya (which has an Imperial warrant but does not advertise the fact) is more appreciated than one from Mitsukoshi.

Regardless of which store you visit, start in the basement where the food department is located. Selling typically Japanese products (seaweed, dried fish, salted vegetables, *tempura*, tea, and so on), hundreds of shouting vendors beckon clients to taste their wares. It is claimed that many Tokyo housewives move from one counter to the next until they have 'had lunch'.

Next, take the elevator directly to the top floor. There is always a terrace on the roof designed for relaxing, complete with bonsai and gold fish exhibits, playgrounds for children, open-air refreshment stands and sometimes even a small temple. In any case, the view is always superb.

The floor below is usually reserved for restaurants. Wander around and look at the various *mihon* (wax or resin copies of food) presented in the windows before choosing where you want to eat. Catering to office workers, the *teishoku* (lunch-time menus) are particularly inexpensive in department stores.

Sometimes a part of this floor is reserved for exhibitions of arts and crafts. At Seibu's branch in Ikebukuro, there is even a museum.

Before leaving the store, go to the departments specializing in kimonos (traditional kimonos can cost well over $15,000!), Japanese paper *(washi)* and calligraphy.

All department stores have telephones and toilets for their customers. These are usually found on landings between the floors.

Department stores are open six days a week 10am-6pm. Unlike the smaller shops, all the department stores in Tokyo are open on Sunday. The different department stores close on different days of the week: Wednesday (Le Printemps, Daimaru, Matsuzakaya, Marui, Isetan and Takashimaya), Thursday (Seibu, Matsuya, Tokyu and Odakyu) and Monday (Mitsukoshi).

The largest *depato* is the Seibu in Ikebukuro.

Fashion

With only a few exceptions, all the major Japanese fashion designers are located in either **Aoyama**, VIII, or **Shibuya**, XI. Listed below are a few of the better-known shops:

Comme des Garçons (Rei Kawakubo), near Shibuya Station in the Parco department store, part 1, 3rd floor, XI, B3, ☎ 3496 2750. *Open daily 11am-8pm*. The men's store is at 5-12-3 Minami Aoyama, Minato-ku, ☎ 498 0921. *Open Tues-Sun 11am-8pm*.

Comme ça du Mode, 3-1-30 Jingumae, Shibuya-ku, XI, B3, ☎ 3478 6761. *Open Mon-Sat noon-11pm, Sun 11am-8pm*.

Hanae Mori, 3-6-1 Kita Aoyama, Minato-ku, XI, D2, ☎ 3400 3301. *Open daily 10:30am-7pm*. The building alone, designed by Kenzo Tange, is worth the visit.

Issey Miyake, 5-3-10, Minami-Aoyama, Minato-ku, VIII, A2, ☎ 3499 6476. *Open daily noon-8pm*.

Junko Shimada, 1-1-4 Aobadai, Meguro-ku, I, A2, ☎ 3463 2346. *Open 11am-8pm*. Junko was one of the first to have invested in the now super-trendy Daikanyama district.

Kansai Yamamoto, 3-28-7 Jingumae, Shibuya-ku, XI, B3, ☎ 3478 1958. *Open 11am-8pm*. Kansai is one of the most original recent designers.

Clothes and shoe sizes

For men, the three most common sizes for clothes are S (small), M (medium) and L (large).

For women, letters are replaced by numbers:

Size in Japan	Size in Great Britain/United States
7	10 / 8
9	12 / 10
11	14 / 12
13	16 / 14

Men's shoes:

$24\frac{1}{2}$	$5\frac{1}{2}$ / 6
26	$7\frac{1}{2}$ / 8
$27\frac{1}{2}$	$8\frac{1}{2}$ / 9

Women's shoes:

24	$4\frac{1}{2}$ / $5\frac{1}{2}$
$24\frac{1}{2}$	$5\frac{1}{2}$ / $6\frac{1}{2}$
$25\frac{1}{2}$	$6\frac{1}{2}$ / $7\frac{1}{2}$

Food

Most Western-style products (coffee, milk, jam, cheese, and so forth) can be found in any Japanese supermarket or department store. Recently, department stores have greatly increased their range of Western goods. If you insist on finding your favourite brand, however, you can go to the following:

Kinokuniya International, 3-11-7 Kita-Aoyama, Minato-ku, VIII, A1, ☎ 3409 1231. *Open daily 9:30am-8pm*. Almost any foreign product can be found here ... at a price!

COMMON GOODS (JAM, BREAD, ETC.) ARE AVAILABLE AT COMMON PRICES AT :

Takano, 3-26-11 Shinjuku, Shinjuku-ku, VI, B1-2, ☎ 3354 2622. *Open daily 10:30am-8pm.* Near Shinjuku Station, this store has a good fresh-food department and an excellent bakery in the basement. On the seventh floor, there is an international restaurant with six different types of cuisine.

Kimonos

New kimonos are very expensive. Once worn, however, their value drops tremendously. It is not in the mentality of the Japanese to wear clothes that have belonged to someone else. As many *gaijin* (foreigners), however, are not concerned by this, the following two shops specialize in selling secondhand kimonos to tourists.

Hayashi Kimono, 1-7 Uchisaiwaicho, Chiyoda-ku, II, BC3, ☎ 3591 9826. *Open daily 9:30am-7pm.* This is one of several specialists in the International Arcade.

The Oriental Bazaar, 5-9-13 Jingumae, Shibuya-ku, XI, C2, ☎ 3400 3933. *Open Wed-Mon 9:30am-6:30pm.* This shop has a large collection of secondhand silk kimonos for women and cotton kimonos for men.

Markets

Flea markets

In Tokyo, there are seven flea markets *(nomi no ichi)* that are held on various days of the month throughout the year. If you are hunting for bargains, go early in the morning.

Roppongi (opposite the Roi Building), VIII, C3, ☎ 3583 2081. *4th Thursday and Friday of every month.*

Sunshine City, Alpha Shopping Arcade, First Basement, Ikebukuro Station, XII, B2. *3rd Saturday and Sunday of every month.*

Temple Araiyakushi, Arai-Yakushimea Station, off map, ☎ 3389 9221. *1st Sunday of every month.*

Temple Hanazono, Shinjuku Station (just behind Isetan), VI, C1. *3rd Saturday and Sunday of every month.*

Temple Nogi, Nogizaka Station, VIII, B2, ☎ 3295 7118. *2nd Sunday of every month.*

Temple Togo, Harajuku Station, XI, C1, ☎ 3425 7965. *1st and 4th Sunday of every month.*

Yoyogi, Yoyogi-Koen Station (between Yoyogi Park and the NHK Building), XI, B2, ☎ 3499 6800. *Once or twice a month on varying dates between February and December.* To know the exact dates, telephone beforehand — in Japanese, of course!

Specialized markets

Dolls and traditional toys

Daruma: a ball-doll

The most famous Japanese doll is a simple ball without arms or legs. It represents the 6th-century Indian monk Bodhi-dharma (called Daruma by the Japanese), who is credited with originating the *dhyana* (meditation) philosophy of Zen Buddhism. According to legend, Daruma meditated so intensely for nine years without stopping that his arms and legs withered away.

The doll, in the image of the sage, symbolizes fortitude and is thought to bring good luck. As a highly stylized representation of the monk seated in deep meditation, the doll is frequently sold without eyes. Instead, there are two empty white circles. The first eye is painted in when a project is undertaken and the second eye is added when the project is successfully completed.

Shops specializing in dolls and traditional toys are concentrated on **Edo Dori** in Asakusabashi (not to be confused with Asakusa) between Asakusabashi Station and Kuramae Station, off map V, A3. This district is also the haunt of sumo wrestlers because of the numerous *chanko-nabe* (see p. 91) restaurants located near Asakusabashi Station.

Wax Food *(Mihon)* and Kitchen Equipment
Kappabashi, V, A2, not far from Asakusa, is the district where all the Tokyo restaurant owners come to buy *mihon* (wax models of food displayed in the windows of Japanese restaurants). Most of the suppliers will sell retail if you ask them. You can also buy outfits worn by Japanese chefs and specialized Japanese kitchen equipment.

Fish
Tsukiji, III, CD3, is the largest fish market in Japan and one of the biggest in the world. Every day in Tokyo, about 450 tons of fish and 30 tons of seaweed are consumed in Tokyo, most of which is sold at Tsukiji. In order to see the fish auctions, you must arrive very early in the morning (between 5am and 6am). The sales take place on the quays where the fishing boats dock. There are numerous *sushiya* (raw-fish restaurants) installed around the market. Despite the early hour, have a bite to eat. It is impossible to find fresher fish anywhere.

Paper *(washi)*
In Japan, paper making is an art that dates from the 7th century AD. Over the centuries, each region has developed its own traditional styles and techniques. Today, *washi* comes in an infinite variety of textures and printed motifs.

Among the better-known paper dealers in Tokyo are the following:

Itoya, 2-7-15 Ginza, Chuo-ku, II, C3, ☎ 3561 8311. *Open daily 9:30am-6pm*. A good selection of *washi* can be found on the 6th floor.

Kyukyodo, 5-7-4 Ginza, Chuo-ku, II, C3, ☎ 3571 4321. *Open Mon-Sat 10am-8pm, Sun 11am-7pm*. This shop also specializes in incense sticks and calligraphy.

Prints *(ukiyo-e)*
Japanese prints *(ukiyo-e)* consist of limited editions of coloured wood-block prints on paper. This typically Japanese art form developed during the Edo period and drew its subject matter from the courtesans and the leisure-life of the rich merchants of Edo. The name *ukiyo-e* literally means images of the floating world.

The best-known *ukiyo-e* masters are Kitagawa Utamaro (1753-1806), Katsushika Hokusai (1760-1849) and Ando Hiroshige (1797-1858). Their works now fetch enormous sums. Real *ukiyo-e* of less well known artists may be obtained, however, for around ¥20,000 to ¥30,000. Do not expect to find a renowned *shunga* (erotic print) on the market. Guarded in private collections, these notorious works are negotiated privately among collectors for astronomical sums.

Sakai Kokodo, 1-2-14 Yurakucho, Chiyoda-ku, II, C3, ☎ 3591 4678. *Open daily 10am-7pm*. One of the better-known dealers, this art gallery has specialized in *ukiyo-e* for over a century.

The **Oriental Bazaar** also sells a few *ukiyo-e*.

Records and cassettes
With the exception of compact discs made in Japan, records and cassettes are not much cheaper than they are in many other countries. The three following stores are by far the best known for their quality and selection of Western and Japanese music:

Disk Union, 3-31-4 Shinjuku, Shinjuku-ku, VI, A2, ☎ 3352 2691. *Open Mon-Sat 11am-8pm, Sun 11am-7pm*.

Kinokuniya, 3-17-7 Shinjuku, Shinjuku-ku, VI, C2, ☎ 3354 0131. *Open daily 10am-7pm; Closed the first and third Wed. of every month*. A large

A fish stand in the covered market at the Ameyoko Arcade in Ueno.

collection of classical and light music can be found on the 2nd floor of the bookstore of the same name (see 'Shopping' p. 64).

Wave, 6-2-27 Roppongi, Minato-ku, VIII, B3, ☎ 3408 0111. *Open daily 11am-9pm.* Several floors of music in this building, one of the most attractive in Roppongi.

Souvenirs *(omiyage)*

Japanese souvenirs *(omiyage),* like their counterparts throughout the world, come in a wide range of tastes and prices. If you have not already picked something up along the way and suddenly realize that you are about to leave Japan empty handed, try one of the following addresses:

Ameyoko Arcade, 4-7-8 Ueno, Taito-ku, IV, B3. *Open Thurs-Tues 10:30am-7pm.* This is a large covered market where everything (Western clothes, perfume, watches, fancy leather goods, souvenirs and so on) can be found for 20% to 50% cheaper than anywhere else in Tokyo. Beware of counterfeited articles and brand names offered for 'incredible' prices.

International Arcade, II, BC3, n° 5a, *Open daily 9am-7pm.* Near the Imperial Hotel in Ginza, this is a group of individual shops specializing in the tourist trade. Kimonos, *yukata* (robes worn indoors or under kimonos), T-shirts and photographic equipment are not any more expensive than elsewhere, and it is possible to buy whatever you choose at *menzei* (duty-free prices), if your bring you passport. Many of the shopkeepers speak English.

The Oriental Bazaar 5-9-13 Jingumae, Shibuya-ku, XI, C2, ☎ 3400 3933. *Open Fri-Wed 9:30am-6:30pm.* For souvenirs, this is *the* place, an immense three-storey store offering a wide range of arts and crafts, both new and old, at reasonable prices. The staff speaks English.

If you wish to buy costume jewelry, there is a large choice in the shops along **Takeshita Dori,** XI, C1, between the Oriental Bazaar and Harajuku Station.

Swords *(katana)*

Swords have been a traditional Japanese speciality since the 15th century. A few craftsmen still produce traditional *katana* (swords) but authentic antique weapons (often signed by master swordsmiths) are the most sought after. Many collectors also collect *tsuba* (metal scabbards used by the samurai), which are frequently as expensive as the swords themselves. One of the best shops is **Nihon Katana** (The Japanese Sword), 3-8-1 Toranomon, Minato-ku, III, A2, ☎ 3434 4321, near Kamiyacho or Toranomon stations.

Toys

The best-known toy shop in Tokyo is **Kiddyland,** 6-1-9 Jingumae, Shibuya-ku, XI, C2, ☎ 3409 3431. *Open Mon-Fri 10am-7pm, Sat-Sun 10am-8pm. Closed the third Tues of every month.* This store, on Omote Sando in Harajuku, is not far from the Oriental Bazaar.

The largest toy shop in Tokyo is **Toy Park** 8-8-11 Ginza, Chuo-ku, III, C2, ☎ 3571 8008. *Open daily 11am-8pm.*

▬ *TELEPHONES (DENWA)*

Telephone area code: 03.

Note: As of January 1, 1991, all 7-digit telephone numbers added a '3' before the existing number and became 8-digit numbers (for example, the number for the JNTO, ☎ 216 1902, became ☎ 3216 1902) The area code for Tokyo remained unchanged.

Very few cities in the world have as many public telephones as Tokyo. They are everywhere: in cafés, in shops, in hotels, in department stores, in banks, in lobbies of large buildings and even in certain trains, such as the *Shinkansen.* It is rare to find a phone that is out of order or one that does not give the right change. To use a phone, simply lift the receiver, insert a ¥10 coin and dial the number as soon as the you hear the dial tone. In Japan, local calls cost ¥10 for three minutes. The machines return all unused coins.

There are four types of telephones in Japan, easily recognized by their colour. **Red** and **blue** phones take only ¥10 coins (a maximum of six) and are best used only for local calls. **Yellow** phones accept up to ten coins of ¥10 and nine of ¥100 (total ¥1000). Use these phones for calls within Japan. **Green** phones have the same coin capacity as the yellow phones but also accept magnetic credit cards, sold in denominations of ¥500, ¥1000, ¥3000, and ¥5000. These machines automatically deduct the amount spent and show the remaining credit. The larger-value cards are perfect for long-distance calls, particularly overseas. Some of the newer green phones accept only credit cards.

For international calls, dial 0051 and ask for your number in English. If you wish to reverse charges, mention it to the operator. Rates are 25% cheaper on Sundays to Canada and the United States.

▬ *TIME*

Tokyo time is 14 hours ahead of that in New York City and nine hours ahead of that in London. When it is 5am in New York City (noon

Greenwich Mean Time in London), it is 9pm in Tokyo. Two or three days may be needed to recover from jet lag after a west-east flight.

All of Japan is in the same time zone. There is no daylight saving time (summertime). In Japan, the 24-hour clock is used more commonly than the 12-hour clock. This is true for restaurants as well as for train timetables.

In each district of Tokyo, bells chime at 5pm every day to alert children that it is time to go home. For tourists, this is a convenient way to keep track of closing times.

TIPPING

Tipping is unknown in Japan. However, a surcharge of 10% is added in restaurants if the bill is over ¥2500 per person and in hotels when it is above ¥5000 per person.

TOBACCO (TABAKO)

Tokyo is a haven for inveterate smokers. Even in the most remote areas of the city, vending machines furnish a seemingly endless supply of cigarettes any time of the day or night. In Japan, the most popular brand is *Seven Stars*, but American cigarettes are also widely available. Uncommon brands can be purchased in international hotels. Do not worry about matches because nearly every restaurant, bar and hotel distributes matchbooks free as publicity.

TOILETS (TOIRE or TE ARAI)

Like telephones, toilets are everywhere in Japan. Always free of charge and immaculately clean, they can be found in subway stations, hotels, cafés, department stores and public buildings.

Recently, an association for the revival of public toilets has taken on the task of putting more comfortable and luxurious toilets at the disposal of the public. You will undoubtedly come across at least one of the deluxe public conveniences during your stay in Tokyo. Some are so grandiose and well cared for that they could easily be mistaken for a temple or a tearoom.

In many private homes, *ryokan* (Japanese-style hotel) and traditional restaurants, a special pair of communal slippers is placed near the toilet door so that you need not walk on the cold tiles. Do not forget to change back into house slippers when you leave the toilet.

In Japan, toilets are normally of the squat type, although international hotels, large department stores and office buildings usually have Western-style facilities as well. Japanese toilets face away from the door and consist of an elongated depression covered at one end.

TOURIST INFORMATION

The Japan National Tourist Organization (JNTO), Tokyo Kotsu Kaikan, 10-1 Yurakucho 2-chome, Chiyoda-ku, III, C1, ☎ 3216 1902, is a semi-official organization that operates several tourist services and publishes numerous pamphlets and booklets.

The Tourist Information Center (TIC), Kotani Building, 6-6 Yurakucho 1-chome, Chiyoda-ku, III, C1, ☎ 3502 1461 *(open Mon-Fri 9am-5pm, Sat 9am-noon; closed holidays)* is near the subway stations Ginza (Sukiyabashi Crossing exit) and Yurakucho. This center, run by the JNTO, is at your disposal should you require any additional information concerning Tokyo, Kyoto or any other major city in Japan. English is spoken.

The **Japan Travel-Phone** is a toll-free, English-speaking service run by the JNTO for foreign visitors. Its purpose is to answer enquiries about traveling and to help tourists in difficulty (particularly with language problems). The service functions daily throughout Japan from 9am-5pm. Below are the telephone numbers for the various regions:

Tokyo area: (03) 3502 1461
Kyoto area: (075) 371 5649
North and east of Tokyo: (0120) 222 800
South and west of Tokyo: (0120) 444 800

In Tokyo and Kyoto, a 24-hour automatic answering **Teletourist Service** gives weekly tourist and cultural information in English, ☎ 3503 2911 (Tokyo) or 361 2911 (Kyoto).

▬ *TRANSPORTATION*

Train/subway

The best way of getting around Tokyo is by the *chikatetsu* (subway). It can conveniently be used in combination with the private train lines that also serve the metropolitan area.

All services within the city run between 5am and midnight. There are trains every two to ten minutes. It is best to avoid the morning and afternoon rush hours which occur between 7:30-9:30am and 5-6pm.

The subway and the JR stations have bilingual signs with the names of the station in Japanese and roman characters. The subway maps in the stations, however, are printed in Japanese only so it is advisable to carry one printed in English with you. These can be obtained at the Tourist Information Center (see p. 71) and at certain of the large hotels.

The Tokyo transport system is similar to that of most other major cities throughout the world. The direction of a train is indicated by the name of the terminus. In the stations, the connections between the different lines are designated by circles corresponding to the colour of the line and the exits are marked by yellow 'Exit' signs.

You will probably use the 'green' **Yamanote Loop Line** often. It encircles the center of Tokyo and connects the principal center of Shinjuku, Harajuku, Shibuya, Yurakucho (the Ginza district), Tokyo, Akihabara, Ueno and Ikebukuro.

The other lines you will probably use often are the **Marunouchi Line** (for Shinjuku), the **Hibiya Line** (for Roppongi) and the **Ginza Line** (for Asakusa).

How to pay in the subway

The fare varies according to the distance traveled. A general plan of the subway network, placed over the ticket-distributing machines, indicates the price for each destination. These signs, however, are written exclusively in Japanese, so you will have to find someone to read them for you. If there is no one around (or if you are too timid to ask), put the minimum amount in the machine ¥120 or ¥150 depending on the line) and pay the rest at the Fare Adjustment Office window on the way out.

To buy a ticket, put either coins or a ¥1000 bill in the machine and press the button corresponding to the amount needed for your destination. The machine gives change. Should any problem arise, press the red button and your money will be immediately returned.

Note that subway *(chikatetsu)* tickets are not valid on the JR Yamanote Line and vice versa. The other private railway lines, such as the Toyoko Line and the Inokashira Sen Line, have their own tickets as well. In the large stations, make sure you have chosen a machine corresponding to the line you intend to take.

The ticket is punched at the entrance and required at the exit. Be careful not to lose it.

If you use the same line frequently, it might be of interest to acquire a magnetic debit ticket. It functions in the same way as a telephone card (see p. 70).

What are they saying?

In the subway, unending messages are constantly being delivered over loudspeakers, both on the platforms and in the trains. Usually, it is only the transport company thanking you for having chosen their line and assuring you that the company has done everything within its power to make your trip as comfortable as possible. On the platforms, certain messages also announce the danger of arriving trains and ask you to stay behind the white line: *'abunai desu kara...haku sen no uchi gawa e osagari kudasai'*. The information given in the trains is more useful. While the train is still moving, the conductor announces, *'Tsugi wa Roppongi desu'* ('Next stop, Roppongi'), and when the doors open, he says, *'Roppongi desui'* ('Roppongi').

Expresses and locals

All the subway trains, as well as the Yamanote Line trains, are locals and stop at every station. Most of the private lines, on the other hand, operate according to a dual system of local and express trains. Sometimes a 'super-express' stops at only two or three stations along the line before arriving at the terminus. The express trains *(kyuko densha)* are recognized by red signs on the front and the rear of the train. Local trains *(kakueki teisha)* merely have the name of the terminus written in black.

The central stations

In the central stations, it is hard not to be intimidated by the massive entanglement of platforms and underground passages; even the Japanese frequently get lost in these concrete labyrinths. The four largest stations in Tokyo are: **Shinjuku,** VI, B2; **Shibuya,** XI, B3; **Ueno,** IV, B3; and **Tokyo,** II, C2. As a visitor, you will most likely use the last two.

On the first of April 1987, Japan National Railways (JNR) was privatized and became *grosso modo* the Japan Railways (JR).

Boat

Boats are no longer a common form of transport in Tokyo. It is still possible, however, to take the 'waterbus' from **Hama-Rikyu Garden,** III, C3, (near Hamamatsucho Station) to **Azuma Bridge,** V, B2 (near Asakusa Station), and vice versa. The journey takes about 40 minutes but is not particularly picturesque. The banks of the Sumida lost much of their charm when a concrete flood wall was built to contain the river.

Streetcars

The streetcars were formerly the pride of the city, but only a single line remains of the once-extensive Tokyo municipal service. The 7.5-mile/12-km journey from Waseda to Minowabashi is a pleasant trip and a good way to see the city. There are several temples and shrines along the way. The Mizu-Inari shrine is not far from Omokagebashi Station and the Zoshigaya Kishibojin (Children's Temple) is near the Kishibojin-mae stop. Those who have read the 19th-century English novelist Lafcadio Hearn (best known for *Kwaidan*) may wish to visit his grave in the Zoshigaya Reien cemetery near Higashi Ikebukuro Yonchome Station.

Bus *(basu)*

Although extensive, the Tokyo bus system is undoubtedly the most difficult means of transportation for anyone who does not read Japanese. All the destinations are written in *kanji* (ideograms), and unless you memorize a few of them, it will be impossible for you to use this efficient network. Moreover, their routes are very complicated, and even Tokyoites are frequently confused. If you have enough time, however, it is possible to use the bus system as a means of visiting Tokyo. Get on any bus at random and go wherever it happens to take you. Unlike the subway system, there is a set price regardless of the distance. Simply get on the front of the bus, put ¥160 in the machine located next to the driver and take a seat. Even though the machines give change, it is best to have the right amount handy as this saves time for both you and the other passengers.

Taxis *(takushi)*

There are over 50,000 *takushi* (taxis) in Tokyo. They are generally large, comfortable cars driven by chauffeurs in white gloves. Some are even equipped with television sets!

A vacant taxi is recognized by a red light in the lower-left corner of the windscreen. A green light indicates that the 30% night surcharge is operational, while a yellow light means that the taxi is answering a radio call. To get a taxi, simply raise your arm. Do not hail a vehicle traveling in the direction opposite to that of your destination. The driver will refuse to make a U-turn (illegal in Tokyo).

As most streets in Tokyo do not have names, a mere address is usually insufficient, and it is best to show the driver a business card with a map or a sketch drawn by a local resident. If this is impossible, indicate a well-known building or a station close to where you are going.

Tokyo is a large, sprawling city, and an average taxi ride can easily cost ¥2000 to ¥3000, if not more. For long journeys, it is more economical — and frequently faster — to take a train or a subway to the nearest station and then take a taxi once you are in the right neighbourhood.

Tips are never given in taxis. At night, there is a 30% increase between 11pm-5am. On Saturday night and on the eve of a holiday, it is nearly impossible to find a taxi in certain districts, particularly Shinjuku, Ginza or Roppongi. At such times, you will see the Japanese conspicuously raise two or even three fingers. This means that they are willing to double or triple the normal price (in company taxi coupons). If you find yourself in the midst of a nocturnal taxi auction and are near a large station, give up the idea of a cab and spend the night in a capsule hotel instead. It will cost about ¥3000 and will be considerably cheaper and less frustrating than trying to find a taxi.

In Tokyo, the passenger door (back left) of a taxi opens and closes automatically. Do not try to open or close it yourself as the mechanism is delicate. Drivers do not like to open their storage space as they keep their own personal possessions there. You are expected to put your luggage on the seat beside you.

▬ *VISITING A JAPANESE HOME OR FACTORY*

If you do not already have an invitation to visit a Japanese home during your stay, contact the TIC, ☎ 3502 1461. They can arrange a visit within 24 hours. The Japan National Tourist Office (see p. 71) publishes a brochure called *Home Visit System,* which is full of useful information and advice. Do not forget to bring a small personal gift for the family. One from your home country will be particularly appreciated.

Japanese factories (automobiles, cameras and electronics) can also be visited on request. Arrangements should be made through the JNTO at least one month in advance.

▬ *WATER (MIZU)*

All tap water in Japan is safe to drink. In Tokyo, however, it has a slightly chlorinated taste to which some people are not accustomed.

When you enter a café, a waiter will bring you a warm towel *(o shibori)* and a glass of ice water even before taking your order. This practice — a welcoming ritual — is performed without exception.

In restaurants, the glass of water is replaced by a cup of tea that is refilled as many times as you request.

The Japanese house

The major factors that originally influenced traditional Japanese architecture were the climate, the abundance of wood and the lack of any other suitable building material. In Japan, winters are mild and summers are hot and humid. Houses were thus designed for summer needs with an emphasis on ventilation rather than on insulation.

The orientation of Japanese houses is very important. In principle, structures should be built along a north-west/south-east axis, but in practice they usually face south toward the land of Buddha. This orientation is not so as to have more sun, but in order to be in contact with the *kami* (gods). The Japanese concepts concerning the virtues of the sun are different from those of many Western cultures as is so vividly expressed in Tanizaki's *In Praise of Shadows.*

Originally, Japanese houses were made exclusively of wood and were covered by large, heavy roofs of thatch or blue or grey tiles. Of prehistoric origin, these low buildings were simple post-and-beam structures without foundations or weight-bearing walls. The boarded floors were covered with *tatami* (straw mats).

Built on one level only, traditional Japanese houses are basically large six-sided structures that tend to be asymmetrical. The shape is based on the dimensions of the *tatami* and all rooms are multiples of standard mat sizes. Separations and entrances are formed by *fusuma* (sliding partitions made of wood and paper) that function as both doors and walls. When the *fusuma* are open or removed, there is no formal boundary between the interior and the exterior. *Fusuma* are normally dismantled in the summer. Traditional Japanese houses are surrounded by exceptionally well cared for gardens. No matter how small the garden is, it must give the impression that the house was built in the middle of the country.

Houses are entered by the *genkan,* a small hall with a low ceiling where shoes are exchanged for slippers. The next room is generally empty except for a low table surrounded by flat cushions *(zabuton).* It is here that guests are invariably served tea. During the winter, the table is covered with a quilted blanket and a small heater *(kotatsu),* placed under the table, diffuses a gentle heat.

The rooms are separated by *fusuma* that slide noiselessly on wooden rails. These sliding walls are so thin that when private conversation is held, the *fusuma* are opened rather than closed, making it impossible for anyone to listen from behind them.

No evidence of any bedding is seen in Japanese houses. During the day, the *futon* (Japanese mattresses) are folded and arranged in deep closets and are taken out only immediately before retiring for the night. All personal objects (clothes, books and so on) are also put away.

Westerners, accustomed to an overabundance of more or less personal objects, are frequently taken aback by the emptiness of a Japanese room. Only in the *tokonoma* (small niche in the wall) may a decorative note, such as a bouquet or a calligraphy, be found.

To the Japanese, this empty — almost abstract — space is an aesthetic ideal that allows the soul to put aside its daily worries and to seek peace.

During the 20th century, the fear of fires and, more recently, the influence of Western building methods, have slowly brought about the replacement of traditional Japanese architecture with ferroconcrete structures. Today, it is necessary to wander extensively through Asakusa or Ueno to find, hidden behind thick vegetation, a traditional Japanese house.

▬ *VOLTAGE*

In Japan, the electrical current is 100 volts AC. The frequency is 50Hz in Tokyo and the north-east and 60Hz in the south-west. Plugs are twin flat pins as in Canada and the United States. Most appliances designed for use in North America will function in Japan. Many hotels have adapters for European appliances.

TOKYO IN THE PAST

The earliest known human occupation of the area that was later to become Tokyo dates from the late Neolithic period (3rd century BC to 3rd century AD). During this period — named the Yayoi period after the street in Tokyo where the pottery that characterized it was first discovered — rice cultivation was introduced from China and the fundamental elements of Japanese society emerged. Other prehistoric sites have since been excavated in various parts of the capital.

Towards the end of the 6th century, Hashino Nakatamo, who had been banished to the area around the estuary of the Sumidagawa (Sumida River), founded a fishing village named Edo and the original Asakusa temple. For nearly 1000 years, Edo remained a small community of about 100 houses, until 1456 when a war lord named Ota Dokan built Edo castle. Dokan was later assassinated, and his estate eventually passed into the hands of the powerful Hojo family. By 1590, General Toyotomi Hideyoshi had completed the unification of Japan and received the title of *kampaku* (civil dictator). Establishing himself at Osaka in order to survey the activities of the Imperial court at Kyoto, he entrusted the province of Kanto to his most loyal ally, Tokugawa Ieyasu, who ousted the Hojo family and took Edo castle as his own fortress.

When Hideyoshi died in 1598, Tokugawa Ieyasu seized power and reestablished the office of shogunate in 1603. Ruling the country from his castle in Edo, the new Shogun was fully conscious of the risks involved in governing Japan so far away from the Imperial court at Kyoto. To reduce the risk of rebellion he instituted a law *(sankin-kotai)* obliging all *daimyo* (landed feudal lords) to reside in Edo at least every other year. Their wives and children, moreover, had to remain behind in Edo as hostages of the shogun whenever the *daimyo* returned to their fiefs or visited the Imperial court in Kyoto. The *daimyo* who were accompanied by small armies of samurai (their retainers and vassals) were responsible for traveling expenses as well as for the cost of maintaining their families in Edo.

The Tokaido Road (East Sea Road), linking Edo to Kyoto, was by far the road most frequently used by the nobles who traveled by horseback or palanquin. Over 370 miles/600 km long, the journey took at least two weeks. The Tokaido was later immortalized by Japan's greatest artists.

An ukiyo-e from the early 19th century when Hokusai, Utamaro and Hiroshige were creating the masterpieces that reflected the epicurean trends of their day.

The power struggle: Emperor vs Shogun

The Emperor

The Imperial family (the Yamato clan) is traditionally said to be descended from Amaterasu, the Sun Goddess and chief deity of the Shinto pantheon. Other important clans traced their ancestry to the lesser gods. The early primacy of the Imperial clan appears to have been more religious than political in nature.

The first Emperor is claimed to have been Jimmu Tenno (Emperor of Divine Valour) in 660 BC. Yet no real records exist prior to about AD 400 when the court at Yamato undertook and partially achieved the unification of Japan. During the formation of the nation the stage was set for a formidable power struggle in Japan. The great clans struggled against one another for over a thousand years up until the Tokugawa shogunate's supremacy.

During the Asuka period, Prince Shotoku (AD 593-622), backed by the Soga clan, became regent *(sessho)* of Japan. In an attempt to end clan rivalry, he changed the government from a system based on clans *(uji)* to an Imperial court with a large complex bureaucracy. The Emperor himself did not actually hold power. During this period of unification and centralization, mainland culture was imported from China and Korea.

In AD 645, the great nobles of Japan were summoned to the Imperial court to hear a proclamation of absolute monarchy. This system, sponsored by the Soga clan, installed a government based on the Chinese model.

During the Nara (710-794) and Heian (794-1185) periods, power was held at the Imperial court (but not necessarily by the Emperor). With the onset of the Imperial state, the Fujiwara clan increased their power. During the Heian period, they ruled Japan as regents without actually ever seizing the throne. Their method was similar to that used by the Soga. Whereas the Soga clan finally developed Imperial pretensions, the Fujiwara preferred to rule as *sessho* or *kampaku* (civil dictator). The Fujiwara family reached the height of its power under Fujiwara Michinaga, who controlled the court from AD 995-1027.

Kyoto's primacy as the economic and political center of Japan, however, was being eroded by new landholding policies and other administrative changes in the rural districts. Between 1068 and 1156, the 'retired Emperors' managed to rule from behind the scenes as the Fujiwara began to decline in favour of the Minamoto and other clans.

The period of Imperial rule ended in civil war in 1156. Eventually, Minamoto Yoritomo set up his *bakufu* in 1192 and established the supremacy of the shogunate that was to last until 1867. A feudal period in Japanese history began.

The Shogun

The shogun (short for *sei-i-tai-shogun* which literally means great general-issimo for the subjugation of the barbarians) was originally one of the many titles under which early Emperors commissioned military commanders for the campaigns against the Ainu of northern Japan. The title first appeared in AD 720 but lost its meaning with the pacification of the northern areas in the 9th century.

Minamoto Yoritomo (1148-99) first used the office of shogun as a means of asserting military and political authority over the country. As the military class acquired increased powers over national and local affairs, the shogun (as chief of the army) became *de facto* the ruler of Japan, although the Emperor continued to retain formal sovereignty.

Minamoto Yoritomo founded a hereditary dynasty of shoguns who ruled from Kamakura (1192-1333). A second line begun by the Ashikaga clan ruled from Kyoto (1338-1573). A third, the Tokugawa, ruled from Edo (1603-1867). Thus, in the name of a powerless Emperor, five great families ruled Japan for seven centuries. The Hojo family, as an exception to this pattern, took control as regents from 1200-1333 when the early Kamakura-based shoguns proved incapable of ruling.

From a Western point of view, the Edo Tokugawa period (1603-1868) appears hostile but for the Japanese it was a period of peace after nearly 1000 years of civil war and clan strife. In the late 19th century, Western intrusion into Japanese affairs renewed the power struggle. The question of authority between the shogun ('tycoon') and the Emperor ('mikado') became an issue once again. In 1868, the Tokugawa shogun resigned and restituted his prerogatives as civil and military ruler to the Emperor.

After a few years of the Tokugawa regime, Edo quickly became the most prosperous city in Japan. From every corner of the land, samurai, merchants, craftsmen and artists poured into the new, unofficial capital to profit from the growing wealth. Here, the tradesmen grew richer, while the *daimyo,* who had to maintain two residences and travel extensively, fell slowly into debt. Edo was now the economic as well as the political centre of Japan.

The social structure of Japan did not allow different castes to live in the same districts. The *daimyo* and their vassal samurai established themselves on the uplands of Yamanote (the Upper Town), while the merchants and artisans crowded into the lower plain of Shitamachi (the Lower Town). This division of class is still visible in the social composition of Tokyo today.

1615-1868: THE TOKUGAWA AND THE POLICY OF ISOLATION

The Tokugawa family ruled Japan peacefully and efficiently for 265 years. Extremely conservative and suspicious of foreign influences, they sealed the country from the outside world. In 1614, a law was instated forbidding the Japanese to leave the archipelago on pain of death. All foreigners were expelled, with the exception of a few licensed Dutch and Chinese merchants. Spanish or Portuguese shipwrecked sailors found on Japanese territory were imprisoned or executed, as were many Spanish, Portuguese and Dutch missionaries. The Japanese who had embraced the Christian faith were persecuted and many suffered martyrdom. This period of absolute, autocratic rule lasted until the Imperial Restoration of 1868.

THE EDO PERIOD: PEACE AND CULTURAL DEVELOPMENT

On the cultural level, however, the Edo period was one of the richest and most progressive in the history of Japan. The rise of a merchant class with money to spend was one of the major keys to this development. Their taste for sensualism gave rise to Kabuki theatre. Its vitality, its extravagant decor, and most of all, its eroticism provided a lively alternative to the old-fashioned and often tedious Noh drama on which it was based.

The authorities, however, considered Kabuki theatre decadent and tried to curb its increasing popularity by forbidding women to appear on the stage. This resulted in the rise of *onnagata* (female impersonators) who played the women's roles. This novel innovation, however, only increased public interest in Kabuki, which became more blatantly obscene than ever before!

The lustful lives of the Edo merchants inspired the artists of the times. The middle class became both subject and patron of a popular new art form, the world-renowned *ukiyo-e.* Interpreting this erotic 'floating world' *(ukiyo)* in a series of colour wood-block prints whose editions ran into the thousands, great masters such as Hokusai, Hiroshige and Utamaro depicted an unrepressed bourgeois society openly devoted to pleasure.

1868: THE MEIJI RESTORATION

By the middle of the 19th century, Europe and the United States had already undergone Industrial Revolutions. Japan, despite its cultural achievements, was still a feudal land ruled by a military clique who literally held the power of life and death over the rest of society.

In July 1853, an American naval squadron under the command of Commodore Matthew Perry entered the fortified harbour of Araga. Perry refused Japanese orders to leave until the shogunate officially accepted certain documents from the American government. These documents were letters of 'advice' to the Shogun concerning his foreign policy and suggested that the Japanese cease their policy of isolation. When the documents were finally delivered, Perry announced that he would call again a year later to receive the reply. In February 1854, Perry reappeared more heavily armed than before and anchored in Tokyo Bay. An agreement, the Treaty of Kanagawa, was reluctantly signed by the shogunate. The treaty, which was actually nothing more than a test of force, stated that American ships would be allowed to call at two minor Japanese ports for fuel and supplies and that shipwrecked sailors would receive better treatment than they had in the past.

Caught between the American gunboats and Japanese isolationism, the Shogun consulted the Emperor for the first time in over 600 years of military rule. Without hesitation, the spiritual leader of Japan demanded that the *namban* (barbarians from the south) be expelled immediately and the agreement be annulled. The Shogun, however, did not have the military means to ignore American pressure and was forced to honour the treaty.

By disobeying the Emperor, who in the eyes of the Japanese was a living god, the Shogun lost the confidence of many of his supporters. Revolt broke out, and the Tokugawa family, confronted with certain military defeat, resigned from office in the hope of a political arrangement. But the shogunal dynasty fell, opening the way for the triumphant restoration of Imperial power; Mutsuhito, who took the name Meiji (Enlightened Rule), became the absolute ruler of Japan at the age of 15. One of his first decisions was to move the Imperial court from Kyoto to Edo, which was renamed Tokyo (Eastern Capital) in 1869. Ironically, it was under the patronage of the Emperor — the oldest of Japanese traditions — that the country was to be catapulted into the modern world.

Since then, a harmony between tradition and progress has been one of the major features of modern Japanese life: Eastern ethics and Western science.

A TOWN FREQUENTLY DESTROYED

Under the Tokugawa, the population of Edo had grown to 1.5 million. The city was not only the largest in Japan but also one of the largest in the world, second only to Beijing. This enormous urban sprawl contained all the attendant problems of hygiene and security. In 1657, a gigantic fire destroyed over half the city. During the reconstruction, large avenues designed to act as fire breaks were built. Owing to such foresight, the fire of 1872 was limited to the Ginza district.

On the other hand, no measures had yet been developed to protect the city against the frequent earthquakes that devastated the region. A violent tremor hit Tokyo in 1703. In 1923, an even more destructive earthquake struck the city and over 100,000 people perished. To make matters worse, this catastrophe occurred at midday when the *hibachi* (charcoal braziers) were in use, causing numerous fires that did more damage than the shock wave itself. As a preventive measure for structural failure, all of the buildings in Tokyo had been built of wood precisely because of the danger of earthquakes!

The city had barely recovered from this cataclysm when it suffered heavy American fire-bombing raids in 1945. At least 140,000 people were killed (more than at Hiroshima), and 760,000 houses (over half the city) were totally destroyed.

At the time of the Japanese surrender in 1945, Tokyo was little more than a heap of ashes. As a result of American investment and a zealous population eager to rebuild their capital at all costs, a new city was rapidly constructed. But it was not until 1964, the year the Olympics were held in Tokyo, that the city — and all of Japan for that matter — truly rose from its ruins.

Today, certain sections of the city are excessively Westernized and resemble an 'oriental New York' complete with neon lights, hamburger restaurants and rock-n-roll clubs. Overpopulated and over-priced (property values rose 300% in the last four years), Tokyo presents the fascinating image of a city without a past.

CHRONOLOGY

Dates	Japan	West
5000 BC-AD 300	Jomon and Yayoi periods (or Japanese Neolithic): In 660 BC, the legendary Emperor Jimmu mounts the throne.	5000 BC-AD 410: Neolithic, Bronze and Iron Ages. Greco-Roman civilizations extend from Scotland to India. In AD 410, Rome falls.
AD 300-552	Kofun period: Large tumulus burials attest to highly organized social structures. At the beginning of the 5th century, the Japanese adopt a system of writing based on Chinese ideograms.	AD 450: Attila and the Huns ravage Europe. 500: Clovis is baptized and establishes the Frankish Kingdom.
AD 552-710	Asuka period: Beginning of the Yamato State. In AD 552, Buddhism is introduced into Japan.	
AD 710-794	Nara period: Invention of a Japanese syllabary *(katakana)*. In AD 794, the capital is moved to Heian (ancient Kyoto).	732: Charles Martel defeats the Arabs at Poitiers.
794-1185	Heian period: The Fujiwara clan rules Japan under the title *sessho* (regent). In 1020, Lady Murasaki writes the *Tale of Genji,* the world's first important novel.	800: Charlemagne is crowned Emperor of the Romans. 1066: William the Conqueror defeats Harold at Hastings. 1095: The First Crusade is proclaimed at the Council of Clermont.
1185-1333	Kamakura period: Minamoto Yoritomo becomes the first shogun in 1192. In 1333, the Hojo family (successors of the Minamoto) are massacred by Emperor Go-Daigo's troops, bringing the Kamakura shogunate to an end.	1215: King John signs the Magna Carta.
1333-1573	Muromachi period: Emperor Go-Daigo's attempt to reestablish Imperial power fails. The Ashikaga clan betrays the Emperor and establishes a new dynasty of shoguns in 1338. In 1549, Francis Xavier and the first Jesuit missionaries arrive in Japan.	1431: Joan of Arc is burned at the stake by the English. 1455: Gutenberg invents the printing press. 1492: Columbus accidentally discovers America while trying to reach Japan by sailing west. The same year, the Moslems are driven from Spain. 1517: Luther nails his protest to the Wittenberg church. 1522: Magellan's expedition first circumnavigates the world.
1573-1603	Momoyama period: Three dictators (Oda Nobunaga, Toyotomi Hideyoshi and Tokygawa Ieyasu) unify Japan.	1588: After an unsuccessful attempt to invade England, the Spanish Armada is destroyed by storms.

)F HISTORICAL EVENTS

Dates	Japan	West
603-1868	Edo period: The Tokugawa family rules Japan from Edo (ancient Tokyo) in the first relatively peaceful reign in over 1000 years. Japan is closed to the outside world. Christians are persecuted.	1649-58: As military dictator, Cromwell rules England. 1776: The American Declaration of Independence is proclaimed. 1789: The Bastille is stormed, and the French Revolution begins. 1804: Napoleon proclaims himself Emperor of France. 1860-65: The American Civil War.
868-1912	Meiji (Enlightened Rule) period: The Emperor regains power (for nearly 1000 years, Emperors were mere figureheads). In 1904, the Japanese attack the Russian fleet at Port Arthur. Japan emerges from the conflict as a world power.	1871: The Franco-Prussian War.
912-26	Taisho (Great Justice) period: Rise of nationalism and militarism. In 1914, Japan declares war on Germany. In 1923, a severe earthquake hits Tokyo, killing between 50,000 and 100,000 people.	1914-18: World War I. In 1917, the Bolshevik Revolution begins.
926-89	Showa (Radiating Peace) period: In 1932, Japan occupies Manchuria. On December 7, 1941, the Japanese attack Pearl Harbor. In August 1945, after Hiroshima and Nagasaki are annihilated by American atomic bombs, Emperor Hirohito acknowledges the defeat of Japan and renounces his divine ascendancy. In 1970, the writer Yukio Mishima commits *seppuku* (ritual suicide) to protest against the disarmament of Japan. Japan maintains good diplomatic relations with most countries except the Soviet Union (estranged over the Kuril Islands dispute). On January 7, 1989, Hirohito dies and is succeeded by his son, Prince Akihito.	1929: The Stock Market crashes, and worldwide recession follows. 1939-45: World War II. In February 1945, the Yalta Conference determines the future of all countries occupied by Allied Forces and the cold war begins. In June, the United Nations in founded. 1950-53: The Korean War. 1959: The Cuban Revolution is followed by the Bay of Pigs fiasco in 1961 and the Cuban Missile Crisis in 1962. 1968: Worldwide contestation of the status quo. Czechoslovakia is invaded by the Warsaw Pact countries. Vietnam peace conference in Paris.
989-present	Heisei period: Akihito becomes Emperor of Japan under the name of Heisi (Peace).	1989: Fall of the Berlin Wall.

TOKYO TODAY

With over 8 million inhabitants (nearly 12 million counting the suburbs), Tokyo is one of the most populated cities in the world. 'Human ant-hill', 'Asian New York' and 'City-planet' are some of the epithets given to this indecipherable conurbation. Who are these men and women who change so easily from a kimono into a three-piece suit or a Chanel outfit and then return from the tea ceremony to the computer?

THE WORLD'S MOST EXPENSIVE REAL ESTATE

A recent poll has shown that nearly 90% of the population of Tokyo is middle class; nevertheless, there is a wide social and economic stratification within the city. Salaries vary enormously and determine the multifarious standards of living evident in the city.

The Japanese are discreet and rarely rebel, as if observing to the letter the Japanese proverb, 'the nail that sticks up gets hammered down'. A recent study revealed that even the managers and owners of Japan's biggest companies are perfectly content with a modest suburban villa.

This may be due in part to the price of property in Tokyo; land-values in Ginza are the highest in the world and can reach up to $1 million per square metre. At this rate, living in the city center is a luxury almost no one can afford. The majority of salaried employees travel 20 to 30 miles/30 to 50 km to and from work, spending over three hours every day on overcrowded public transportation.

NEARLY CRIMELESS

Miraculously, the incredibly high density of Tokyo's population has not given rise to street crime as it has in other cities, such as New York. In fact Tokyo's crime rate is one of the lowest in the world. This may be explained by the high level of education in Japan. Despite having one of the most complicated

The Asakuja Jinja, one of Tokyo's most well known Shinto shrines.

systems of writing in the world, Japan's literacy rate is said to be 99.7%. Furthermore, the world economic crisis — which is responsible for a great deal of petty crime — has not affected Japan as much as it has many other nations.

Tokyo also has one of the largest police forces in the world, and they patrol every neighbourhood 24 hours a day from the local *koban* (miniature police station). Thanks to these preventative measures, a woman can walk down almost any street in Tokyo at 2am without fear of being attacked.

Identity checks are nearly unheard of in Japan, which is convenient because the Japanese do not carry any identification apart from their *meishi* (calling cards). As a foreigner, however, you are obliged to carry valid identification.

NEIGHBOURHOOD LIFE

Tokyo is officially divided into 23 *ku* (wards). These, however, are more an administrative division than a physical reflection of the city's social structure. Tokyoites prefer to speak in terms of smaller and more human units: districts and neighbourhoods. They might work in Harajuku, live in Ikebukuro and dine in Shinjuku. In Tokyo, there are dozens of such 'city centers', each with its own personality and function.

The character of a neighbourhood in Tokyo may change radically depending on the time of day. Shinjuku, for example, is a respectable district of offices and large department stores during the day but becomes a haven for the perverse at night, when sex shops and massage parlours appear as if out of the darkness. Shibuya, more respectable, is frequented at all hours by a moneyed, trendy set who buy their clothes at Parco (Tokyo's fashionable department store) and eat at McDonalds — considered chic in the land of sushi!

Roppongi is the foreigner's district. Towards midnight, it is possible to see Swedish or American models nibbling on *mochi* (rice cakes) as they leave a local disco. Ginza is the area for important businesses and exclusive shops, while the more traditional Asakusa is the home of *tatami* and bamboo. Harajuku is the favourite meeting place for Japan's punk rockers, Aoyama is the high-fashion district and Ueno has the finest museums in Japan.

This brief survey of Tokyo's many centers is an indication of the astonishing diversity of the city. All tastes and budgets can be satisfied in Tokyo, as is apparent, for example, in the vast number of restaurants offering every major cuisine of the world — from Turkish *shish kebabs* to French *bœuf en daube,* not to mention innumerable Japanese specialities (see Japanese Cuisine p. 89).

ARCHITECTURE

The wide variety of architectural styles in Tokyo is no less suprising. Destroyed twice during the 20th century, the city was quickly rebuilt on both occasions. It now encompasses every style

— from traditional Japanese single-storey wooden houses to contemporary streamlined ferroconcrete towers soaring into the sky. Between these extremes, there is a full range of buildings in every style, from the simplest to the most Baroque. This complete liberty of expression sometimes gives rise to curious aesthetic contradictions, such as the view of a colossal Bavarian castle rising out of a group of traditional Japanese houses.

Tokyo, as many Japanese urban planners have pointed out, has no overall inclusive plan or general perspective. Unlike large European cities, it is made up of a number of disconnected smaller urban units that coexist without ever integrating with one another, making the city a compilation rather than composition.

The Italian writer Fosco Maraini, who lived for a number of years in Tokyo, said that in building their cities, 'the Japanese take a hidden pleasure in making them hideous, as if they wish to protect their real treasures by surrounding them with ugliness'.

Neither temples nor pagodas soften this grim and implacable logic of concrete. Rampant and sprawling, Tokyo is a city that shows its teeth before its heart. To discover the human and refined aspects of the place, you must first brave the confusing maze of highways and towering buildings.

A FINANCIAL AND CULTURAL CAPITAL

In this 'creative chaos' the Japanese are feverishly preparing for the 21st century.

With seven television channels, over 100 private radio stations and as many daily papers (of which two print over 10 million copies a day), Tokyo is one of the best-informed capitals in the world. Information goes hand in hand with business. Registering a recent annual turnover of $2500 billion, the city has become the second most important financial capital of the world, just after New York. With a growth rate three times that of the Big Apple, Tokyo could very soon usurp the leading role. The 1987 stock market crash did not effect the Japanese economy in the least; on the contrary, foreseen by experts well in advance, it confirmed the solidity of the yen.

The Japanese, however, are not merely content to play the role of the world's bankers. Cultural developments in Japan have been stimulated by the growing economy, and the country is now developing and exporting 'civilization' and art as well as technology.

Without abandoning their own heritage (which is increasing in popularity outside Japan, as witnessed recently the worldwide interest in Kabuki theatre, sumo wrestling and the martial arts), the Japanese have invested heavily in all fields of traditional Western arts and skills. In many of these domains, Japanese students have quickly become masters. In the realm of fashion, for example, Hanae Mori, Kenzo and Kansai have achieved success on a par with Christian Dior, Hermes and Cardin.

Japanese cinema is also recognized as one of the most original and expressive in the world.

Summary of Japanese cinema

Although it has recently experienced a slight decline, Japanese cinema continues to be productive. Four large companies share the market: Toho, Toei, Shochiku and Nikkatsu. Between them, they own all the cinemas in Tokyo.

Five Japanese directors have archieved international recognition: Yasujiro Ozu — *The Taste of Mackerel* and *Tokyo Story;* Kenji Mizoguchi — *Sisters of Gion* and *The Tales of the Silvery and Vague Moon after the Rain* (British title); *Ugetsu* (US title); Akira Kurosawa — *Seven Samurai* and *The Lower Depths;* Shoei Imamura — *The Ballad of Narayama;* and Nagisa Oshima — *The Realm of the Senses.*

Other directors such as Teinosuke Kinugasa, Mikio Naruse and Hiroshi Teshigara, although less famous in the West, figure among the best known in Japan.

In the last few years, modern Japanese artists have been influential in the realms of graphics, design and video. Seething with ideas, talent and — most of all — money, Tokyo holds all the trumps for becoming the beacon city of the planet by the year 2000.

Yet as long as you can still hear the whining of bicycles and the sweet-potato vendor singing his melancholic refrain, you will still feel the village origins of Tokyo.

JAPANESE CUISINE

Rice forms the basis of the Japanese diet, accompanying almost every meal and served boiled. The second most important food is fish — an abundant natural resource of the island, that is eaten both raw and cooked. Meat, on the other hand, is very expensive and has not yet been fully adopted by the Japanese. Before the Meiji Restoration of 1868, Buddhism forbade its consumption, and anyone who worked in the meat trade was considered impure. Even today the descendants of these meat workers are often victims of discrimination. On the whole, Japanese cooking is light, fat free and rich in minerals. This diet is a major contributing factor to the life expectancy of the Japanese, which is among the highest in the world.

The incredible variety of culinary specialities in Japan strikes the visitor immediately. Among the best-known dishes are: *yakitori* (grilled chicken), *sashimi* (raw fish), *tonkatsu* (breaded pork cutlets) and *tempura* (fish and vegetable fritters). Foreign-style Japanese cooking includes Korean, Chinese, Thai, French and Italian dishes that have frequently been "Japonized" beyond recognition.

Japanese food goes well with beer (Kirin and Sapporo are excellent brands), hot sake or *ocha* (green Japanese tea). In restaurants, tea is served free of charge. Japanese wines, despite their pretentious French names and fancy labels, are disappointing and do not suit the subtle taste of Japanese food.

With about 80,000 restaurants, Tokyo is certainly one of the world's easiest cities in which to eat. Most restaurants open for lunch around 11:30am and remain open until 9pm. Except in certain animated districts, such as Shinjuku and Roppongi, it is difficult to be served any later.

Generally, you can eat at any time during the day, but in order to take advantage of the *teishoku* (lunchtime, fixed-price menu), you must arrive before 2pm. The menu is set and you are not obliged to choose from a variety of dishes you do not know anything about in the first place. Just look around at what the rest of the customers are eating. Nine times out of ten they will have ordered the *teishoku*.

Although Tokyo is an important international city, the foreign population is not large. As a result, restaurants — particularly those located outside the important centers — are not accustomed to serving tourists. The arrival of a *gaijin* (foreigner) almost always provokes mass panic in the establishment: will the staff understand the customer's order? Will the guest like Japanese food? The Japanese are so convinced of being 'different' that they are extremely surprised when a foreigner admits liking raw fish. Any foreigner capable of eating *natto* (fermented soyabean), becomes a *henna-gaijin* ('strange' foreigner).

Even if you do not speak Japanese, it is usually easy to make yourself understood in a restaurant. Many establishments have *mihon* (wax imitations of food) on display. Merely point to your choice. Others, catering to a foreign clientele, have menus printed in English and/or with pictures. In restaurants where the entire menu is in Japanese, however, it becomes more complicated. Below is an alphabetically arranged list of different specialities from which you can choose while getting to know the various culinary delights of Japan.

Most of the restaurants listed below are marked on the maps at the beginning of this guide. If they are not, the nearest subway station is given. Ask at the nearest *koban* (police-box) and a police officer will help you find the way. A more complete selection of restaurants, arranged by districts, is found, in the 'Tokyo Addresses' chapter at the end of this guide (see p. 217).

Table manners

At the beginning of the meal

If you dine with Japanese friends, they will undoubtedly start the meal by wishing you *'itadakimasu'*. You simply reply with the same word. Formerly, the expression was much longer and plates were lifted above the diner's head in order to be blessed by the gods.

During the meal

While eating, the Japanese observe a relatively strict etiquette based on religious beliefs. Chopsticks are placed on or next to the rice bowl but never left in the bowl as this gesture is reserved for the dead. Food is never passed from chopsticks to chopsticks because this, too, is a ritual gesture used at funerals — after cremations, the bones of the dead are handled in this manner.

Traditionally, boiled rice is served plain and is never mixed with sauce. If served in any other manner (such as a pilaf or a curry), it is no longer called *gohan* a term reserved for white rice, but *raisu* (derived from the English word 'rice'). To the Japanese, it is no longer considered rice but a totally different food.

If you eat noodles (whether *udon, soba* or *ramen*), you will find your Japanese hosts aspirating them noisily. Considered impolite in other countries, this is not only permitted in Japan but also recommended. If you do not make a certain amount of noise, your host might ask if you dislike the dish.

No matter what beverage you have chosen — and this is particularly true for sake, beer and whiskey — never serve yourself. Hold your glass in one hand while your host serves you, then take the bottle or carafe, and serve him or her in turn. This rule holds true throughout the entire meal.

At the end of the meal

At the end of a good meal, it is normal to say *'Gochiso sama deshita'* which roughly means 'We have eaten well'. If you wish to be the perfect guest, tell the host or the owner of a restaurant, *'mata kimasu'* ('we will come again'). It will be most appreciated.

POPULAR SPECIALITIES

Chanko-nabe: Sumo wrestlers' fare

If you have ever had the opportunity to watch a sumo wrestling contest, you may have wondered how the fighters attain such enormous proportions. The answer is simple. They sleep 14 hours a day and eat *chanko-nabe,* a special soup that calls for 6.6 lb/3 kg of fish, 2 whole chickens, 4.4 lb/2 kg of beef, a dozen eggs and 4.4 lb/2 kg of broad beans per serving!

If you enjoy substantial meals, do not hesitate to join the *sumotori* (sumo wrestlers) in their favourite restaurants. Most of these are located around Ryogoku Station in the district where the wrestlers train and where the matches are held.

Suggested addresses

♦♦♦ **Kashiwado,** 4-1-15 Tsukiji, Chuo-ku, III, C2, ☎ 3542 3951. Higashi-Ginza Station, *Open daily 11am-10pm.* This is one of the best known *chanko* in Tokyo, near Higashi-Ginza Station with a choice of beef, chicken or fish *nabe.* If you do not wish to appear a lame duck next to the pony-tailed wrestlers wolfing their meals beside you, it is best to skip a meal beforehand.

♦♦♦ **Tomoegata,** 2-17 Ryogoku, Simuda-ku, I, B2, ☎ 3632 5600. *Open Mon-Sat 11:30am-10pm; Sun noon-10pm.* Run by the son of a former *sumotori* this colourful restaurant near Ryogoku Station is full of atmosphere. It is possible to order from photographs on the menu.

Fugu (pufferfish)

Known by a variety of names (puffers, balloonfish, globefish and blowfish to mention just a few), *fugu* is the Japanese equivalent of Russian caviar or French *foie gras.* It is very rare and is served only in specialized restaurants where a meal may reach the astronomical sum of ¥30,000 or more per person.

Fugu is more than just a food, it is a gamble. The *diodon* (the scientific name of the pufferfish) is, in fact, unfit for human consumption as it contains tetrodotoxin, a deadly poison. The fish can be eaten only after the ovaries and other glands containing the toxin are carefully removed. Only qualified chefs, specially licensed by the government, are allowed to open and operate a *fugu* restaurant.

This distinct fish is served either raw as *sashimi* or cooked with vegetables as *nabe.* An authentic *fugu* meal consists of both these dishes accompanied by *hirezake,* warm sake in which a grilled *fugu* fin is floated. The meal usually ends with *zosui,* warm rice and egg mixed with *fugu* bouillon. Nothing of the puffer is wasted.

Do not be surprised to find that for an hour or so after eating the fish your lips are slightly painful. This sensation is normal and much appreciated by *fugu* lovers.

Fugu is a cold-weather speciality and is served only between October and the end of March.

Warning: Even qualified chefs are not always successful at removing the toxin, and every year many people die from *fugu* poisoning. Frequently referred to as a 'gourmet's Russian roulette', this fish is to be eaten at your own risk.

Suggested addresses

♦♦♦ **Nibiki,** 3-7 Shitaya, Taito-ku, IV, B1-2, ☎ 3872 6250. Uguisudani Station. *Open Mon-Sat 4pm-9pm. Closed April to Sept.* This extraordinary, 100-year-old restaurant serves the cheapest *fugu* in Tokyo. It offers a fish market atmosphere combined with tradition (low tables and *tatami*) and hospitality. The *sashimi* and *nabe* menus are an unforgettable experience. It is wise to make reservations.

♦ **Tentake,** 6-16-6 Tsukiji, Chuo-Ku, III, B2, ☎ 3541 3881. Tsukiji Station. *Open Mon-Sat noon-10pm. Closed the first and third Wed of* *every month as well as from April to Sept.* This is another inexpensive restaurant compared to prices usually charged elsewhere.

Kaiseki ryori: tea ceremony cuisine

Kaiseki ryori is Japanese *haute cuisine.* Originally limited to two or three dishes served at the tea ceremony, as a means of protecting the stomach against burning, today it has become the pride of Japanese cuisine. A *kaiseki* meal consists of a number of highly elaborate miniature servings meant to please the eye as much as the palate.

This cuisine is the most expensive in Japan, and a bill of ¥15,000 is in no way unusual for a meal. Many *kaiseki* restaurants will not accept clients unless they have already been 'presented' by one of their regular customers. The meal is almost always served in a special room complete with *tatami.*

Suggested addresses

♦♦♦♦ **Takamura,** 3-4-27 Roppongi, Minato-ku, VIII, C2, n° 1c, ☎ 3585 6600. *Open Mon-Sat noon-3:30pm, 5-10:30pm.* The decor is outstanding, and there is a traditional Japanese garden, a feature that is becoming more and more difficult to find in Tokyo.

♦♦ **Tatsumiya,** 33-5 Asakusa, Taito-ku, V, B2, n°11, ☎ 3842 7373. Asakusa Station. *Open Tues-Sun noon-2pm, 5-9pm.* Opened in 1980, this restaurant puts *kaiseki* cuisine within the reach of everyone. A complete meal, consisting of seven dishes that vary according to the season, is quite inexpensive. Reservations are essential.

Okonomiyaki

Okonomiyaki is a speciality of Hiroshima. Beef, vegetables and seafood are coated with a batter of flour, water and eggs and then fried on a hot plate in front of you. Once cooked, *okonomiyaki* resembles a large omelette and is served accompanied by a sweet brown sauce that is 'painted on' according to your taste. *Okonomiyaki* is one of the cheapest and most nourishing dishes you can find in Japan. There is always a wide selection of ingredients from which to choose. In certain restaurants, you cook your own *okonomiyaki.* This is not difficult and can be amusing.

Suggested address

♦ **Tambo,** 2-27-8, Asakusa, Taito-Ku, V, AB1, n°29. Asakusa Station. *Open Tues-Sun 5-9pm.* This is the most traditional *okonomiyaki* in Tokyo. Seated on *tatami,* you prepare your own omelette.

Okonomiyaki, as well as *yaki-soba* (fried noodles) and *tako-yaki* (octopus croquettes), are also sold on the street by vendors. These are frequently among the best that can be found in Tokyo.

Robata yaki

Exclusively Japanese, *robata yaki* is as much a show as it is a meal. Imagine a large rustic hall with all types of seafood and vegetables stacked in the middle of the room. Cooks kneel before you and prepare on open fires whatever you may happen to point to. When cooked, your meal is passed to you on a long bamboo shovel. To enhance the atmosphere, the personnel shout the orders at the top of their lungs. The meal ends with *onigiri,* grilled rice balls dipped into *shoyu* (soy sauce). The feeling of an open market, where the vendors are selling off the last of their stock at closing time, is realistically recreated.

Suggested addresses

♦♦♦ **Gonin Byakusho,** Roppongi Square Building, 4th floor, 3-10-3 Roppongi, Minato-Ku, VIII, C3, n° 4c, ☎ 3470 1675. Roppongi Station. *Open daily 11:30am-2pm, 5-11pm.* The name of the restaurant, which means the 'Five Peasants', clearly indicates the ambiance of this establishment. When you enter, your shoes are put in a box and a hostess gives you an immense key in exchange, undoubtedly to 'open' your appetite.

The art of Japanese cooking lies in its taste and its presentation. Above, a meal from the Shizuoka region.

♦♦♦ **Inakaya**, 7-8-4, Roppongi, Minato-Ku, VII, C2, n° 7c, ☎ 3405 9866. Roppongi Station. *Open daily 5pm-5am*. This is the best-known *robata yaki*, at least among tourists. The cook's showmanship is astonishing.

Sashimi/sushi: raw fish

This is the Japanese speciality par excellence. In Japan, raw fish is eaten in many ways: as *sashimi*, simply sliced and lightly dipped in *shoyu* (soy sauce); as *onigiri sushi*, a slice of fish placed on a slightly vinegary rice ball; or as *maki sushi*, rolled with rice in *nori* seaweed. Raw fish is always filleted and served with ginger marinaded in vinegar.

A typical assortment *(ichi nin mae)* generally consists of eight to ten pieces of fish, including *maguro* (bluefin tuna), *toro* (fatty tuna), *sake* (salmon), *ebi* (shrimp), *ika* (squid), *saba* (mackerel), and a sort of Japanese omelette, called *tamago*. The variety of fish and shellfish *à la carte* is almost infinite and depends on the day's catch. The *sushiya* (raw-fish restaurants) of Tokyo buy fresh provisions every morning at the Tsukiji fish market. Among the more unusual types of fish used are *anago* (conger eel), *uni* (sea urchin eggs) and *awabi* (abalone). Other varieties are completely unknown in the West.

A fish meal *à la carte* can easily cost ¥5000 or more per person without being extravagant by Japanese standards. To stay within a reasonable budget, it is best to eat in a *sushiya* for lunch, when the *teishoku* (lunch time menu) is inexpensive. There are also numerous 'turning' *sushi*, where the various dishes pass by on a conveyor belt. Choose those that have just been placed on the belt by the chef as they are undoubtedly the freshest. Take as many dishes as you like, and stack the empty plates in a pile next to you. These are counted when you pay. In certain 'turning' *sushi*, different-coloured plates indicate different prices.

Suggested addresses

♦♦♦ **Sushi Sai,** 1-7-5 Jinnan, Shibuya-ku, XI, B3, n° 24, ☎ 3493 6333. *Open Mon-Sat 5:30pm-1am; Sun 4-10pm.* This Art Déco restaurant specializes in 'natural' *sushi,* such as *sushi* and *tofu* (soy bean curd) and *sushi* with *shiso* (beefsteak plant leaves). The fish is particularity fresh. Estimate between ¥5000 and ¥7000 per person .

♦♦ **Sushi-han,** on Sakura Dori in Shinjuku (Kabukicho), VI, C1, n° 25, ☎ 3200 9427. *Open daily until 9pm.* This *sushiya* is one of the best in Shinjuku and specializes in rare shellfish. Reasonable.

♦♦ **Takeno,** 21-2 Tsukiji 6-chome, Chuo-ku, III, D2, n° 9a, ☎ 3541 8698. Tsukiji Station. *Open Mon-Sat 11am-8:30pm.* This is an excellent restaurant just next to the Tsukiji fish market. The *tempura* (fritters) are as good as the *sushi.* The lunch menus are varied and inexpensive.

Soba, udon and *ramen:* noodles

In Japan, noodles are a favourite lunch meal. Each type of noodle has a particular name and is often served in specialized restaurants.

Soba noodles are made of buckwheat. They are eaten either hot in soup — of which there are over ten types — or cold, sprinkled with onions and *nori* (purple seaweed). Cold noodles are served in a bamboo box accompanied by a soy-based sauce.

Udon, thick white noodles made from wheat, are always eaten hot in a bowl of beef or pork soup.

Ramen, Chinese in origin, are also eaten hot in soup. They may be served with *giyoza* (grilled ravioli) that are dipped into a hot sauce.

Suggested addresses

♦ **Entotsuya,** 34-30, Minami-Aoyama, Minato-ku, VIII, A1, ☎ 3475 6337. Gaienmae Station. *Open Mon-Sat 11am-5pm.* This Chinese restaurant is probably one of the cheapest in Tokyo. An enormous and delicious *gomoku ramen* (noodle soup) costs about ¥500 per person.

♦ **Nanaki,** 13-2 Nishi Ebisu, Shibuya-ku, ☎ 3496 2878. Ebisu Station. *Open Mon-Sat 11:30am-9:30pm.* The *soba* served here are handmade according to an ancient traditional method from the Nagano Prefecture. The speciality of the house is *misuzu soba,* a dish made with noodles, eggs, fried *tofu* (bean curd) and thinly sliced pork. The *sansai soba* (noodles with vegetables) and the *soba gaki* (noodle croquettes) also are excellent. The bill will rarely exceed ¥2000 per person.

♦ **Yabu soba,** 10 Awajicho, Chiyoda-ku, II, C1, n°6a, ☎ 3251 0287. Awajicho Station. *Open Tues-Sun 11:30am-7pm.* Established over a century ago, this restaurant is both the oldest and the best *soba* restaurant in Tokyo. The service and presentation are irreproachable, even for a simple 'bowl of noodles'. The *anago namban* (noodles and conger eel) is an inexpensive delicacy not to be missed.

Sukiyaki/shabu-shabu

Although not really an indigenous dish, *sukiyaki* (along with raw fish and *tempura*) is one of the best-known Japanese specialities outside of Japan. Apart from the preliminary cutting of the meat and vegetables, this dish is prepared entirely at the table. It is undoubtedly due to this novelty that *sukiyaki* is so popular.

Thin slices of beef are grilled in a *sukiyaki-nabe* (cast-iron pan) and then covered with a slightly sweet soy-based bouillon. Vegetables and *tofu* are then added. These delicate morsels are dipped into raw egg, which cools the food and enhances its flavour. *Sukiyaki* (pronounced 'skiyaki') is always served with white rice.

Shabu-shabu is a variant. The ingredients are the same as for *sukiyaki* but the stock is different and Japanese noodles are added at the last minute.

Suggested addresses

♦♦♦♦ **Iseju**, 14-9 Nihombashi-Kodenmacho, Chuo-ku, II, D1, ☎ 36637841. Kodenmacho Station. *Open Mon-Sat noon-8pm*. The Takamiyama family has run this restaurant since 1869! It is unquestionably the oldest *sukiyaki* restaurant in Tokyo as well as one of the best. To ensure the use of high-quality beef, the restaurant has its own butcher shop just across the street. Prepared according to traditional methods, the *sukiyaki* at Iseju's is cooked at your table on a charcoal fire.

♦ **Chin'ya**, 1-3-4 Asakusa, Taito-ku, V, B2, n°1, ☎ 38410010. Asakusa Station. *Open Thur-Tues 11:30am-9:30pm*. For over 100 years, this restaurant has served excellent *sukiyaki*. The prices are very reasonable.

Tempura: fritters

Tempura is one of the few Japanese specialities that is of foreign origin. The Portuguese imported this means of cooking food in the 16th century, and the Japanese quickly adapted it to their own taste. The delicacy of *tempura* has little in common with the sodden, deep-fried cod of Lisbon.

Here again, the *teishoku* (lunch menu) is recommended. It generally consists of five or six pieces of fish and vegetables served one after another on paper towels which absorb the excess oil. *Tempura* is generally dipped into *tentsuyu*, a soy-based sauce made with *daikon* (radish) and *mirin* (sweet sake).

Suggested addresses

♦♦♦ **Inagiku**, 9-8 Nihombashi-Kayabacho 2-chome, Chuo-ku, III, C2, n°17, ☎ 36695501. Kayabacho Station. *Open daily Mon-Sat 11:30am-3pm, 5-11pm*. This is definitely *the* place for *tempura*. It is also very expensive because the oil is changed for each customer. The quality of the ingredients is irreproachable. The meal itself follows an impressive ritual where every detail is important, including the shape of the finished *tempura*. There are 18 different types from which to choose.

♦ **Tsunahachi** is a chain of *tempuraya* (*tempura* restaurants) known for the freshness of their ingredients and the quality of their batter. One of the best branches is in Shinjuku, 3-31-8 Shinjuku, Sinjuku-ku, VI, B2, ☎ 33521011. *Open daily 11:30am-10pm*. Equally good is the branch in Ginza at the top of the Matsuya department store, III, C1, n°15. The lunch time menu is a real bargain.

Teppan-yaki: 'iron-fry'

Teppan-yaki is as much a performance as a meal. Before each table, a chef juggles meat and shrimp over a hot griddle. When cooked, these are covered with lemon juice and flamboyantly salted and peppered. It is simple and delicious mouth-watering food. The menu usually consists of a small first course, a grilled meat, rice and a dessert.

Suggested address

♦♦♦ **Holytan**, 2-2 Uchisaiwaicho, Chiyoda-ku, II, D3, n°3, ☎ 35012454. *Open Mon-Sat 11am-3pm, 5-8:45pm*. This restaurant specializes in Matsuzaka beef (one of the best varieties in Japan), which is served with whatever vegetables are in season. The lunch menu is as good as the evening meat at a quarter the cost.

Tofu and buddhist cuisine

Tofu ryori is a vegetarian cuisine based on *shojin ryori* (the cuisine of the Buddhist monks). Almost all the dishes, which vary according to the season, are based on *tofu* (bean curd). An acquired taste, *tofu* is both rich in protein and low in calories. Even more so than raw fish, the extreme subtlety of *tofu* is removed from Western taste. It is difficult to switch from a diet of meat and potatoes to the more frugal diet eaten by Zen monks! It should definitely be tried, however, even if only for the extraordinary settings of the three restaurants listed below.

Suggested addresses

♦♦ **Goemon,** 1-26 Hon-Komagome, Bunkyo-ku, I, A1, ☎ 3811 2015 or 3812 0900. Hakusan Station. *Open Tues-Sat 5-10pm; Sun 4-10pm.* In this restaurant (with a garden of its own) the preparation of *tofu* is raised to the level of an art. While waiting for the main dish to cook, customers nibble on tidbits such as *goma dofu* (*tofu* and sesame) or *tomoe dengaku* (kebabs of *tofu* covered with a sweet sauce). It is best to make reservations.

♦ **Sankoin,** 1-36 Honmachi 3-chome, Koganei-chi off map, ☎ (0423) 81 1116. *Open Fri-Wed, lunch only.* From Shinjuku Station, take the Chuo Line to Musashi Koganei Station. The journey takes about 40 minutes. Leave the station and walk down Koganei Kaido Avenue. After ten minutes or so, you will come to a service station on the right side of the road. Turn right and continue walking as far as the Sankoin mae bus stop. The temple is on the left at the end of an alley. There are two sittings a day: noon and 2pm. The Sankoin is not a restaurant but a Buddhist temple where the cooking is done by resident monks. Its cuisine is so well known that reservations must be made at least two weeks in advance, although a month is preferable. Write to the temple (in English) stating the size of your group and the day and the hour you have chosen.

Served in a special room fitted with *tatami* the meal itself is preceded by *macha* (the tea ceremony). This is followed by a stream of small dishes (essentially based on vegetables and *tofu*) that vary according to the season. The presentation of the dishes is so refined that it seems sacrilegious to destroy them with chopsticks. For merely ¥3000, this is definitely the most extraordinary meal available in Tokyo.

♦ **Sasanoyuki,** 2-15-10 Negishi, Taito-ku, IV, B1, n°4a, ☎ 3873 1145. Uguisudani Station. *Open Tues-Sun 11am-9pm.* The decor is a little less sophisticated than that at Goemon but the food is just as good, and the atmosphere popular and friendly. A menu of eight different dishes provides an inexpensive meal.

Tonkatsu

Although pork (like other meat) is rare in traditional Japanese cooking, *tonkatsu* is a typically Japanese way of preparing this food. A cutlet is dipped in an egg-based batter, rolled in *panko* (coarse bread crumbs) and then deep fried. There are many *tonkatsu* restaurants in Tokyo, but only a few offer an unforgettable gastronomic experience. There are a number of different types of *tonkatsu,* of which the fillet is the best. It is always served with a salad of finely chopped cabbage with either *amakuchi* (a sweet sauce) or *karakuchi* (a hot sauce). *Katsudon* is the only traditional Japanese dish where sauce is put on rice. The pork and the rice are served in the same bowl with an egg and grilled onions.

Suggested addresses

♦♦ **Katsu Kichi,** IX, B1, ☎ 3812 6268, is on Shiroyama Dori, just across from Suidobashi Station. *Open daily 11am-10pm.* Not only is the meat of exceptional quality, but also the rice may be ordered garnished with *shiso* (beefsteak plant leaves), a real delicacy. The restaurant's setting is perfect. The decor is totally of wood, and a fabulous collection of cups is displayed on the walls. The atmosphere is both popular and select and the price is very low, considering the quality of the cuisine.

♦ **Tonki,** 1-1-2 Shimo-Meguro Ichome, Meguro-ku, I, A2, ☎ 3491 9928. One minute from Meguro Station. *Open Wed-Mon 4-11pm.* This is unquestionably the best *tonkatsu* in Tokyo. The batter is so crisp and light that the recipe remains a jealously guarded secret, and the meat is perfection itself. The only drawback is that the restaurant is so popular that it is frequently necessary to wait an hour before finding a place to sit down. If you wish to taste this wonder (and the word is not an exaggeration), skip lunch and arrive at 4pm. Order a *hire daboru* (double fillet) to compensate for your fast.

鬼あられ
二〇〇グラム
六〇〇円

月見
二〇〇グラム
六〇〇円

These salted delicacies, made of rice, are a perfect accompaniment to beer and sake.

Unagi: grilled conger eel

Unagi (eel) is one of the great Japanese specialities. On no account should you miss trying it. Although some restaurants serve eel along with other dishes, it is best to go to an authentic *unagiya* (eel restaurant), where the fish is treated with reverence and where many of the recipes are centuries old (some date from the 13th century).

Eel cooked in the Japanese style does not resemble the fish as it is cooked in the West. In Japan, it is split lengthwise and then threaded on small bamboo skewers. First steamed, it is then basted with a sweet sauce and grilled. The taste can be heightened with *sansho*, a hot pepper used uniquely for this dish.

Grilled *unagi* is frequently served in a lacquered box on a bed of white rice. This is called *kabayaki teishoku* (grilled eel menu). If you are hungry, order a side dish of *kimoyaki* (grilled eel liver), which is served on skewers accompanied by ginger. In the evening, a *unagi* meal will cost between ¥3000 and ¥4000 per person but the lunch *teishoku* will rarely exceeds ¥2000.

Eel-eating is a popular pastime in August and is thought to protect the brain from the undesirable effects of summer heat. At any rate, it is a good excuse for the Japanese to indulge in one of their favourite foods.

Suggested addresses

♦ **Akimoto**, 3-4 Kojimachi, Chiyoda-ku, VII, C2, n°13, ☎ 3261 6762. Kojimachi Station. *Open Mon-Sat 11:30am-2pm, 5-8pm. Closed holidays.* Excellent and inexpensive.

♦ **Tambaya,** 3-2 Kojimachi, Chiyoda-ku, VII, D2, n°11, ☎ 3261 2633. Kojimachi Station. *Open Mon-Sat 11am-8pm*. Established over 200 years ago, this reputable restaurant is the haunt of all true lovers of grilled eel. The *kabayaki teishoku* is remarkable, and the soup served on this menu is made from *kimo* (eel liver).

Yakitori: grilled chicken

Yakitori (grilled chicken) consists of food grilled on bamboo skewers over a charcoal fire. Although most of the kebabs served in this type of restaurant are based on chicken (breast, wings, livers, gizzards, and so on), a *yakitori kosu* menu always includes vegetables as well. Some restaurants, such as the Nanbantei chain, even serve beef or pork kebabs.

Yakitori is usually eaten without rice. At the end of the meal, *nigiri* (rice balls) wrapped in seaweed are served. They are either dipped in a slightly sweet sauce or sprinkled with lemon according to taste. A variant of *yakitori* from Osaka, called *kushi-age* or *kushi-katsu*, consists of deep-fried floured kebabs. This dish is made with a greater variety of ingredients, pork being one of the most common.

Suggested addresses

♦ **Kan Jin Cho,** 1-24-7 Shibuya, Shibuya-ku, XI, C3, n°25, ☎ 3400 6777. Shibuya Station. *Open daily 5-11pm*. A novel *yakitoriya* where the kebabs are served accompanied by grated *daikon* radish. *Konyaku* (devil's tongue), a translucent tuber-root cake served with a sweet sauce, or a salad goes particularly well with this original *yakitori*. There are three menus, all between ¥2000 and ¥3000.

♦ **Kushinobo** is a chain of *kushi-age* restaurants which offers a series of menus (8 to 12 kebabs). Their specialities include pumpkin, lotus root, crab and rhubarb. There is a branch in Ginza, Rikka Building, III, CD1-2, ☎ 3571 3060. *Open Mon-Sat* 11:30am-10pm. There is another branch in Shinjuku, Isetan Building, VI, C2, ☎ 3356 3865. *Open Thurs-Tues 11:30am-10pm*.

♦ **Nanbantei** is 'the' chain of *yakitoriya* (*yakitori* restaurants). There are branches absolutely everywhere in Japan. All of them offer three excellent menus (A, B and C) that differ in the number of kebabs offered. There is a branch in Roppongi, 4-5-6 Roppongi, Minato-ku, VIII, C2, n°19, ☎ 3402 0606. *Open daily 5:30-11:30pm*.

▬ RARE SPECIALITIES

This section provides addresses where you can find (and taste) some of Japan's more unusual dishes.

Catfish

♦♦ **Namazu-ya,** 2-31-16 Okubo, Shinjuku-ku, I, A1, ☎ 3200 0283. *Open Mon-Sat noon-2pm, 5-11pm*. From Okubo Station, turn left and walk for about three minutes. Then turn left at Dunkin' Donuts. Catfish is reputed to be 'effective' for men and to make women more beautiful. Whatever the case, this restaurant is unique in Japan.

Crab

♦♦♦ **Kani Doraku,** 1-7-7 and 1-7-9 Kabukicho, Shinjuku-ku, VI, C1, n°27a, ☎ 3208 0061 or 3208 0068. Shinjuku Station. *Open daily 4pm-3am*. This chain of seafood restaurants is easily recognized by the large crab suspended above the entrance of each branch. *Kani-nabe* (crab casserole) and *kani no sashimi* (raw crab) are among the many dishes in which to indulge.

Macrobiotic Food

♦ **Temmi,** Daiichi Iwashita Building, 2nd floor, 1-10-6 Jinnan, Shibuya-ku, XI, B3, n°15, ☎ 3496 9703. *Open Mon-Sat*

11:30am-2:30pm, 4:30-7:30pm; Sun 11:30am-6pm. Closed on the third Thurs of every month. This is one of the few macrobiotic restaurants in Tokyo. The principles of Georges Oshawa (*yin* and *yang*) are applied with finesse and wisdom. The food served is excellent (whole grains, fish and salted vegetables).

Miso

♦♦♦ **Suginoya,** Shinko Building B 1, Kabukicho, Shinjuku-ku, VI, C1, n°28a, ☎ 3200 7546. *Open daily 6pm-3am.* This unique establishment offers over ten varieties of *miso* soup (soy-based) served with vegetables, red mushrooms, eggs or numerous different sorts of small mollusks. The restaurant also serves *fugu* (see **warning** p. 91) and copious salads.

Sardines

♦♦♦ **Iwashiya,** 7-2-17 Ginza, Chuo-ku, III, C2, n° 27a, ☎ 3571 3000. This is probably the only sardine specialist in Tokyo. The infinite variety of dishes offered is overwhelming but the prices are high.

Suppon: turtle

♦♦♦ **Murakami Suppon Hompo,** 4-2-2 Higashi Ueno, Taito-ku, IV, B3, n°2a, ☎ 3841 9831. Ueno Station. *Suppon ryori* (cuisine based on turtle) is one of the most delicate and sought-after cuisines in Japan. In general, it is very expensive, and prices vary according to the catch. It is wise to eat *suppon* on a lunch menu.

Tongue

♦♦ **Shinobu,** 16 San'eicho, Shinjuku-ku, VII, B2, ☎ 3355 6338. Yotsuya Station. *Open Mon-Sat 5-11pm, Sun 5-10pm. Closed the third Sun of every month.* It is best to arrive early as this friendly, popular bistro is always crowded. Beef tongue is served grilled, boiled and even raw as sashimi.

Wild boar

♦♦♦ **Momonja,** 1-10-12 Ryogoku, Sumida-ku, I, B1, ☎ 3631 5596. Ryogoku Station. *Open daily noon-9:30pm.* This restaurant, over 300 years old, specializes in wild game.

▬ REGIONAL CUISINES

Each region of Japan claims at least one speciality. Not all are available in Tokyo but, with a little effort, most of the principal cuisines can be sampled without leaving the capital.

Hiroshima region, southern Honshu

♦♦ **Suishin,** top floor of the Isetan department store, 3-15-17 Shinjuku, Shinjuku-ku, VI, C2, n°21, ☎ 3352 8721. Shinjuku Station. *Open daily 11am-10pm.* Seafood specialist. Moderate prices.

Kyushu region, southern Japan

♦♦ **Satsuma,** Ginza Building, 9-8-5 Ginza, Chuo-ku, III, BC2, ☎ 3572 0955. Shimbashi Station. *Open Mon-Sat noon-2pm, 5-10pm.* This restaurant offers excellent cooking from Kagoshima, including specialities of *sushi* and *tofu*. About 40 different varieties of alcohol (sake and *shochu*, including a potato alcohol) are offered. Prices average around ¥3000 to ¥4000 per person. Reservations are recommended.

♦♦ **Yukun Sakagura,** Kyowa Bank Building, Basement, 16-14 Shimbashi 1-chome, Minato-ku III, B2, n°15, ☎ 3508 9296. Shimbashi Station. *Open Mon-Fri 11:30am-1:30pm, 5-10pm.* If the menu of this restaurant is totally incomprehensible to you, console yourself with the fact that it is just as confusing to the great majority of Tokyoites. The language of Kyushu, in the south of Japan, is a totally different dialect from that spoken in Tokyo. This is immaterial, however, as dishes are chosen from a counter and there are many regional seafoods found only offshore in the waters of the Kyushu region. The prices (¥3000 to ¥4000 maximum) are reasonable.

Nagoya region, central Honshu

Shirakawa Go, 29-10 Kabukicho, Shinjuku-ku, VI, C1, n°26a, ☎ 3200 5255. Shinjuku Station. *Open daily 1-11pm.* This restaurant was totally dismantled in the 1950s and transported piece by piece from the Gifu Prefecture to Tokyo. Three different menus ranging from ¥3000 to ¥4000 include an excellent Gifu-style chicken and an appetizing grilled fish.

Wakamatsu-an, 5-18-17 Shinjuku, Shinjuku-ku, VI, B2, ☎ 3200 5987. Shinjuku Station. *Open Mon-Sat 11am-7:30pm.* This restaurant specializes in noodles and offers over 40 handmade kinds. There is even an alcohol *(soba shochu)* made from *soba* noodles!

Okinawa, the southern extremity of Japan

Omoro, 1-13 Nishi Ikebukuro, Toshima-ku, XII, A2, n°8a, ☎ 3982 0236. Ikebukuro Station. *Open Mon-Sat 5-11pm.* A charming inn with a thatched roof, this restaurant serves specialities from the island of Okinawa, which is located at the southern extremity of the Japanese archipelago. Raw pigs ears or pork tail stew awaits you for about ¥2000 to ¥3000, sake included.

The Island of Shikoku, southern Honshu

♦♦♦ **Neboke,** 7-6-8 Ginza, Chuo-ku, III, C1, ☎ 3572 9640. Ginza Station. *Open Mon-Sat 11:30am-10pm.* Seafood from the region of Tosa holds the place of honour here. It is best to make reservations.

♦ **Iyoji,** 1-5-13 Okubo, Shinjuku-ku, I, A1, ☎ 3209 6830. Shin-Okubo Station. *Open Mon-Sat 11am-9pm.* This is one of the best *udon* (wheat noodle) restaurants in Tokyo. There are over 30 kinds served Kagawa-style (with duck, herring, oysters or clams). The bill will rarely exceed ¥2000 per person.

SAKE

Sake *(nihon shu)*, brewed from fermented rice, is the national drink of the Japanese. There are over 2500 kinds produced in Japan. They range from the purest *(junmaislu)*, nearly impossible to find and prohibitively priced, to the most common *(sanbaizoshu)*, frequently nothing more than low-grade liquor. *Honjozoshu* is a middle-range, quality sake and should not contain more than 25% fortified alcohol. Regardless of the quality, sake is either *amai* (sweet) or *karai* (spicy). Whether consumed *kanzuke* (hot) or *hiya* (cold), it is always served in small cups. This means that guests are served constantly, a ritual much appreciated by the Japanese. Sake can be ordered in any establishment that serves Japanese cuisine but not in those serving foreign food.

It should be noted that in Japanese the word 'sake' means 'alcohol' and also includes wine and whiskey. When ordering sake, ask for *nihon shu* (Japanese wine).

In restaurants, sake is almost always served warm in small carafes *(nihon shu ippon)*. About 6 fl oz/180 ml, a carafe will usually cost ¥300-500. Sometimes an assortment of small cups are offered, from which the customers choose the size and colour of their preference. One of the best places to buy sake in Tokyo is at **Yanagiya Saketen** in Kanda-Kajicho, II, CD1, ☎ 3265 5001. This is *the* sake boutique par excellence.

As part of the tea ceremony, the cup is delicately turned around to appreciate the potter's work before drinking.

If you wish to taste rare sake, go to **Sasashu**, 2-2 Ikebukuro 2-chome, Toshima-ku, XII, A1, n°10, ☎ 3971 9363. *Open Mon-Sat*. This very well-known *nomiya* (a place to drink on the premises) offers 40 different varieties of sake. Note that prices may reach ¥2000 per carafe!

Another typical Japanese speciality manufactured from fermented rice is *amazake* (sweet sake). Made from sake rice lees (sediment) and practically non-alcoholic, this beverage has the consistency of porridge and is drunk like yogurt. It is found in certain restaurants, including **Amanoya**, 2-18-15 Soto-Kanda, Chiyoda-ku, IX, CD3, ☎ 3251 7911. *Open Mon-Sat 9am-6pm*. Unquestionably the most traditional establishment *amazake*.

▬ THE TEA CEREMONY

In Japan, *macha* (the tea ceremony) is an art as highly esteemed as archery and flower arranging. All are inspired by Zen Buddhism. Religious in origin, the tea ceremony is conducted in a special room, with appropriate equipment.

The cups used are frequently collectors' items. In order to appreciate the work of the master potter, you should hold the cup in your hands and turn if before it si filled with tea.

You can take part in the tea ceremony at **Sakurai-Kai** (Tea Ceremony Service Center), 2-25 Shimo-Ochiai 3-chome, Shinjuku-ku, off map, ☎ 3951 9043. Mejiro Station. Participation costs ¥600 and a lesson costs twice the price. This ceremony takes place every Thursday and Friday. Arrive at 11am.

Many of the large hotels also hold tea ceremonies. You do not have to be a guest of the hotel to attend. These are a few:

♦ **Hotel New Otani**, 7th floor, 4-1 Kioicho, Chiyoda-ku, VII, C3, ☎ 3265 1111, extension 2567. *Open Thur-Sat 11am-4pm*.

♦ **Hotel Okura**, 7th floor, 2-10-4 Toranomon, Minato-ku, III, A2, ☎ 3582 0111. *Open daily 11am-5pm*.

♦ **Imperial Hotel**, 4th floor, 1-1-1 Uchisaiwaicho, Chiyoda-ku, II, B3, ☎ 3504 1111. *Open Mon-Sat 10am-4pm*. By appointment only.

If you wish to taste Japanese tea without participating in the ceremony, try the Gencho-an room at the **Suntory Museum**, 11th Floor, Tokyo Suntory Building, Asakusa, Taito-ku, VII, C3, ☎ 3470 1013. *Open Tues-Sun 10am-4pm*.

Ukai Toriyama: The Mountain of Birds.

For the relatively reasonable sum of ¥5000 per person, you can treat yourself to an unforgettable meal in one of the most incredible settings imaginable: the restaurant is a series of small tea houses clinging to the mountainside, nearly lost among luxuriant and exotic vegetation.

A waitress in a *kimono* takes your order as you wait seated on *tatami* in a private room. While advising you, she lights a small brazier in the centre of the table upon which you will cook your own chicken brochettes and then season them with lemon. A multitude of small dishes (mainly fowl), each more surprising than the last, accompanies the main course.

The landscape that you can see from the tea houses is meticulously cared for. Simply slide open the *shoji* (wood-and-paper door) and discover a delightful Japanese garden where cherry trees flower in April.

Afterwards you may want to stroll around the area. Mount Takao is well known for its rich plant and animal life.

Ukai Toriyama, 3426 Minami Asakawacho, Hachioji-shi, ☎ (0426) 61 0739. *Open daily 11am-9:30pm*.

From Shinjuku Station, take the Keio Line to Takaosanguchi Station, the terminus. The journey is about 50 minutes. From the station, take a taxi to the restaurant. On Saturday and Sunday, a shuttle service runs from the restaurant to the station.

GETTING TO KNOW TOKYO

Unlike most other major cities in the world, Tokyo does not have one particular city center; several areas of the town could be considered the center for different reasons. The following eight itineraries explore independent and yet complementary districts.

With a pair of sturdy legs and a minimum of organization, you can see everything in Tokyo in about a week, but at a rather rapid rate. Ideally, you should plan to spend 10 to 15 days getting to know the city.

If you have only a day, visit **Asakusa** (p. 103) in the morning, **Ginza** (p. 104) in the afternoon and **Shinjuku** (p. 107) in the evening.

With two or three days, you should also be able to include the **Imperial Palace** (p. 110) and the museums in **Ueno** (p. 111).

Four or five days will allow you to add the **Shibuya** (p. 113), **Harajuku** (p. 114) and **Aoyama** (p. 116) districts to your itinerary.

If you have a week or more, it will also be possible to visit **Roppongi** (p. 116) and **Ikebukuro** (p. 117). To some extent, these last two districts resemble Aoyama and Shinjuku and are not essential for a general survey of the town.

━━ ASAKUSA

This itinerary takes half a day.

Access: the simplest way to get to Asakusa is by subway (Asakusa Station, V, B3). An alternative possibility is the *suijo basu* (waterbus), a passenger ferry service that links the **Hamarikye**** gardens, III, C3 (see p. 128), to Asakusa Park. A boat leaves the Takeshiba pier (located between the Hamamatsucho and Shimbashi stations) every 40 minutes, and the journey along the Sumida takes about half an hour. Once at Sumida Park Waterbus Station, go through Sumida Park to Asakusa Station.

Asakusa is the heart of the Lower Town. Real 'Old Tokyo' lovers claim that only in Asakusa (pronounced 'Asaksa') can the essence of Edo still be found. The district, although largely destroyed by fire-bombing raids in 1945, was rebuilt in wood and tile rather than in concrete and glass.

During the time of the shoguns, the 'little people of Edo' lived on the lower plain in Shitamachi (the Lower Town), while the aristocracy and their retainers lived on the drier high ground in Yamanote (the Upper Town). Even today, the inhabitants of Asakusa have the reputation of being more open and straightforward than 'those who live up there'. The low houses, the charming ancient shops (some of which are centuries old), the astonishing restaurants and the great number of religious feasts *(matsuri)* held here make Asakusa one of the most frequently visited districts in Tokyo, by foreigners and by Japanese tourists alike. With its theatres, cabarets and all-night restaurants, it is one of the liveliest nightspots in Tokyo. There is even a small and exclusive geisha area.

From Asakusa Station, walk to the **Kaminarimon*** (Thunder Gate), the entrance to the Senso ji temple, V, B2. Walk down **Nakamise Dori***, a long gallery lit by hundreds of paper lanterns and lined on each side by shops selling souvenirs, combs, kimonos and other traditional Japanese wares. The adjacent streets, particularly those to the left, are interesting to wander through, if you have the time. Note the statues of the fearsome gods of wind and thunder, thought to frighten evil spirits away from the temple, at the entrance of Nakamise Dori.

Senso ji*, or Asakusa Dera, more commonly called the Kannon temple, was founded in AD 628 and is dedicated to the goddess Kannon, a female reincarnation of Buddha. Three fishermen are said to have caught a golden statue of the goddess in their nets in that year (see p. 122).

To the right of Senso ji temple is the **Asakusa Jinja***, V, B2. Every year on May 17 and 18, this Shinto shrine hosts one of the three most important religious festivals in Tokyo (see p. 122).

To the left of Senso ji temple is Asakusa Park, which contains the Gojuno-to, a five-storey pagoda, and the **Denboin temple**, V, B2. The temple possesses a very fine 17th-century landscape garden designed by Kobori Enshu. Special written permission, however, is required in order to visit it. If you are interested in doing so, you should inquire at the Tourist Information Center (see p. 71). To the north of Asakusa Park, the former plant market, **Hanayashiki Yuenchi**, V, B2, dating from 1853, has been turned into an amusement park.

If you wish to get an idea of what daily life was like on the banks of the Sumida River during the Edo period, pay a visit to the **Fukagawa Edo Museum*** (see p. 137) across the river in Koto-ku.

To the north of Asakusa (about 0.9 mi/1.5 km from the station) is the notorious **Yoshiwara*** district, off map V, B1, the 'land of pleasures' and prostitution — or what is left of it. During the Edo period, there were over 300 'houses' here employing a total of about 3000 girls. In 1956, when prostitution was made illegal, many of these establishments were transformed into *toruco* (Turkish baths) in order to remain (in appearances at least) within the limits of the law. The clients were brought into bathrooms, instead of bedrooms, where the masseuses went to work.

In 1984, the Turkish Embassy lodged an official complaint to protest against the use of the word 'Turk' as a qualifier for these dubious establishments. Anywhere else in the world, this incident would have remained a diplomatic joke, but the respectful Japanese now call these establishments 'soapland'.

The **Matsubaya House***, 4-31-1 Senzoku, Taito-ku, V, A1, ☎ 3874 9401, is one of the rare *toruco* that has kept the tradition of *hikitechaya* (where the clients dine beforehand). Today, it is possible to watch a tourist-orientated *oiran* (courtesan) show every evening at 9:20pm.

▬ *NIHOMBASHI-GINZA*

This itinerary takes one day.

Access: Nihombashi Station, II, D2. To get to Nihombashi (Bridge of Japan) from the station, walk towards the Nihombashi River.

The **Nihombashi Bridge***, V, D2, spans the Nihombashi River at its intersection with Chuo Dori, not far from the Mitsukoshi department store. It is a convenient point of departure from which to visit the museums, art galleries and shops that line Chuo Dori, the most important avenue in the district.

The Shinjuku skyscrapers are specifically designed to withstand earthquakes.

First constructed in 1604, the bridge served for centuries as the 'zero' reference point from where all distances from Tokyo to other towns were measured. It figures on many 18th- and 19th-century Japanese prints. The bridge was originally built in wood, but the present structure is made of granite and dates from 1911 (one year before the death of the Emperor Meiji). The fact that today the bridge — which only a century ago was the symbolic centre of Japan — is covered by a hideous highway is apparently not disturbing to the Japanese mind.

From Nihombashi, follow Chuo Dori south. On the left of the avenue is the world renowned **Takashimaya**** department store, II, D2. A veritable institution dating from the Meiji period, it is the most luxurious department store in the district. Just across the avenue from Takashimaya is **Maruzen***, an international bookstore that offers a good selection of books on Japan in English.

The Bridgestone Building, on the corner at the Yaesu Dori intersection, houses the **Bridgestone Museum*****, II, D3, which possesses one of the best collections of Western art in Japan (see p. 129).

Continue south to Kyobashi Station and cross the large avenue that intersects Chuo Dori. If you are interested in art, go down the first street on the left or the next one parallel to it, II, C3. Numerous art galleries are installed in this little area. The best known are: **Kaneko***, 3-17-13 Kyobashi, Chuo-ku, ☎ 3564 0455, specializing in drawings; **Tsubaki***, 3-2-11 Kyobashi, Chuo-ku, ☎ 3281 7808, showing young Japanese painters; and **Nantenshi***, 3-6-5 Kyobashi, Chuo-ku, ☎ 3563 3511, dealing in well-known artists, particularly Europeans and Americans.

Continue following Chuo Dori to the expressway. On the far side is Ginza. The district draws its name from the fact that it was once the site of a shogunal mint (*gin*, meaning 'silver'; *za*, meaning 'seat'). As the major shopping center in Japan, Ginza has become the most expensive real estate in Tokyo — if not in the world — currently valued at roughly US $1 million per square metre. Needless to say, the majority of the shops and restaurants are prohibitively expensive, and more window shopping is done than any other kind. The Japanese verb for this is *ginbura* (to 'stroll in Ginza'). Throughout Japan, numerous shopping centers have been christened Ginza.

One of the most interesting shops in the area is **Itoya****, III, C1, a stationery shop offering an impressive choice of postcards, rare Japanese papers *(washi)* and very sophisticated office equipment. In the basement, you can order bilingual calling cards; they take about one week to be printed.

Just after Itoya are two well-known department stores, **Matsuya** and **Mitsukoshi**. Both of them have restaurants that offer inexpensive *teishoku* (lunch menus). **Tempura Tsunahachi**, on the top floor of Matsuya, is reputed for the delicacy of its *tempura*.

After lunch, try a coffee at **Kimuraya****, III, C1. Just opposite Mitsukoshi, this bakery was the first to introduce French bread into Japan. It is most famous for its *han-pan* (small, round breads filled with red bean paste), which have been held in high repute for over five generations.

At Mitsukoshi, turn left onto Harumi Dori and walk to Showa Dori. On the left, after the next intersection, is the **Kabuki za***** (Kabuki Theatre), III, D2. Originally founded in 1624, it was rebuilt in 1950 and now seats 2200 spectators (see p. 48).

Turn down the first street on the left after the theatre and continue walking towards the next intersection. The handsome modern building on the left is the **Magazine House***, III, D1-2, the headquarters of numerous Japanese magazine publishers. The first two floors are open to the public and contain a large selection of magazines from around the world. These may be read on the premises, even over a cup of coffee in the adjoining cafeteria. Have the courtesy to replace the magazines in their proper place before leaving the building.

Leave the Magazine House, turn right and then cross Showa Dori. On the left is **Musashiya,** a shop specializing in *tabi* (Japanese socks). They separate the large toe from the rest of the foot and allow the wearer to slip on *geta* (wooden clogs) or *zori* (straw sandals). *Tabi* are usually white for women and black or blue for men. They make amusing and inexpensive gifts.

Continue to the end of the street. You should be facing the **Sukiyabashi** shopping center, III, C1. Nearby is the Toei cinema, which specializes in *yakuza* (gangster) films. On your right, after the cinema, is **Le Printemps,** III, C1, a branch of the Parisian department store.

Retrace your steps to **Sukiyabashi Crossing,** III, C1. As the most important intersection in Ginza, it is here that political parties (particularly the extreme right) come to howl their philosophies over loudspeakers turned up full blast.

Cross the intersection and walk in the direction of the Sony Building, which houses two of the most expensive restaurants in Tokyo: **Maxim's de Paris,** III, C1, n°1, ☎ 3572 3621, and **Sabatini di Firenze,** III, C1, n°2, ☎ 3573 0013. The **Pub Cardinal,** just next door, is a convenient up-market meeting place.

Walk by Hankyu department store, just opposite the Sony Building, and take the first right. The **Riccar Museum**,** III, C1, (see p. 138) is on the left about 109 yd/100 m down the street. This is the best place in Tokyo to see *ukiyo-e* (Japanese prints).

End this urban excursion on a green note. From the museum, cross the railway tracks and walk toward **Hibiya Park*,** III, B1. Laid out in 1904, Hibiya was the first Western-style park in Japan (see p. 127).

▬ *SHINJUKU*

Count on one day for this itinerary.

Access: Shinjuku Station, VI, B2.

On a giant television screen, a geisha gives you the eye. All around multicoloured neon lights flash. Ideograms light up and then disappear to the rhythm of disco music. From somewhere down the road, the street is filled with the infernal racket of *pachinko* machines, and a crooner in a nearby bar begins to intone the lament of the abandoned *salaryman*.

This is Shinjuku, the pulsating heart of Tokyo. Here, amid the seemingly ageless stalls of *takoyaki* (octopus fritters) vendors and in the tiny bars where four is a crowd, the year 2000 — electronic and robotized — is already half installed. Life in Shinjuku is most intense at night, when light-hearted *salarymen* come in bands to get drunk after work. By around midnight, the district offers a hallucinating spectacle reminiscent of Roman orgies. If you have only one night to spend in Tokyo, do not miss Shinjuku.

By day, Shinjuku is transformed into a district of large department stores and fancy shops, offering the tourist a number of interesting excursions.

Shinjuku by day: skyscrapers and department stores

Shinjuku is geologically more stable than the rest of Tokyo. The first skyscrapers constructed in the city after the 1923 earthquake were built here. More recently, giant buildings have sprouted in a park-like setting to the west of Shinjuku Station in an area known as 'New Shinjuku'. Due to the frequency of seismic tremors in Tokyo, Japanese architects have employed a wide range of technical innovations and have succeeded in producing structures that are (theoretically) capable of resisting the strongest earthquakes.

To get to Shinjuku take a train or subway to Shinjuku Station, then leave the station by the West Exit. The Odakyu department store should be in front of you. Turn left in the direction of the big buildings that dominate the district to the west, IV, AB2. All of these structures can be visited, but only a few are of any real interest unless, of course, you happen to be an architect. For the lay person, the most interesting buildings are these:

● **Shinjuku NS Building***,** VI, A2. Opened in 1982, this 30-storey structure is undoubtedly the most handsome building in the area and has the peculiarity of being hollow in the center. A glass roof of more than 6000 panes admits daylight into the center of the structure. For a touch of fantasy, the architect added on the ground floor a giant clock and on the 29th floor a small foot bridge that spans the hollow centre of the building from one side to the other. One entire floor of the Shinjuku NS Building is devoted to computers. Nineteen manufacturers have installed showrooms here, and it is possible to test the latest equipment and ask the company representatives any technical questions you might have concerning their models.

● **Shinjuku Mitsui Building****, VI, A2. Built in 1974, this 55-storey building is easily recognized by its blue-tinted, mirrored façade towering to a height of 735 ft/224 m. Have something to drink on the terrace of the Go-Go Plaza, among the trees and the waterfall.

● **Yasuda Kaisai Building****, VI, B1-2. This building houses the **Seiji Togo Art Museum**. The collection consists of about 100 works of Seiji Togo, a famous female portraitist. The view from the museum, on the 42nd floor of the building, is one of the best in Tokyo.

Other good views of Tokyo can be seen from the 53rd floor of the **Shinjuku Center Building***, VI, B2, and the 50th floor of the **Shinjuku Nomura Building,** VI, B1. Both are free of charge. The latter contains a large number of restaurants.

Anyone interested in photographic equipment should pay a visit to **Yodobashi Camera****, VI, B2, behind the bus station. Do not be taken aback by the militaristic music; it is only the store's theme song. A gentler voice will soon greet you in English, French, Italian and Russian. Absolutely anything in the world of cameras and lenses can be found here at interesting prices.

The eastern half of Shinjuku offers more down-to-earth attractions. First retrace your steps to Odakyu department store, VI, B2. Then take Koshu Kaido Avenue and cross over the railway tracks in front of the station. Once on the east side of the station, turn down any one of the small streets on the right. This little area, with its small bars and narrow streets, is reminiscent of pre-war Tokyo. After wandering through it, you will eventually come to the Alta Building, easily recognized by a giant television screen that covers its façade. The large avenue on the right is Shinjuku Dori, the main commercial thoroughfare in the district. It is closed to traffic on Sunday, when it teems with pedestrians.

On the left is **Kinokuniya****, VI, C2, a book shop that serves as a meeting place for *gaijin* (foreigners). Its international department on the 6th floor is well stocked with books in English and other foreign languages.

A little farther on, on the same side of the street, is **Isetan,** VI, C2. This department store has an aquarium, a playground for children and (like all Tokyo department stores) numerous restaurants on the second-top floor. Catering to local office workers, the *teishoku* (lunch menus) are good and inexpensive. The Isetan Art Museum is on the 8th floor.

Leave Isetan and continue down Shinjuku Dori to Shinjuku-gyoenmae Station, VI, D2. Turn right after the station and walk toward **Shinjuku Gyoen*****, VI, CD2-3. *Open Tues-Sun 9am-4pm.* The entrance to these gardens is a little to the left. Do not confuse this park with Shinjuku Central Park, near 'New Shinjuku'.

Now classified as a National Garden, Shinjuku Gyoen originally belonged to the Naito family. This district is sometimes referred to as 'Night-Shinjuku' because in Japanese the word 'night' is pronounced 'naito'. Later the land came into the hands of the Imperial family, who held the Imperial Cherry Bud and other garden parties here. The park has been open to the public only since the end of World War II.

The second-largest park in Tokyo, after Yoyogi Koen, Shinjuku Gyoen has the originality of combining both Western and Japanese styles in a single setting. It is possible to stroll from the formal French gardens (designed in 1906 by Henri Martinet, the head gardener at Versailles) into the Japanese chrysanthemum gardens just a few steps away. In April, about 2000 cherry and plum trees, including some of the rarest varieties in Japan, flower in a multitude of colours. There is also an English garden with a wide expanse of lawn, tropical greenhouses and a large collection of cacti.

Before starting your night in Shinjuku, return to the station. Just before reaching Meiji Dori, you will come across a traditional Japanese pastry shop, **Dango Oyumake***, 1-2-8 Shinjuku, Shinjuku-ku, VI, C2, ☎ 3364 2201. Refresh yourself with tea and *abekura-mochi*, a Japanese pastry.

On the corner near Isetan, turn right, cross the Yasukuni Dori and go down Meiji Dori a few paces. On the left is **Hanazono Jinja***, VI, C1. A haven of peace, this shrine is totally incongruous with the surrounding fury of Shinjuku. The Japanese come here to pray to the 'god of bargains and good deals'. Considering the number of tradespeople in the neighbourhood, the shrine certainly must not lack worshippers.

Tori-no-ichi (Cock Festival), also called Rake Fair, takes place at the shrine in November. Because the date varies slightly from year to year, it is necessary to inquire in advance. During the festival, vendors sell small bamboo rakes *(kumade)* that symbolize the money 'to be raked in' during the year. The ceremony is well worth attending.

A flea market is held at the entrance of the shrine on the first Saturday and the third Sunday of every month.

Shinjuku by night: the Kabukicho

As night falls, flashing neon lights bathe faces already flushed with alcohol. Visitors to this area start early and drink fast.

Just a few steps away from the Hanazono Jinja shrine is one of the most amazing districts in Tokyo, the **Golden Gae*****, VI, C1. This 'village', where the streets are barely wide enough for two people to walk abreast and where three-quarters of the doors lead into tiny bars, has remained unchanged for the last 50 years. Unfortunately, the future of this animated district is uncertain. In 1987, one of the large department stores bought the whole area for land-speculation purposes.

Unless you are with Japanese friends or happen to be fluent in Japanese, it is best to limit your excursion to a simple stroll. The owners of these tiny bars speak only Japanese and tend to refuse service to foreigners. They have their own regular customers and do not accept casual trade. Stick to the places that are accustomed to *gaijin* (foreigners). On Yakusuni Dori, just opposite the Kabukicho, the **Café Jazz Dug***, VI, C1, serves all types of alcoholic beverages as well as coffee and soft drinks.

Once you have quenched your thirst, cross the street to the **Kabuki-cho***** (Kabuki district), VI, BC1. The area acquired this name just after the war when a proposal to reconstruct the Ginza Kabuki-za theater in this neighbourhood was announced. The project, however, was quickly abandoned due to widespread public protest.

Today, the Kabukicho district is one of the hottest spots in Tokyo. Sex shops, nightclubs, discos, cinemas and thousands of restaurants attract large crowds every night. Contrary to an initial impression, it is not the peep shows but the sing-song bars that attract the most people (particularly after a law voted in 1986 forbade touters to solicit on the streets). A favourite pastime of the Japanese is to sing love songs to the sound of prerecorded music in front of other customers. This national mania is called *karaoke*. If you happen to wander into such a place, you will undoubtedly be asked to take the microphone. The owner always has a little booklet of lyrics handy . . . unless, of course, they are preregistered on a videoscreen. At the **Young Karaoke Bar,** VI, B1, Western voices are highly appreciated.

Try the more typically Japanese bars at your own risk. Some of these establishments (particularly where 'entertainment' and 'company' are provided) are the haunts of the *yakuza* (Japanese underworld), and ¥38,000 for a beer is not unheard of.

There are also a number of discotheques in the district. These are concentrated around the **Koma Theater,** VI, B1, in the center of Kabukicho. The entrances fees are rather steep (¥3000 to ¥4000) but cover as many drinks as you can handle. Sometimes a buffet is provided as well. Alternatively, a more relaxed atmosphere is available at an excellent jazz club called the **Shinjuku Pit Inn****. It is located in the YK Building, 2-16-4 Shinjuku, Shinjuku-ku, VI, B2, ☎ 3354 2024. *Open* *daily 11:30am-11pm.* There are concerts every day at noon, 3pm and 7:30pm.

No matter where you choose to spend the evening, you will be confronted with an apocalyptical vision on leaving. Every night, thousands of *salarymen* 'do the rounds' from bar to bar, and by midnight almost everyone wandering the streets — or lying in them — is completely drunk. They hobble around in twos and threes, bawling drinking songs at the top of their lungs. As a foreigner, you will most likely be accosted by one or more of these inquisitive individuals who have temporarily shed their inhibitions. Don't worry — even when drunk, the Japanese retain their sense of propriety.

If you are not staying in the neighbourhood, remember that the last train leaves at about half past midnight. After this time, there is a mad rush for taxis, and it is frequently impossible to find one, particularly on Saturday nights. If this should happen, resign yourself to finding a capsule hotel near Shinjuku Station. For about ¥3500, you will be able to get a good night's sleep provided that you are not too claustrophobic.

▬▬ THE IMPERIAL PALACE

Half a day is necessary for this itinerary.

Access: Otemachi Station, II, C2.

The Imperial Palace (or Kokyo) has been called the 'empty center' of Tokyo. Surrounded by wide moats and almost totally forbidden to the public, the palace consists of numerous buildings scattered around an immense park that takes two to three hours to walk around. The Emperor and his family live in the middle of this sacred enclosure.

Start your visit with **Kokyo Higashi Gyoen***** (East Imperial garden), II, B1-2. *Open daily 9am-4pm.* This 52-acre/21-hectare park was opened to the public in 1968. It contains 250,000 trees from every province of Japan and is one of the richest botanical gardens in the country. It was here that the Tokugawa originally had their castle in the 17th century. The foundations of the *tenshudai* (keep) are still visible. There is also a Chinese zigzag bridge, designed to prevent evil spirits (which can travel only in straight lines) from entering the palace grounds. In the middle of the park, there is a lake and a teahouse as well as the **Ninomaru****, a beautiful Japanese garden originally designed in 1630 by Kobori Enshu. The easiest way to reach Higashi Gyoen is through the Otemon Gate located five minutes from Otemachi Station.

Leave Higashi Gyoen by the Kitahanebashimon Gate and enter **Kitanomaru Park****, II, AB1, to the north. This part of the palace grounds has been open to the public since 1969 on the occasion of Hirohito's 60th· anniversary. The park contains three museums: the **Science Museum** (see p. 138), the **Tokyo National Museum of Modern Art** (see p. 134) and the **National Archives Museum.** Near the northern entrance of the park is the **Nippon Budokan,** the largest concert hall in Japan. This polygonal building, originally designed for judo contests, was built for the 1964 Olympic Games.

On the left, beyond the Taysumon Gate and across Yasukuni Dori, is the **Yasu kini Shrine****, II, A1. Dedicated to the Japanese who died for Japan from the Meiji Restoration to World War II, this shrine is the controversial rallying point for Japanese nationalists. It contains a small war museum (see p. 142).

Retrace your steps toward the Imperial Palace. Cross the avenue and turn south towards **Chidorigafuchi Aquatic Park****, II, A1. When the cherry trees bloom in April, this is one of the most popular spots in Tokyo. It is possible to rent boats for rowing on the moat.

Continue south, go past the Hanzomon Gate and re-enter the park through the **Sakurada mon Gate***, II, B3, at the southern extremity of the Imperial Palace enclosure. Walk along the inner moat until you come to a second gate, the **Sakashita mon***, which leads to the **Nijubashi**

Bridge***, the official entrance of the Imperial Palace. The bridge was constructed from the stones of the old feudal castle.

Leave the palace grounds and cross the outer moat. On the far side of Uchibori Dori, turn left. In front of you is **Hibiya Park***, II, B3, the oldest Western-style park in Japan (see p. 127). It is famous for its azaleas (in April) and chrysanthemums (in November). In the middle of the park, there is a restaurant where you can eat on a terrace in the summer — a rarity in Tokyo.

Leave the park and head east in the direction of the Imperial Hotel. Its silhouette is visible from afar. Continue past the hotel to the end of the street. Near the railway tracks is the **International Arcade****, II, BC3, a market offering duty-free souvenirs, jewelry and electronic equipment.

Yurakucho Station is three minutes away on foot. You are also very near Ginza (see p. 104), where you could spend the evening.

UENO

Plan half a day for this itinerary; if you want to visit the museums, you will need a full day.

Access: Ueno Station, IV, B3.

Ueno, with its park, its museums and, above all, its history, is not to be missed. One of the main centres of activity in Tokyo, it is also the site of Ueno Station, where most provincials and many tourists arrive in the capital.

Ueno (literally 'plain on high') was formerly of strategic importance. It was from this slightly elevated area that the shogunate's guards surveyed the surrounding area. At the beginning of the 17th century, the *daimyo* (obliged to reside in Edo on the Shogun's orders) built their homes on the higher ground of Ueno. During the Kanei period (1624-44), they were displaced by Shogun Iemitsu, who took possession of the land and built a number of temples for himself and his family. Almost all of these buildings were destroyed in a major battle that occurred here in 1868 between the *shogitai* (the shogun's partisans) and the Imperial troops. One of the great heroes of the battle was Saigo Takamori (1827-77), whose sad story is superbly recounted by Ivan Morris in *The Nobility of Failure: Tragic Heroes in the History of Japan*.

In 1873, the idea of a public park began to take root. The first in Japan, it was finished in 1890. The municipality then gave it to the Emperor Meiji as a gift. Hirohito finally returned it to the city in 1924 on the occasion of his wedding.

Leave Ueno Station and walk toward the statue of **Saigo Takamori***, IV, B3. Continue walking in the direction of the Shinobazu pond and then turn right. The **Shitamachi Museum***** (Shitamachi Fuzoku Shiryokan), is on the left of the path at the southern end of the pond. It provides an excellent introduction to the Ueno and Asakusa districts (see p. 137). Stroll around the pond on the northern side toward the principal entrance to the park.

The park's main path is bordered by hundreds of cherry trees. During the week when they bloom (usually around the beginning of April), they attract millions of visitors. Entire families come and picnic on straw mats under the boughs, drinking, dancing and singing late into the night. This ritual, called *o hanami* ('looking at the flowers'), occurs throughout Japan wherever cherries, plums or apricots bloom. Any stranger who happens to wander past one of these joyous parties is swept into the revelry and encouraged to celebrate the arrival of spring.

The first building on the left is the **Toshogu****, IV, A2. This temple is dedicated to Ieyasu Tokugawa, the founder of the Tokugawa shogunal dynasty. The present building was built in 1651 and is the only temple in Tokyo to be classified as a National Treasure. The path that leads to it is lined by stone lanterns that were offered by various *daimyo* at the inauguration of the temple.

Schoolgirls in the lively Harajuku district.

Continue towards the north. Just behind the Tokyo Metropolitan Art Museum is the **Ueno Zoo****, IV, A2. It is worth a visit if only to see the giant pandas Ton Ton and Wan Wan. They are national stars in Japan, and the television frequently broadcasts news of them. The length of the line in front of the cage demonstrates the degree to which the Japanese are infatuated by these animals.

Nearby is the **National Museum*****, IV, B2. At least half a day is needed to visit it. It is best to go on a Thursday, if possible, as that is the only day — and even then on the condition that it is not raining — that the Horyuji Treasury is open (see p. 132).

Bypass the museum for now and walk toward **Kanei ji***, IV, B1. The original structure of the temple was destroyed in 1868. In 1875, the central building of a temple in the Saitama Prefecture was reconstructed here. Not far away is the **Tokugawa cemetery,** where 6 of the 15 Tokugawa shoguns are buried. A little farther to the north is the **Jomjoin temple,** famous for its 20,000 images of Jizo (the god of pilgrims and 'Saviour of the Damned').

Yanaka Cemetery, IV, A1, just across Kototoi Dori, is a few minutes walk to the north-west of Ueno Park. During the cherry blossom season in April, the cemetery is invaded by flower worshippers, and its daytime population greatly increases.

Offer yourself the pleasure of ending the day's excursion near **Shinobazu Pond****, IV, A3. The sunsets are often magnificent, particularly in the summer, when the entire lake is covered with waterlilies and the evenings present a free concert... of frogs. Between July 13 and 16, the nearby **Bentendo temple** celebrates *O-Bon,* a festival dedicated to ancestors. In autumn, lovers rent pedal boats and glide in and out among the thousands of migrating ducks that invade the pond at this time of year. At the northern end of the pond, there is an **aquarium** containing a large collection of exotic fish.

Before leaving Ueno, go to **Ameyoko****, IV, B3. Across from the southern exit of Ueno Station, this is a large covered market where everything is 20% to 50% cheaper than it is anywhere else in Tokyo. The word *ameyoko* means 'the American side', and it was here that the GIs started the black market after the war, during the American Occupation. Counterfeited objects are not uncommon, so beware of good 'brands' at bargain prices.

Nearer the railway tracks, Ameyoko becomes a fantastic food market, offering fish, seaweed, tea, *tsukemono* (salted vegetables) and other ingredients required to prepare an excellent Japanese meal. Many Japanese householders come to Ameyoko to stock up in preparation for *Shogatsu* (New Year). They buy provisions for the three-day-long holiday. The prices fall as the hour advances. The vendors of this cheerful and popular market are so persuasive that legend has it they sold 22 lb/10 kg of tuna to an anorexic bachelor.

At Ueno Station, you are only a stop away from the **Kappabashi district****, V, A2, near Inaricho Station. The kitchen suppliers' neighbourhood, this is the best place to buy a *mihon*, the famous mouth-watering 'false food' in resin or wax that is displayed in so many of Tokyo's restaurants.

▬ *SHIBUYA, HARAJUKU AND AOYAMA*

You will need a day or two and a good pair of walking shoes to visit these three districts.

Shibuya: large stores and small restaurants

Access: Shibuya Station, XI, B3.

Shibuya is a popular, teeming district. This area is centered around Shibuya Station, which — although smaller than Shinjuku Station — is more confusing than Shinjuku. It is possible to walk around for hours without finding any exit — let alone the right one. The station is a city within itself, containing various department stores and hundreds of small shops, on several levels. Over 700,000 commuters use Shibuya Station every day, making it the third most important station in Japan. Four railway lines (the Yamanote, the Shintamagawa, the Inokashira and the Tokyu Toyoko) and two subway lines (the Hanzomon and Ginza) meet at the station.

A dog's life

Towards the end of the 1920s, a university professor (whose name is now forgotten) had a dog named Hachiko. Every morning, the dog would follow his master to Shibuya Station. In the evening, he would return to the station to wait for his master's return. One day the professor died in an accident. No one informed Hachiko, who continued to come to the station every day for seven years to wait for his master.

When Hachiko died in 1935, the story hit the headlines. A collection was organized, and a statue was erected for the dog who had been so loyal to his master.

During the war, the statue was melted down but was replaced by another monument in 1948.

On every holiday, Hachiko is decorated as a divinity with bonnets and ruffles. People touch the statue, treating it as a good luck charm. The spot has become the neighbourhood's (and even Tokyo's) number-one rendez vous. On some Saturday nights, the poor dog is nearly completely lost among the milling crowd — a crowd so huge that the meeting place itself seems from afar to have disappeared.

Wander around the station for a while and when you have had enough of being 'lost', ask someone how to find the statue of **Hachiko** the dog, XI, B3, *('Sumimasen, Hachiko doko desu ka')*. When you have found the statue (see box), walk in the direction of his gaze. On the corner, near a cylindrical building named Fashion Community 109 ('109' in Japanese is pronounced 'Tokyu' and is the name of a chain store), turn right and walk down any of the small pedestrian streets opposite the station. There are numerous coffee shops and small restaurants, generally frequented by middle-class students and Westernized young people, where you can relax for a while. Alternatively, there are department stores that offer a choice of cafés and restaurants with inexpensive *teishoku* (lunch menus).

Apart from **Seibu***, XI, B3 (similar to its other branches), there is **Parco****. This store is always on the forefront of fashion, both for its constantly changing interior decoration and for its choice of products. Clothes, gadgets, leather goods or just paper — anything that trendy Japan has to offer, is on sale here. Note that there are three different Parco buildings, each with its own specialities. A little farther on is **Tokyu Hands** XI, B3 — the sign is a giveaway — a large store offering everything necessary for drawing, writing and calligraphy as well as for outfitting the kitchen and the bathroom and for cultivating bonsai.

From the intersection near Parco, continue down Koen Dori for two more blocks. On the right is the **Museum of Tobacco and Salt** (Tabaco To Shio Hakubutsukan), XI, B3, ☎ 3476 2041. *Open Tues-Sun 10am-6pm.* Tobacco was first introduced into Japan in the middle of the 16th century. Its use, in typical Japanese fashion, engendered a number of rituals explained in this museum. Non-sectarian, the museum has devoted an entire floor to the subject of tobacco in the world, and it contains a good international collection of cigarette packages. On the 3rd floor, the history of salt in the world and in Japan is presented. Unfortunately, the explanations are given exclusively in Japanese (see p. 141).

Leave the museum, turn right and walk about 330 yd/300 m. In Yoyogi Park you will find the **National Yoyogi Olympic Gymnasium*****, XI, B2. The interior is *open daily 10am-4pm except when competitions are being held.* Designed by Kenzo Tange for the 1964 Olympic Games, it is considered one of the finest examples of the architecture of the last few decades. Attempting to reconcile traditional Japanese architecture with the avant-garde, two huge pillars support the metallic roof that is also held up by cables in a manner reminiscent of the Wedded Rocks of the Ise Jingu, one of Japan's most sacred shrines. It contains two swimming pools, one of which is open all year long, and an ice-skating rink *(open daily Oct 15-Apr 1 10am-8pm)*.

To the left of the Yoyogi Gymnasium is a massive green tower covered by radar antennae. This is the **NHK (Nihon Hoso Kaisha)***, XI, B2, the national radio and television network. The studios can be visited. *Open daily 10am-5pm. Closed the 4th Mon of every month.*

Harajuku: the Champs-Élysées of Tokyo

Access: Harajuku Station, XI, C2.

Just over the railway line, to the north-east of the Yoyogi Gymnasium, lies the Harajuku district. This area is frequented by adolescents playing at being rockers and punks before settling down to become gallant *salarymen*.

From the main exit of the station, take the large avenue that descends towards Aoyama Dori. This is **Omotesandodori****, XI, CD2. Resembling a Parisian boulevard, it is one of the few tree-lined streets in Tokyo, and as such it is a popular avenue for strolling and café life.

On a back street to the left is the **Ota Museum****, XI, C2 (see p. 138). It has a collection of 12,000 *ukiyo-e* (Japanese prints), including some works by great masters such as Utamaro and Hiroshige, exhibited in rotation.

Harajuku's main street near Yoyogi Park is closed on Sundays for the weekly get-together of Tokyo's rockers... 50s style.

Continue down Omotesandodori to its intersection with Meijidori. Take note of a large building called La Forêt. It will serve as a landmark at the end of your walk. A short way down the avenue on the right side is **Kiddy Land★**, XI, C2, one of the largest toy stores in Tokyo. It sells traditional toys (kites, tops and so on) as well as the latest electronic novelties. The local kids come here just to spend the afternoon. Worth seeing, even if you don't buy anything.

A little farther down on the same side of the street is the **Oriental Bazaar★★**, XI, C2, the souvenir shop par excellence. Collectors' stamps, Japanese antiques (real or fake depending on your budget), traditional crockery, secondhand kimonos, T-shirts and the like, all can be purchased at reasonable prices. If you are in Tokyo for only a short time, this is the ideal place to buy everything you want at once.

Heart of a rocker

On every Sunday, Harajuku's main street near Yoyogi Park is closed to traffic and becomes the temple of rock'n'roll — Japanese style, of course, with a maximum of order and a minimum of violence. Groomed and geared like Buddy Holly, swaying their hips like Elvis Presley, groups of young people with names such as The Wild and The Tokyo Rockers get together and dance the full repertoire of the 1950s. The younger *takenokozoku* (bamboo shoots) gather nearby. Dressed in multicoloured silks and with feathers in their hair, as many as 50 of these Japanese 'punks' dance to the same rhythm as their rock elders. Feel free to photograph them — they thrive on it!

Numerous stalls along the avenue offer a large choice of delicious specialities. Particularly good are the *yakisoba* (fried noodles) accompanied by a little ginger and the aromatic *takoyaki* (small grilled croquettes filled with octopus). With such fare, you can easily forget about lunch and just nibble all afternoon.

Aoyama: fashion and design

Access: Aoyama Station, off map XI, D2

Although Aoyama is largely a residential area with many schools and embassies, it is also the fashion district of Tokyo. The following detour considerably lengthens the excursion mentioned above, but anyone interested in architecture and/or design should continue down the avenue. On the same side of the street is the **Hanae Mori Building****, XI, D2, designed by Kenzo Tange. Continue down Omotesandodori and turn left on Aoyama Dori. This is where the big fashion designers, such as Issey Maiyake and Comme des Garçons, have their outlets.

Walk to the intersection with Gaien-Nishi Dori. **Killer Street****, VIII, A1 (so named by the designer Junko Koshino) is on your left when you arrive at the Aoyama Belle Commons Building. If you are interested in folklore and handicrafts, the **Japan Traditional Crafts Center** is on the adjacent corner. For refreshment there is a minuscule bar called the COD that serves an excellent espresso just opposite the Nicole Building.

Retrace your steps back to the La Forêt Building, XI, C2, and turn right at the intersection. About 330 yd/300 m farther on, turn left into the narrow **Takeshitadori*****, XI, C1, the Carnaby Street of Tokyo. The **Le Ponte gallery** (just opposite McDonald's) will give you a good idea of the sorts of things that can be found in Harajuku: clothes, badges, stickers and jewelry.

From here, Harajuku Station is convenient for reaching both Shinjuku and Shibuya, depending on where you plan to spend the evening.

▬ ROPPONGI

You will need half a day and an evening for this itinerary.

Access: Roppongi Station, VIII, C3. For the Tokyo Tower, VIII, D3, take the Toei Mita Line to Shiba-Koen Station and walk through Shiba Park.

Roppongi literally means 'six trees'. The area was once owned by six *daimyo* whose names all ended in '*gi*', the Japanese word for 'tree'.

Today, with its discotheques, cabarets, English pubs and chic restaurants, Roppongi is one of the trendiest districts in Tokyo and attracts a variety of nocturnal characters from chic to punk. Similar to London's Soho, it is also an expensive residential area with a number of embassies.

As far as tourist attractions are concerned, the district has little to offer apart from two temples. On the other hand, it is an ideal neighbourhood for 'doing the rounds' (pub crawling), one of the nation's favourite pastimes.

The main site of interest in the district is the **Tokyo Tower*** (Tokyo Tawa), VIII, D3. It is a graceless imitation of the Eiffel Tower (according to the French), but the proud Japanese point out that Tokyo Tower is, nonetheless, 36 ft/11 m taller than its French counterpart. Constructed in 1958, when it was billed by its sponsors 'the wonder of Asia', the tower is 1093 ft/333 m high. It houses a wax museum, a science museum and an aquarium with 800 different species of fish. From the observation platform 768 ft/234 m above the ground, there is a panoramic view of Tokyo and — on clear days — Mount Fuji. Because Tokyo is a relatively flat city however, so is the view, sometimes amounting to not much more than a bird's perspective on a bank of smog. Try to avoid the Sunday crowds. See 'Access' above for the most direct way to get to the tower.

The **Zojo ji***, III, A3, in the middle of the park, is the Kanto headquarters of the Jodo Buddhist sect. Like many of Tokyo's temples, it has been destroyed and rebuilt on numerous occasions. The main building dates from 1974. Although nothing remains of the original 1393 structure, the entrance gate dates to 1605, and the temple contains a rare image of a 'Black Buddha'.

From the Tokyo Tower, follow the Gaien-Higashi Dori to **Roppongi Crossing,** VIII, C2, The walk takes about 20 minutes if you do not stop to gaze at the numerous fancy shops and the Baroque and futuristic buildings along the way. The Soviet Embassy, on the left side of the street, just after the Sakuradori intersection, is permanently guarded by the police.

The Roppongi Crossing is the heart of the district. On one side is **Almond,** VIII, C2, a confectioner's and tearoom that serves as a meeting place for foreign fashion models; the violet façade of the shop is hard to miss. On the other side of the intersection is an international bookstore that offers a variety of English and American magazines. In typical Japanese fashion, an elevated expressway has been built right through the middle of the intersection.

To the north of the expressway is the **Nogizaka district,** VIII, BC2. Walk along Gaien Higashidori and pass the famous Boecho (Ministry of Defense). Turn down the first street on the right and enter **Nogi Park.** The park contains Nogi Jinja, a shrine dedicated to General Nogi, who disemboweled himself at the beginning of the century in order 'to follow Emperor Meiji to the tomb'. His wife, after slitting her husband's throat, then killed herself in turn. It is possible to visit the general's house, including the room where he committed his act of *seppuku* (ritual suicide).

Cross the Gaien Higashidori in the direction of Nogizaka Station and follow the larger of the streets to **Aoyama Cemetery**** (Aoyama Reien), VIII, B2. One of the largest in Tokyo, it is unlike most cemeteries in Japan, in that it is not affiliated to a Buddhist temple. It contains the ashes of many famous Japanese, including those who participated in the Meiji Restoration. There are about 100,000 tombs along the long, shady aisles where some of the most beautiful cherry trees in Tokyo bloom in April.

Leave the cemetery on the Nogizaka side. Take the avenue on the left back to Roppongidori — easily recognized by the elevated expressway. Turn left at the intersection, cross to the opposite side of the avenue and walk for about 10 minutes until you arrive at **Wave*,** VIII, B2, a branch of the Seibu department store. One of the best examples of successful modern architecture in Tokyo, this store sells records and ultramodern objects. There is a good selection of art books on the 4th floor. In the basement, a projection room called the Ciné-Vivant shows French avant-garde films.

If you are going to be in Japan for only a short time, dine at **Inakaya**,** VIII, B2, n° 7c. A bit touristy perhaps, this is nevertheless an extremely lively *robata yaki* restaurant (see 'Tokyo Addresses' p. 234). For the rest of the evening, Roppongi offers all kinds of entertainment, from jazz to disco, as well as American bars and English pubs (see Tokyo Addresses' p. 235).

▬▬ *IKEBUKURO*

This itinerary should take three to five hours.

Access: Ikebukuro Station, XII, A1-2.

The district takes its name from a lake *(ike)* that once existed here and had the form of a sack *(bukuro).*

Today, Ikebukuro is an important commercial and recreational center **Sunshine City**,** XII, B2, the tallest building in Japan, was constructed here in 1978 and has greatly modified the social make-up of the area. A mixture of enormous modern skyscrapers and small (slightly unkempt) streets, the district resembles Shinjuku (see p. 107) but is more popular and less expensive.

Start your visit of the district at the monstrous **Seibu**** department store, XII, A1-2. Entirely covering Seibu Ikebukuro Station, it is the largest department store in Japan. The food section, in the basement, resembles an enormous covered market and contains everything from the culinary specialities of Shikoku Island to the finest French wines. The French caterer Lenôtre has opened an outlet here that has become a fashionable place to eat chocolate cake and drink chicory coffee.

The Seibu Museum of Art is on the 12th floor. Several different exhibitions of modern painting, photography, masks and so on are mounted each year.

Leave Seibu and head toward Parco. Turn left at the first corner and then immediately to the right. You should be facing the **Tokyo Bio Radon Center***, 1-39-11 Higashi Ikebukuro, Toshima-ku, XII, B1, ☎ 3981 2441. This establishment is unique in Japan. Unlike in *sento* baths (see p. 62), you may actually wash here as well as socialize. A series of hot, cold and steam baths concludes with carbonated radon water said to open the pores of the skin. You can follow this circuit as many times as you like. Between baths you can have a drink or watch television. Soap, towels and a *yukata* (robe) are provided at the entrance.

Behind the Tokyo Bio Radon Center, there is a little neighbourhood that — with its nightclubs, bars and small restaurants — resembles the Kabukicho district in Shinjuku (see p. 107). Despite its appearance, this district is quite safe. Stroll around and discover this interesting neighbourhood. The **Bungeiza cinema**, XII, B1, runs old American and French films with their original soundtracks.

Cross Meiji Dori and walk down Ekimae Dori. Near the intersection at the end of the avenue is Bic Camera, one of the cheapest stores in Tokyo for cameras, videos and computers. Turn left just after the store and take the pedestrian street toward Sunshine City. This area contains numerous shops and restaurants as well as the infamous *abec hoteru* (love hotels), easily recognized by their Baroque appearance. As their name indicates, these hotels are used by couples in the afternoon or early evening. Designed to encourage amorous adventure, the rooms are decorated in rather poor taste. One of the oldest love hotels in Ikebukuro, the Guru-Chateau is in the shape of a European manor house. Discretion is guaranteed: the hallways are arranged in such a manner that clients never come face to face with one another.

After wandering through the pedestrian area, cross under the Shuto Expressway and walk toward **Sunshine City**, XII, B3. Built in 1978 on the site of the famous Sugamo Prison, this complex comprises four buildings totaling 646,000 sq ft/60,000 sq m. The Sunshine 60 Building rises 787 ft/240 m above the street. The elevators take exactly 35 seconds to reach the 60th (top) floor. The view is so impressive that some people claim to be able to distinguish the curvature of the earth.

A city within itself, Sunshine City contains a hotel, a cultural center and dozens of shops and restaurants. The **aquarium****, on the 10th floor, ☎ 3989 3466, *open daily 10am-5pm,* is one of the best in the world and is well worth seeing. Every hour there is an amazing circus of trained fish. On the same floor, there is also a superb **planetarium*** with a 36 ft/11 m dome.

If you still have a little time left, visit the **Gokoku ji***, I, A1. You can either walk or take the Yurakucho Line to Gokokuji Station, the second stop after Ikebukuro. From the exit of the station, the temple is clearly visible. One of the largest temples in Tokyo, it belongs to the Shingon Buddhist sect. Built in 1681 by Tsunayoshi, the fifth Tokugawa shogun, the temple contains several noteworthy treasures, including a Kamakura period mandala and an Indian Kannon with amber eyes.

Walk in the opposite direction of the temple toward the Kanda River. Near Shin Edogawa Park is **Saint Mary's Cathedral*****, 3-16-5 Sekiguchi, Bunkyo-ku, I, A1. Designed by Kenzo Tange, the building is entirely covered with steel. From the ground level, the structure ressembles a crane, the symbol of Japan, while from above, the building forms an immense Latin cross. The cathedral was constructed in 1964 to commemorate the 100th anniversary of the recognition of Catholicism by the last shogun.

OFF THE BEATEN TRACK

You have been in Tokyo for 10 days (or more). Shinjuku, Ginza and Roppongi are now 'classics', and you ask yourself what remains to be discovered. The answer is simple: Everything. Tokyo is so vast it would take a lifetime to get to know it well. Listed below are five districts that are off the beaten track and are not generally dealt with in tourist guides. These are the 'villages' of Tokyo.

Den'enchofu***

This visit should take half a day.

Access: From Shibuya Station, take the Toyoko Line to Den'enchofu Station. The journey takes about 15 minutes.

Den'enchofu, an exclusive suburb of Tokyo, is an entirely residential area, flooded in greenery, where the smallest shack costs millions. Leave the station on the west side. The station itself is a charming little maisonnette that faces a square surrounded by trees. Three avenues can be seen. Take the one just opposite the station and walk for as long as you like. Venture down the side streets. In the springtime, the exuberant vegetation from the private gardens flows over into the streets. The scent of the flowers and the trees ensures you an unforgettable walk.

Apart from those on the square near the station, there are no shops or restaurants in Den'enchofu.

Jiyugaoka**

Plan half a day for this trip.

Access: From Shibuya Station, take the Toyoko Line to Jiyugaoka Station.

Jiyugaoka is not far from Den'enchofu, and it is easy to visit them both on the same day. With its shopping streets and covered arcades around the station, Jiyugaoka is a village best explored slowly.

Leave the station by the north exit, cross the square and take the pedestrian street directly opposite. You will soon come across the **Kuhombutsu Temple***, dating from 1678. This is not a tourist attraction but a neighbourhood temple visited almost exclusively by worshippers. Stroll around the gardens that surround the four temple buildings.

Leave the temple, turn left and then take the first right in order to circle the station on the north. Cross two sets of railway tracks and turn right again. Not far off is the **Okusawa Shrine***, whose symbol is a serpent. Every year on September 14 and 15, the shrine celebrates its annual festival.

Dalloyau, a French tearoom on the station square, serves excellent coffee and cakes. Another pleasant spot to eat is **Hanakyabetsu** (cauliflower), a café specializing in pancakes, ☎ 3724 0310. *Open daily 8am-11pm.*

Kichijioji**

This itinerary will take you one day.

Access: From Shibuya Station, take the Inokashira Sen Line to Kichijioji Station, the terminus. If you take the *Kyuko* (rapid), which stops at only every third station, the journey should take about 20 to 30 minutes.

Kichijioji is an up-and-coming district. Every Saturday night, young people from all over Tokyo come to dance and drink (in Japan, drinking is a major attraction in itself). They find this district more amusing than Shinjuku, less snobbish than Shibuya and much less expensive than Roppongi.

Leave the station on the south side and walk toward Inokashira Park. You will go through a pleasant neighbourhood of small tradespeople where the atmosphere is partly working-class (dubious small cafés) and partly trendy (flashy cafés and clothing shops).

Inokashira Park**, about 10 to 15 minutes from the station, is known for its long, narrow lake and for the magnificent cherry trees that, in April, shed their petals onto the water. There is a small floating temple in the middle of the lake, and small boats and pedal boats are available for use any time of the year.

You can either go back to Shibuya Station from Inokashira Station by leaving the park on the south side, or you can visit the northern part of Kichijioji (delineated by the Seibu, Parco and Marui department stores) by going back to the Kichijioji Station. The covered arcade opposite the station is well known for its inexpensive clothing shops.

Shimokitazawa**

Half a day is needed for this visit.

Access: Take either the Inokashira Line from Shibuya Station or the Odakyu Line from Shinjuku Station to Shimokitazawa Station. Allow 15 minutes.

Many young Tokyoites dream of living in Shimokitazawa. With a rural atmosphere, it is a friendly neighbourhood on a human scale.

Start your visit in Kitazawa (the northern section), with its market and shopping center, and then return to Shimokitazawa (southern section), with its maze of little streets animated at both day and night. It is here, in a little restaurant without a name or a telephone, that the best *okonomiyaki* in Tokyo can be found (see 'Japanese Cuisine' p. 89).

Just opposite the Inokashira Line exit is **Natural House,** a shop selling natural foods as well as wholewheat bread (very rare in Japan).

Tsukudajima-Monzen Nakacho**

This is a one-day trip.

Access: Take either the Yurakucho Line to Shintomicho Station or the Hibiya Line to Tsukiji Station. Cross the Sumida River on the ungainly Tsukuda-Ohashi Bridge.

Before World War II, a ferryboat connected Tsukudajima, located in the middle of Tokyo Bay, to the mainland. Since then, two bridges have connected the island to Tokyo and as a result, some of its charm has been lost but the island is still worth a visit.

Tsukudajima was given by the Shogun Ieyasu Tokugawa to a group of fishermen from Osaka who had rendered him a service. These families formed a distinct population with customs and traditions quite different from those of Tokyo.

Not much remains of this heritage today except for a local speciality, *tsukudani* (fish conserved in soy sauce), that can still be bought at **Tenyasu,** 1-3-14 Tsukuda, Chuo-Ku, ☎ 3531 3457. *Closed on the 1st and 3rd Sat of every month.*

Only a single street on the whole island has managed to fully retain its 19th century ambiance. With a bit of luck, you may see the flower vendors who sing as they pull their little carts along. Here, as elsewhere in Tokyo, promoters are greedily eyeing this last piece of Edo's heritage.

Leave the station and head for the immense (and hideous) Tsukuda-Ohashi Bridge that straddles the Sumida River. Cross the river on the right side of the bridge. Once on the island, take the first street on the right and then the first on the left. A little farther, on the right, is the last traditional street of the island, easily recognized by the arcades on both sides.

Cross under the bridge and go to the **Sumiyoshi Jinja*,** the religious center of the island. Not far from here, on the point of the island, is **Tenyasu,** which has fabricated its famous *tsukudani* since 1837. Now cross the small red bridge that spans the canal. Turn left, then right and walk straight on toward Kiyosumi Dori. Take bus 33 to the 6th stop, **Kiyosumi Teien Gardens***.** *Open daily 9am-4:30pm.* Completed in 1878, the Kiyosumi Teien is undoubtedly one of the most beautiful gardens in Tokyo. Among other attractions, it contains rocks from every part of Japan.

The **Fukagawa Edo Museum** is not far from the gardens. Opened in 1986, this museum offers a re-creation of the daily life of the district during the time of the shoguns (see p. 137).

Now take bus 33 in the opposite direction (for two, a taxi is about the same price) or walk for about 20 minutes along Kyosumi Dori until you come to Monzen Nakacho Station. Near the subway entrance is an immense red portico marking the entrance to the Fukagawa Fudo temple. As at Asakusa, numerous shops line the alley leading to the religious buildings. *Manju* (small cakes filled with red bean paste) are the local specialty and can be bought at **Miyagestudo,** on the right at the beginning of the lane.

Do not miss visiting the **Tomioka Hachimangu Shrine**** just across the street from the temple. Sumo tournaments were formerly held here. There is a traditional market on the 1st, 15th and 18th of every month.

Leave by the principal alley and turn right at Eitai Dori to reach the Monzen Nakacho Station.

TEMPLES AND SHRINES

The religious monuments of Tokyo have suffered heavily over the years. Revolts, fires, earthquakes (particularly that of 1923) and bombing raids have all taken their toll, and very few buildings of any historic interest remain today. In contrast to the temples of Kyoto, many of which are centuries old, most of those in Tokyo were built in the last 40 years.

A temple or a shrine?

In Japan, a distinction is made between Buddhist temples and Shinto shrines. Buddhism and Shintoism, however, are not contradictory to the Japanese. Shintoism was the indigenous religion of Japan; Buddhism was introduced from India via China and Korea.

A Buddhist temple is called *ji* or *tera;* the name of a Shinto shrine is always followed by the word *jinja* or, more rarely, *taisha* or *jingu.*

It is not always easy at first glance to distinguish a temple from a shrine. Frequently the only feature that differentiates one from the other is a wooden portico *(torii).* This ceremonial entrance resembles an immense perch and is a key feature of Shinto architecture. According to legend, a village cock perched on a similar roost lured the sun-goddess from hiding and restored daylight to the world. A thick, plaited cord made of rice straw *(shimenawa)* hung from the *torii* identifies a Shinto shrine; this cord is the 'barrier' that wards off evil spirits. A small bell or gong, used by the faithful when addressing a god, is sometimes placed near the entrance of the sanctuary.

Orthodox Shinto architecture is marked by basic simplicity and is of purely Japanese origin. Usually, a Shinto shrine consists of a *honden* (principal building) reserved for the congregation and a *haiden* (oratory) open to the public. Linked by a corridor, these two structures are traditionally constructed of raw wood and rest on large pillars that are visible from the exterior. An enormous thatched or shingled roof covers the shrine. Shinto priests are easily recognized by their long white robes and their high black headdresses.

Buddhist architecture, on the other hand, is imported and frequently evokes its Chinese origins. The pagoda is the ultimate Buddhist form. Most of the larger temple complexes open to the public consist of a number of small buildings surrounded by gardens, as at Kyoto and Nara. They frequently contain ancient statues visible behind a grille, as at Horyuji in Nara. In Japan, Buddhist monks wear black.

Temples and shrines almost always charge an admission fee, and sometimes permission to visit them must be obtained in advance. A five-day waiting period and a fee of ¥3000 are required to visit the celebrated moss gardens of the Saihoji temple in Kyoto. This, however, is an exception. The usual fee is about ¥300.

On entering a shrine or temple (or for that matter, any other traditional Japanese building), you must remove your outdoor shoes and put on special slippers. Usually, arrows indicate the route of the visit. Unless otherwise specified, photographs are permitted.

Asakusa Jinja (Sanja Sama)***

Access: Asakusa Station, V, B2.

This small shrine, also known as Sanja Sama, was built just behind the Senso ji by Iemitsu (1623-51), the third Tokugawa shogun, in homage to the three fishermen who found the statue of the goddess.

Sanja Matsuri (see p. 52), the annual shrine festival and one of the most important celebrations in the capital, is held between May 16 and 19 and attracts thousands of Tokyoites. On May 18, young people in traditional costumes carry enormous *mikoshi* (portable shrines) through the streets of Asakusa. This event should not be missed if you are lucky enough to be in Tokyo at this time of year.

Meiji Jingu***

Access: Harajuku Station, XI, B1.

This shrine, built in 1915, is dedicated to the memory of Emperor Meiji (1854-1912). It consecrates his entrance into the pantheon of Shinto deities and is the focus of one of the most popular pilgrimages in Japan today. Enormous crowds gather here on New Year's Day. The shrine complex includes a huge main shrine, an oratory, a treasury, several minor shrines and a 178-acre/72-hectare garden. This Inner Garden is planted with 130,000 trees presented by the people from every province of Japan and contains the famous Iris Garden, where over 80 species flower in late June and early July. The garden alone is worth the visit. The main shrine, built in pure Shinto style, was destroyed during a bombing raid in 1945, along with the oratory and other smaller buildings. First replaced by a temporary structure immediately after the war, it was completely restored to its original plan by 1958. The enormous *torii* (entrance gate) is made of 1700-year-old *hinoki* trees from Taiwan.

Senso ji***

Access: Asakusa Station. V, B2.

This temple, also known as the Asakusa Kannon temple and the Asakusa Dera, is one of the most impressive in Tokyo. It is said to have been founded in AD 628 when three fishermen caught a small golden statue of Kannon, the goddess of mercy, in their nets. Among the three fishermen was Hashino Nakatomo, the legendary founder of Tokyo.

The original structure, dating from 1692, was destroyed by fire-bombing raids in 1945. The present temple, constructed in 1958, contains frescoes by contemporary artists. The neighbouring area, 'Old Tokyo', with its small shops, pilgrims and peddlers, is also well worth visiting.

Kanei ji**

Access: Ueno Park, Ueno Station, IV, B1.

Under the Tokugawa regime, the Kanei ji was one of the most important Buddhist centres in the capital. The original building, built in 1625 on the site of the present National Museum, was burned down at the time of the Imperial Restoration in 1868 during a battle between the Emperor's and the Shogun's troops. To replace it, in 1875 the Daijiin (the former main building of the Chorakuji temple at Serata in the Gumma district), was dismantled and rebuilt stone by stone on the temple's present site. Today the Kanei ji belongs to the Tendai sect.

Behind the Kanei ji is the Jomjoin Temple, famous for its 20,000 Jizo (images of Buddha).

A Buddhist monk outside the Asakusa Jinja asking for contributions.

Nezu Jinja**

Access: Nezu Station, IV, A2.

This shrine is dedicated to four Shinto gods and to Sugawara Michizane — the patron of scholars. A statesman and poet of the 9th century AD, Michizane was deified as the god of literature under the name Tenjin. Entirely rebuilt in 1706 under the orders of Shogun Tokugawa Tsunayoshi, this shrine is one of the most impressive in Tokyo. The best time to visit is toward the end of April, when the 3000 azaleas in the surrounding garden are in flower.

Sengaku ji**

Access: Sengakuji Station, X, C3.

This temple was founded in 1612 by Tokugawa Ieyasu. It contains the graves of the 47 *ronin* condemned to *seppuku* (ritual suicide) in 1701 for avenging their master, who had suffered the same fate for drawing his sword in the shogun's palace against another *daimyo* who had gravely offended him. The Kabuki theatre has immortalized the heroes of this story, whose memory is still cherished by the Japanese. The oldest of the *ronin* was 77, and the youngest was 15. A statue of their leader, Oishi Yoshino, was erected near the Sammon (Great Gate). The basin where they washed their enemy's bloody head before bringing it to their master's grave stands in the courtyard.

Toshogu**

Access: Ueno Park, Ueno Station, IV, A2, near Ueno Zoo.

The Toshogu is dedicated to the memory of Shogun Tokugawa Ieyasu. Founded in 1626 and modified in 1651, this meticulously decorated shrine is the only Shinto building in Tokyo to be classified a National Treasure. Of major architectural importance, the Toshogu has miraculously survived the wars, fires, earthquakes and air raids that proved fatal to the majority of Tokyo's monuments. The path that leads to the main shrine is lined with over 250 stone-and-bronze lanterns offered by various *daimyo* to the memory of the Shogun. The Toshogu is built in a particular Chinese style of which the only other examples in Japan are found at Nikko. The annual feast takes place on April 17. The Karamon (Chinese Gate) in front of the shrine is thought to have been carved by Jingoro Hidari, Japan's most famous sculptor. The treasury contains military weapons and letters from the Tokugawa shoguns.

Nearby stands the remains of the original Kanei ji, a five-storey pagoda that was moved here in 1957.

Yasukini Jinja**

Access: Kudanshita Station, II, A1.

Built in 1869 on Kudan Hill in orthodox Shinto style, this shrine commemorates Japan's war heroes and all those who have died for the nation since the Meiji Restoration. A small war museum was opened after the 1945 defeat. Because this is a symbol of Japanese nationalism, all career-minded politicians gather here during the annual shrine festival *(matsuri)*, held from July 13 to 16. Free open-air performances of Noh drama take place during the festival. The *torii* (portal), built in 1933, is the largest marble *torii* in Japan. An ablution basin *(temizuya)*, where worshippers wash their hands and rinse their mouths before entering the sacred precinct, stands in the courtyard. The shrine itself is reserved for religious rites and is not open to the public.

Zempuku ji**

Access: Hiro-o Station, X, C1.

This temple is said to have been founded in AD 832 by Kobo Daishi. The treasury contains sacred formulas written by him in addition to Buddhist scriptures and paintings. Destroyed by fire on several occasions, the previous temple was burned down during fire-bombing raids in 1945. Built after the war, the present building is less interesting than the gigantic gingko tree near the entrance. According to legend, this tree sprouted from the walking stick of Shinran, a famous 13th-century priest of the Amida sect who introduced the idea of Paradise to the common man. The tree is so impressive that the municipal authorities have declared it a natural monument. The Zempuku ji temple housed Townsend Harris and the first American Legation to Japan (1859-70). Since 1901, when Fukazawa Yukichi, the founder of the University of Keio, was buried here, droves of students come here on pilgrimage prior to taking university entrance examinations.

Religion

It is often said that the Japanese are born Shintoist and die Buddhist. In reality, they practice both religions throughout their lives. Shintoism is the elder of the two and indigenous to Japan, whereas Buddhism was imported from China at the beginning of the Asuka period (AD 552-710).

Shintoism is a polytheistic religion without dogma that venerates the forces of nature through a cult of *kami* (gods). There are thousands of such deities, each with his or her own domain and function. Sometimes the heroes of Japanese history are pronounced *kami* at death — a practice that resembles the Roman Catholic tradition of bestowing sainthood. Bells situated near the entrance of shrines are rung to attract the attention of the gods whenever prayers are addressed to them. If there is no bell, the worshipper claps his or her hands a few times instead.

It is common to call on the aid of a Shinto priest when a store is opened or a building is constructed. In ceremonial dress, he purifies the site and chases away evil spirits, ensuring a successful venture.

Based on the tenets of Japan's early agricultural society, Shintoism has always been supported by the state and is at the core of Japanese patriotism. The cult of the Emperor is a typical Shinto phenomenon. Buddhism, on the other hand, has had a more checkered history.

Buddhism was brought to Japan in the middle of the 6th century by the Soga clan, as a means of introducing discipline and Chinese culture to a nation just beginning to emerge from a tribal society based on the clan *(ugi)*. Embracing the comprehensiveness, purity and merciful charity of Buddhism, the Japanese nonetheless rejected all parts of the doctrine that conflicted with their traditional beliefs, including its negation of the personality. A sectarian Japanese Buddhism developed, devoid of intellectual speculation and harsh monastic rule. The vast majority of the Japanese adopted the precepts of the Great Vehicle *(Mahayana)* with its simple emotional appeal: life is to be lived, not from the head, but from the heart.

Buddhism split into a number of sects in Japan; there are now over 60 (13 major ones), of which the Jodo (Pure Earth) and the Soka Gakkai (Value Creating Society) are the most popular. The latter claims over 15 million members throughout the world and is militantly nationalistic.

To many Westerners, Zen is synonymous with Japan, but in reality it constitutes only a single branch of Japanese Buddhism. Zen was introduced from China in the 12th century by the monk Eisai (1141-1215), who had traveled to China to study. There he was initiated in the techniques of mental concentration called *Ch'an* (pronounced 'Zen' in Japanese) that had developed out of the Dyana sect. Zen emphasizes the practice of *zazen* (seated meditation) as a means of obtaining *satori* (illumination). Today, Zen claims a total of about 5 million members in Japan.

It is also the form of Japanese philosophy that has most attracted Western intellectuals. Among the first to expose Westerners to Zen was writer Eugene Harrigel, who recounted his experience of Japan in a marvelous little book entitled *Zen and the Art of Archery*. The British philosopher and writer Alan Watts, along with D. T. Suzuki, also figured importantly in bridging the gap to the West.

Confucianism also plays an important role in the moral life of Japan. Introduced in the 4th century AD from China, it still serves as the foundation of the nation's ethical, social and political theories. Paternalistic in nature, it is seen as the 'Outer Gate' to the Buddhist 'Inner Gate' and is the basis for the samurai Code of Warriors *(Bushido)*.

Zozo ji** III, B3

Access: Shiba-Koen Station, near the Tokyo Tower, III, A3

Originally founded in 1393, this temple became the property of the Tokugawa family and was one of the largest Buddhist centres in Edo, along with the Kanei ji. Today, it is the headquarters of the Jodo Buddhist sect for the Kanto region. Destroyed on numerous occasions, the present structure dates from 1974 and is without much interest except for a rare Black Image of Buddha. The Sammon (Main Gate), a red-lacquered portal dating from 1605, is the only surviving element from the Edo period.

The prehistoric site of Maruyama was discovered just south of the temple.

▬ PARKS AND GARDENS

Although Tokyo is not reputed for its greenery, numerous parks and gardens dot the capital. Frequently very attractive, they aerate the town and allow the inhabitants to go — generally en masse — to admire the cherry blossoms (o hanami) in April. In general, the parks are open Tuesday to Sunday, 9am-4:30pm; the Shinjuku Gyoen and a few others close at 4pm. There is almost always an entrance fee.

Koishikawa Korakuen Garden***

Access: Korakuen Station, IX, A2.

This 17-acre/7-hectare garden is one of the best in Tokyo. Begun in 1629 by Shogun Tokugawa Yorifusa, it was heavily influenced by Shu Shin Sui (1600-59), a Chinese scholar who had taken refuge in Japan under the shogunate. Tokugawa Iemitsu later added a lake and the famous Full Moon Bridge, a semi-circular arch that is reflected in the water. With its pond and tiny stone bridges, it is a perfect example of a 17th-century, Chinese-influenced Japanese garden. Not to be missed on any account, it is near the Tokyo Dome and the Korakuen amusement park.

East Imperial Garden*** (Kokyo Higashi Gyoen)

Access: Takebashi Station, II, B2.

This garden has been opened to the public only since 1968. It contains the ruins of the ancient Edo castle (see 'Imperial Palace' p. 110).

Meiji Sanctuary Inner Garden*** (Meiji Jingu Gyoen)

Access: Harajuku Station, XI, B1.

Adjoining Yoyogi Park, this is one of the best known gardens in Japan. Every New Year's Day, millions of worshippers come to pray at the Meiji shrine located in the middle of the park. Cultivated in a special garden, over 100 varieties of iris bloom in the early summer. The garden contains a pond and over 100,000 cherry trees from all over Japan.

Shinjuku Imperial Garden*** (Shinjuku Gyoen)

Access : Shinjuku Station, VI, CD2-3.

About 15 minutes on foot from the eastern exit of Shinjuku Station and the Kabukicho district, this is one of the largest parks in Tokyo (see 'Shinjuku' p. 107).

Ueno Park***

Access : Ueno Station, IV, AB2.

This park contains numerous monuments and museums (see 'Ueno' p. 111 and 'Museums' p. 129) and was the site of a decisive battle between the Emperor's and the Shogun's armies in 1868.

Yoyogi Park***

Access: Harajuku Station, XI, AB1-2.

This park is adjacent to Meiji Jingu Gyoen and contains the Yoyogi Olympic Stadium. It is, along with Shinjuku Gyoen, one of the largest parks in Tokyo (see 'Shibuya' p. 113).

Celebrating the blossoming of the cherry trees in Ueno Park on o hanami day in the spring.

Chidorigafuchi Aquatic Park**

Access: Kudan Kita Station, II, A1.

To the north-west of the Imperial Palace, this park is a 10-minute walk from the station. During the cherry blossom season, it is a favourite among Tokyoites. Small boats are available for rowing on the lake.

Hibiya Park**

Access: Hibiya Station, II, B3.

Opposite the Imperial Hotel, this was the first Western-style park in Japan. There is a children's playground, a fountain, a restaurant with a terrace, an open-air concert hall, a library and several ponds.

Kitanomaru Park**

Access: Kudanshita Station, II, AB1.

To the north-east of the Imperial Palace, this park was opened to the public in 1969. Inside you will find the Tokyo National Museum of Modern Art, the Science Museum and the Nippon Budokan Concert Hall (see p. 134, 138).

Koishikawa Botanical Gardens** (Koishikawa Shokubutsen)

Access: Hakusan Station.

Originally a medicinal herb garden for the Tokugawa shogunate, this garden now belongs to the science faculty of Tokyo University. About 6000 different species are cultivated on the 40 acres/16 hectares.

There is a tropical greenhouse and a lake.

Cherry blossoms (sakura no hana)

Every year in spring (usually early April), Tokyoites flock en masse to the parks of the town for *o hanami* ('see the flowers'). Cherry flowers hold a very profound symbolic meaning for the Japanese. The ancient samurai, and more recently the *kamikaze* ('divine winds') pilots, were fascinated by this flower, whose life is so short that it is blown away even before it has a chance to fade. For these warriors, who dreamed of sacrificing their lives for a noble cause, the cherry blossom was an ideal model for a short but glorious life.

Certain people, even today, see *sakura no hana* as the very essence of the soul of Japan.

Korakuen Amusement Park** (Korakuen Yuenchi)

Access: Suidobashi Station, IX, B2. *Open Tues-Sun 10am-7pm.*

Korakuen Yuenchi is an amusement park to the east of the Korakuen Gardens. The district is geared toward entertainment and includes a swimming pool, an ice-skating rink, a gymnasium that seats 3800 spectators, the Hosho Noh Theater, the Tokyo Dome (or Big Egg), a velodrome and the Kodokan (an important judo centre).

Hama Detached Palace Garden* (Hama Rikyu Teien)

Access: Shimbashi or Hamamatsucho Station, III, C3.

Hama Rikyu Teien is an authentic example of a *daimyo* garden of the Edo period. On the edge of Tokyo Bay, this park contains about a dozen small ponds, around which are planted cherries, azaleas and iris. Near the *suijo basu* (waterbus) terminus, the garden includes a pine-bordered beach and a lake that rises and falls with the tide.

Kyosumi Garden* (Kiyosumi Teien)

Access: Monzen-Nakacho Station, I, B2.

A 15-minute walk from the Monzen-nakacho station, this beautiful 19th-century landscape garden is famous for its rhododendrons and even more for its rock collection. The rocks come from every province of Japan. Although a little out of the way, this garden is worth a visit.

Meiji Shrine Outer Garden* (Meiji Jingu Gaien)

Access: Gaienmae Station, VIII, A1 and VII, A3.

This is essentially a sports centre and has a baseball field, a rugby pitch, a municipal gymnasium and a sports museum. It was here that the funeral of the Emperor Meiji was held in 1912. The Meiji Memorial Picture Gallery, in the centre of the park, is devoted to his life. Do not confuse this with the Meiji Jingu Inner Garden (see above).

MUSEUMS IN TOKYO

O ver the last decade, a museum mania seems to have hit the Japanese. Frequently financed by private enterprises, dozens of highly specialized museums — dealing with everything from cameras to kites and from handbags to bicycles — have been opened to the public.

Tourists visiting Japanese museums are confronted with two major problems: the first is that very few foreigners are familiar with Japanese aesthetics; the second is the fact that almost all the explanations are in Japanese.

Furthermore, Japanese art museums are rarely pedagogically organized. It is assumed that visitors are well acquainted with the subject matter and its historical context. Museum objects and works of art are often presented without any explanation, not even in Japanese!

Listed below, grouped according to subject matter, are some of the most interesting museums in Tokyo:

ART

Bridgestone Museum*** (Bridgestone Bijutsukan) II, D3
1-10-1 Kyobashi, Chuo-ku, ☎ 35630241. *Open Tues-Sun 10am-5:30pm.*

Access: Tokyo Station

This museum is devoted to Western art. The painting collection contains Western masters from the 17th century to the present (Rubens, Rembrandt, Van Gogh, Renoir, Cézanne, Monet, Matisse and Picasso), as well as works of 19th-century Japanese artists inspired by the West. The sculpture collection ranges from ancient Egyptian and Sumerian to works by Rodin and Despiau. The museum also has engravings by Rembrandt, lithographs by Toulouse-Lautrec and etchings by Picasso, as well as antique ceramics and Roman copperware.

Chronology of Japanese art

Prehistory   There is evidence (core and flake tools) of a Palaeolithic occupation in Japan around 30,000 to 10,000 BC. The origins of the early colonization of the islands are obscure, but a hunting, non-agricultural Neolithic people inhabited the archipelago by the 5th millennium BC.

1000 BC-200 BC   Neolithic period (Jomon Culture or Early Japanese Neolithic). The word *jomon* means 'rope drawing' and is derived from the corded wares (handmade, rope-marked pottery) that characterized this period. At this time, Japan was a food-gathering society with no domesticated animals apart from the dog. *Dogu* (totemistic figures) and stone formations attest a basic social organization.

250 BC-AD 250   Bronze Age (Yayoi Culture). The first wheel-turned wares appeared. This pottery was simpler and less ornately decorated than the ceramics of the preceding period. Bronze-casting and irrigated rice cultivation were introduced from the mainland around the beginning of the Christian era. Bronze swords, *dotaku* (bronze bells), Chinese Han dynasty mirrors and dolmen burials appeared.

AD 250-552   Iron Age (Yamato or Tumulus Culture). During this period, the Japanese built *kofun* (tumuli) — gigantic keyhole-shaped tombs that served as burial monuments for emperors and other important military leaders. These grave mounds, some larger than the Egyptian pyramids, were surrounded by as many as 20,000 *haniwa* (clay figurines). At first simple, hollow clay cylinders, they evolved into more elaborate animal and human forms without ever losing their tubular shape. Other characteristic pieces of the Yamato Culture include *magatama* jewelry, mirrors and swords. This period was marked by the extensive use of iron tools and weapons, the rise of social classes and widespread warfare.

552-710   Asuka period. Both Buddhism and writing were introduced into Japan from the continent. Japanese art and architecture were heavily influenced by Chinese and Korean styles. The Suiko style (AD 593-AD 628) sculptures visible in the *kondo* (main hall) of the Horyu ji temple are from this period.

710-784   Nara (or Tempyo) period. This was the golden age of Japanese sculpture. Dry-lacquer, wood, bronze and clay sculptures were specialities of this period. Buddhist influences totally dominated Japanese art. Murals appeared. The earliest surviving examples, dating from AD 763, are those of the Golden Hall at the Horyu ji monastery near Nara. In the 8th century, the first wood-block prints were made.

794-897   Early Heian (or Jogan) period. Wooden sculpture and *sumi-e* (China ink drawings) characterize diverse aspects of Buddhist philosophy. The esoteric Shingon and Tendai sects played a predominant role in the development of Japanese art. Secular paintings, mostly decorated screens and panels, were also influenced by the Chinese schools, particularly the late T'ang style.

895-1185   Late Heian (or Fujiwara) period. The Fujiwara family played a dominant role in Japanese history for nearly 1000 years. During this period, official relations with China were suspended, and an insular style of Japanese art developed. *Yamato-e* (Japanese picture) and the *emakimono* (horizontal picture scrolls) are characteristic of this style. Wooden sculpture became more refined and the works of this period are considered to be the most impressive in the history of Japanese art. Remarkable examples are conserved at the Horyuji in Nara. Romantic aestheticism gave rise to the *raigo* ('coming to welcome') school of painting. These vividly painted images of Amida Buddha are associated with the Jodo and Tendai sects. The first scrolls with animals drawn in China ink also appeared.

1185-1333   Kamakura period. The military-based society and its realistic approach to life favoured the development of a bold linear style of *Yamato-e. Raigo* paintings pictured a Buddha rising in glory. 'Chinese' portraits by various masters, such as Fujiwara Takanobu (1142-1205), made their appearance. The introduction of Zen Buddhism, at the beginning of the 13th century, profoundly influenced the artistic styles of the period, particularly Zen-inspired ink-paintings on *kakemono* (vertical scrolls). The first Zen 'dry' rock-and-sand gardens also appeared.

1335-1573   Muromachi period. Zen philosophy influenced all levels of Japanese art and architecture, particularly painting, where *suiboku* (the use of lines to evoke volume) was combined with wash drawing, colour and *sumi* (ink sketches). The *yamato-e* school, now called the Tosa school, degenerated into mannerism. The Kano school, freed from Zen influence to unite Japanese and Chinese mural techniques, became the dominant form of art.

1574-1603   Momoyama period. When the Ashikaga shogunate was overthrown in 1573, there was a radical change in taste. Formerly austere, the large palaces of the great war lords were now decorated with ornate sliding panels and folding screens, often painted on a background of gold leaf. After their first contact with Europeans, Japanese artists represented these *nanban* (barbarians from the south) on screens called *nanban byobu.* Under the influence of Kano Motonobu, the Kano school continued to develop.

1603-1867   Edo period. While the traditional schools of painting (Kano, Tosa and Nanga) developed and became the official styles of the nation, a new technique arose during the second half of the 17th century. This was the *ukiyo-e,* better known in English as the Japanese print. Geared entirely toward a rising middle class, this art form consisted of coloured wood-block prints, depicting the daily life of ordinary people and their leisure activities. *Ukiyo-e,* meaning 'images of the floating world' drew its inspiration from the epicurean trends of the time. According to a manual published in Kyoto in 1661, *ukiyo* is 'the ephemeral but intense pleasure based on experience: to sing, to drink, to drift with the tide or to follow the current of the river.'

1868-present   The Meiji, Taisho, Showa and Heisei periods. Following the Imperial Restoration, Japan was opened to the West, and the Japanese began to travel; after two and a half centuries of isolation, they discovered Western art. Realism was introduced, including techniques of perspective and shading. A diverse range of styles developed. These are generally classified, according to the medium used, into Western styles and Japanese styles. The Western schools took their inspiration from realism and later Impressionism. Many Japanese artists went abroad to France or Italy, returning home to be crowned with fame. Traditional schools returned to the older Chinese styles or continued to produce Japanese prints. After World War II, subjectivism heavily influenced the young Japanese artists.

Eisei Bunko Foundation** (Eisei Bunko) I, A1

1-1-1 Mejirodai, Bunkyo-ku, ☎ 3941 0850. *Open Mon-Fri 10am-4pm.*

Access: Edogawabashi Station.

From the subway station, follow the right bank of the river for about 10 minutes until you come to a stone stairway on the right side of the street. The museum is at the top, in a warehouse behind a dilapidated house.

Although a little out of the way, this museum is certainly worth visiting. Originally belonging to the Hosokawa family, *daimyo* (warlord) of the Ashikaga shogunate, this fabulous collection contains paintings by such 15th-century masters as Sesshu, Takuan and Tessai, as well as ancient Japanese scrolls, ceramics, robes and masks that are exhibited alternately. Armour and weapons of the Hosokawa, as well as numerous Chinese objects, including jade, also are on display.

Goto Art Museum** (Goto Bijutsukan) I, A2

3-9-25 Kaminoge, Setagaya-ku, ☎ 3703 0661 *Open Tues-Sun 9:30am-4:30pm.*

Access: Kaminoge Station.

Located in a handsome garden, the Goto Museum is best known for the 10th-century painted scrolls illustrating scenes from the *Genji monogatari* (the most-famous work of classical Japanese literature). Known throughout Japan, these scrols are exposed only once a year for a week in May. The museum also contains *emakimono* (horizontal scrolls), ceramics, lacquerware, calligraphy, archaeological material and a very fine collection of Japanese and Chinese paintings.

Hatakeyama Museum*** (Hatakeyama Kinenkan) I, A2

2-20-12 Shiroganedai, Minato-ku, ☎ 3447 5787. *Open Apr 1-Sept 15, Tues-Sun 10am-5pm; Oct 1-Mar 15, Tues-Sun 10am-4:30pm.*

Access: Meguro Station.

This is an important museum for Japanese traditional arts. It includes an impressive collection of paintings, sculptures, calligraphies, ceramics and lacquerware, as well as costumes and numerous objects related to the tea ceremony (some of which belonged to the 16th century master of the ceremony Sen no Rikyu).

The museum is behind the gardens of the Hannya-en restaurant.

Idemitsu Museum** (Idemitsu Bijutsukan) II, B3

Teikoku Theatre, 9th floor, 3-1-1 Marunouchi, Chiyoda-ku, ☎ 3213 3111. *Open Tues-Sun 10am-5pm.*

Access: Hibiya Station.

This collection contains paintings, ink drawings, *ukiyo-e*, bronzes, lacquerware and a large collection of Buddhist calligraphy, in particular the works of the Zen monk Sengai. There is also a large collection of ceramics from around the world.

National Museum*** (Tokyo Kokuritsu Hakubutsukan) IV, B2

13-9 Ueno Koen, Taito-ku, ☎ 3822 1111. *Open Tues-Sun 9am-4:30pm. The Koryuji Treasury (Horyu ji Homotsuden) is open Thurs on condition that it is not raining and that the relative humidity is below 70%.*

Access: Uguisudani Station.

Do not be put off by the austerity of the building's exterior. This museum, the largest in Japan, contains the most complete collection of Japanese art and archaeology in the world. There are 86,000 catalogued items in all, of which over 80 pieces (paintings, sculptures, armour, sabers, ceramics and lacquerware) are classified as National Treasures.

The museum is divided into the following four sections:

The **Honkan,** at the center, is the principal building and houses Japanese works of art. It contains: sculptures from the Nara, Heian and Kamakura periods; paintings covering the evolution of Japanese painting from the 8th century to the 19th century; masks and costumes from Noh theatre; ceramics; metal objects including swords, armour, mirrors and articles for the tea ceremony; architectural scale models; lacquerware; calligraphy; and *ukiyo-e* (wood-block prints).

The **Toyokan,** to the right, is devoted to non-Japanese Asian art and covers the area from the Mediterranean to the Pacific. Chinese and Korean art are well represented, particularly Neolithic pottery (2500-2000 BC). The basement is reserved for temporary exhibitions.

The **Hyokeikan,** to the left, is devoted to archaeological material. The 1st floor deals with Japanese prehistory from the Palaeolithic period onward, while the 2nd floor concentrates on the Kofun Culture. A large number of *haniwa* (ceramic figurines) and *dotaku* (bronze bells) are on display.

The **Horyu ji Treasury** (Horyu ji Homotsuden), on the far left, conserves the treasures of the Horyu ji temple near Nara. Most of these objects date to the 6th and 7th centuries AD. Apart from sculptures, there are calligraphies, textiles, religious objects in bronze and wood, sacred mirrors, lacquerware, *gigaku* masks, musical instruments and paintings. One of the many famous treasures it contains is the Shotoku Taishi Eden, a series of panels painted in 1069 recounting the life of Prince Shotoku.

National Museum of Western Art*** (Kokuritsu Seiyo Bijutsukan) IV, B2

7-7 Ueno-Koen, Taito-ku, ☎ 3828 5131. *Open Tues-Sun 9:30am-5pm.*
Access: Ueno Station.

This museum consists of two buildings, the elder designed by Le Corbusier and built in 1959. The painting collection contains a large number of works by Cézanne, Cottet, Courbet, Degas, Delacroix, Gauguin, Manet, Monet, Pissarro and Renoir. There are also bronzes by Rodin exhibited on the parvis of the museum. The core of this collection was purchased by the perspicacious Kojiro Matsukata (1865-1950), an art collector of the early part of the century who, on his numerous travels to Europe, bought anything that took his fancy, regardless of its price.

Nezu Museum*** (Nezu Bijutsukan) VIII, A3

6-5-36 Minami Aoyama, Minato-ku, ☎ 3400 2536. *Open Tues-Sun 9:30am-4:30pm.*
Access: Omotesando Station.

This museum contains a very fine collection of Japanese traditional art, including paintings, scrolls, textiles, signed *Katana* (swords), calligraphy, ceramics and lacquerware. The Chinese section includes bronzes, Sung paintings and gilded bronze Buddhas. The museum is located in a small park, and there are a number of fine teahouses scattered around the grounds. You can attend a tea ceremony and even take a lesson if you wish.

Okura Museum** (Okura Shukokan) III, A2

2-10-3 Toranomon, Minato-ku, ☎ 3583 0781 *Open Tues-Sun 10am-4pm.*
Access: Kamiyacho Station.

Just opposite the Okura Hotel, this museum was founded in 1927 by Baron Okura Kihachiro, the hotel's owner. It contains Japanese paintings, sculptures, ceramics, costumes, scrolls (*kakemono* and *emakimono*), calligraphy and Noh masks, as well as a fine collection of Chinese, Indian and Tibetan works.

Suntory Museum** (Suntory Bijutsukan) VII, C3

Suntory Building, 11th floor, 1-2-3 Moto-Akasaka, Minato-ku, ☎ 3470 1013. *Open Tues-Sun 10am-5pm.*
Access: Akasaka-Mitsuke Station.

This is primarily a collection of Japanese traditional art containing lacquerware, ceramics, paintings and prints dating from the 15th century onward. Excellent tea is served in a room reserved for the tea ceremony.

Tokyo Metropolitan Art Museum* (Tokyo-to Bijutsukan) IV, AB2

8-36 Ueno Koen, Taito-ku, ☎ 3823 6921. *Open Tues-Sun 9am-5pm.*

Access: Ueno Station.

Constructed in 1975, this recent museum houses about 1000 contemporary works, mainly Japanese. Paintings, sculptures, calligraphy and handicrafts are exhibited alternately. There are also numerous temporary exhibitions.

National Museum of Modern Art** (Tokyo Kokuritsu Kindai Bijutsukan) II, A1

3 Kitanomaru-Koen, Chiyoda-ku, ☎ 3214 2561. *Open Tues-Sun 10am-5pm.*

Access: Kudanshita Station.

Just opposite Kitanomaru Park, this museum is devoted to Japanese art since the Meiji. It contains about 3000 works, including paintings, Japanese prints, sculptures and handicrafts.

Yamatane Museum* (Yamatane Bijutsukan) II, D2

Yamatane Building, 8th floor, 7-12 Kabutocho, Nihombashi, Chuo-ku, ☎ 3669 7643. *Open Tues-Sun 10:30am-5pm.*

Access: Tokyo Station.

This museum shows modern and contemporary Japanese paintings dating from the Meiji period to the present.

▬ *ARTS AND CRAFTS*

Furniture Museum* (Kagu No Hakubutsukan) I, B2

JFC Building, 3-10 Harumi, Chuo-ku, ☎ 3533 0098. *Open Thur-Tues 10am-4:30pm.*

Access: From Ginza Station, take a bus to the Harumi no Yubinkiyoku bus stop.

This museum contains chests, chairs, trunks and Japanese tables — everything from the simplest to the most Baroque in Japanese furniture.

Japan Folk Crafts Museum*** (Nihon Mingeikan) I, A1

4-3-33 Komaba, Meguro-ku, ☎ 3467 4527. *Open Tues-Sun 10am-5pm.*

Access: Komaba-Todaimae Station.

Soetsu Yanagi, who founded this museum in 1936, defended the idea that an object is all the more beautiful if it is not expressively intended as 'art'. True artists, he claimed, are the artisans (particularly those of the Edo period) who make everyday objects: bowls, sake bottles, plates, cases and kimonos. The museum contains over 20,000 objects that are displayed alternately in a typical Japanese house. A visit to this museum is indispensable for anyone interested in Japanese folk art. In November, the museum shop sells folk art from every region of Japan.

Japan Paper Museum** (Nihon Kami Hakubutsukan) I, A1

1-1-8 Horifune, Kita-ku, ☎ 3911 3545. *Open Tues-Sun 9:30am-4:30pm.*

The most beautiful Japanese prints can be seen in the Ota and Riccar Art museums.

Access: Oji Station.

This museum is said to be the only one of its kind in the world. It covers various aspects of Japanese paper making and possesses an impressive collection of ancient and modern papers.

Tokyo Metropolitan Museum of Decorative Arts** (Tokyo Teien Bijutsukan) I, A2

21-9 Shirokanedai 5-chome, Minato-ku, ☎ 34430201. *Open daily 10am-6pm.*

Access: Meguro Station.

Formerly a residence of Prince Yasuhiko, this building was entirely renovated in 1932 by the French architect Henri Rapin, who attempted to combine Art Deco with traditional Japanese architecture. The only building of its kind in Tokyo, it was opened to the public in 1983, and it is certainly worth a visit.

▬ *CALLIGRAPHY*

Calligraphy Museum* (Shodo Hakubutsukan) IV, B1

2-10-4 Negishi, Taito-ku, ☎ 3872 2645. *Open Tues-Sun 10am-4pm. Closed June 15-July 15.*

Access: Nippori Station.

This museum covers the history and evolution of calligraphy from its Chinese origins to the present day.

Japan Calligraphy Museum* (Nihon Shodo Bijutsukan) I, A1

1-3-1 Tokiwadai, Itabashi-ku, ☎ 3965 2611. *Open Wed-Sun 11am-5pm.*

Access: Itabashi-Honcho Station.

This museum contains contemporary 20th-century calligraphy.

▬ *COMMUNICATIONS*

Communications Museum* II, C2

2-3-1 Otemachi, Chiyoda-ku, ☎ 32703841. *Open Tues-Sun 9am-4:30pm.*

Access: Otemachi Station.

This museum recounts the history of modern communications in Japan. It covers every aspect of the field, from air mail and submarine cables to satellites.

NHK Broadcasting Museum* (NHK Hoso Hakubutsukan) III, A2

2-1-1 Atago 2-chome, Minato-ku, ☎ 34335211. *Open Tues-Sun 9:30am-4:30pm.*

Access: Kamiyacho Station.

It was from this building that the first radio broadcast in Japan was transmitted. The museum deals more with radio than with television.

Nippon Telephone and Telegraph (NTT) Museum* II, C2

2-2-2 Otemachi, Chiyoda-ku, ☎ 32418080. *Open Tues-Sun 9:30am-4:30pm.*

Access: Otemachi Station.

This museum is the showcase of the powerful NTT. The latest computers and the most recent telecommunications equipment are regularly displayed here. It is not far from the Communications Museum (see above).

HISTORY AND ARCHAEOLOGY

Ancient Oriental Museum* (Kodai Oriento Hakubutsukan) XII, B2

Sunshine City, 7th floor, 3-1-4 Higashi Ikebukuro, Toshima-ku, ☎ 3989 3491. *Open Tues-Sun 10am-5pm.*

Access: Higashi Ikebukuro Station.

This is the only museum in Japan that deals with Middle Eastern archaeology.

Fukagawa Edo Museum** (Fukagawa Edo Hakubutsukan) I, B2

3-28 Shirakawa 3-chome, Koto-ku, ☎ 3630-8625 *Open daily 10am-5pm.*

Access: Monzen-Nakacho Station.

Completed in 1986 and housed in a specially designed building, this is one of most recent and modern museums in Tokyo. Dealing with 19th-century life in Edo, it contains a little port with antique boats and an entire neighbourhood reconstructed in the style of the Fukagawa district around 1840, complete with shops and houses into which visitors may wander and even handle the furnishings. This is a living museum and you will certainly not regret your visit.

Meiji University Archaeological Collection* (Meiji Daigaku Kokogaku Chinretsukan) IX, BC3

Meiji Daigaku, 1-1 Surugadai, Kanda, Chiyoda-ku, ☎ 3296 4432. *Open Mon-Sat 10am-4:30pm. Closed during school vacations.*

Access: Jimbocho or Ochanomizu stations.

Located on the Meiji University grounds, this archaeological collection consists of two sections, one covering China (prehistory to the Tang) and the other concentrating on Japan (prehistory to the Kofun Culture).

Shitamachi Museum*** (Shitamachi Fuzoku Shiryokan) IV, AB3

2-1 Ueno-Koen, Taito-ku, ☎ 3823 7451. *Open Tues-Sun 9:30am-4:30pm.*

Access: Ueno Station.

Located in Ueno Park, this is one of the most interesting museums in Tokyo. On the ground floor, visitors can enter the houses of a detailed reconstruction of a 19th-century Asakusa street. On the 2nd floor, photographs and documents recount the history of Asakusa in the 1940s-50s. This is a rarity in itself; normally the war years are deliberately 'forgotten' in Japan. This museum should not be missed.

JAPANESE PRINTS (UKIYO-E)

Coloured wood-block prints, or *ukiyo-e* (images of the floating world), developed during the Edo period (1600-1868) from traditional techniques. Closed to the outside world and relatively free from internal strife, the life-style of urban Japan was then geared entirely toward pleasure, art and the joy of living. The great masters of this art form include Hokusai, Utamaro and Hiroshige. In Japan, *shunga* (erotic prints) are never shown publicly in museums, mostly because they are jealously guarded in private collections and reach astronomical prices. One of the major themes treated by the artists was the Tokaido Road (see p. 192). This great road, linking Kyoto and Edo, was often traveled by the errant *daimyo* (feudal war lords) on their journeys between the imperial and shogunal capitals.

Ota Museum*** (Ota Kinen Bijutsukan) XI, C2

1-10-10 Jingumae, Shibuya-ku, ☎ 3403 0880. *Open Tues-Sun 10:30-5:30pm. Closed from the 25th to the end of every month.*

Access: Meiji-Jingumae Station.

Lodged in a small, traditional Japanese building just behind the La Forêt building, the Ota Museum houses a private collection of 12,000 prints and 900 folding screens and also a library of 200 books on Japanese prints. The prints are displayed in rotation and include some by such masters as Utamaro and Hiroshige. A rock garden surrounded by bamboo benches allows the visitors to meditate over the works.

Riccar Museum*** (Rikka Bijutsukan) III, C1

2-3-6 Ginza, Chuo-ku, ☎ 3571 3254. *Open Tues-Sun 11am-6pm.*
Access: Ginza Station (Sukiyabashi Crossing exit).

This is undoubtedly one of the better-known *ukiyo-e* collections. Thematic exhibitions are held in a quiet and serene atmosphere. The museum contains a good collection of old prints as well as the wood blocks from which they were made. A small library also is open to the public.

▬ SCIENCE

National Science Museum* (Kokuritsu Kagaku Hakubutsukan) IV, B2

7-20 Ueno-Koen, Taito-ku, ☎ 3822 0111. *Open Tues-Sun 9am-4:30pm.*
Access: Ueno Station.

Larger and older than the Science Museum, the National Science Museum is a pedagogical institution, similar to its counterparts in New York and London, with departments of zoology, botany, geography, physics, chemistry, astronomy, meteorology, oceanography, space, electricity and mineralogy.

The museum has an annex, **The National Park for Nature Study,** at 5-21-5 Shiroganedai, Minato-ku, ☎ 3441 7176. **Access:** Meguro Station. *Open Tues-Sun 9am-4:30pm.* The 50-acre/20-hectare park is a center for the ecological study of insects, birds and plants. The dense vegetation of this woodland park is a vestige of the pre-urban forest of the Kanto region.

Science Museum** (Kagaku Hakubutsukan) II, B1

2-1 Kitanomaru Koen, Chiyoda-ku, ☎ 3212 8471. *Open Tues-Sun 9:30am-5pm.*
Access: Kudanshita Station.

The most recent scientific discoveries and the latest industrial equipment are exhibited in this constantly updated museum. Opened in 1964, it is more contemporary and less historical than the National Science Museum in Ueno Park.

▬ SPORTS

Baseball Museum* (Yakyu Hakubutsukan) IX, A2

1-3-61 Koraku, Bunkyo-ku, ☎ 3811 3600. *Open daily 10am-5pm.*
Access: Suidobashi Station.

You may have noticed, by watching television or by walking through parks, that the Japanese are great baseball fans. This entire museum is devoted to the sport.

Sumo Museum** (Sumo Hakubutsukan) I, B1

1-3-28 Yokoami, Sumida-ku, ☎ 3622 0366. *Open Mon-Fri 9:30am-4:30pm.*
Access: Ryogoku Station.

Installed since 1985 in the new *kokugikan* (sumo wrestling center), this small museum covers the history of sumo wrestling through photographs, trophies and other objects related to the sport.

TRANSPORTATION

Bicycle Museum* (Jitensha Kaikan) III, A2

1-9-3 Akasaka, Minato-ku, ☎ 3584 4530. *Open Tues-Sun 10am-4pm.*

Access: Toranomon Station.

On the 1st floor of this museum, there are films and exhibitions concerning the bicycle. The latest models may be tested. On the 2nd floor, the history of the bicycle is recounted in sculptures and paintings. There are also old models — including a bicycle belonging to the Emperor! On the 3rd floor, computers and videos scientifically explain the physics of cycling.

Subway Museum* (Chikatetsu Hakubutsukan) I, B2

3-1 Higashi-Kasai 6-chome, Edogawa-ku, ☎ 3878 5011. *Open Tues-Sun 10am-5pm.*

Access: Kasai Station.

Opened in July 1986, this is one of the most recent museums in Tokyo. Located under Kasai Station on the Tozai Line, it covers all aspects of urban rail transport from its origins to the present. The first subway train in Tokyo, which ran from Ueno to Asakusa, is displayed in a reconstruction of the old Ueno Station while in another room the techniques of urban tunnel-boring are explained. Visitors may 'drive' a moving train from a simulated engineer's compartment with a panoramic view of the city. Explanations are given in English.

Transportation Museum* (Unyu Hakubutsukan) IX, D3

1-25 Sudacho, Kanda, Chiyoda-ku, ☎ 3251 8481. *Open Tues-Sun 9:30am-5pm.*

Access: Akihabara Station.

Although it concentrates on railroads, this museum contains about 20,000 objects dealing with virtually every means of transportation possible or imaginable. There are several miniature reproductions of stations and trains from various periods as well as of the first locomotive used in Japan (made in England), which went into service in 1872.

OTHER MUSEUMS

Ace Museum* (Seikai No Kaban Kan) V, B3

1-8-10 Komagata, Taito-ku, ☎ 3843 8141. *Open Mon-Sat 10am-4:30pm. Closed the 1st and 4th Sat of every month.*

Access: Asakusa Station.

This museum displays 330 handbags, suitcases and briefcases from 31 different nations, including crocodile handbags, attaché cases from the 1950s and hollow-bottomed smuggler's trunks. This original museum is sponsored by Ace, a leading Japanese handbag company.

Bunka-Gakuen Costume Museum* (Bunka-gakuen Fuku-shioku Hakubutsukan) VIII, A3

3-22-1 Yoyogi, Shibuya-ku, ☎ 3370 3111. *Open Mon-Fri 10am-4:30pm; Sat 10am-3pm. Closed June 23.*

Access: Sangubashi Station.

This museum has a large collection of traditional Asian costumes, as well as European and American clothes dating from the 18th and 19th centuries.

Daimyo Clock Museum* (Daimyo Tokei Hakubutsukan) VIII, A3

2-1-27 Yanaka, Taito-ku, ☎ 3821 6913. *Open Tues-Sun 10am-4pm. Closed July 1-Sept 30.*

Access: Nezu Station.

Watches were introduced into Japan at the beginning of the Edo Period just before the Tokugawa shogunate closed the door to the outside world. During the two centuries that followed, the Japanese adapted the watch to fit their needs, the museum exhibits about 400 from the Edo Period.

Kite Museum* (Tako No Hakubutsukan) II, D2

Taimenken Building, 5th floor, 1-12-10 Nihombashi, Chuo-ku, ☎ 3275 2704. *Open Mon-Sat 11am-5pm.*

Access: Nihombashi Station.

Kites are a traditional craft in Japan, and many are works of art. Every year at the beginning of February, hundreds of magnificent kites are launched during the annual festival at the Oji Inari temple. If you are in Tokyo at this time of year, do not miss this event; if not, console yourself with a visit to this little museum that contains over 2000 kites from around the world. A kite association affiliated to the museum will gladly give you details concerning all kiting events organized in Japan.

Meiji Shrine Treasury* (Meiji Jingu Homotsuden) VIII, A1

Yoyogi Park, 1-1 Kamizonocho, Yoyogi, Shibuya-ku, ☎ 3379 5511.

Access: Gaien Mae Station.

Located in the Meiji Jingu Inner Garden, this little museum contains objects, photographs and written documents pertaining to the Emperor and Empress Meiji.

Meiji University Museum of Crime* (Meiji Daigaku Keiji Hakubutsukan) IX, C3

Meiji daigaku, 1-1 Kanda-Surugadai, Chiyoda-ku, ☎ 3296 4431. *Open Mon-Sat 10am-4:30pm. Closed during school vacations.*

Access: Jimbocho or Ochanomizu stations.

This museum belongs to Meiji University and contains weapons and court exhibits associated with famous criminal cases. There are also numerous instruments for punishing the offenders, including a guillotine.

Musashino Academy (Museum of Musical Instruments)** I, A1

1-13 Hazawa, Nerima-ku, ☎ 3992 1121 ext. 243. *Open Wed 10am-3pm.*

Access: Ekoda Station.

A little off the beaten track, this museum is definitely worth the detour for anyone interested in the history of musical instruments. It contains a remarkable collection of antique instruments, Western as well as Japanese. Many of them are rare items, such as a Napoleonic piano of surrealistic design and a magnificent 'bird-sitar' from India.

Oyama Collection* IX, B1

20-12 Hongo 4-chome, Bunkyo-ku, ☎ 3813 7441. *By appointment only.*

Access: Kasuga or Karakuen stations.

This is a private collection that contains over 300 dolls from 100 different countries. You can arrange a visit by calling Mrs Oyama (who speaks English) before 10am or after 4pm. She will most likely send someone to meet you at the station.

Photography Museum* VIII, B3

3-21-20 Nishi-Azabu, Minato-ku, ☎ 3401-2186. *Open Mon-Sat 10am-5pm.*

Access: Hiroo Station.

This is the only photography museum in Japan. It contains an impressive collection of old cameras, as well as an amusing series of espionage equipment that includes cameras hidden in match boxes and pens.

An adjoining gallery regularly organizes exhibitions of contemporary photographers.

Sword Museum** (Token Hakubutsukan) VIII, A3

4-25-10 Yoyogi, Shibuya-ku, ☎ 3379 1386. *Open Tues-Sun 9am-4pm.*
Access: Sangubashi Station.

During the rule of the shoguns, only the samurai (called *bushi* by the Japanese) had the right to carry swords. Many of these weapons were forged and signed by master swordsmiths. Containing over 1000 exceptional swords, scabbards and other related items, including 30 classified as National Treasures, this museum is the only one of its kind in Japan.

Sugino Costume Museum** (Sugino Hakubutsukan) I, A2

4-6-19 Osaki, Shinagawa-ku, ☎ 3491 8151. *Open Mon-Sat 10am-4pm. Closed holidays.*
Access: Meguro Station.

Opened in 1957, this museum is run by a nearby pattern-cutting school. European clothes from 1850 to the present are displayed on the 1st floor. Costumes of the Middle Ages and of non-Japanese Asian nations (China, Indonesia, Malaysia and so on) are on the 2nd floor. The history of Japanese clothing from the Ainu (the first inhabitants of the islands) to modern paper garments is recounted in a magnificent collection on the 4th floor.

Tobacco and Salt Museum** (Tabaco To Shio Hakubutsukan) XI, B3

1-16-8 Jinnan, Shibuya-ku, ☎ 3476 2041. *Open Tues-Sun 10am-6pm.*
Access: Shibuya Station.

On the first two floors, the history of tobacco (in the world in general and in Japan in particular) is illustrated through drawings, photographs and numerous other objects. The floors above give an account of the origins and use of salt. The explanations, unfortunately, are in Japanese only.

Toy Museum* (Omocha Ya Bijutsukan) off map I, A1

2-12-10 Arai, Nakano-ku, ☎ 3387-5461. *Open daily 10:30am-4pm.*
Access: Nakano Station.

A former toy restorer transformed his workshop into a museum with thematic exhibitions that generally last about six months. Children are actually permitted to play with the toys on display, much to their delight.

Waseda University Tsubuchi Memorial Theatre Museum* (Waseda Daigaku Tsubuchi Hakase Kinen Engeki Hakubutsukan) I, A1

Waseda daigaku, 1-6-1 Nishi-Waseda, Shinjuku-ku, ☎ 3203-4141. *Open Mon-Fri 9am-4pm; Sat 9am-2pm. Closed during school vacations.*
Access: Waseda Station.

The only museum in Japan devoted exclusively to the stage, it covers both Japanese (Noh drama, Kabuki theatre and *bunraku*) and Western theatre. The museum is dedicated to the dramatist (and translator of Shakespeare), Tsubuchi Shoyo (1859-1935).

Yasukuni Jinja Museum* (Yasukuni Jinja Homotsu Ihinka) VII, D1

3-1-1 Kudan-Kita, Chiyoda-ku, ☎ 3261-8326. *Open daily 9:30am-4:30pm.*

Access: Ichigaya Station.

This museum, belonging to the Yasukuni Jinja shrine, is a war memorial commemorating the dead. Dramatic objects displayed include a kamikaze airplane and a flag painted in human blood.

ENVIRONS OF TOKYO

Several interesting day excursions are possible from Tokyo. Kamakura, Yokohama, Disneyland, Mount Fuji and Nikko are the most popular.

Although each of these places may be visited in a day, it is more relaxing to stay overnight in a *ryokan* (Japanese-style hotel). Far more enjoyable than rushing to catch a train, staying in one of these hotels will let you experience the full flavour of authentic Japanese hospitality.

KAMAKURA

Map coordinates refer to the map pp. 144-145.

From 1192 to 1333, Kamakura was the seat of the feudal government of Japan. After defeating the Taira clan, Minamoto Yoritomo (1147-99) was granted the title of *sei-i-tai-shogun* (Great Generalissimo for the Subjugation of the Barbarians) in 1192. He installed his *bakufu* (tent government) in this remote corner of Kanto in reaction to the decadence of the Imperial court at Kyoto. The military government's ascetic, martial ideology was heavily influenced by Zen Buddhism, then rapidly spreading through Japan. This rise of militarism resulted, in turn, in the establishment of feudal rule in Japan and the supremacy of the shogunate over Imperial power that was to last until the Imperial Restoration of 1868.

Minamoto Yoritomo, who had murdered members of his own family in order to secure power, died in 1199 after falling off his horse. The Hojo family seized power from his heirs and ruled as regents until 1333. In that year, a renegade general of the shogunate, Ashikaga Takauji (1305-58), attacked the city and murdered the Hojo family. In 1335, he deserted his newly acquired Imperial lord, drove the Emperor's forces from Kamakura and was proclaimed Shogun by a new puppet emperor whom he had installed on the Imperial throne. In order to keep the activities of the Imperial court under his control, Ashikaga Takauji moved his government to Kyoto the following year. By 1603, when the Tokugawa family became the masters of Japan, Kamakura was a quiet backwater.

Today, the town is an exclusive residential area and a seaside resort for urban Tokyoites. With its beaches and mild climate, it is only 51 mi/32 km from Tokyo, to which it is linked by frequent trains.

Temples and shrines

In many ways, Kamakura can be considered the home of Zen Buddhism in Japan. Introduced to Japan by the priest Eisai and spread by his disciple Dogen, Zen is derived from the Chinese Ch'an sect, which developed in the 7th century out of the earlier Indian Dhyana (Meditation) School. There are five major Zen temples in Kamakura:

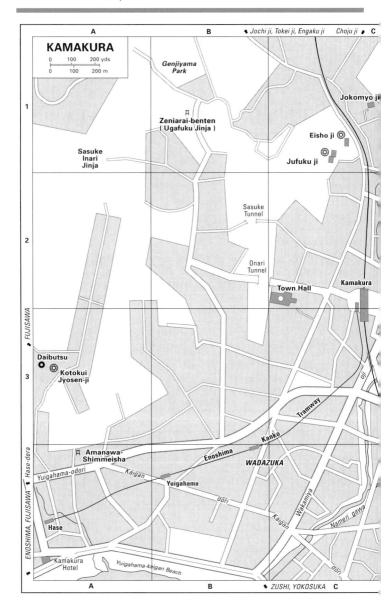

The **Kencho ji*****, E1, is the most important of the Zen temples. Founded in 1253 by Hojo Tokiyori for the Chinese priest Daigaku Zanji, this temple was destroyed by fire in 1415 and was not rebuilt again until the beginning of the 17th century. The *hondo* (Main Hall) and the Karamon (Chinese Gate) date from 1646. Surrounded by dense vegetation, including many *hinoki* (Japanese cedars), the Kencho ji is one of the loveliest temples in Kamakura. The bronze bell, cast in 1255, is classified a National Treasure.

The **Engaku ji****, C1, founded in 1282, was built in pure Zen Karayo (Chinese) style, imported directly from the mainland. Many of the original

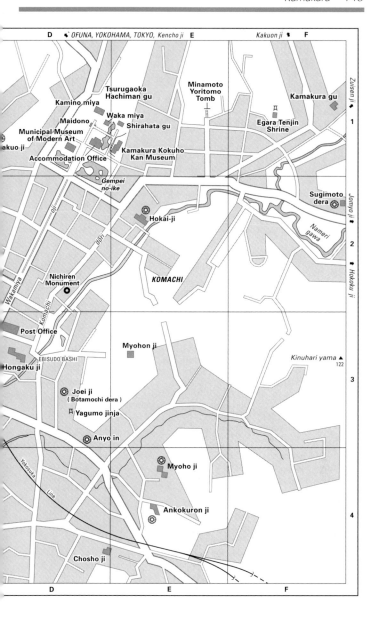

buildings were destroyed in the great 1923 earthquake. The *shariden* (Holy Relics Hall), erected in 1285, houses a tooth said to be that of Buddha Gautama. The bronze bell dates from 1301.

The **Jochi ji,** B1, formerly one of the most important Zen temples of the region, was founded in 1283 and placed under the control of the Chinese priest Funei. Largely destroyed by the Great Kano earthquake of 1923, little remains of its former greatness. Its main attractions today are the irises that flower in May and a statue of Jizo, attributed to Unkei — one of the best-known sculptors of the Kamakura period.

The **Jufuku ji★**, C1, is the oldest Zen temple in Kamakura. Originally placed under the direction of Eisai, the priest who had introduced both Zen Buddhism and tea growing to Japan, it was founded in 1200 by Masako Hojo, Minamoto Yoritomo's wife, who is buried in the grounds along with her son, Shogun Sanetomo (1203-19). The temple possesses Kamakura-period wooden sculptures, including statues of Eisai and Jizo.

The **Jomiyo ji***, F2, although founded in 1251, is one of the least-visited of the Kamakura Zen temples. The oldest remaining building dates from 1756, and there is not much to see apart from a stone stairway covered with moss and, in May, an immense mass of flowers.

The **Tsurugaoka Hachimangu****, E1, is the largest Shinto shrine in Kamakura. Founded in 1063, it was moved to its present site during the 12th century on the orders of Minamoto Yoritomo. Located on a hill in the center of a large park, the present buildings date from the Momoyama and Edo periods. The grounds are the focal point of the complex and contain several non-religious buildings, including the Kamakura Municipal Museum and the Kamakura Kokuho Kan Museum.

If you still have a little time left, take a taxi to the **Zuisen ji*****, F1. The temple and garden were founded in 1327 by the Zen priest Soseki, who had a special talent for integrating gardens with their surrounding environment. During the month of May, an incredible variety of flowers may be seen here. There is a view of Mount Fuji from the summit of Kimpei San, the hill on which these gardens are laid out.

The great Buddha (Daibutsu)*** A3

From Kamakura, take the Enoden Line to Hase Station. The journey takes about five minutes.

Considered artistically superior to the older and larger Buddha at Nara, the Buddha of Kamakura is 37 ft 5-in-11.4 m high (without the base) and weighs about 124 tons. Representing Amida Buddha (Eternal Light), this impressive statue, attributed to Ono Goroemon, dates from 1252 and replaced an earlier wooden colossus. Originally housed inside the Kotokuin temple, it has been in the open air since 1495, when a huge tidal wave swept away the temple. You may visit the interior of the statue, but do not expect to discover the secret of Amida Buddha's serenity there — particularly during holidays!

Access

Take the Yokosuka Line of the JR (Japanese Railways) from Tokyo Station, Shinagawa Station or Shimbashi Station. Because most of the temples and monuments are located between Kamakura and Kita-Kamakura, you can get off at any one of these stations. The journey takes about an hour.

Accommodation

If you are planning to spend the night in Kamakura, try Japanese-style accommodation. Both *Ryokan* and *minshuku* (lodging in a private home) are available.

▲▲ **Minshuku Ai**, 2-22-3 Hase, Kamakura-shi, ☎ (0467) 25 5859. Hase Station. Two minutes from the station. The price is about ¥4000 per person, including breakfast. Only women are accepted.

▲▲ **Ryokan Ushio**, 2-3-9 Komachi, Kamakura-shi, ☎ (0467) 22 716. Kamakura Station. A three-minute walk from the station. The price is ¥4500 per person, including breakfast.

Festivals

The **Kamakura Festival** takes place between April 7 and 14. The star attraction of this celebration is a samurai parade that features historical characters associated with the town including Minamoto Yoritomo and his wife, Masako Hojo. The procession starts at Yuigahama Beach and proceeds to the Tsurugaoka Hachimangu shrine. The Kamakura Festival takes place during *o hanami* (the cherry blossom period), when the town literally disappears under a cloud of white and pink blossoms.

The **Yabusame Festival** is held at the Tsurugaoka Hachimangu shrine between September 14 and 16. The major event is a tournament of mounted archers whose equestrian skill alone is worth the excursion.

Food

The restaurants, cafés and souvenir shops in Kamakura are concentrated on the two major streets: Wakayama Oji, C3-4, and Komachi Dori, DE2-3.

Particularly recommended is **Hachinoki,** 7 Yamanouchi, Kamakura-shi, ☎ (0467) 228719. A very fine Japanese meal is offered for ¥4000 per person.

▬ *YOKOHAMA*

Up until 1859, Yokohama was nothing more than an insignificant fishing village. In that year, this little port was opened to foreigners. In 1872, the first railway line in Japan linked Yokohama to Tokyo, and the village rapidly became Japan's principal international port. Destroyed twice in the 20th century, first by the Great Kano earthquake on September 1, 1923, and then by American bombers on May 29, 1945, Yokohama has again risen to be one of the most important trading centers in Japan.

Today, with a population of over 3 million, Yokohama is the second-largest city in Japan, after Tokyo. To meet the challenge of the future, the municipality has embarked on an ambitious project of reclaiming 460 acres/186 hectares of land from the sea.

Entirely geared toward commerce, Yokohama has very little to offer the tourist. The principal centers of interest are listed below:

Motomachi — Yokohama's equivalent to Ginza — is a commercial pedestrian street that is always animated.

The **Foreigner's Cemetery,** on the northern side of Yamate Hill (also called the Bluff), contains the graves of 4200 foreigners from over 45 different countries.

The **Santonodai Archaeological Museum** contains a good collection of material from a nearby Jomon period excavation illustrating daily life in Neolithic Japan (2500-250 BC).

Chinatown, just opposite Ishikawacho Station, is a miniature Chinese city. The restaurants and tearooms are more authentic here than they are in Tokyo. The pastries are particularly good.

The **Silk Center Building,** Yamashita Cho, Naka-ku, ☎ (045) 6410841, was inaugurated in 1959 on the 100th anniversary of the port of Yokohama. The Silk Museum, on the 2nd and 3rd floors, deals with every aspect of the industry from silkworms and raw cocoons to the weaving of beautiful fabrics. The **Silk Exchange,** *open daily 9:30-11am, 1:30-3pm,* is on the 4th floor. Yokohama's tourist information center is on the ground floor.

The **Soji ji Temple,** near Tsurumi Station, is one of the most important Soto Zen Buddhist temples in Japan and is a particularly fine example of Kamakura-period architecture. The extensive grounds contain the tomb of the Emperor Go-Daigo.

Yamashita Koen Park is located on the waterfront near the Silk Center. From the top of a 348 ft/106 m lighthouse, there is a view of the port and Tokyo Bay.

Sankeien (Three Little Valleys) Park is one of the most impressive landscape gardens in Japan. Several traditional buildings (pagodas, shogun villas and teahouses) dating from the Edo period have been reconstructed here. Mount Fuji can be seen from the top of a three-storey, 15th-century pagoda located in the park.

Access

Yokohama can be reached from Tokyo by the Yokosuka Line of the JR (Japanese Railways). This is the same line you use to get to Kamakura but the journey is shorter, taking only about 20 minutes. Trains leave from Tokyo, Shimbashi and Shinagawa stations. Alternatively, you can catch a train from Shibuya Station on the Toyoko Line, but this takes twice as long.

Festivals

The **Yokohama Festival** is held on the first Sunday in June. Among other attractions, a 33 ft-/10 m-long paper snake is carried through the streets of the town to ward off evil spirits.

O-Sannomiya Festival, from September 13 to 15, features *kagura* (ritual dances). *Mikoshi* (portable shrines) are carried through the streets of the town.

On **October 10** (as well as on May 13 and August 25), Chinatown is on parade, featuring street events with Chinese masks and dragons.

Food

There is a large Chinatown in Yokohama. The following two restaurants are among the best-known:

Manchinro, 153 Yamashita Cho, Naka-ku, ☎ (045) 681 4004.

Junkaikaku, 147 Yamashita Cho, Naka-ku, ☎ (045) 681 1324.

In Motomachi, try **Mutekiro,** 2-96 Motomachi, Naka-ku, ☎ (045) 681 2926. This is a fine restaurant serving French specialities.

DISNEYLAND

Opening hours vary according to the time of the year. For more information call beforehand, ☎ (0473) 54 0001 or (03) 366 5600.

Located about 35 minutes by bus from Tokyo Station, the amusement park can also be reached by a shuttle bus from Urayasu Station, the terminus of the Tozai Line.

Since Disneyland's opening in April 1983, hoards of visitors have flocked to this 114 acre/46 hectare amusement park, the first Disneyland outside the United States. Essentially a copy of its American counterparts, this park offers the same attractions and atmosphere.

It is formally forbidden to bring food into the amusement park. Unless you plan on a hunger strike, you will be forced to eat in one of the restaurants in the World Bazaar. When Mickey is around, Uncle Scrooge is never far away!

MOUNT FUJI AND THE LAKE REGION

World-renowned, Fuji San is the symbol of eternal Japan. The highest elevation in the country at 12,388 ft/3776 m, this symmetrically shaped volcanic cone conforms to the Japanese aesthetic ideal: a perfect natural form.

Geologically, Mount Fuji is very young. Originally two mountains that were formed about 600,000 years ago at the beginning of the Quaternary (Ice Age) period, volcanic activity later covered them with lava, which cooled to form a single peak. There have been 18 recorded eruptions. The last, in 1707, covered Edo (ancient Tokyo), 60 mi/100 km away, with a thick layer of ash. The name Fuji is thought to come from an Ainu word for the goddess of fire and the hearth.

Climbing Mount Fuji

The official climbing season is from July 1 to August 31. There are six main trails that lead to the summit. The ascent takes five to nine hours, and the descent takes three to five. Ideally, you should plan to reach the summit for *goraiko* (a Fuji sunrise). To arrive at dawn, you will need to spend the previous night on the mountain. Numerous refuges line the trail, and accommodation is no problem. The gradients are steep but not difficult. Every year 300,000 people reach the summit. Temperatures at the summit, however, rarely exceed 43° F/6° C and winds can be very strong. A woolen sweater is a real comfort, even in August, and heavy boots are essential.

For the less adventurous, a bus takes you to the 5th stage of the Yoshida Trail from which point the climb to the summit is reduced to a 'mere' four hours.

No matter which itinerary you choose, do not expect solitude. Every year, about 3 million Japanese pilgrims (and thousands more foreign tourists) joyfully tackle the trails of the sacred mountain, leaving behind them thousands of tons of tin cans and greasy papers that distract somewhat from the bucolic charms of the hike. Fortunately, at the end of each season, a force of volunteer students cleans the holy trails.

The five lakes

To the north and west of Mount Fuji are five famous lakes: **Kawaguchiko, Yamanakako Saiko, Shojiko** and **Motosuko.** The first three are particularly well known for the splendid view they offer of Mount Fuji.

In the summer, it is possible to hike, camp, fish or boat. In the winter, ice-skating and cross-country skiing are possible.

Kawaguchiko Station is a good base from which to visit the area.

Access

Train

The train from Shinjuku Station to Kawaguchiko, at the foot of Mount Fuji, takes 2 hours and 10 minutes.

Bus

The bus also leaves from Shinjuku Station. The terminal is in front of the Yasuda Building near the east exit of the station. Buses leave every Sunday (and every day during August) at 7:45 am and 8:45 am.

▰ *HAKONE AND THE SURROUNDING REGION*

Located about an hour and a half from Shinjuku Station, Hakone is a popular outdoor resort among Tokyoites. Apart from its magnificent lake, lush vegetation and mountain scenery, Hakone is the closest *onsen* (natural spring) to Tokyo. There are also several historic sites in the area.

The Hakone hot springs

The Hakone region, between Mount Fuji and the sea, lies on the remains of an extinct volcano, the paleo crater of which is 25 mi/40 km in circumference. Local geothermic activity is manifested by the numerous hot springs in the area, of which 12 are of major importance. Many of the springs are sulfurous, and almost all of them are attributed therapeutic properties. At Tonosawa Onsen, the temperature of the springs varies from 110° F/44° C to 153° F/67° C and the waters are recommended for rheumatism, nervous illnesses and dermatological complaints.

The region was important historically, both for its strategical position as the gateway to Edo and for the Tokaido Road (see p. 192).

Mount Fuji, Fuji San, the symbol of eternal Japan.

Miyanoshita, the best-known spa in the region, is only two hours from Tokyo by train or bus. The center of the district, it is a convenient point of departure for Lake Ashi or Mount Sengen. There are numerous hotels and restaurants in the area.

Kowakidani (Valley of the Lesser Boiling), a 15-minute walk from Miyanoshita, is famous for its boiling springs as well as for its cherry trees and azaleas.

Gora Park and the Open-Air Museum

Take the Hakone Tozan Line to Gora Station. There is a rock garden and a nature museum with exotic plants and birds.

The Hakone Open-Air Museum is a 10-minute walk from Gora Park. *Open daily 9 am-5 pm.* In a 7 acre/3 hectare park, a small covered museum presents an exhibit of modern sculpture from Rodin to Maillol. Permanent exhibitions of Rodin, Bourdelle, Giacometti, Moore and Zadkine are exhibited in the garden.

Owakudani

Owakudani (Valley of the Greater Boiling), also known as O Jigoku (The Great Hell), is 13 minutes away from Sounzan Station by cable car. The major attraction is Mount Kamiyama. A restaurant over the station offers an inexpensive lunch for ¥1,500 and a superb view of Fuji-Hakone-Izu National Park.

Lake Ashi

At 2,372 ft/723 m, Lake Ashi (Lake of the Reeds) lies at the bottom of a vast crater. The lake itself has a 11 mi/17.5 km circumference and covers 1,705 acres/690 hectares. Swimming, trout fishing and boating are the major attractions. Motorboat excursions of the lake may be taken from Moto-Hakone, a spa on the south-east shore. Nearby is the Hakone Jinja shrine, originally founded in AD 757. It was here that Minamoto Yoritomo took refuge after his defeat at Odawara in 1180. The *torii* (portal) is built in the lake.

Access

From Shinjuku Station, take the Odakyu Line to Hakone Yumoto. Trains depart every 30 minutes, and the journey takes about an hour and a half.

Accommodation

Hakone is a tourist center and hotels and *ryokan* are expensive. There is a 50% price increase during the winter vacation and in July and August.

▲▲▲ **Kagetsuen Hotel,** Sengokuhara, Hanoke-Machi, ☎ (0460) 48621. This is a small Western-style hotel with rooms starting at ¥12,000 per night for a double room.

▲▲▲ **Seihokaku Terumoto,** 1320 Gora, Hanoke-Machi, ☎ (0460) 23177. This *ryokan* costs about ¥12,000 per person including lunch and dinner.

Festivals

Koji-sai (Lake Festival) is held on July 31. In the evening, thousands of lanterns are lit and reflect off Lake Ashi. The ceremony takes place at the Hakone shrine.

Torii Matsuri (Torii Festival) is held on August 5. A large wooden *torii* (portal) is installed in the middle of the lake and burned.

Daimyo Gyoretsu (Daimyo Procession) occurs on November 3. Over 200 people dressed as *daimyo* in 17th-century costumes reenact the voyage of the shogun's vassals along the old Tokaido Road between Yumoto and Tonosawa.

Food

Hagehachi, 594 Yumoto, Hanoke-Machi, ☎ (4060) 55558. This is a good *sushiya* (raw-fish restaurant).

Hatsuhana, 635 Yumoto, Hakone-Machi, ☎ (4060) 58287. An excellent *soba* (buckwheat noodle) restaurant.

▬ *NIPPON MINKA-EN*

If you are not planning to travel around Japan to any great extent, go to Nippon Minka-en (Japan Farmhouse Garden). *Open daily 9:30 am-4 pm.* This museum, devoted to traditional Japanese rural architecture, contains 15 old farmhouses from different parts of Japan. The oldest dates from 1688. The visit takes about half a day and is one of the most interesting excursions from Tokyo.

Access

From Shinjuku Station, take the Odakyu Line to Mukogaoka-Yuen Station. The journey takes about half an hour. The village is a short walk from the station.

▬ *NIKKO*

Since the 8th century AD, Nikko (Sunny Splendour) has been an important Buddhist center. In AD 767, the priest Shodo Shonin founded the first temple in this deserted region and declared that the older Shinto spirits of the mountains were merely different manifestations of Buddha. One hundred years later, there were dozens of sub-temples, and by 1220 the temple was receiving an annual revenue of 180,000 *koku* (almost 1 million bushels) of rice. At the end of the 16th century, however, the town underwent a temporary decline. In 1590, Toyotomi Hideyoshi punished Nikko because the monks there had taken up arms against him during his unification of Japan. He confiscated the temple's domains, and all but nine sub-temples were dismantled and moved elsewhere.

However, in 1617, Shogun Tokugawa Iemitsu selected Nikko as the place to honour Ieyasu, his grandfather and the founder of the Tokugawa shogun dynasty. The Toshogu, erected in 1636, is probably the most lavishly decorated temple in Japan. Gilt, highly ornate Chinese-style roofs, columns and balconies with complex motifs combine to create a masterpiece of Baroque architecture in total opposition to Zen philosophy.

The anti-Buddhist policy of the Meiji government was a second shock for Nikko. The Toshogu was converted into a Shinto shrine and opened to the public.

Nikko is a center for both summer and winter vacations. **Nikko National Park** and the surrounding area offer yachting, boating, trout fishing, camping, hiking, mountain climbing, skiing and ice-skating as well as numerous *onsen* (hot springs).

Toshogo★★★

The Toshogu is the principal attraction of Nikko. Allow at least two hours for the visit. Start with the five-storey (105 ft/32 m) pagoda and finish with the treasury and the mausoleum of Iemitsu Tokugawa. Do not miss the world-renowned Yomeimon Gate, the main entrance to the temple.

Kirifuri Falls

Kirifuri Falls (a double waterfall of 230 ft/70 m), only 3 mi/5 km north of Nikko, can be reached easily by a short bus trip.

Lake Chuzenji

Take a bus from Nikko Station to Chuzenji-Onsen. The sinuous road reveals some marvelous views. Once at the lake, you can either take a boat tour or take an elevator to the bottom of the Kegon waterfall (Kegon no taki), famous as a site for romantic suicides; numerous frustrated lovers have leapt together from the 328 ft/100 m height.

Access

The quickest way to get to Nikko is to take the Tobu Line from Asakusa Station to Tobu-Nikko Station. There is a train about every half hour. The journey takes 1 hour and 45 minutes.

Accommodation

If you reserve well in advance, it is possible to stay in either of these excellent *ryokans*.
▲▲ **Konishi Bekkan,** 1115, Kami-hachi ishi cho, Nikko, ☎ (0288) 54 1105.
▲ **Turtle,** 2-16, Takumi cho, Nikko, ☎ (0288) 53 3168. This is a little less expensive than the Konishi Bekkan.

Food

If you feel adventurous, try **Ebisuya,** 955 Shimo hatsui shi, Nikko, ☎ (0288) 54 0113. It is just behind the town hall. The cuisine is based on *yuba,* dried soy paste used by the monks.

If you don't feel adventurous, a steak awaits you at **Meiji no Yakata,** 2339 1 Sannai, Nikko-shi, ☎ (0288) 53 3751.

KYOTO

Kyoto was saved from destruction during World War II by the French Orientalist, Serge Elisseeff. Informed of the American High Command's intention of bombing Kyoto, he implored the Americans to spare the ancient capital, the very soul of Japan. Fortunately, Kyoto was not bombed and, unlike most other large towns in Japan, suffered no damage.

Today, Kyoto is considered the museum of Japan. Nearly 20% of Japan's National Treasures are found in the temples and shrines of the Kyoto region, which are among the oldest surviving structures in the country. With nearly 1.5 million inhabitants, Kyoto is the seventh-largest city in Japan. Its 1000-year-old history makes it the spiritual capital of the nation.

794-1185: HEIAN AND THE RISE OF THE FUJIWARA

In AD 794, the Emperor Kammu moved his court from Nara to the nearby village of Uda, which he renamed Heiankyo (Capital of Peace and Tranquility). The new town was modeled on the Chinese capital of Ch'ang-an, with large avenues intersecting at right angles. Very quickly, the political life of Heiankyo (one of Kyoto's many names) became dominated by a single family, the Fujiwara. By systematically marrying their daughters to the crown princes, young emperors and other important members of the Imperial family, the Fujiwara managed to dominate the Imperial court for nearly 1000 years. They proclaimed themselves *sessho* (regent) and forced the newly crowned emperor to abdicate in favour of his son who, too young to rule, needed a *sessho* to govern until his maturity. In this manner the Fujiwara effectively remained masters of Japan.

A few emperors, such as Go Sanjo, actually managed to retain power. Known as 'retired emperors', they abdicated in favour of their sons but took advantage of this retirement to escape from the complicated ceremonies and involvements of the court in order to wield power from behind the scenes. On the whole, however, such cases of Imperial dominance were rare, and the Fujiwara, under a variety of pseudonyms, managed to hold the real power at the court for 10 centuries.

Even though the emperor officially incarnated the supreme function of the head of state, Japan was rife with power struggles and clan animosity. The 12th century was marked by a bitter rivalry between the Taira and the Minamoto families, whose history is recounted in numerous Kabuki plays.

1185-1392: KAMAKURA AND THE FIRST SHOGUNS

In 1185, the victorious Minamoto clan established its *bakufu* (camp government) in Kamakura, while a Fujiwara was named *sessho* (regent) at the Imperial court in Kyoto. During the Kamakura period, the control of Japan was in the hands of the military government at Kamakura.

At the beginning of the 14th century, General Ashikaga Takauji managed to seize power. Originally sent by the Hojo family (who at that time dominated the Kamakura government) to fight the Imperial forces of Go-Daigo, Ashikaga deserted to the emperor's cause but later threw Go-Daigo off the throne, installing a puppet emperor in his place. In 1336, Ashikaga Takauji was named shogun by the puppet emperor and moved his government to Kyoto.

The Ashikaga family ruled a war-torn Japan until 1567. By then, clan strife had reduced Kyoto to a ruined and defenseless capital, mercilessly pillaged by bandits. At the head of 20,000 determined soldiers, Oda Nobunaga, a minor warlord, took the opportunity to invade the capital. Seconded by the generals Toyotomi Hideyoshi and Tokugawa Ieyasu, Oda then took control of the rest of Japan but later committed *seppuku* when he was betrayed in 1582. Hideyoshi then seized power as *kampaku* (civil dictator) and installed his government in Osaka, from where he could closely survey the Imperial court in Kyoto.

During the 14th and 15th centuries, various art forms inspired by Zen Buddhism developed in Kyoto: the tea ceremony, flower arranging and the art of gardening. The Golden Pavilion, the Silver Pavilion and the moss garden of Kokedera also date from this period.

1603-1868: EDO AND THE TOKUGAWA

In 1603, Tokugawa Ieyasu was proclaimed shogun and established his government in Edo, where he owned a castle. Kyoto, however, remained the Imperial capital and even recovered some of the splendour of its former pre-Ashikaga times. The Tokugawa ran the country without interruption for over 250 years, while the powerless emperors succeeded one another in domestic tranquility. Apart from religious roles, the Imperial family had absolutely no power.

1868: THE MEIJI RESTORATION

In 1868, the Emperor Meiji restored the Imperial prerogative. This sealed Kyoto's fate as the capital of Japan. The Emperor decided to move his court to Edo, which was then renamed Tokyo (Eastern Capital).

KYOTO TODAY: THE GUARDIAN OF TRADITION

After over 1000 years of loyal service as the Imperial capital, Kyoto remains today the guardian of Japanese tradition. It is an important center for tourism and traditional arts and crafts (essentially pottery and weaving). But most of all, Kyoto is the city of the Geisha.

The neighbourhoods of Gion and Pontocho are known throughout the world for the extreme sophistication of their *zashiki* (places where clients meet geisha) and for the *maiko* (young geisha) who receive formal and authentic instruction.

Kyoto is not an economic capital and has no intention of rivaling Osaka, only about 25mi/40km away. The provincial character of the city is one of Kyoto's charms and life flows by far more peacefully here than in Tokyo, the 'city of madness'.

Ikebana: flower arranging

In Japan, flower arranging is both an art and a discipline. It is beautiful, yet as rigorous and precise a form as archery. In existence since the 7th century AD, *ikebana* developed most under the Ashikaga (1333-1582) and, above all, the Tokugawa (1603-1868) shogunates with the appearance of two separate styles: the *rikka* (huge sheaves evoking legends or suggesting emotions) and the *chabana* (sparser bouquets designed for tearooms).

Today, there are over 300 different schools, each with its own particular style and 'philosophy'. One of the most popular is the *ten-chi-jin* (sky-man-earth) school, where every composition has three basic elements representing the three 'levels of life'.

As with other Japanese artistic domains, the art of flower arranging is based on aesthetic rules that are in total opposition to those that prevail in the West. As followed by Zen masters, the fundamental idea is to 'let the void circulate between the flowers'.

Since the 15th century, all traditional Japanese houses have had an alcove *(tokonoma)* reserved for a bouquet, behind which is placed a painted scroll *(kakemono)*. Each season or stage in life has its own appropriate flower arrangement. It is often said that a trained eye is capable of reading the housewife's mind by the way she has arranged her flowers.

KYOTO:
PRACTICAL INFORMATION

Telephone area code: 075
Map coordinates refer to the maps pp. 162-163, 166-167.

▬ ACCESS

Kyoto is 304 mi/489 km south-west of Tokyo. The three most convenient ways to get there are by train, plane and bus.

Train

A *Shinkansen* (Bullet Train) leaves every 4 to 16 minutes (10 minutes on the average) in either direction. The first southbound train leaves Tokyo at 6am and the first northbound train leaves Kyoto at 6:30am. The journey takes from three to three and a half hours, depending on whether the train is a *hikari* (direct) or a *kodama* (local). The fare is ¥11,800 for a one-way ticket. As in all Japanese trains, the first five cars are not reserved.

Plane

From Tokyo, the plane is not much faster than the train. As Kyoto does not have its own airport, you must fly to Osaka and then take a bus or taxi to Kyoto. In all, the journey takes about three hours and does not justify the difference in price (about ¥4,000 more than the train). Osaka International Airport is, however, convenient for foreign visitors coming from abroad who do not plan to go to Tokyo.

Bus

The bus is the cheapest way to get to Kyoto, but it is also the longest and the least comfortable. The journey takes all night but costs only ¥7,800, including a reservation. The buses leave form the Yaesu exit of Tokyo Station at 11pm and arrive in Kyoto at 7:45am the following morning. These buses are very popular with the Japanese and it is best to reserve well in advance (¥1,500). The Japanese Railways operate this service and the Japan Rail Pass (JRP) can be used.

▬ ACCOMMODATION

See p. 217 for hotel classification.
Finding a Western-style hotel in Kyoto is not a problem. The city has about 50 such establishments in every price range. It would be a shame, however, not to take advantage of your stay in the ancient capital of Japan — the cradle of tradition — by trying a Japanese-style inn *(ryokan)* or lodging with a family *(minshuku)*. Unless, of course, you feel like

A young girl drinking water as part of a traditional purification ritual before entering a temple.

spending a night in a Buddhist temple. To do this, contact the Tourist Information Center near Kyoto Station (see 'TIC' p. 71). A night in a monastery, with two meals included, costs between ¥3,000 and ¥5,000. The hours are a bit spartan: lights out at 9pm and wake-up call at 5am.

Around the station

Hotels

▲▲▲ **Kyoto Grand Hotel,** Horikawa Shiokoji, Shimogyo-ku, II, C2 ☎ 341 2311. 573 rooms. Modern hotel with conference facilities, sauna, hairdresser and shops.

Ryokan

▲▲ **Ohtomo Bekkan Inn,** Akezu Dori, Nanajo Agaru, Shimogyo-ku, II, C2, n°25, ☎ 341 6344. Traditional and inexpensive.

▲▲ **Riverside Takase,** Shoshijicho, Kaminoguchi-agaru, Kiyamachi Dori, Shimogyo-ku, II, C1, n°23, ☎ 351 7920. 25 rooms. Reasonably priced for a double room with a view of the Takasegawa Canal.

▲ **Hiraiwa,** 314 Hayacho, Kaminoguchi-agaru, Ninomiyadori, Shimogyo-ku, II, C1-2, n°24, ☎ 351 6748. 16 rooms. The rooms are small but the personnel is friendly. Near the river.

The East, northern half

Hotels

▲▲▲▲ **Hotel Miyako,** Sanjo-Keage, Higashiyama-ku, I, D4, ☎ 771 7111. 480 rooms. This is one of the best-known hotels in Kyoto. A double room costs at least ¥20,000 per night.

▲▲ **Kyoto Traveller's Inn,** 91 Enshojicho, Okasaki, Sakyo-ku, I, D4 ☎ 771 0225. A decent hotel for less than ¥4,000 per night.

▲ **Kyoto Gion Hotel,** Gion, Higashiyama-ku, I, C4 ☎ 551 2111. Simple and inexpensive.

Ryokan

▲ **Three Sisters' Inn,** 81 Higashi Furaukawa, Okazaki, Sakyo-ku, I, D3, n°31, ☎ 771 6336. For those not obsessed by material comfort, this is a very inexpensive yet pleasant *ryokan*.

The East, southern half

Ryokan

▲▲ **Iwanami,** Higashiiioji, Nishi-iru, Shinmonzen Dori, Higashiyama-ku, II, D1, n°39, ☎ 561 7135. A traditional and very calm *ryokan* near Shirakawa Canal where room with breakfast costs ¥7,000 per night.

▲ **Kiyomizu Sanso,** 3-341 Kiyomizu Sanso, Higashiyama-ku, II, D1 n°39, ☎ 561 6109. This is one of the least expensive *ryokan* in Kyoto. It is indispensable to make reservations well in advance as there are only a few rooms available.

Gion and the center of town

Hotels

▲ **Fujita,** Nishizume, Nijo-Ohashi, Nakagyo-ku, I, C4, ☎ 222 1511. 195 rooms. Very well located, this luxury hotel overlooks the Takasegawa Canal.

▲▲▲▲ **International,** Nijo Sagaru, Aburanokoji Nakagyo-ku, I, C4, ☎ 222 1111. 334 rooms. Located just opposite Nijojo Castle, this luxury hotel is one of the most renowned in Kyoto. There is a magnificent Japanese garden inside the hotel. Estimate about ¥20,000 to ¥30,000 per night for a room.

▲▲ **Sun Hotel Kyoto,** Sanjo Sagaru, Kawaramachi Dori, Nakagyo-ku, I, C4, ☎ 241 3351. A good hotel with average prices. Between ¥4,000 and ¥7,000 per room.

Ryokan

▲▲▲ **Yoshima,** Yamato Oji, Higashi iru, Shinmonzen, Higashiyama-ku, I, C4, n°1, ☎ 561 2620. A very good *ryokan* in the center of the Gion district. With two meals, the bill will come to about ¥15,000 to ¥20,000 par person.

▲ **Gion Umemura,** 102 Hakata, Shijo Yamato Oji Sagaru, Higashiyama-ku, I, C4, n°2, ☎ 525 0156. A small *ryokan* where a room with two meals will not exceed ¥12,000.

The West, the southern half

There are not many Western-style hotels in this part of Kyoto. There are, however, numerous Japanese-style establishments *(ryokan and minshuku)*.

▲ **Kyoto,** 1-4 Taiteshi Cho, Saga Tenryu ji, Ukyo-ku, I, A3, n°46, ☎ 882 1817. This family inn is just next to Arashiyama Station. About ¥5,000 per person for a room and breakfast.

▲ **Saga no sato,** 42-2 Kitatsukurimichi Cho, Saga Tenryu ji, Ukyo-ku, I, A3, n°47, ☎ 882 0623. Many foreigners frequent this *minshuku.* The owner speaks English. A room and two meals costs about ¥5,000 per person. It is best to reserve well in advance.

CURRENCY EXCHANGE

It is possible to change money (preferably US dollars) in the large hotels or at the **Bank of Kyoto,** Karasuma Dori, Matsubara, I, C4 ☎ 361 2221.

FESTIVALS

January

New Year is celebrated from January 1 to 3. In Kyoto, as in the rest of Japan, it is one of the most important religious celebrations of the year, particularly in Shinto shrines. The Heian Jingu and Yasaka Jinja are the center of these festivities.

Toshiya (an archery tournament) is held on January 15 at the Rengeoin temple, more commonly called Sanjusangendo. About 600 archers attempt to shoot as many arrows as possible the full length of the hall. The record dates from 1696 when a contestant sent 8,153 arrows to the opposite end of the 390 ft-/119 m-long hall.

February

Fushimi Inari Shrine Festival, an important Shinto feast, is celebrated on February 3. The entire area around the shrine becomes very animated.

March

Hinamatsuri (Doll Festival) is on March 3. The best dolls are displayed at the Hokyo ji temple to the north-west of the Imperial Palace.

Otaimatsu, a torch procession commemorating the death of Buddha, is held on the March 15 at the Seiryo ji temple in Arashiyama in honour of Shakakumi, the founder of Japanese Buddhism. This is the only day of the year that his statue is exposed to the public.

April

Miyako Odori (Cherry Dance) is performed at the Kaburenjo theater in Gion during the month of April. The geisha of the Gion district give four

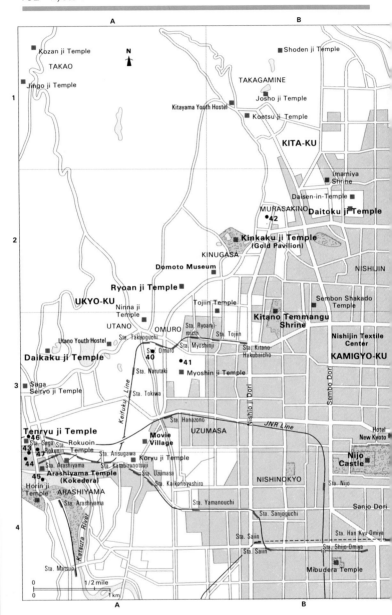

KYOTO I: NORTH

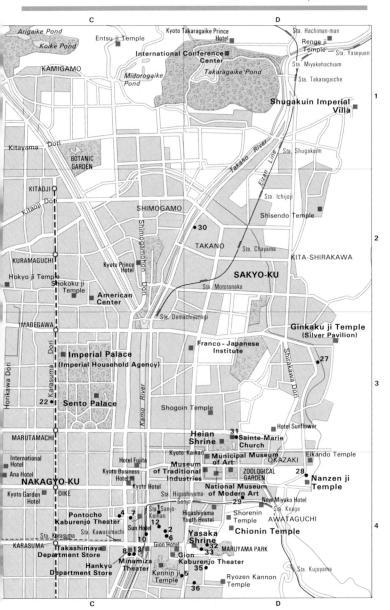

performances a day. The entrance fee is ¥3,000 and includes the right to take part in the tea ceremony.

Yasurai Matsuri takes place at the Imamiya Ebisu Jinja shrine not far from the Daitoku ji temple on the 2nd Sunday of the month. There are dances, including the Dance of Demons, traditionally believed to ward off the plague, and costume parades. Arrive around 3pm.

Hana Matsuri (Flower Festival), coinciding with the anniversary of the birth of Buddha, is celebrated on April 8. In Kyoto, the most colourful celebrations are held at the Chionin and Nishi Hongan ji temples.

Mibu Kyogen, a drama festival of comedy and mime that dates to the Middle Ages, is held from April 21 to 29. Originally intended to teach Buddhism to the common person, the festival consists of many short plays. It is well worth attending. Performances are held at the Mibu Dera temple at 1pm and 3pm. Take bus n°26 or 28 from Kyoto Station.

May

Kamogawa Odori (Kamo River Dance) is held from May 1 to 24. During this period, the geishas of the Pontocho district give three performances a day at the Pontocho Kaburenjo. There is an entrance fee of ¥3,000.

Aoi Matsuri (Hollyhock Festival), a superb Heian-period costume parade, takes place on May 15. The procession leaves the Imperial Palace at 10:30am and follows the Kamo River to the Shimogamo shrine. After a religious ceremony, it then heads toward the Kamigamo shrine, where a second ceremony is performed by Shinto priests.

Mifune Matsuri (Boat Festival), or Shuyusai, is held in Arashiyama on the 3rd Sunday of the month. This is one of the most spectacular events of the year in Kyoto. Around 1pm, a procession of people in Heian costume leaves the Kurumazaki Jinja shrine for Nakanoshima Park. About an hour later, it embarks on 32 richly decorated boats on the Oi River, accompanied by traditional music.

June

Takigi Noh is held on June 1 and 2 at the Heian Jingu shrine, where Noh drama performances are given by torchlight *(takigi no)*. Performances start at 5:30pm and cost ¥2,300.

July

Gion Matsuri, the biggest *matsuri* (festival) in Kyoto and one of the largest in Japan, is celebrated from July 16 to 24. The activities are centered at the Yasaka Jinja shrine, but involve a large area of the town. Over 1 million people participate in this festival, which was started in 869. There are several costume parades and, on July 17, a procession of huge floats that takes over the entire city of Kyoto.

August

Daimonji Okuribi (Daimonji Festival) is held on August 16. Large bonfires in the shapes of Chinese ideograms are lit on the five mountains that surround Kyoto, in order to 'light the way for the dead' who, according to Buddhist tradition, return at this time of year to visit the living. The largest of these fires, on Mount Nyoigatake, is in the shape of the Chinese ideogram *dai* ('great' or 'large') and elsewhere, small lanterns are lit, while the city lights are turned off for the occasion. The best place to watch is from Shogun-zuka Hill or Yoshida-yama Hill.

October

Kamogawa Odori (Kamo River Dances) are performed between October 15 and November 7. This second session (see 'May' above) takes place at Pontocho Kaburenjo.

Jidai Matsuri (Festival of the Eras), commemorating the founding of Kyoto in AD 794, is held on October 22. A procession of over

2,000 people dressed in costumes from the 13 historical eras of Kyoto's past (including samurai in full armour), leaves the Imperial Palace at noon and arrives at the Heian Shrine around 2:30pm.

Kurama no Hi Matsuri (Kurama Fire Festival) is held — much to the terror of local property owners — the same evening. Young people dressed in traditional costumes burn gigantic torches and then carry *mikoshi* (small portable shrines) through the streets of Kurama near the Yuki Jinja shrine on Mount Kurama.

November

Momiji Matsuri (Maple Festival) is held near Arashiyama Park on the 2nd Sunday of the month. Dressed in costumes of the 10th century nobility, men and women boat down the river, playing traditional musical instruments.

December

An exceptional tea ceremony is held on December 1 at the Kitano Tenmangu shrine. The religious service is at 10:30am, but the tea ceremonies continue until 3pm in the shrine's seven teahouses. The entrance fee of ¥1,500 entitles you to taste over 100 different types of Japanese cakes!

▬ FOOD

See p. 217 for restaurant classification.

Considering the number of Buddhist temples (around 1650) located in the Kyoto region, it is not surprising that the local cuisine is heavily influenced by religious principles. Strict Buddhism implies vegetarianism, and *Kyo ryori* (the cuisine of Kyoto) contains only vegetables and seafood with the total exclusion of meat. The most-common ingredient by far is *tofu* (bean curd), which is served in dozens of different ways.

Kyo ryori is a mixture of three different traditions: *yusoku ryori* (Imperial cuisine), *kaiseki ryori* (tea ceremony cuisine) and *shojin ryori* (Buddhist cuisine). It is perhaps the most aesthetically pleasing style of cooking in Japan, with its balanced, coloured compositions neatly presented on black-lacquered tableware. Real *Kyo ryori* is served only in *ryotei* (first-class establishments) and costs a minimum of ¥15,000 per person. This refined cuisine, however, can be sampled for less at lunch. Between 11am and 3pm, the *ryotei* usually offer a *o bento* (platter lunch) with an assortment of specialities for ¥2,500 to ¥3,000.

Kyoto is also an international gastronomic capital in its own right and cooking schools from the world over are represented there.

Around the station

The station district is not ideal for eating. If you do not have time to go into the center of town, eat in the basement of the station. *Sushi,* eel, *tempura* and steak are available. Almost all national and international specialities can be found here as well.

The Center

Restaurants

◆◆◆◆ **Mikaku,** I, C4, n°12, ☎ 525 1129. *Sukiyaki* (vegetables and meat cooked at your table). Perhaps the best beef in Kyoto.

◆◆◆ **Edogawa,** I, C4, n°4, ☎ 221 1550. Grilled eel.

◆◆◆ **O Edo,** I, C4, ☎ 221 7301. Breaded pork.

◆◆◆ **Le Français,** I, C4, n°7, ☎ 221 8661. A French bar and grill with good regional dishes.

◆◆◆ **Yagenbori,** I, C4, n°1, ☎ 551 3331. Clients are served an exceptional Kyoto cuisine. Private rooms.

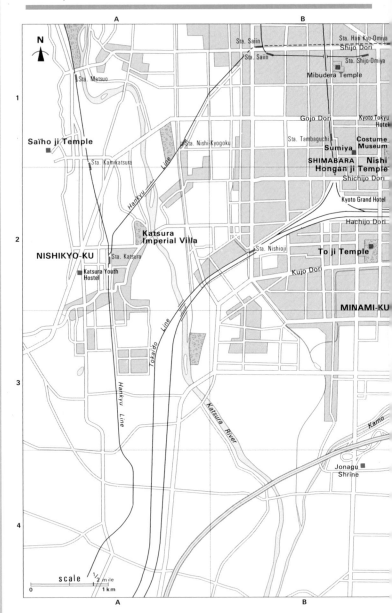

KYOTO II: SOUTH

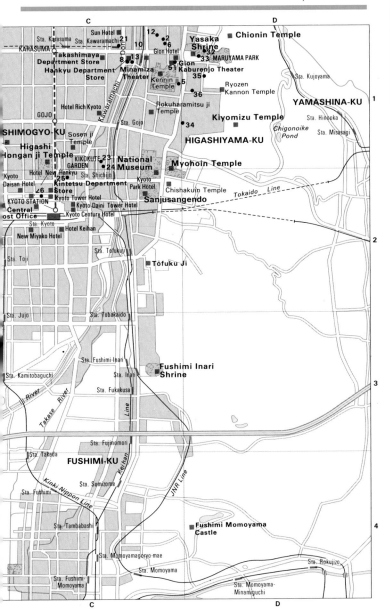

C   D

Sta. Karasuma   Sta. Kawaramachi   Sun Hotel
KARASUMA
Takashimaya
Department Store
Hankyu Department
Store

12
2
6
10
Gion Hotel

■ **Chionin Temple**

21
8 13
Minamiza
Theater
5
Kennin ji
Temple

■ **Yasaka**
Shrine
32
33 ■ **MARUYAMA PARK**
■ **Gion**
Kaburenjo Theater
35

YAMASHINA-KU

Ryozen
Kannon Temple

Sta. Kujoyama

1

Hotel Rich Kyoto
GOJO
SHIMOGYO-KU
Higashi
Hongan ji Temple

Kawaramachi Dori

Sta. Gojo

Sosen ji
Temple

Rokuharamitsu ji
Temple
34

36

Kiyomizu Temple

HIGASHIYAMA-KU

Chigonoike
Pond

Sta. Hinooka
Sta. Misasagi

Kyoto
Daisan Hotel
Hotel New Hankyu
25
KYOTO STATION
Central
Post Office

KIKOKU
GARDEN
23
24
26
Sta. Shichijo
Kinetsu Department
Store
Kyoto Tower Hotel
Kyoto Daini Tower Hotel

■ **National**
Museum
Kyoto
Park Hotel
Chishakuin Temple
Sanjusangendo

Myohoin Temple

Tokaido Line

2

Sta. Kyoto
Hotel Keihan
New Miyako Hotel

Sta. Toji

Kyoto Century Hotel

Sta. Tofukuji

■ **Tōfuku Ji**

Sta. Jujo
Sta. Tobakaido

Takase River

Sta. Kamitobaguchi

Sta. Fushimi-Inari
Sta. Inari
Sta. Fukakusa

Kinki-Nippon Line

■ **Fushimi Inari**
Shrine

3

Sta. Fujinomori
Sta. Takeda
FUSHIMI-KU
Sta. Sumizome
Sta. Fushimi

Keihan Line

JNR Line

Sta. Tambabashi

■ **Fushimi Momoyama**
Castle

4

Sta. Fushimi-
Momoyama

Sta. Momoyamagoryo-mae
Sta. Momoyama

Sta. Rokujizo

Sta. Momoyama-
Minamiguchi

C   D

♦♦ **Tonchinkan**, I, C4, n°5, ☎ 531 0480. Breaded pork.

♦ **Akasatana**, II, C1, n°8, ☎ 255 1920. *Ramen* (noodles).

♦ **Gombei**, II, C1, n°6, ☎ 561 3350. Excellent traditional *soba* (noodles). Try the *anago-soba*.

♦ **Takasebune**, I, C4, n°13, ☎ 351 4032. One of the best and least expensive *tempuraya* (*tempura* restaurant) in Kyoto.

Bars and tearooms

♦♦ **Ishibei**, I, D4, n°14, ☎ 525 0558. A typical bar.

♦♦ **Kagizen Yoshifusa**, I, C4, n°16, ☎ 561-1818. An astonishing tearoom. Tea ceremony and Japanese cakes.

Pastry shops

♦ **Tsukimochiya Naomasa**, I, C4, n°18, ☎ 231 0175. A specialist in *tsukimochi* (moon cakes) — small, round rice cakes in the shape of the moon (*tsuki*). The shop has existed since 1804!

♦ **Umezono**, I, C4, n°17, ☎ 221 5017. This shop sells *mochi* (rice cakes) that have been cooked on skewers over a charcoal fire and then dipped in a sweet sauce. They are very popular in Kyoto.

The East, northern half

Restaurants

♦♦♦ **Minokichi**, I, D4, n°29, ☎ 771 4185. With a view over a magnificent park, this restaurant offers an excellent *Kyo ryori*. It is best to reserve well in advance.

♦♦ **Omen**, I, D3, n°27, ☎ 771 8994. This *udon* (wheat noodle) restaurant is one of a kind. It is so popular that the owner has opened a branch in New York.

♦ **Okutan**, I, D4, n°28, ☎ 771 8709. Near the Nanzenji temple, this is one of the best *tofu* restaurants in Kyoto. The bucolic setting is also unique. Service stops at 5:30pm.

Tearoom

Kanoshoju an, I, D3, n°30, ☎ 751 1077. This tearoom, between the Ginkakuji (Silver Pavilion) and the Honenin temple, holds tea ceremonies at 10am and 3:30pm. Seated on traditional *tatami* (floor mats), clients are served their tea accompanied by *nama-gashi* (red bean pastries).

The East, southern half

Restaurants

♦♦♦♦ **Minoko**, II, D1, n°35, ☎ 561 0328. Another restaurant famous for its delicious *kaiseki ryori* cuisine. Customers eat on *tatami* in a private room with a view of a magnificent garden. An evening meal will cost between ¥10,000 and ¥15,000. At lunch, an *o bento* is inexpensive.

♦♦ **Nakamura Ro**, I, D4, n°33, ☎ 531 3328. This is said to be the oldest restaurant in Japan. In the evening, *kaiseki ryori* is available. Between 11am-3pm, you can order an inexpensive *o bento*.

♦♦♦ **Ashiya**, II, D1, n°34, ☎ 531 3328. An excellent meat restaurant.

♦♦♦ **Hirano Ya**, I, D4, n°32, ☎ 561 1603. This century-old restaurant serves a very original *Kyo ryori*. Try the *ebi-imo* (a potato in the shape of a shrimp) or the *bodara* (a type of fish found only in Japan).

♦ **Ikkyu-an**, II, D1, n°36, ☎ 561 1901. Chinese-style *shojin ryori*. A unique experience for a reasonable price. There is a free view of the Yasaka pagoda.

Tearoom

♦♦ **Bunnosuke Jaya**, II, D1, n°37, ☎ 551 1376. If you have not already tasted *amazake* (a dessert made of sweetened fermented sake lees), this is the ideal place to do so. You can also take part in the tea ceremony while admiring a splendid garden designed by Kobori Enshu, Japan's most famous landscape gardener.

Bars

◆ **Ishibei**, II, C1, n°14, ☎ 525 0558. An excellent and friendly little Japanese bar.

The West, northern half

Restaurants

◆◆ **Plum Creek**, I, A3, n°40, ☎ 461 5524. Grilled foods.

◆◆ **Torin in**, I, A3, n°41, ☎ 463 1334. This is an extraordinary *shojin ryori* restaurant located in the Myoshin ji temple.

◆◆ **Wakadori**, I, B2, n°42, ☎ 722 0771. A traditional Japanese restaurant specializing in chicken but not a normal *yakitoriya* (grilled chicken restaurant). A *kosu* (menu) consists of chicken *sashimi* and five or six delicious other little dishes. Wakadori is five minutes north of the Golden Pavilion. If you take a taxi, ask for the village of Shozan and make sure that you mention *'kinkaku ji no chikaku'* ('next to the Golden Pavilion').

◆ **Izusen**, ☎ 491 6665. In the Daitoku ji temple complex, this is one of the most authentic Zen cuisines (vegetarian) available in Kyoto.

The West, southern half

Restaurants

◆◆◆ **Nishiki**, I, A4, n°45, ☎ 881 8888. This restaurant, with its elegant setting near the water's edge on an island in the Katsura River, offers *kaiseki ryori* for reasonable prices. It is wise to make reservations.

◆◆ **Nishiyama Sodo**, I, A3, n°43, ☎ 861 1609. A feast awaits *tofu* lovers.

◆ **Sagano**, I, A4, n°44, ☎ 871 0277. An incredible restaurant set among bamboo and ancient statues. Try the succulent *yudofu* (*tofu* cooked Kyoto-style).

GETTING AROUND KYOTO

Bus

Buses run every day from 6:30am to 10pm and are the most practical way of getting around Kyoto. With this extensive service, it is possible to get to any of the sites listed below from the main station, **Kyoto Station (Kyoto Eki)**, II, C2, the terminus of all the bus routes in and around town.

Tickets may be bought either beforehand from an automatic distributor or on the bus itself. The fare is generally around ¥160 but may be a little higher for destinations outside the city center. If you plan to stay in Kyoto for several days, it is worth buying a booklet of 10 tickets. You may also purchase for ¥890 a day pass that is valid on both the bus system and Kyoto's single subway line.

To board a bus, get on the back and take a fare-zone ticket (not to be confused with the fare ticket bought before boarding) from the automatic distributing machine. This is marked with the number of the fare zone and will determine how much you owe when you arrive at your destination. You pay just before getting off the bus. To pay, go to the front of the bus and slide both tickets into the machine next to the driver. It is also possible to pay with coins. The machines give change.

The stations are announced in advance. To request a stop, simply press the violet button.

Subway

There is only one subway line in Kyoto, a fact that considerably reduces your chance of getting lost. It goes from Kyoto Eki (or Kyoto Station) to Kitaoji Station, near the botanical gardens to the north of the Imperial Palace. The fare varies from ¥140 to ¥170. The day pass sold for the bus system is also valid on the subway.

Trains run every day from 5:30am-11:30pm.

Renting a car

It is worth having a car for a day or two if you plan to visit Mount Hiei and the scenic region around Lake Biwa.

Nippon Rent-a-Car, ☎ 6810311, is the most important rental agency. Its office is just next to the west exit of Kyoto Station.

Renting a bike

This is a good compromise between walking and taking the bus and is an excellent way to discover the town. There are numerous bicycle rental agencies in Kyoto, including these:

Nippon Rent-A-Cycle, II, C2, is just opposite the Hachijo exit of Kyoto Station.

Rent-a-Cycle Heian is at the intersection of the Karasuma and Shimochojama avenues.

You can also call **Shin and Steve,** ☎ 464 2028, who will gladly deliver a bike to your hotel. Prices range from ¥1,200 to ¥1,500 per day.

▬ NEWSPAPERS

An English-language monthly, *Kansai Time Out,* gives the cultural progam for the entire region (Kyoto, Osaka, Kobe and Nara). It can be obtained at Kyoto's only international bookstore, **Maruzen,** I, C4, on Kawaramachi Dori, between Shijo Dori and Sanjo Dori.

▬ NIGHTLIFE

In Kyoto, nightlife is dominated by geishas and *maiko* who meet their clients in *ryotei* (traditional restaurants) or *zashiki* (reception rooms). Kyoto also has nightclubs and Western-style bars. They are concentrated around Gion and Pontocho, the only districts that are lively at night.

▬ POST OFFICE

The **Central Post Office** in Kyoto, 843-12 Higashi Shiokoji, Shimogyo-ku, II, C2, ☎ 361 4151, is just next to Kyoto Station. It is here that all Poste Restante (General Delivery) should be addressed. Collectors' stamps *(kinen kitte)* are sold on the 2nd floor.

▬ SHOPPING

Kyoto has been a major center for handicrafts of quality for over 1,000 years. Today, the city is best known for its ceramics, lacquerware and fine fabrics — including silk, brocades and *nishijin* (indigo cloth). There are also many other beautiful regional products, including dolls, wooden combs, parasols and bronzes.

Listed below is a selection of traditional shops offering authentic products produced by Kyoto artisans.

The shopping arcades on Shijo Dori, the main avenue in Gion.

Fans

Miyawaki Baisen An, Tominokoji, Nishi iru, Rokkaku Dori, Nakagyo-ku
I, C4, n°22, ☎ 221 0181. *Open daily 9am-5pm*. This shop has specialized
in fans for Noh drama, the tea ceremony, sumo tournaments and geisha
dancers for 150 years.

Japanese prints

Nishimura, Tera machi, Kado, Sanjo Dori, Nakagyo-ku, I, C4, n°19,
☎ 211 2849. *Open daily 1-9pm*. Nishimura is the oldest shop in Kyoto
specializing in *ukiyo-e* prints. Authenticity is guaranteed.

Kimonos (secondhand)

Komachi House, Ichijo-agaru, Inokuma Dori, Kamigyo-ku, I, B3, n°22,
☎ 451 6838. *Open daily 9am-5pm*. A large choice of kimonos at
reasonable prices.

Lacquerware

Monju, Hanamikoji Higashi iru, Minami gawa, Shijo Dori, Higashiyama-ku,
I, C4, n° 51, ☎ 525 1617. *Open Fri-Wed 10am-7:30pm*. If you are not
sure of being able to distinguish fine lacquerware from imitation plastic,
go to Monju. All the objects sold here are guaranteed authentic Kyoto
lacquerware. There is a large selection of platters, boxes and chopsticks
at a wide range of prices.

Paper parasols

Kasagen, 284 Gion machi, Kitagawa, Higashiyama-ku, I, C4, n°52,
☎ 561 2832. Since 1861, Kasagen has sold the most beautiful as well
as the most solid parasols in Kyoto. The handmade paper is oiled to make
it rainproof.

Wooden combs

Jusan Ya, Otabi-cho, Shinkyogoku Higashi iru, Shijo Dori, Shimogyo-ku,
I, C4, n°21, ☎ 221 2008. *Open daily 10am-7pm*. This family business has
made combs since the reign of the Emperor Meiji. They are all handmade
from various types of wood. The store sells mostly to geishas and Kabuki
theater actors.

Dolls

Fuji Kei Shoten, Shimbashi, Nawate Dori, Higashiyama-ku, I, C4, n°50, ☎ 561 7863. *Open daily 10am-6pm.* This is an established shop dealing in both antique and new dolls.

Nakanishi Toku Shoten, 359 Motocho, Yamatooji Higashi iru, Furumonzen Dori, Higashiyama-ku, II, C1, n°49 ☎ 561 7309. *Open daily 10am-6pm.* This is one of the better-stocked shops. It sells dolls from Kyoto *(Kyoningyo)* as well as masks for Noh drama and dolls for the Ningyo Matsuri festival.

Indigo cloth

Aizen Kobo, Omiya Nishi iru, Nakasuji Dori, Kamigyo-ku, I, B3, n°48, ☎ 441 0355. *Open daily 9am-5:30pm.* After visiting the Nishijin Textile Center, not far from the Imperial Palace, you can buy traditional hand-dyed cloth at Aisen Kobo, one of the oldest cloth dealers in the Nishijin district.

Markets

In Kyoto, there are two monthly flea markets:

Toji temple, II, B2. On the 21st of every month. Near Kyoto Station.

Kitano Tenmangu Shrine. On the 23rd of every month. In the north-west part of town (bus 50 or 52 from terminus B2 at Kyoto Station).

A ceramic and porcelain market is held at **Gojozaka** (bus 206 from terminus A2) August 7-10. Pottery may also be bought at any time of the year on **Gojo Dori,** II, C1, between Gojozaka and the Kamo River.

▬ *TELEPHONE*

As in Tokyo, the post office and telephone service are separate organizations. Telephone boxes are the only places to make a call; do not try to phone from the post office (see p. 70).

To call Kyoto, the code is 075 from anywhere in Japan. To call Tokyo from Kyoto, you must dial 03 first and then the number.

▬ *TOURIST INFORMATION*

Whatever your plans are concerning Kyoto, first go to the **Tourist Information Center** (TIC), Kyoto Tower Building, Higashi-Shiokojicho, Shimogyo-ku, II, C1-2, ☎ 371 5649. *Open Mon-Fri 9am-5pm; Sat 9am-noon. Closed holidays.* The TIC is located just opposite Kyoto Station.

The **Japan Travel-Phone** (see p. 72) in Kyoto is operated by the TIC from the number above.

The **Teletourist Service,** ☎ 361 2911, gives prerecorded information in English 24 hours a day on the week's cultural and religious events.

▬ *VISITING A JAPANESE HOME*

As in Tokyo, it is possible to visit a Japanese private home in Kyoto for a few hours. Simply contact the **Kyoto City Government Tourist Section** at least 48 hours in advance: Kyoto Kaikan, Okazaki, Sakyo-ku, ☎ 752 0215. Do not forget to bring a small personal gift from your home country when you visit the family.

GETTING TO KNOW KYOTO

U nlike Tokyo, Kyoto has remained human in scale. Covering a total area of about 230 sq mi/600 sq km, the city is administratively divided into 11 *ku* (wards): Kamigyo-ku, Kita-ku, Nakagyo-ku, Shimogyo-ku, Minami-ku, Ukyo-ku, Sakyo-ku, Higashiyama-ku, Fushimi-ku, Yamashina-ku and Nishikyo-ku.

The principal businesses (department stores, hotels and restaurants) are concentrated in the middle of town, near the intersection of Shijo Dori and Kawaramachi Dori, not far from Kawaramachi Station and the Kamo River.

The street plan of Kyoto is extremely simple: based on early Chinese chessboard models, 10 principal thoroughfares (numbered 1 to 10) traverse the city from east to west, intersected by three large roads running north to south — Horikawa Dori, Karasuma Dori and Kawaramachi Dori. Even if you have no sense of direction you will find it almost impossible to get lost in Kyoto.

You really need a minimum of a week to get to know all the districts of Kyoto. If your time is limited, however, do at least visit the Golden Pavilion (see p. 184), the Ryoanji Zen temple (see p. 184-185) and the Imperial Palace (see p. 179). Also try to reserve an evening for either Gion (see p. 176) or Pontocho (see p. 178), the two geisha districts of the ancient capital.

■■ AROUND THE STATION

Map coordinates refer to the maps pp. 162-163, 166-167.

Staying at a hotel or *ryokan* in the area around Kyoto Station is a wise idea. Centrally located, this district is an ideal base from which to visit the city and the surrounding region. For day trips, there are frequent trains to Nara, Kobe and Osaka, while any destination in Kyoto itself can be reached by bus. The bus terminal is in front of the station.

Another advantage of this district is its proximity to the Tourist Information Center (TIC) where you can get information on hotels, exhibitions, cultural programs, maps and so on (see p. 172).

Start your visit of the town on foot and stroll around the area near Kyoto Station. The **To ji**** (East Temple), II, B2, is less than 0.6 mi/1 km to the south-west of the Karasuma exit. *Open daily 9am-4pm.* Officially called the Kyoogokoku ji, the To ji is located in an extensive park-like enclosure. Founded in AD 796 by the Emperor Kammu, the present temple complex is composed of buildings from various periods and contains one of the largest Momoyama-period buildings in existence. The *kondo* (Main Hall) dates from 1599 and the *hozo* (Treasure Hall) from 1197. The 180 ft/55 m five-storey pagoda, reconstructed in 1644 on the orders of Tokugawa Iemitsu, is the tallest pagoda in Japan. A flea market is held on the 21st of every month.

About 0.6 mi/1 km to the north of Kyoto Station's main exit (Chuo exit) is the **Higashi Hongan ji Temple****, II, C1. *Open daily 9am-4:30pm.* Founded in 1602 by Tokugawa Ieyasu in order to balance the power of the influential Jodo Shinshu sect at the Nishi (West) Hongan ji temple, the Higashi (East) Hongan ji temple is the headquarters of the dissident Otani school of the Jodo Shinshu (True Pure Earth) Buddhist sect.

Japanese religious architecture

The architecture of Japan is fundamentally different from that of the West. Based on wooden columns and beams rather than on masonry arches and vaults, it is less durable and more susceptible to fire but tends to harmonize better with a rural environment.

Shinto shrines

Shinto architecture is based on simple post-and-lintel prehistoric house designs that evolved during the Neolithic period. The shrines are basically rectangular buildings with posts sunk into the ground. Usually built in scenic settings, they range from large national shrines to obscure roadside oratories. They are generally made of raw, undecorated wood and are covered by thatched roofs. Most are dedicated to deities but some honour celebrated historical figures such as Emperor Meiji and General Nogi. Under the influence of Buddhism, Shinto shrines after the Nara period adopted several stylistic features including curved roofs, painted exteriors and ornamented gables. They remained, nevertheless, far less ornate than Buddhist temples.

The typical shrine is composed of two principal units, the *honden* and the *haiden.* The *honden,* or Main Hall, is the inner shrine. According to Shintoism, the deity is present here and only the priest and his attendants are permitted to enter this sacred room. The *haiden* is the oratory and is usually open to the public.

Larger shrine complexes have a *noritoden* (Prayer Hall), *heiden* (Offerings Hall) and *kaguraden* (Liturgical Dance Hall).

The sacred compound is delimited by a simple gate, the *torii.* These ceremonial gateways are distinctively Shinto features. A stylized *torii* is made of raw wood and consists of two vertical wooden posts with a horizontal beam projecting from them and a shorter second beam underneath, butting against the uprights.

Upon entering, worshippers wash their hands and mouths in an ablution basin, the *temizuya.*

Buddhist temples

In Japan, the architectural standards for this originally Indian religion were based on Chinese models. Buddhist temple monasteries in China were solidly framed buildings with tile roofs that stood on masonry terraces. They consisted of a main hall with a courtyard that was entered through a formal gateway. The layout was symmetrical and orientated toward the south. Based on the design of Imperial palaces, the only specifically Buddhist feature of the temple was the pagoda, derived from the Indian *stupa.* Unlike palaces, monasteries of course required quarters for monks and large refectories or *jikido* (Eating Halls).

The temples of the Nara period were copies of Chinese models and built on flat plains near cities. During the Heian period, the new esoteric Tendai and Shingon sects favoured mountain retreats, and a less rigidly symmetrical architectural ideal developed. Due to the heavy rainfall in Japan, covered entrance halls were added, making Japanese temples deeper and darker than their Chinese counterparts.

During the Kamakura period, several new styles of architecture developed that prevailed until modern times: *Wayo* (Japanese or 'native'), a compilation of earlier Japanized styles; *Tenjikuyo* (Indian) with massive roofs; and *Karayo* (Chinese), by far the most eleborate and the one to become standard for Zen halls. Most buildings since the Kamakura period combined these three styles.

During the Muromachi, Momoyama and Edo periods, temples were rebuilt according to the original plans and are frequently careful copies of the former buildings.

Among the buildings found in the temple monastery complexes are: *kondo* (Golden Hall, that is Buddha Hall), *kodo* (Lecture Hall), *kyozo* (Library), *shoro* (Belfry), *daibutsuden* (Great Buddha Hall), *shinden* (sleeping place) and *chaseki* (Teahouse).

The *daishodo* (Founder's Hall), Kyoto's largest wooden building, has the largest wooden roof in the world. It houses a statue of Shinran attributed to the priest himself. In the *hondo* (Main Hall), there is a rope made of women's hair that was used to pull up the wooden beams during the hall's reconstruction in 1895.

The **Nishi (West) Hongan ji Temple****, II, B2, is just opposite the Higashi Hongan ji temple. *Open daily 10am-4:30pm. Guided tours of the inner quarters (the only way to see the interior) are given Sun-Fri 10am, 11am, 1:30pm, 2:30pm; Sat 10am, 11am.*

Ho Onko, the temple festival, is held January 9-16 in this magnificently preserved temple belonging to the Jodo Shinshu sect. The buildings are considered among the finest examples of Buddhist architecture in Japan, and the interiors of the rooms are decorated with paintings from the Kano school.

Just across Horikawa Dori, near the north-east corner of the Nishi Hongan ji, is the **Costume Museum***, 5th floor, Izutsu Building, II, B1. This collection includes originals and replicas of Japanese costumes from the prehistoric period up until the Meiji.

About 0.6 mi/1 km east of Kyoto Station's main exit is the **Rengeoin Temple*****, II, CD2, commonly called the Sanjusangendo. *Open daily 8am-5pm.* Originally founded in 1164, this temple is dedicated to the goddess of compassion, Kannon Bosatsu. The main temple consists of a vast hall 390 ft/119 m long, which is divided into 33 bays (*sanjusangen* means '33'), representing the number of successive reincarnations of Kannon. The temple is known best for the 1001 life-size statues of the goddess that crowd the bays, and for a 10 ft/3 m eleven-headed statue of Kannon Bosatsu in the center of the hall. All these statues date from the 13th century and are the works of such great masters as Unkei, Tankei (Unkei's son), Kozyo and their assistants. All the faces of the smaller statues are different and it is customary to give a donation if you happen to resemble one of them. A large archery contest called *toshiya* is held on January 15.

The **Kyoto National Museum*****, II, C1-2, is located in the northern half of the park, just across Shichijo Dori from the Sanjusangendo. *Open Tues-Sun 9:30am-4:30pm.* Exceptionally rich, the collections contain archaeological material, sculptures and paintings from every period of Japanese art from the prehistoric origins of Japan (*haniwa* of the Kofun culture) to the 17th century (painted screens by Sotatsu, the founder of the Korin school). The museum is particularly well known for its sculpture collections, which are among the best in Japan and cover the Nara, Heian and Kamakura periods. Allow at least two hours for the visit. As in most Japanese museums, the collections are exhibited in rotation due to lack of space.

The **Tofuku ji temple*****, II, C2, is 0.9 mi/1.5 km south-east of Kyoto Station. Take either bus 208 from Terminal A2 or the JR train to Tofukuji Station. *Open daily 9am-4pm.*

Unknown to most tourists, this temple is one of the most refreshing surprises awaiting you in Kyoto. Founded in 1236 by the monk Ben'en, the temple was progressively enlarged during the 14th, 15th and 16th centuries. Apart from the main temple, which was entirely rebuilt in 1911 following a fire, the complex contains three magnificent Zen gardens designed by Shigemori Mire in 1938. The symmetrical composition of the rocks, vegetation and raked sand, is at the same time modern and respectful of Zen traditions. The *sammon* (Main Gate) dates from around 1250 and contains 11th-century Buddhist sculptures said to have been carved by the priest Jocho. The temple also possesses a number of 14th- and 15th-century paintings. A covered bridge spans a deep ravine on a path that leads to the Founder's Hall.

Just in front of Kyoto Station rises the ungainly Kyoto Tower, II, C2 a sort of red-and-white 'lighthouse'. You can climb to the summit (430 ft/131 m) if you wish.

▬ GION AND THE CITY CENTER

Access: Take bus 206 from Terminal A2 at Kyoto Station to the Gion bus stop.

Compared to Tokyo, Kyoto seems very provincial. Even the main avenue, Shijo Dori, with its traffic jams, theaters and shopping arcades, cannot attenuate this impression of a large country market town.

The city center, bisected by the Kamo River, is bound on the south by the Shijo Dori, on the west by Nijojo Castle, on the north by the Imperial Palace and on the east by Maruyama Park. It can easily be covered on foot.

Start at **Gion★★★**, the geisha district. With its old wooden houses, this is one of the most ancient districts in Kyoto and is protected by special laws against disfiguring architectural changes. Formerly the 'pleasure-seeker's quarter', a large number of antique dealers and artisans have more recently installed their shops here.

From the Yasaka shrine with its unmistakable vermilion portal, walk toward the shopping arcades on Shijo Dori. The traditional shops that line this street, as well as the tearooms, restaurants and pastry shops, may be hard to resist. Turn left into Hanamikoji Dori and follow the signs to Gion Corner. The anonymous façades of the buildings frequently hide *zashiki* (teahouses where geisha entertain their clients) or *machiya* (courtyards grouping several houses with a common central alley).

Gion Corner★, I, C4, is a theater for tourists. Performances take place twice a day. The show is a compilation of different Japanese arts: *bunraku* (see p. 48), the tea ceremony, court music and the like, all of dubious authenticity.

Geishas

Contrary to popular belief, geishas are not prostitutes. They are primarily performing artists (*gei* meaning 'art'; *sha* meaning 'person') who know how to dance and play traditional instruments (*koto* and *shamisen*) to perfection. Most of the time, their role consists of enlivening a gathering of gentlemen by punctuating the conversation with witty remarks or proposing various divertissements (sometimes slightly erotic) to the guests.

The evening is expensive. A large part of the money goes directly to the school in order to support the singing and dancing lessons given throughout the year. Since the end of the World War II, the number of geishas has been in constant decline. In Gion, there are now only 140, of which 20 are *maiko* (apprentice geisha). The majority of geishas do not earn a living by the price of the entertainment which barely covers their expenses (kimono, coiffeur and so forth) but from the generosity of *danna-san* (sponsors). This tradition dates back to when the geishas were bought and owned in order to escape prostitution.

For the non-Japanese, it is not always easy to arrange an evening with a geisha. However, many of them speak English and do not systematically refuse foreigners. If the price does not dash your hopes, contact the Tourist Information Center or your hotel for a list of *ryotei* (traditional restaurants) where geishas are found. For a party of four to six people, two geishas and a *maiko* are generally required.

Every year from May 1 to 24 and October 15 to November 7, the geishas of Gion dance the Kamogawa Odori (River Dance) at the Pontocho Kaburenjo Theater, located at the end of Pontocho. In April, the *maiko* come to dance in the Gion Kaburenja — a tradition that is over a century old.

A geisha in Gion: the neck is considered the most erotic part of the body.

Just behind the theatre is the **Kennin ji temple****, I, C4. *Open only in the morning. It is necessary to ask permission to visit it at least 24 hours in advance (contact the TIC, p. 71).* Founded in 1202 by the priest Eisai (1141-1215) after his second visit to China, this was Kyoto's first Zen temple, and is thus the oldest in Japan. All that remains of its original form, however, is the Chokushimon (Imperial Messenger's Gate). The *hojo* (Superior's Quarters), dating to the 14th century, actually comes from a temple near Hiroshima and was moved here in the 18th century. The temple contains a number of National Treasures, including several painted scrolls. The Ryosoku gardens belong to the temple and are well worth the visit; Eisai, the founder of Zen Buddhism, is buried here.

On the other side of Shijo Dori is a much more modern Gion, where nightclubs, Turkish baths and 'love hotels' are legion. It is not a dangerous or even shady neighbourhood and it is quite safe to stroll down the streets at night amid flashing neon ideograms to discover the *mizu-shobai* (water commerce, or those who work in bars).

Continue down Shijo Dori to the **Minamiza Theater,** I, C4, the oldest theater in Japan. Performances, including kabuki, are held throughout the year. As the center of the district, it provides an excellent meeting place.

Cross the bridge and turn down the first street on the right. This is **Pontocho*****, I, C4, a charming district of restaurants and teahouses wedged between the Kamo River and the Takasegawa Canal.

Continue down the Shijo Dori to its intersection with Kawaramachi Dori, I, C4. This is the second most important road in town. The two largest department stores in Kyoto, Hankyu and Takashimaya, are not far away.

A little farther down on the right is a double arcade, **Shinkyogoku****, I, C4. As busy as Pontocho, this area is, however, much more commercial. In the second arcade is **Daishodo,** a bookstore that specializes in *ukiyo-e* and old books. If you are hungry, try **Izumo,** a *sushi* restaurant just opposite the bookstore.

Nearby is **Nishikikoji Dori*****, I, C4, a fascinating covered market that sells a great variety of fish, vegetables and condiments totally unknown in the West.

End your tour of the city center with a visit to **Nijo Castle*****, I, B3-4. *Open daily 8:45am-4pm.* It is five minutes by taxi or bus from Pontocho. As the monument is very popular, arrive early in the morning to avoid the crowds.

This impressive structure dates from 1603 and was built by Kobori Enshu on the order of Tokugawa Ieyasu. Because it was the official Kyoto residence of the Tokugawa shogunate, several shoguns resided here until the abdication of the Tokugawa clan in 1867. It was here that the Emperor symbolically issued the proclamation abolishing the shogunate. The following year, the Nijo Castle became the seat of the new Imperial government. When the Emperor moved his capital to Edo the following year, it became the seat of the Kyoto Prefecture which it remained until 1884. Since 1893, the castle has belonged to the municipality. Now an historic monument, it is open to the public.

The Nijo Castle consists of five principal buildings spread out among the gardens. The Ninomaru (Main Palace) is a National Treasure. Almost all the rooms were decorated by 16th-and 17th-century masters (Hidari Jongoro, Kano Sanraku, Kano Tanyu, Kano Naonobu, Kano Koi). In the *O Hiroma* room, a small wax museum has been installed. The scene represents a shogun giving orders to *daimyo* dressed in costumes from different provinces of Japan. The palace garden was designed by Kobori Enshu and is among the best in Japan.

Although it is called a castle (*jo* means 'castle'), the Nijo is reallly a luxurious palace with very few military defense works. A more subtle form of protection — from intrigue rather than from invasion — was required in feudal Japan. Master carpenters developed the infamous *uquisubari* (bush warbler or nightingale floors) that 'chirped' when walked on, thus indicating the presence of intruders. Made of *hinoki* (Japanese cypress), the technique of their construction is now lost.

THE IMPERIAL TOUR

Although the emperor has not lived in Kyoto since 1868, the former residences of the Imperial family have remained sacred. Written permission is necessary to visit the three Imperial sites in Kyoto: the Imperial Palace, the Katsura Imperial Villa and the Shugakuin Imperial Villa. Authorization can be obtained easily from the **Imperial Household Agency**, I, C3, situated west of the Seisho Mon, the entrance gate to the palace. Come to the agency with your passport 30 minutes before the palace tour in order to fill out an application form. For groups of 10 or more, apply at least 24 hours in advance. At the same time, you may also choose the days to visit the Imperial Villas. For all three sites, escorted tours are obligatory but entirely free of charge.

Imperial Palace (Kyoto Gosho)*** I, C3

Open Mon-Fri at 10am and 2pm (for individuals) and 11:30am and 3:30pm (for groups of 10 or more). Closed Sat afternoon, Sun, holidays, and Dec 25-Jan 5.

Access: From Kyoto Station, take either bus 2 or bus 36 to the Imperial Palace or the subway to Imadegawa Station.

Set like a jewel in the heart of a magnificent 208-acre/84-hectare park, most of the Imperial Palace is inaccessible to the public. Escorted by an interpreter and a guard, visitors are allowed only to circulate between a few of the buildings, the ones with doors left open so that the interiors can be seen. Among the rooms exhibited are: the Shodaibu no ma (Dignitaries Room), the Seiryo den (Hall of Ceremonies), the Shishin den (Main Hall and Coronation Room),the Gogakumonjo (Hall for Poetry Readings) and the Otsune Gote (Imperial Apartments).

The first Imperial Palace was built in AD 794 when Kyoto (then called Heiankyo) replaced Nara as the Imperial capital. Destroyed by fire on numerous occasions, the palace was rebuilt in the original Heian style in 1788 on the present site. It burned down again in 1854. The present structure dates from 1855. The emperors of Japan lived here until the Imperial Restoration of 1868, when they moved to Tokyo. The highlight of the visit is the *Oike no niwa*, a Japanese garden. The palace gives an idea of what Kyoto must have looked like during the Chinese-inspired Heian period, before the houses were built closely together and the city became crowded.

The **Sento Gosho** (Palace of the Retired Emperors), to the south of the Imperial Kyoto Palace, requires a separate authorization from the Imperial Household Agency. Originally built in 1600 for the retired Emperor Gomizuno, it was entirely destroyed in 1708, rebuilt, and then destroyed again before its final completion in 1854. The Emperor himself designed the gardens of the Sento Gosho under the supervision of the famous landscape architect Kobori Enshu. It is one of the most beautiful gardens in Japan.

Katsura Imperial Villa (Katsura Rikyu)*** II, A2

Access: From Kyoto Station, take bus 33 or bus 60 from Terminal C6 to Katsura Rikyu Mae Station.

Written permission to visit the Katsura Imperial Villa must be obtained in advance from the Imperial Household Agency (see above).

Built on the banks of the Katsura River for Toshihito Hachijo (1579-1629), the younger brother of the Emperor Go Yozei (1571-1617), the Katsura Imperial Villa is the work of Kobori Enshu. Considered the best villa of its period with the most perfect Japanese garden, its conception was entirely novel at the time; the design of its garden marked a major step in the development of Japanese gardens. Even today the Katsura Villa is an important reference for anyone interested in landscape architecture; it has had a profound effect on American post-war architecture. Its style, called *shibui*, is elegant and simple; every element is considered and yet appears natural. Entirely designed for visual effects, the villa consists of several pavilions, each with a particular purpose: flowers in the garden can be admired from the Shoka Tei (tea pavilion), while the moon can be contemplated from the *shoin*, or the main building. Extraordinarily well preserved, the Katsura Rikyu is a gem of Japanese heritage. Numerous buildings, including the Hall for Imperial visits, a moon-viewing platform, a teahouse and living quarters, were built between 1620 and 1624. In 1642, the main house was extended by Prince Toshitada in the same sober style as the other buildings.

Shugakuin Imperial Villa (Shugakuin Rikyu)*** I, D1

Access: From Kyoto Station, take bus 5 from Terminal A1 to Shugakuin Rikyu Michi Station.

Built on the site of a former Buddhist temple, the Shugakuin (learning) Imperial Villa lies at the foot of Mount Hiei. It was commissioned by the Tokugawa shogunate for the retired Emperor Gomizuno (1596-1680) when he abdicated in 1629. The Emperor himself drew up the plans for these tea pavilions under the direction of Kobori Enshu. There are three pavilions, each with its own garden. The Shimo no chaya (Lower Villa) is an 1824 replica of the original structure. The Naka no chaya (Middle Villa) was built for the Emperor's daughter and contains the House of Bliss, famous for its paintings. The Kami no chaya (Upper Villa) is of particular interest for its gardens — less formal and austere than most Zen-inspired gardens. From the Cloud Pavilion in the Upper Villa, there is a magnificent view of the central lake and grounds, extending as far as Kyoto and the surrounding hills. Here again, the villa demonstrates Japanese genius for organizing form and space.

▬ THE NORTH-EAST

The path that leads from Ginkaku ji (Silver Pavilion) to the Nanzen ji Temple is frequently called the 'path of enlightenment' due to the fact that for centuries monks from the nearby temples have been coming to meditate here. Every year millions of lay people also make this pilgrimage — usually at the beginning of April when the cherry trees are in bloom.

Traditionally, the walk starts at the Silver Pavilion and proceeds south toward the city center, but there is no reason not to do it backward starting at the Heian shrine.

The Silver Pavilion (Ginkaku ji)*** I, D3

Open daily 9am-4:30pm.

Access: take bus 5 from Terminal A1 at Kyoto Station to Ginkaku ji Michi bus stop. Walk up the Higashi-Imadegawa Dori to the Jisho ji temple, the Buddhist temple that contains the Silver Pavilion.

The Silver Pavilion was built for Shogun Ashikaga Yoshimasa in 1482 after he fell from power. On abdicating, the retired dictator devoted his life entirely to leisure and art, staging incense-burning parties, watching the moon, viewing flowers and generally indulging in the most refined pleasures. His taste for luxury was such that he planned to cover the pavilion with silver to compete with the Golden Pavilion, constructed by his grandfather, Ashikaga Yoshimitsu. Although he died before putting the project into effect, the name has remained ever since. Upon his death, the building became a Buddhist temple, the Ginkaku ji. The garden, one of the best in Kyoto, was designed by Soami, a famous artist of the times. One section contains piles of sand to be viewed by the moonlight!

After leaving the Silver Pavilion, visit the **Sonso gardens.** *Open 10am-5pm.* The house, dating from 1916, formerly belonged to the painter Kansatsu Hashimoto. You will be served a cup of ceremonial tea accompanied by cakes in a traditional room covered with *tatami*. The view of the garden and pond is exceptional.

Honenin* I, D3

This pleasant little temple is dedicated to the monk Honen Shonin, founder of the large Jodo (Pure Land) Buddhist sect. Honen devoted his life to making Amidist Buddhism a religion of the common people. He taught that faith, and not wisdom, was the way to salvation.

The present structure, formerly part of Hideyoshi's castle in Fushimi, was given by the Tokugawa shogunate to the temple shortly after it was founded in 1640. It is not always possible to visit the interior of the temple; the hours and days vary. The simple gardens contain beds of raked sand, stone lanterns and azaleas.

Zenrin ji (Eikan do)** I, D4

Open daily 9am-4pm.

This temple was founded in AD 856 but is named after the monk Eikan, who lived during the 11th century. The present structures date from the 15th century. The temple is most famous for its statue of Buddha Amida, the *Mikaeri no Amida* (Amida 'looking back'). This depicts Amida looking over his shoulder — a very rare posture explained by the legendary meeting of Buddha and Eikan. One day, while the monk was praying, he became aware that Buddha was sitting next to him. Taken aback, he stopped praying. Buddha then turned toward him and asked, 'Why have you stopped praying, Eikan?' The monk answered that he merely wished to make sure that he was not dreaming.

You can visit the various rooms of the temple, climb up the pagoda, and see a magnificent view of Kyoto. The gardens alone are worth the visit, particularly in autumn.

Nanzen ji *** I, D4

Open daily 9am-4:30pm.

The Nanzen ji (Temple of Enlightenment), one of the most important monasteries in Kyoto, belongs to the austere Zen Rinzai sect. The original temple was founded in 1291 when the Emperor Kamenaya (1259-1305) donated a large villa that he had had built on the site. The oldest structures still standing date from the 16th century.

The *hondo* (Main Hall) was rebuilt after a fire in 1895. The *daihojo* (Great Superior's Quarters) was moved here from the Imperial Palace in 1611 and is classified as a National Treasure, while the *shohojo* (Smaller Superior's Quarters), with the famous Tiger Rooms, came from Hideyoshi's castle in Fushimi. The temple houses several famous painted *fusuma* (sliding doors) of the Kano school as well as a Heian-period statue of Kannon, the goddess of Compassion. The ceiling of the Sammon (Great Gate), dated to 1628, is decorated with paintings of the Kano and Tosa schools.

The grounds, planted with cedars, contain 12 sub-temples scattered on the unspoiled, wooded mountainside. Three sub-temples can be visited, including the Konchiin, with its beautiful 17th-century garden designed by Kobori Enshu, and the Nanzenin, with a landscape garden dating from the 14th century.

Heian Shrine (Heian Jingu)** I, D3

Open daily 8:30am-5pm.

The Heian Jingu was erected in 1895 to commemorate the 1100th anniversary of the founding of Heiankyo (ancient Kyoto). Built in pure Heian style, this brightly coloured shrine is a 60% scale reduction of the original AD 794 Imperial Palace. The shrine is dedicated to Emperor Kammu (AD 736-805) and Emperor Komei (1831-67), respectively, the first and last emperors to reside in Kyoto. The huge 75-ft/23-m *torii* (portal) at the entrance of the shrine is the largest in Japan. In 1976, considerable damage resulted from a fire of mysterious origin.

From Heian Jingu, it is possible to take bus 5 or bus 206 to the city center or to Kyoto Station.

THE SOUTH-EAST

Higashiyama-ku, not far from the center of town, offers the tourist with a tight schedule the chance to see as much as possible in a short time. In two hours, you will see five temples — including some of the most famous — a pagoda and a shrine. There are also a number of souvenir shops along the way.

Start your visit at the Kiyomizu temple and slowly work your way toward the Heian shrine.

Kiyomizu Temple*** II, D1

Open daily from sunrise to sunset.

Access: Take bus 206 from Terminal A2 at Kyoto Station to the Kiyomizu Michi bus stop.

The Kiyomizu Temple (or Seisui ji), founded in AD 798 at the request of the priest Enchin, belongs to the Hosso sect. The present buildings were erected in 1633 on the orders of Tokugawa Iemitsu. Perched on the slopes of Mount Kiyomizu, this temple is best known for its *hondo* (Main Hall), built on pillars and overhanging a cliff. From its wide veranda, there is a superb view of Kyoto. Dedicated to the goddess Kannon Bosatsu (Kannon-of-the-Eleven-Heads), the temple's Treasury contains a statue of the Eleven-Faced-Thousand-Armed goddess that is exposed only once every 33 years (next time in 1997) and is traditionally attributed to Enchin. There is an interesting *shoro* (belfry) with a bell that was cast in 1478. The gardens of this popular temple are particulary appreciated during the cherry blossom season and in the autumn. Worshippers come here to pray to the goddess of Compassion for safe childbirth — and for divine punishment to rain down on their enemies!

Going north you will pass the **Yasaka shrine***, II, D1. Originally constructed in 1440 by Ashikaga Yoshinori, the present five-storey structure, rebuilt in 1618, measures 128 ft/39 m high and was formerly used to watch troop movements.

A little farther on is the **Ryozen Kannon Temple***. The main point of interest is the 79 ft/24 m cement statue of the goddess Kannon. This colossus, erected in 1955, is dedicated to the unknown soldier of World War II.

Kodai ji** II, D1

Open daily 9am-4pm.

This temple was founded in 1606 by Toyotomi Hideyoshi's widow, Yodogimi (1569-1615), in memory of her husband. The *kaisando* (Founder's Hall) possesses early-17th-century paintings of the Kano and Tosa schools. A mortuary chapel, built in the same year, is decorated in *tatamaki-e* (three-dimensional lacquerwork). The Omotemon (Main Gate) was brought here from Hideyoshi's castle in Fushimi. The gardens were designed by Kobori Enshu.

Maruyama Park and Yasaka Jinja*** II, D1

Covering 25 acres/10 hectares, Maruyama Park is the largest public park in Kyoto. Spread out on the slopes of Higashi Yama, it contains two huge temples and a famous shrine as well as many restaurants and souvenir shops. Particulary beautiful in April when the cherries bloom, it attracts large numbers of Kyotoites in the spring. Gion Matsuri, Japan's largest festival, takes place here on July 16.

The Yasaka Jinja, also called the Gion shrine, was founded in AD 876, but the present buildings date to 1654. The main shrine is the namesake of the Gion style. The shingles are made of *hinoki* (Japanese cypress), Japan's most-prized wood. The Treasury contains two interesting 13th-century wooden statues of Komainu (a mythological dog-lion). The stone *torii*, dating from 1646, is one of the largest granite examples in Japan. Both Gion Matsuri and Okera Mairi (the New Year's Eve fire-lighting ceremony) are celebrated here.

Chionin** II, D1

Open daily 9am-5pm.

Founded in 1234 by the priest Genchi, the present temple buildings date from 1633. The Chionin is the headquarters of the powerful Jodo (Pure Land) Buddhist sect, one of the most important in Japan. The founder of this sect, who is buried on the grounds, was Honen Shonin (1133-1212), also known as Genku. His statue, believed to be a self-portrait, stands in the Miedo, the temple's most important building. The Chionin is an active temple and not just a museum, and you have every chance of observing Buddhist ritual in practice.

The Sammon (Main Gate), built in 1619, is 79 ft/24 m high and is the tallest in Japan. Surmounted by an upper storey, it is the most perfect example of its kind. The other curiosity of this temple is an enormous 74-ton bell, the largest in Japan. Cast in the 17th century, it is 17 ft/5 m high and 9 ft/2.7 m in diameter. Seventeen bell-ringers are required to put it into motion during the festival in honour of Honen's birth (April 19-25). Paintings of the Kano school may be seen in the *hojo* (Superior's Quarters). The gardens were designed by Kobori Enshu in 1644. The parquet of the corridor behind the Miedo is *uguisubari* (nightingale flooring) — designed to warn the warrior-monks against intruders.

Shorenin** I, D4

To the north of Chionin, the Shorenin temple, also known as the Awata Palace, was once the headquarters of the Tendai Buddhist sect. The present buildings are of recent construction. The *hondo* (Main Hall) houses several painted *fusuma* (folding screens) of the Kano school. The splendid gardens, designed by Soami and Kobori Enshu, are the highlight of the visit and should not be missed on any account.

Return on foot to the city center by Sanja Dori. In the extreme south-east corner of Kyoto is the Daigo ji Temple.

Daigo ji (Samboin)** II, D4 (off map)

Open daily 9am-4pm.

Access: From the center of town, take the JR Line from Kyoto Station to Rokojizo Station and then bus 26 to the Daigo bus stop.

The Daigo ji Temple, founded in AD 874 by Shobo (AD 832-909), belongs to the Shingon sect. It has several interesting features, including one of the most famous landscape gardens in Japan.

The pagoda, normally closed to the public, contains several important Heian-period paintings including the oldest known mandala on wood. Other works of art from the Heian, Kamakura and Muromachi periods (mostly Buddhist paintings and sculptures and a fine collecton of *sutra* and calligraphy) can be seen in the Reihokan (Sacred Treasury), which is open only in October, November, April and May.

The Samboin Villa, built by Toyotomi Hideyoshi, is a perfect example of 17th-century architecture. The Momoyama-style garden contains several teahouses, of which the Chinryutei (Pillow-on-the-Stream-Teahouse) and Shogetsutei (Moonlit-Pines Teahouse) are the best known. There is also a smaller dry garden and the Fujito Stone, the most legendary stone in Japan and the subject of a Noh play. It was instrumental in the death of an innocent fisherman and is said to have brought a curse on the powerful Minamoto clan.

The Junhokan, a building specifically designed for entertainment, is set near a small stream that was used to float cups of sake and love poems from person to person as they sat on the rocks and socialized.

THE NORTH-WEST

North-western Kyoto also contains a large concentration of monuments in a relatively small area. A full day, however, is needed to visit this part of town.

Start at the Daitoku ji, to the north, and walk toward the Golden Pavilion and the Ryoan ji. The latter contains the most famous Zen garden in Japan.

Daitoku ji*** I, B2

Open daily 9am-5pm.

Access: take bus 205 from Terminal B3 at Kyoto Station to the Daitoku ji mae bus stop.

The Daitoku ji (Great Virtue Temple), founded in 1319 by the priest Daito Kokushi (1282-1337) at the request of Emperor Go-Daigo (1287-1338), belongs to the Rinzai Zen Buddhist sect. The temple burned once in 1453 and again in 1468. Most of the present buildings date from the 16th and 17th centuries. Spread over 27 acres/11 hectares, the Daitoku ji is an active temple complex of 23 sub-temples, seven of which can be visited. Each sub-temple has a separate entrance fee. (The temple administration has been criticized for the commercialization of the complex.)

If you have time to see only one sub-temple, go to the Daisenin temple. It contains painted *fusuma* (sliding doors) of the Kano school in the *hojo* (Superior's Quarters) and has three very fine Zen *karesansui* (dry gardens). Attributed to Soami, these gardens are among the best-known in Japan.

The Butsuden (Buddha Hall) of the Main Temple, dating from 1664, is a fine example of Zen architecture. Well worth visiting, it contains a superb collection of statues of Buddha, including an imposing statue of Shaka (the historical Buddha) in addition to a ceiling painted by the Kano school.

The Hoshunin sub-temple is known for its garden (designed by Kobori Enshu) and for a magnificent pavilion built in 1617, the Donko Kaku.

Within the Daitoku ji temple complex there is a Zen restaurant, **Isuzen** (see p. 169), serving authentic Buddhist vegetarian cuisine.

Golden Pavilion (Kinkaku ji)*** I, B2

Open daily 9am-5pm.

Access: the road that leads from the Daitoku ji Temple to the Golden Pavilion is not very interesting. Hail a taxi or take bus 12. The distance is under a mile / 1500 m.

Set beside a large pond at the foot of Mount Kinugasa, the Golden Pavilion was constructed in 1394 as a retreat for retired shogun Ashikaga Yoshimitsu (1358-1408) but later became a Buddhist temple, the Rokuon ji (popularly called the Kinkaku ji). The building survived over 500 years of tumultuous Japanese history, only to be deliberately set on fire in 1950 by a deranged young monk who subsequently committed suicide. The present structure is an exact replica of the original Muromachi-period building and dates from 1955. The pavillion was recovered with gold foil in 1987. The gardens contain the famous 17th-century Sekka Tei tea pavilion built by Emperor Gomizuno-o.

Ryoan ji*** I, A2

Open daily 8am-5pm.

Access: from the Golden Pavilion, it is easy to walk the 0.7 mi/1200 m to the Ryoan ji Temple. If you are in a hurry, take a taxi; there are no direct buses.

The Golden Pavilion (Kinkaku ji), an exact replica of the original 14th-century construction, is a superb example of delicacy and balance in architecture.

The Ryoan ji (Peaceful Dragon Temple), originally founded in 1473, was rebuilt on numerous occasions following wars and fires. The *karesansui* (Zen dry garden) of the Ryoan ji is considered the most perfect Zen garden ever designed. Attributed to Soami (1472-1523), it is a rock-and-sand garden composed of 15 rocks in five groups, skillfully placed in a bed of raked white sand. The scenery changes as soon as you move, and only 14 of the rocks are visible at any one time. Conceived for meditation, it has lost much of its appeal due to excessive commercialization.

The Ryoan ji is also a temple in its own right. There are numerous paintings in the temple buildings, and the grounds (covering 100 acres/40 hectares) contain landscape and moss gardens, groves of trees, a lake dug in the 12th century and a giant *moku-gyo* (wooden gong).

Under no circumstances should you miss this masterpiece. It is best to visit this temple, however, on a weekday (provided it is not a public holiday). You will avoid the inevitable Japanese weekend 'group meditation'.

Ninna ji* I, A2

Open daily 9am-5pm.

The Ninna ji, also called the Omuro Palace, is 880 yd/800 m south-west of the Ryoan ji.

Most of the buildings are 20th-century copies of the Momoyama-style originals that were built in AD 886. Apart from its garden and the Ryokaku Tei tea pavilion, the Ninna ji Temple is not of great interest to the tourist.

Myoshin ji* I, B3

Open daily 9:10am-3:40pm.

The Myoshin ji is a 20 minute walk to the south-east of the Ninna ji.

Founded in 1337 on the site of an Imperial Villa, this huge monastery and its sub-temples — the largest Zen headquarters in Japan — belong to the Rinzai Zen Buddhist sect. It is crammed with works of art, including numerous paintings of the Kano school, particularly 16th-century landscapes and various works depicting episodes in Chinese history. The bell of the *shoro* (belfry), cast in AD 698, is the oldest in Japan.

Uzumasa Eiga Mura** (Movie Village) I, A3

Open daily 9am-5pm; in winter 9:30am-4pm.

Access: take bus 61, 62 or 63 from the Myoshin ji temple to the Hachigaoka Cho bus stop.

The Movie Village is unique in Japan. This curiosity belongs to the Toei Company, one of the major Japanese filmmaking firms. In order to produce samurai films ('easterns'), an entire village of the Edo period has been constructed in traditional Japanese style. With a bit of luck, you can watch a battle charge of armoured soldiers or the suicide of a weeping geisha. You can also visit the miniature towns and the little museum that explains special effects, and then take your pick of the many restaurants on the set. There are also numerous activites for children.

Koryu ji*** I, A4

Open daily 9:30am-4pm.

Just to the south-west of the Movie Village, is the Koryu ji Temple (also called the Uzumasa Dera), most famous for its important collection of early wooden sculptures.

The temple was founded in AD 622 by Hata Kawatsu in honour of Prince Shotoku (AD 572-621). The *kodo* (Lecture Hall), dating from 1165, is the second-oldest surviving structure in Kyoto. It contains three important wooden statues, one of Buddha and two of Kannon. The Taishido, built in 1720, houses the alleged self-portrait of Prince Shotoku, said to have been carved in AD 606 when he was 33 years old. The Keiguin, built in 1251, contains another self-portrait of the prince, this time at the age of 16, and images of Amida and Nyoirin Kannon. The Reihokan (Treasury) houses numerous wooden statues of the Heian period, including the famous Miroku Bosatsu, the oldest sculpture in Kyoto. Classified as the most precious of all National Treasures, it dates from the Asuka period (AD 552-710) and represents Buddha-of-the-future. The strong Korean features of the work indicate that it may have come from the Korean kingdom of Silla.

From the Koryu ji, you can take bus 71, 72 or 73 back to Kyoto Station.

▬▬ *THE SOUTH-WEST*

You will need at least two days in order to visit this part of town. A morning should be spent at the Daikaku ji temple, an entire day in Arashiyama — which deserves even more time — and half a day at least at the famous Kokedera moss garden. To visit the Kokedera, you must make arrangements with the Saiho ji Temple at least five days in advance (see below).

Daikaku ji*** I, A3

Open daily 9am-4:30pm.

Access: take bus 28 from Terminal C4 at Kyoto Station to the Daikaku ji bus stop.

Founded in AD 876 by the Emperor Junna on the site of an older Imperial Villa, this temple is famous for its five Buddhist statues, attributed to Kobo Daishi (AD 774-835). It also contains several paintings of the Kano school. Its garden alone, one of the oldest in Japan, is worth the visit. Blending harmoniously with the hills of Arashiyama, its design was inspired from the Chinese landscape around Lake Dongtinghu.

Arashiyama I, A4

Open daily 8:30am-5pm.

Access: take bus 28 from either Kyoto Station or, in the other direction, from the Daikaku ji temple to Arashiyama.

At the foot of Mount Arashiyama (1230ft/375m), the town spreads out on both banks of the Hozu River at a point where the torrent emerges from a gorge and becomes the Katsura River. Here, amid groves of pine, maple and cherry trees, the waters widen out and form a narrow lake. Boating is possible, either on the calm lake waters or on the famous Hozu rapids, and there are also hot springs. If you can ignore the burgeoning commerciality of kabab venders, boat-renters, and so on, you will find the spot relatively well preserved. It is pleasant just to wander in the surrounding forest, and in Iwadeyama Park, where monkeys freely roam the slopes. Around Arashiyama Station, bicycles can be rented for around ¥800 per day.

● **Kyoto Arashiyama Museum (Kyoto Arashiyama Hakubutsukan)****, 33-22 Tsukurimichi-cho, Tenryuji, Saga, Ukyo-ku. *Open Tues-Sun 9am-4pm.*

The museum is divided into two parts. One section contains an important collection of ancient armour, helmets, swords, halberds and other weapons as well as a fine collection of ornate lacquerware. The other section contains oddities from World War II, including old machine guns, a Kamikaze plane, a gun barrel from a sunken Japanese battleship, a midget suicide submarine and the only Zero fighter plane in Japan (fished out of Lake Biwa in 1978).

● **Tenryu ji*****, *Open daily 9am-5pm.*

The Tenryu ji (Celestial Dragon Temple), one of the five major Zen temples in Kyoto, was founded in 1339 by Shogun Ashikaga Takauji in honour of Emperor Go Daigo (1287-1338). All the present buildings are modern, but the magnificent Muromachi-style garden with a 'dry waterfall' of rocks and a little pond in the shape of the ideogram *kokoro* (heart, mind or spirit) should not be missed. The garden is attributed to Soseki (1271-1346), who also designed the famous moss gardens at the Saiho ji Temple.

Japanese gardens

Japanese gardens developed as a response to the 'sacred space' around the temples. Although their form and philosophy have evolved over the centuries, certain immutable concepts are common to all of Japan's great gardens.

In general, Japanese gardens are intended to stylize natural landscapes and at the same time blend into the surrounding environment, separated from it only by a low wall or a row of trees. This trend is typified by the Zen *shibumi* school, with its nearly imperceptible subtleties. Except for the Chinese-influenced *shinden* gardens of the Heian period, traditional Japanese gardens are never symmetric and its flowers are never planted. On the other hand, the few trees they do contain are carefully pruned. Frequently, the overall pattern of the garden or the central lake may evoke an animal or an ideogram, such as a heart.

Historically, records show that Imperial palaces had gardens by the 5th century and that by the 6th century 'the art of gardening' had been introduced from the Asian mainland. The oldest known Japanese gardens developed around AD 710 at the beginning of the Nara period. Inspired by Chinese models, they represented a scene set around a central lake. Unfortunately, there are no surviving examples of this type. During the Heian period (AD 794-1185), small bridges were added, straddling the streams that serpentined between the various pavilions scattered around the garden. The Byodoin in Uji (to the south of Kyoto) is one of the few survivors of this style.

The militarism that prevailed during the Kamakura period (1185-1333) heavily influenced the philosophy of the garden, and the art of gardening greatly increased. Under the influence of Zen Buddhism, the strolling garden fell from favour, and garden retreats (such as the Daitoku ji in Kyoto) were designed for meditation and religious contemplation. This trend reached its climax with the Zen-inspired dry gardens of the Muromachi (1333-1573) and Momoyama (1573-1603) periods. Both the famous Kokedera moss garden and the Ryoan ji garden in Kyoto date from this era. Zen, the tea ceremony, meditative gardens and flower arranging are oddly enough all associated with the militarism of the Kamakura period.

Under the influence of Kobori Enshu (1579-1647), a master of the tea ceremony and a great landscape architect, another style of garden developed — the *cha-seki* (tea garden). These gardens revolutionized the philosophy of Japanese gardening. They consist of numerous pavilions for the tea ceremony *(chanoyu)* linked by skilfully arranged winding paths. The Katsura Imperial Villa in Kyoto is a masterpiece of this classical style.

The center of garden design gradually shifted from Kyoto to Edo, and the Edo period (1603-1868), geared entirely toward pleasure, reinstated the strolling garden. There was even a utilitarian development of duck ponds and gardens for military supplies (such as reeds for arrows). Larger than the gardens of the previous periods, these strolling gardens somewhat resemble Western parks. The major difference is their layout; Classical Western gardens play on perspective, while Japanese gardens depend on visual diversity and change. The Imperial Palace at Kyoto, which dates from 1790, is a prototype of this Edo style. Public parks were encouraged after 1873 and provided safety for tens of thousands during the Great Kano earthquake in 1923.

Since the Meiji period (1868-1912), Western influence has been so strong that very few pure Japanese gardens were created. The Tofuku ji in Kyoto, designed in 1938, is a major exception to this rule.

Some of the more impressive gardens in Kyoto are: Daichi ji, Imperial Palace, Jonangu, Katsura Rikyu, Nijo Castle, Ryoan ji, Saiho ji, Tenryu ji and Tofuku ji.

The Kokedera garden in Kyoto contains more than one hundred different types of moss.

Saiho ji (Kokedera)*** II, A1

Open daily 9am-5pm. Written permission is required.

Access: take bus 73 from Kyoto Station (in front of the post office) to the Kokedera bus stop. There is only one bus per hour. It generally leaves at a quarter to the hour and the journey takes about an hour each way.

In order to visit this temple, you must request permission at least five days in advance. The necessary forms may be picked up at the Tourist Information Center (see p. 172) in Kyoto. You can also write directly to the temple (Saiho ji, Kokedera, Ukyo-Ku, Kyoto, Japan/Saiho ji, 56 Kamigatani, Matsuo, Nishikyo-ku, Kyoto-shi, Japan) from your hometown before leaving. Write in English and state your name, address, age, occupation and the date and hour (between 9am and 5pm) that you wish to visit the gardens. Do not forget to include a stamped envelope addressed to your hotel in Kyoto. For the 'privilege' of visiting the temple, you are expected to give a donation of ¥3,000. This entitles you to leave a wish written on a wooden tablet at the temple.

This exorbitant price is due not so much to the desire to make money but to the desire to limit the number of visitors by dissuading those who have no real interest in the temple. Thousands of tourists used to visit the Kokedera each year raising so much dust by tramping around that the survival of the mosses was endangered. The gardens were formerly so popular that the neighbours of the temple lodged an official complaint.

The Saiho ji, popularly called the Kokedera (Moss Temple), is a Zen monastery lodged at the foot of a little mountain. Originally founded in AD 731 by the priest Gyoki (AD 670-749) on the site of a house belonging to Prince Shotoku, it was reconstructed by Muso Kokushi in 1339 during the Kamakura period. For 700 years, Zen monks have lived here and kept a meditation garden. The moss garden itself, with over 100 different species of shade-loving bryophytes, is of relatively recent origin as there was initially no canopy of foliage under which they could grow. The path leads around a little pond in the shape of the Chinese ideogram *kokoro* (heart). The mosses, lit by an oblique sunlight, change colour with the hour and the season. The best time to visit the Kokedera is in the spring, particularly after a rain shower.

▬ ENVIRONS OF KYOTO

O'Hara**

Access: take bus 17 or 18 from Kyoto Station (near the post office).

O'Hara, a pleasant little village to the north-east of Kyoto, offers an excellent day trip from Kyoto. From here, you can visit the Sanzenin Temple and Jakkoin Temple. There are a number of restaurants and souvenir shops nearby. The village is a curiosity in itself, local women carry loads on their heads, an unusual practice in Japan.

The **Sanzenin Temple** was founded in the 9th century by the priest Saicho. The *hondo* (Main Hall), dating from AD 985, was decorated by Eshin (942-1017). These paintings, unfortunately, are in very poor condition.

The **Jobon Rendai ji** Temple, near Yawata, contains a rare example of early *emakimono* (illuminated scrolls), a Chinese-influenced style of painting that dates to the 8th century.

Mount Hiei and Enryaku ji**

Open daily 9am-4pm.

Access: From Kyoto Station, take the bus marked 'Mont Hiei' to the Enryaku ji temple. The journey takes about 1 hour and 20 minutes.

The Enryaku ji Temple was built in AD 788 by the monk Saicho (AD 767-AD 822), the founder of the Tendai sect. Intended to protect the new capital of Heiankyo (ancient Kyoto) from evil spirits that were thought to attack from the north-east, the temple grew into an organization of 3000 sub-temples. By the 11th century, it had its own private army of several thousand armed monks — a force larger than any that the government could muster. The temple was damaged on numerous occasions by various rival Buddhist sects whose internal fighting terrorized the capital. In 1571, Oda Nobunaga destroyed the Enryaku ji Temple complex because of its military importance. He burned every temple to the ground and killed most of the monks. Rebuilt by Toyotomi Hideyoshi and supported by the Tokugawa shogunate, the temple prospered, although it never regained its former prominence. Today there are over 100 sub-temples affiliated to the Enryaku ji.

The Komponchudo (Fundamental Center Hall) is the main building of the temple and is classified a National Treasure. Rebuilt in 1642 on the site of the original structure, it contains three lanterns claimed to have been lit by Saicho himself in AD 788. Legend has it that they were hidden in 1571 when the temple was razed and have never been allowed to go out in over 1200 years. The Shakado, a 13th-century building, was moved here on the request of Hideyoshi after the destruction of 1571. It contains the sacred statue of Sakyamuni by Saicho, which is usually kept hidden; a copy is on display. The Hokkedo (Lotus Sutra Hall), built in 1595, contains an image of Fugen Bosatsu seated on an elephant.

From the western side of the monastery, walk toward the Mount Shimeidake (2,753 ft/839 m) Observatory, where you have superb views of Osaka Bay and Lake Biwa, the largest lake in Japan. There are several restaurants near the observatory.

From the observatory, take a cable car to Mont Hiei (2,782 ft/848 m). Near the summit, there is an amusement park with a rotating observation platform, a botanical garden, a natural science museum and a different view of Lake Biwa and the surrounding region.

From Mount Hiei, you can return to Kyoto by taking a cable car to Yase and a second cable car to Demachiyanagi Station, from where the Keifuku Line runs to the city center.

Uji and the Byodoin

Access: to get to Uji, take either the JR or Keihan line from Kyoto Station. About 12 mi/19 km south of Kyoto, Uji is famous for its Byodoin Temple, green tea and *ukai* (night time cormorant fishing) that takes place June 11-August 31. The tea from Uji is claimed to be the best in Japan and was once reserved exclusively for the Imperial household.

Byodoin**

Originally a villa belonging to Minamoto Toru (9th century), Byodoin later became an estate of Fujiwara Michinaga. In 1052, it was converted into a Buddhist temple-palace but continued to be occupied by members of the Fujiwara family.

The principal attraction is the Hoodo (Phoenix Hall), built in 1053. A classical example of Heian *shinden* architecture, the structure represents a phoenix about to land. The image of the building is reflected in a man-made artificial lake. The Hoodo contains an 11th-century sculpture of Amida (Amitabha) seated on a lotus pedestal. Attributed to the priest Jocho, this work is an assemblage of individually carved pieces (*yosegi* technique).

The Kannondo (Kannon Hall) contains a Late Heian statue of Kannon, and is also known as the Tsuridono (Angling Hall) because it was once possible to catch fish in the Uji River from it.

The Byodoin Homotsukan (Byodoin Treasure House) contains an impressive collection of paintings, sculptures and bronzes. Because it is open only two months in the spring and two months in the autumn, telephone beforehand, ☎ 22 3920, or contact the TIC (see p. 172).

To the north of the Byodoin Temple is the Uji bridge, said to have been built originally by the priest Docho in the 7th century. Of strategic importance during the Heian and Kamakura periods, the bridge was the site of many important historical battles.

Nearby is the Uji shrine, the oldest standing Shinto building in Japan. Founded in AD 313, the present structures date from the 10th century.

Mampuku ji, to the north of the town, is a classic example of Chinese Ming architecture. Built during the 17th century by the Chinese priest Ingen, this temple houses the 60,000 wood blocks used to print the *sutra* of the Obaku sect. This sect was introduced into Japan from China in the mid-17th century.

Tokaido

The Tokaido (East Sea Road) is one of the great highways built during the Kamakura period. It is world famous as a result of the sketches of the 'Fifty-three Stages of the Tokaido' by Ando Hiroshige (1786-1858), now in the National Museum.

These roads radiated from the shogun capital to the various provinces of Japan. The Tokaido, which linked Kamakura to Kyoto, was the most important. When Edo became the seat of power in the 17th century, the Tokaido was extended to the new shogun capital. With the instigation of *sankin-kotai* (a law requiring *daimyo* to reside every other year in Edo), the Tokaido became the most frequently used road in Japan.

Today, the N1 highway and the tracks of the *Shinkansen* (Bullet Train) run more or less parallel to the old Tokaido Road. An 855-mi/1376-km signposted trail, with excursions into several National Parks, has been created along this old route. In central Japan, it passes through the heartland of the nation, a region famous for tea and oranges. Nearer Tokyo, the Tokaido can be visited in the Hakone region. There is a tariff wall at the Hakone Gate which served as a lookout post for Edo and the Kanto plain.

The first guidebook of the Tokaido, complete with maps, was published in 1658!

NARA

In AD 710, Nara was chosen as the first permanent capital of Japan. Known then as Heijokyo (Capital of Peace), the city ws constructed with wide streets, according to plans based on the chessboard pattern of the Chinese capital of Ch'ang-an. Heijokyo remained the seat of Imperial power until AD 784.

With the passing of time, the monarchs who ruled from Nara have become legendary figures, from the Empress Regnant Gemmyo, who founded the city, to the Emperor Kammu, who moved the capital to Heian (ancient Kyoto) in AD 794. But the most famous of all is the twice-empress Shotoku, whose dealings as head of state were so notorious that women were banished from ruling for 1000 years afterwards.

The Nara period (AD 710-794), although relatively short, was one of the richest artistically in the history of Japan, even though widespread poverty due to overtaxation and an outbreak of smallpox in AD 737 devastated the country. Nara is considered by many to be the birthplace of Japanese culture, literature and sculpture in particular. It was in AD 760 that the first important volume of Japanese poetry, the *Manyoshu,* was published. The *Kojiki* (AD 712) and *Nihongi* (AD 720), the earliest commissioned histories, also were compiled at Nara.

However, it was in the domains of architecture and, above all, sculpture that artistic achievement reached its zenith. Today, the Todai ji Temple (housing a 53-ft/16-m bronze statue of Buddha) stands as the principal monument to the glory of the Nara period. It took nearly 20 years to build, employing over 2.5 million labourers, artisans and artists.

Considered the Golden Age of Japanese sculpture, the Nara period was heavily influenced by Chinese Buddhism, which was spreading through the country at that time. Never again were Japanese sculptors to capture the same clarity of traits or simplicity of expression as is found in the religious work of this period. The countenance of the monk Ganjin in the Toshodai ji and the strange, smiling expression of Yakushi Nyorai (Buddha-the-Healer) in the Kofuku ji Temple are perfect examples of this style.

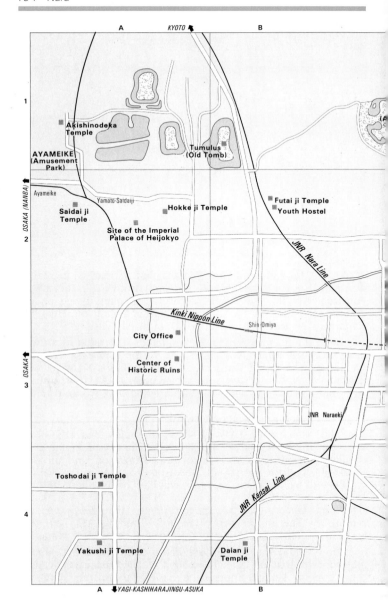

NARA

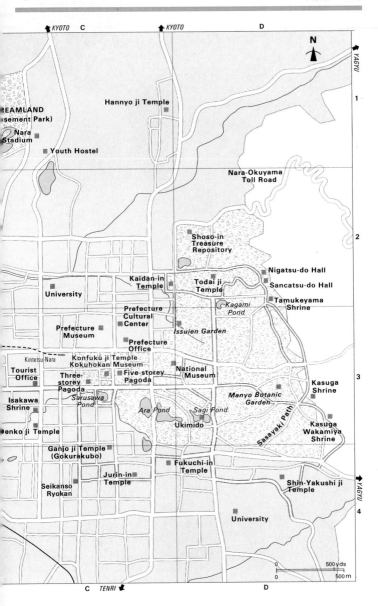

↑ KYOTO C ↑ KYOTO D

N

→ YAGYU

REAMLAND
(?sement Park)

Nara
Stadium

Youth Hostel

Hannyo ji Temple

1

Nara-Okuyama
Toll Road

2

Shoso-in
Treasure
Repository

Kaidan-in
Temple

University

Todai ji
Temple

Nigatsu-do Hall

Sancatsu-do Hall

Tamukeyama
Shrine

Kagami
Pond

Prefecture
Cultural
Center

Prefecture
Museum

Issuien Garden

Prefecture
Office

Kintetsu-Nara

Konfukū ji Temple
Kokuhokan Museum

Tourist
Office

Three-
storey
Pagoda

Five-storey
Pagoda

National
Museum

Kasuga
Shrine

Isakawa
Shrine

Sarusawa
Pond

Manyo Botanic
Garden

Ara Pond

Sagi Pond

Ukimido

Kasuga
Wakamiya
Shrine

enko ji Temple

Sasayaki Path

Ganjo ji Temple
(Gokurakubo)

Fukuchi-in
Temple

→ YAGYU

Jurin-in
Temple

Seikanso
Ryokan

Shin-Yakushi ji
Temple

University

3

4

0   500 yds
0   500 m

C TENRI ↓ D

▬ *PRACTICAL INFORMATION*

Telephone area code: 0742.

Access

From Kyoto, it is possible to make an excursion of a day or two to Nara. Trains from Kyoto Station take 35 minutes by the Kintetsu Line and a little over an hour by the JR (Japanese Railways).

Accommodation

See p. 217 for hotel classification.

Western-style hotels include the following:

▲▲▲▲ **Nara**, Nara Koen Nai, Nara, C3 n°6, ☎ 26 3300. This is generally considered to be the best hotel in town but is not within everyone's budget. Near Nara Park, its windows overlook the park's pond, where the sacred fallow deer come to drink. The building is over 70 years old and has 73 rooms. Expect to pay a minimum of ¥20,000 per night.

▲▲ **Sun Route**, 1110 Takahatacho, Nara, C3 n°10, ☎ 22 5151. A notch or two below the Nara, this business hotel is much less expensive, with rates rarely exceeding ¥7,000 to ¥8,000 per person.

There are also a number of *ryokan* in Nara:

▲▲▲▲ **Kiku Sui Ro**, Takahata Bodaimachi, Nara, C3 n°3, ☎ 23 2001. The most expensive *ryokan* in Nara, costing ¥25,000 per person, including two meals a day.

▲ **Matsumae**, 28-1 Higashi-Terabayashicho, Nara, C3 n°9, ☎ 22 3686. This is the least expensive *ryokan* in town and costs half the price of the Kiku Sui Ro.

Festivals

January

Burning of the Hill Festival (or Grass Fire Ceremony) takes place on January 15 on Wakakusayama (Young Grass Mountain), just outside of Nara. Toward 6pm, fires are lit at the Todai ji and Kofuku ji temples to commemorate a land dispute settlement between these two temples in the 8th century.

February

Mando-e (Lantern Festival), on February 3 and 4, is held at the Kasuga Jinja. Over 3,000 lanterns are lit, and dances take place by lamplight.

March

Omizutori (Water-Drawing Festival) is celebrated during the first two weeks of the month. On the evening of March 12 (at 2am on March 13), a ceremony, accompanied by music, takes place at the Todai ji Temple in front of thousands of spectators. The water drawn from the sacred well is claimed to cure illness and protect the temple from fire.

Kasuga Matsuri (Kasuga Festival) is held on March 13 at the Kasuga shrine. This festival has been celebrated for over 12 centuries and is one of the most sumptuous in Japan. There are classical Heian dances performed in the streets to ancient court music, as well as Heian costume parades.

May

Shomu Sai Festival, on May 2, is held in honour of Emperor Shomu (AD 701-756). In the afternoon there is a costume parade at the Todai ji Temple.

The tanuki, *a badger, is a good luck charm in Japan, often found at the entrance to restaurants. Its rounded belly symbolizes prosperity.*

The Noh Theater Festival is held on May 11 and 12 at the Kofuku ji Temple. From 4pm onward, there are open-air performances by the four national schools of Noh drama.

August

The Dai Bonfire Festival is held on August 14 and 15. The 3,000 lanterns of the Kasuga shrine are lit for the second and last time of the year. Around 8pm on the evening of the August 15, a large bonfire in the shape of the ideogram *dai* ('large') is set ablaze on Mount Koezan.

September

The Noh Drama Festival is held on September 15 in Nara Park.

December

On Matsuri (On Festival) is celebrated from December 16 to 18. A large and colourful procession of Shinto dignitaries from the Kasuga Wakamiya shrine take the shrine's *kami* (god) to the top of a neighbouring mountain. The next day, they retrieve it in the presence of a 'messenger of the sun' chosen from among the descendants of the Fujiwara family.

Food

See p. 217 for restaurant classification.

The cuisine of Nara is similar to that of Kyoto. Nara, however, has two specialities: *kaki no ha zushi* (raw fish and rice wrapped in a kaki leaf) and *cha gayu* (soup made from rice and Japanese tea).

♦♦♦♦ **Kiku Sui Ro,** C3 n°3, ☎ 23 2001. This is one of the most famous *kaiseki ryori* (tea ceremony) restaurants in Nara.

♦♦♦ **Shiki tei,** C3 n°4, ☎ 22 5531. This restaurant serves all types of Japanese specialities as well as *kaiseki ryori*.

♦♦♦ **Tono Cha Ya** and **Yanagi Cha Ya,** two sister establishments, serve the famous *kaki no ha zushi* and *cha gayu*.

♦♦ **Hira so,** C3 n°2, ☎ 22 0866. This is one of the best places in town for *sushi* (raw fish).

It is also possible to eat quite well and at reasonable prices in the restaurants of certain hotels. Try **Fujita,** C3 n°5, ☎ 23 8111; or **Kasuga,** C3 n°7, ☎ 22 4031.

Shopping

Most of the souvenir and crafts shops are concentrated on Sanjo Dori. Nara is famous for its excellent writing brushes. **Sho Ko Kan,** C3 n°8, specializing in calligraphy, is well worth the visit. The alley that leads to the Todai ji Temple is lined with little stalls selling the specialities of the town.

Tourist Information

Japan Travel Bureau, C3 n°5, Kitagawa Building, is next to the Kintetsu Nara Station, ☎ 26 6355.

The **Prefectural Tourist Office,** C3, is located in Noborigi Cho, ☎ 23 3300.

The **Nara City Tourist Information Office** is on the first floor of Kintetsu-Nara Station.

The Tourist Information Center in Kyoto (see p. 172) also has useful printed information pamphlets concerning Nara.

Voluntary guides

In Nara, there is an association of English-speaking Japanese who will guide you around the city — for free! Call in advance, ☎ 26 4753, between 10am and 4pm, in order to take adavantage of this service.

GETTING TO KNOW NARA

Although you need to take a bus to visit Toshodai ji, you can easily cover most of Nara on foot. From Kintetsu-Nara Station, Sanjo Dori leads directly to Deer Park, so called for the thousands of beloved fallow deer that live there in complete liberty. From the park, it is possible to visit the following:

Kofuku ji and Kokuhokan*** (Kofuku ji Temple and Treasury) C3

Open daily 9am-5pm.

Founded in AD 669 at Yamashina near Kyoto, the Kofuku ji (Happiness Producing) Temple was moved to its present site by Fujiwara Fuhito in AD 710. Belonging to the Hosso sect, it became one of the seven most important Buddhist centers in Nara during the Tempyo period (AD 729-748), possessing 175 different buildings. The Taira clan destroyed the temple in 1180. Over the centuries, fires and political decline have considerably reduced the size of the complex. The oldest surviving building, the three-storey pagoda with the Thousand Buddhas decoration, dates from 1143.

The Kokuhokan (treasury), a modern concrete structure, contains a large number of important statues from the Asuka, Nara, Heian and Kamakura periods — all classified as National Treasures. The oldest is a head of Buddha, probably Yakushi Nyorai (Buddha-the-Healer), dating to the 7th century. Nara period sculptures include the famous Eight Guardians of Shaka Nyorai. In dry-lacquer technique, they date from AD 734 and include a rare image of Ashura, the god of hunger and anger. The Unkei school of the Heian period is particularly well represented. The paintings in the museum include an 11th-century portrait on silk of the priest Jion.

Nara National Museum** (Nara Kokuritsu Hakubutsukan) C3

Open Tues-Sun 9am-4pm.

This museum is composed of two buildings. The older building houses the prehistoric and archaeological collections, including swords and *haniwa* (ceramic figurines). The modern building contains works of art (paintings and sculptures for the most part) organized along recent museological lines. Temporary exhibitions of selected works covering over 1000 years of Japanese history, from the Asuka (AD 538-645) to the Muromachi (1338-1573) periods, are displayed alternately.

Yamato Bunkakan Museum**

Open Tues-Sun 10am-5pm. Closed Dec 28-Jan 4.

Opened in 1960, this is one of the most important private collections in Japan. There are constantly changing exhibits of Asian art, including paintings, sculptures, China-ink drawings, calligraphy, *emakimono* (horizontal scrolls) and other Japanese arts, as well as ceramics, pottery, bronzes and metal objects from China and Japan. The collection includes works by such masters as Korin, Kenzan, Kanzan, Sotatsu and Okyo.

Shin Yakushi ji* D4

Open daily 8:30am-4pm.

The Shin Yakushi ji Temple was erected on the command of the Empress Komyo (AD 701-760) in AD 747 to thank the gods for having restored her husband, the Emperor Shomu, to health. The *hondo*, one of the oldest buildings in Nara, contains a 9th-century statue of Yakushi Nyorai (Buddha-the-Healer) carved from a single piece of wood. The Buddha is surrounded by the Juni Shinsho (Twelve Celestial Guardians), which are made of earth covered with *gofun* (calcium carbonate) and then gilded.

Kasuga Shrine*** D3

Located on the eastern edge of Nara Park at the foot of Mount Kasuga, this shrine is one of the oldest in Japan. Founded in AD 768 as the tutelary shrine of the Fujiwara family, it became the prototype of the Kasuga style. The building, painted bright red, is in striking contrast with the surrounding forest of tall pines. The shrine possesses over 3000 stone lanterns that are lit twice a year (see 'Festivals' p. 197). The treasury contains a fine collection of ancient weapons and masks. In the courtyard, there are four small Kasuga-style shrines that were periodically rebuilt according to Shinto custom.

Todai ji*** D2

The Todai ji (Great Eastern) Temple, in the northern part of the park, is the most important Buddhist edifice in Nara and perhaps in all of Japan. Founded by the Kegon sect on the order of Emperor Shomu, the temple has remained their headquarters ever since. It took nearly 20 years and over 2.5 million labourers, carpenters and metalworkers to complete the Todai ji, which was inaugurated in AD 752.

The Daibutsuden (Great Buddha Hall), 187 ft/57 m long and 195 ft/48.5 m high, is the principal building of the temple. The largest single wooden structure in existence, it houses the world's largest bronze statue, the Daibutsu (Great Buddha). This enormous statue of Buddha Vairocana, 53 ft/16.2 m tall, was cast in AD 749 by the Korean master Kimimaro. Considered less refined than the younger 13th-century Amida Buddha at Kamakura, it has been seriously damaged over the ages. In AD 855, its head fell off during an earthquake, and it later burned twice, first in 1185 and again in 1692. Mediocre restoration has taken its toll as well.

Nearby is a curious building, the Shosoin, built on piles in the *azekura* style (without nails). Originally the temple treasury, it is now administered by the Imperial Household Agency and contains treasures belonging to the Imperial Family. It is open to the public only a few days each year (in April and October), but some of its collections are on display at the Nara National Museum. The Shosoin contains an important collection of objects assembled during the Tempyo period, including decorated screens, ceramics, weapons, masks, furniture, cloth and garments, as well as objects from India, Persia, Greece, Byzantium and China. It is considered the world's oldest museum.

Many of the surviving sub-temples, masterpieces in themselves, contain statues classified as National Treasures.

The Kaidenin, which contains 8th-century clay statues of the four heavenly guardians, stands on a small hill about 330 yd/300 m west of the Daibutsuden; the earth for this man-made mound came from China.

The Nigatsudo (Temple of the Second Month) possesses two sacred statues of Kannon-of-Eleven-Heads that are kept hidden from the public. Their size is unknown, but legend has it that the smaller one is warm to the touch.

The Sangatsudo (Temple of the Third Month) dates from AD 747 and is the oldest surviving building of the temple complex. It houses several remarkable dry-lacquer statues of the Tempyo period, including one of Kannon with a halo made of 20,000 pearls and other gems.

To the west of the station there are also two important temples, Toshodai ji and Yakushi ji.

Toshodai ji** A4

Open daily 8:30am-4pm. The Treasury is open only Mar 20-May 19 and Sept 15-Nov 5.

Access: take bus 52 or 63 from the Todai ji Temple or Kintetsu-Nara Station.

The Toshodai ji is regarded as one of the most perfectly designed temple complexes in Japan. Miraculously, it has suffered no damage — by war or fire — since its founding in AD 759 by the Chinese priest Ganjin (the

A statue at the entrance to the Horyu ji temple near Nara.

blind founder of the Risshu sect). It still serves as headquarters for the sect and is considered the foremost Buddhist seminary in Japan. There is a polychrome statue of Ganjin in the Mieido (Founder's Hall) shown once a year on June 6.

The *kondo* (Main Hall), strongly influenced by Chinese architecture, contains numerous dry-lacquer works that are classified as National Treasures, including a 10-ft/3.3-m painted and gilded image of Buddha Vairocana, Kannon-of-the-Thousand-Hands and Yakushi Nyorai.

During the 8th century, the Toshodai ji was heavily influenced by Chinese styles in art and architecture. And in 1981, over 1200 years later, the temple accepted a monument presented by the People's Republic of China.

The 'Path of History', so named for the great number of historical figures who took it, leads from the Toshodai ji Temple to the neighbouring **Yakushi ji Temple*** A4. The latter was founded in AD 680 but was destroyed on several occasions. The principal attractions are a three-storey pagoda built in AD 698, a statue of Buddha-the-Healer dating from AD 696 and a footprint claimed to be that of Buddha.

ENVIRONS OF NARA

Horyu ji***

Open daily 8am-4pm.

Access: take bus 52 from the Todai ji Temple or Nara JR Station to the Horyu ji-mae bus stop. The journey should take about 50 minutes.

The Horyu ji (Noble Law) Temple is the oldest temple in Japan. In AD 601, Prince Shotoku (AD 572-621) built a palace here, and a small temple, dedicated to Yakushi, was completed in AD 607. In AD 739, the monk Gyoshin Sozu constructed the Dream Pavilion, one of the oldest existing wooden buildings in the world.

The Horyu ji, heavily influenced by 7th-century Chinese and Korean styles, was spared the wars and fires that destroyed most of the works of this period. It is the most impressive surviving temple of the Asuka period and, as such, is one of the most important examples in Japan of early Buddhist art and architecture. Today, many of the temple's treasures are housed in a specially designed building in the Tokyo National Museum (see p. 133).

Enter the temple grounds by the Nandaimon (Great South Gate). Go through the Chumon (Middle Gate) that marks the entrance to the Saiin (West Temple). In front of you is the *kondo* (Main Hall), entirely rebuilt in 1949 following a fire. Built in Sino-Korean style, this structure contains a bronze statue of Yakushi Nyorai (Buddha-the-Healer) said to date from AD 607 and the bronze Shaka trinity cast in AD 623. Both are from the Asuka period and show strong Chinese influences. To the left of the *kondo* is the 107-ft/32.5-m five-storey Gojunoto pagoda, and to the right is the *daikodo* (Lecture Hall), moved here from Kyoto in AD 990. It houses a Fujiwara-period wooden statue of the Yakushi Trinity.

Now proceed to the Toin (East Temple) where you will see the Yumedono (Dream Pavilion), the oldest octagonal religious building in Japan. It contains the famous Guze Kannon (Saviour of the World) statue in camphor wood and gold leaf, an 8th-century dry-lacquer of Gyoshin Sozu and a 9th-century clay statue of the monk Dosen Risshi.

The **Daihezoden,** built in 1941, is the temple's museum of treasures and contains the best examples of Tempyo-period statues to be seen in Japan. This museum alone is worth a trip to Nara.

The Chugu ji nunnery, moved to its present site in the 15th century, contains several treasures from the Asuka period. The most famous are a magnificent wooden statue of Miroku Bosatsu (Buddha-of-the-Future), claimed to have been carved by Prince Shotoku himself, and the Tenjukoku Mandara embroidery, the oldest in Japan, dating from AD 662.

KOBE

With nearly 1.5 million inhabitants, Kobe is the sixth most populated city in the country. The largest container port in the world, it is the second most important port in Japan, after Yokohama. Located on the Minato River at the head of Osaka Bay, Kobe is opposite the island of Shikoku at the eastern end of the Inland Sea.

In the 4th century, Kobe was a small fishing village that already had contacts with the mainland, but it remained unimportant until 1868 when, because of its deep harbour, it became an 'open' port for foreigners. It was in Kobe that the first Europeans, or *nanban* ('barbarians from the south'), had landed in Japan over 300 years earlier. Even today, it is the most cosmopolitan city in Japan, with a particularly strong British influence.

At the outbreak of World War II, Kobe was the largest port in Japan, but because it was a military and economic target, over two-thirds of the city was destroyed by bombing raids in 1945. Today, Kobe appears to the visitor as an oversized modern 'small town'. Hemmed in between the mountains and the bay, the municipality is currently reclaiming land from the sea and leveling hills to prepare for its future needs. Unless you are visiting friends or are on business, you will find that one day is ample to see the town.

▬ PRACTICAL INFORMATION

Telephone area code: 078.

Access

From Tokyo, the *Shinkansen* takes 3.5 hours, and costs about ¥12,000. Get off at Shin Kobe Station and take a bus from opposite the station to Sannomiya, the city center.

From Osaka, the easiest and cheapest way to get to Kobe is to take the Tokaido Line. It takes slightly over 30 minutes and arrives in Sannomiya.

From Kyoto, there is either the *Shinkansen,* which takes 35 minutes and costs ¥2600, or the Tokaido Line (arrival in Sannomiya), which costs half the price but takes twice as long.

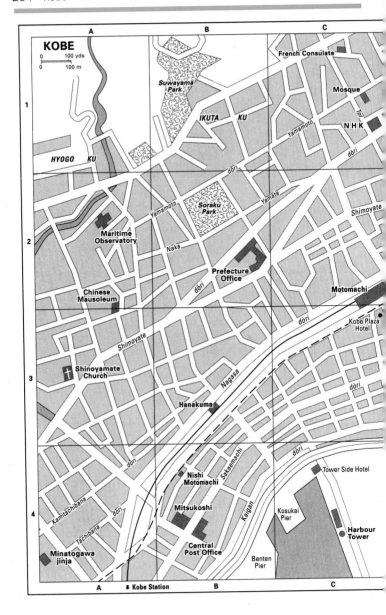

KOBE

0 ___ 100 yds
0 ___ 100 m

Suwayama Park

French Consulate

Mosque

IKUTA　KU

N H K

Yamamoto dōri

dōri

HYOGO　KU

dōri

Yamamoto

Shimoyate

Soraku Park

Yamate

Maritime Observatory

Naka

Prefecture Office

dōri

Motomachi

Chinese Mausoleum

Kobe Plaza Hotel

Shimoyate

dōri

Shinoyamate Church

dōri

Nagasa

Hanakuma

dōri

dōri

Tower Side Hotel

Nishi Motomachi

Sakaemachi

Kamitachibana

Mitsukoshi

Kaigan

Kosukai Pier

dōri

Harbour Tower

Tachibana

Central Post Office

Minatogawa jinja

Benten Pier

↓ Kobe Station

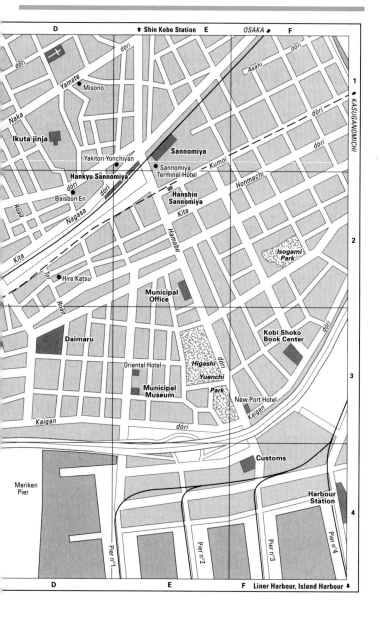

KASUGANOMICHI

dori
Asahi
dori
dori
Yamate
Misono
Naka
Ikuta jinja
Yakitori Yonchiyan
Sannomiya
Kumoi
Honmachi
Hankyu Sannomiya
Sannomiya Terminal Hotel
Baisbon En
Nagasa
Kita
Hanshin Sannomiya
Kita
Hamabe
Isogami Park
Road
Jor
Hire Katsu
Road
Municipal Office
Daimaru
Oriental Hotel
Higashi Yuenchi Park
Kobi Shoko Book Center
dori
Municipal Museum
Kaigan
dori
New Port Hotel
Kaigan
Customs
Meriken Pier
Harbour Station
Pier n°1
Pier n°2
Pier n°3
Pier n°4

Accommodation

See p. 217 for hotel classification.

▲▲▲ **Oriental Hotel**, 25 Kyomachi, Chuo-ku, E1, ☎ 331 8111. A very good hotel near Sannomiya Station; it is quite expensive.

▲▲▲ **Sannomiya Terminal Hotel**, 8 Kumoidori, Chuo-ku, E1 ☎ 291 0001. Very central with prices about the same as those at the Oriental.

▲▲ **Kobe Plaza**, 1-13-12 Motomachi Dori, Chuo-ku, C3 ☎ 332 1141. Very comfortable. Located near Motomachi Station.

Food

See p. 217 for restaurant classification.

♦♦♦ **Misono**, D1, ☎ 331 2890. This excellent beef restaurant is rather expensive. It is claimed that the animals are massaged with beer to tenderize the meat!

♦ **Bai Shun En**, D2, ☎ 331 7854. *Open daily 4pm-2am*. Taiwan cuisine. There is a counter downstairs and a dining room on the 1st floor.

♦ **Hire Katsu**, D2, ☎ 331 2237. You can lunch and dine here (up to 8pm) quite inexpensively. The house specializes in *tonkatsu* (breaded pork).

♦ **Yakitori Nonchiyan**, D1, ☎ 332 1651. *Open daily 4-10pm*. Good, clean and inexpensive, this restaurant offers *sashimi* (raw fish) followed by grilled chicken brochettes.

Useful Addresses

Bank of Kobi, 56 Naniwacho, Ikuta-ku.

Bank of Tokyo, 24 Kyomachi, Ikuta-ku.

Central Post Office, 6-9 Sakae-Machi Dori, Ikuta-ku.

Japan Travel Bureau, JR Sannomiya Station, ☎ 231 5115.

Kobe Tourist Information Center, Kobe Kotsu Center building, 2nd floor, JR Sannomiya Station, ☎ 331 8181.

▬ GETTING TO KNOW KOBE

Temples and shrines

For lovers of Japanese religious architecture, Kobe does not have much to offer. The town has only three Shinto shrines, all of recent construction.

The most important shrine is **Ikuta Jinja**, D1. Near Sannomiya station, it is dedicated to the patroness of the city, Wakahirume-no-Mikoto. Originally founded in the 3rd century by the Empress Jingu, this brightly coloured post-war shrine is set in the midst of camphor and cedar trees.

Minatogawa (or Nanko) Jinja, A4, is the city's second most important shrine. Built in 1871, it was destroyed in 1945 and was reconstructed in 1953. Near Okurayama Station.

Nagata Jinja is dedicated to Kotoshionushi-no-Mikoto, the patron of good fortune. Near Nagata Station.

Chinatown (Nankin machi)** C3-4

Kobe's Chinatown is very small in comparison to that of Yokohama. Located between the port and the Motomachi district, it is a good spot to find a pleasant Chinese restaurant.

Kitano* C1

Formerly the foreigner's district, this is now a trendy part of town. Thirty-five *ijikan* (American-style houses), most dating from the Meiji period, have been renovated, and some are even open to visitors. Start your tour of the area by walking up Tor Road and exploring the little streets on the bluff where you will find a mosque, a synagogue and a Catholic church.

In Kitano there are numerous craft shops and foreign restaurants. If you are hungry, try **Wang**, ☎ 222-2507, the only Thai restaurant in the Kansai region; it is particularly good.

Port Island F4

Port Island is a massive man-made island covering 1075 acres/ 435 hectares. It was built to extend the port facilities and house about 20,000 people. The project was completed in 1981 in time for the International Portopia Exhibition. The fair grounds have since been transformed into a science museum and an amusement park. Port Island can be reached by the 'port-liner' that leaves from Naka Pier *(between 11am-4pm)*. This ferry can also be used to tour the port without getting off at Portopia. Near the pier is the Port Tower (338 ft/103 m) with its observation platform.

A second artificial island, Rokko Island, is currently under construction.

Sake Museum (Hakutsuru Hakubutsukan)
Open Mon-Sat 9am-noon, 1-4pm.

Access: Take the Hanshin Line from Sannomiya to Uozaki. From there, walk under the highway to Sakagura (the sake district). The Hakutsuru museum is nearby. There are two other sake museums, much less sophisticated, run by the Masamnue and Sawanotsuru breweries.

Kobe is claimed to have the best water in Japan for the manufacturing of *nihon shu* (Japanese wine, or sake).

Hakutsuru, one of the most reputed manufacturers in Japan, has opened a museum in its factory. The museum traces the complete process of sake manufacturing from the rice to the finished product. Entrance is free, and it is possible — after tasting various kinds of sake — to buy the famous *senshu* (pure sake), which is practically impossible to find on the market.

Hakutsuru Art Museum (Hakutsuru Bijutsukan)
Open Tues-Sun.

This museum has an excellent collection of Chinese and Japanese bronzes. The Chinese collection, dating back to the early Chou period, is particularly good.

▬ ENVIRONS OF KOBE

Mount Rokko and Mount Maya

Access: From Sannomiya Station, take the Hankyu Line to Rokko Station. From there, cable cars can be taken to the summit of either mountain.

Mount Rokko and Mount Maya, not far from Kobe, allow the inhabitants of the city to receive a bit of fresh air on the weekends.

Mount Maya (2293 ft/699 m) is named for the mother of Buddha, Maya Bunin, whose statue may be seen in the Toritenjo ji Temple. Founded in AD 646 by the Indian priest Hodo, this temple is pleasantly located in a grove of cedars on the slope of the mountain. On the summit, there is a French restaurant, **La Tour d'Or**, which offers one of the most outstanding views of Kobe.

Mount Rokko (3058 ft/932 m) is part of Seto Naikai National Park. It has a garden of Alpine plants, a platform and the oldest golf course in Japan (1903).

OSAKA

With nearly 3 million inhabitants, Osaka is on its way to becoming the second-largest city in Japan. Municipal authorities have intensified efforts to attract capital, and many companies have established headquarters here; commercially, Osaka is surpassed only by Tokyo. Located at the delta of the Yodo River at the head of Osaka Bay, this huge town is wedged between the mountains and the bay (like its neighbour Kobe) and has no option for expansion but to reclaim land from the sea.

The earliest historical reference to Osaka is from an account of Emperor Jimmu's odyssey on the Inland Sea in the 7th century BC. By the 4th century AD, Osaka, then known as Naniwa (fast-floating waves), was already an Imperial residence. Osaka was also the first site in Japan to obtain statues of Buddha, sent by the king of Korea in AD 553. More importantly, the town developed into the main port serving the ancient capitals of Nara and Kyoto. In 1583, when Toyotomi Hideyoshi established his headquarters in Osaka, he built a castle and forced large numbers of merchants to move to the town. Under the Tokugawa (see p. 79), Osaka prospered and became the main commercial center in the country.

Although Osaka has expanded rapidly in the last few years, it has nevertheless retained a provincial character. Osaka residents are more open and direct than those of Tokyo. In the street, people will address you boisterously or blow their horns good-naturedly. Osaka compensates for its lack of cultural sites by a profusion of bars, restaurants and commerce of all types. If you want to see the Japan of the year 2000, then Osaka is the place to come. With an amazing mixture of disco and *shamisen,* geishas and rockers, of neon and softened lights, the small streets of Osaka have a charm which is impossible to find anywhere else in Japan.

The opening of a theater in the Namba district of Osaka.

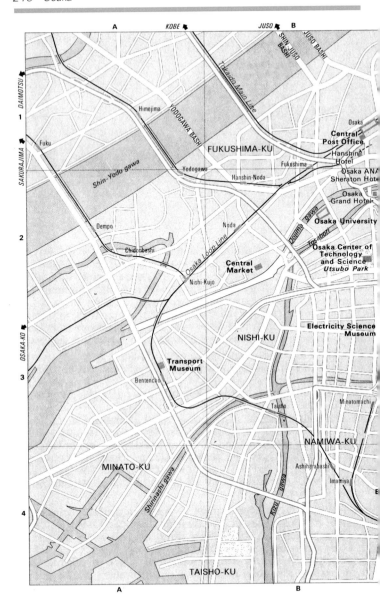

OYODO-KU

Sekime

N

KYOTO

Temma   Sakuranomiya

Noe

Piscine

KITA-KU

Sakuranomiya
Park

Koyobashi

Bank of
Japan   Temmangu   Fujita Museum   Kyobashi

Katamachi

Municipal Office
Yodoyabashi
Air France   Temmabashi   HIGASHI-KU

Midosuji

Osaka
Castle   Osakajo

Prefecture
Office   Municipal   Park
Museum

Chuo-odori   Municipal
Gymnasium   Hokoku Jinja

Nissei Stadium

MINAMI-KU   HIGASHI-NARI-KU

Morinomiya

Nagahori-dori Ave.

Tanimachisuji Ave.
Uchommachisuji Ave.

Tamatsukuri

Asahiza
Theater   Kosugu

Osaka Loop Line

NARA

Shin-   Bunraku   Sennichimae-dori
Kabukiza   National
Theater   Theater   Ikutama Jinja   Tsuruhashi

Gymnasium

Osaka Stadium

Japanese Craft
Industry Museum   TENNOJI-KU

Imamiya
Ebisu Jinja
Jinja   Momodani   IKUNO-KU

Shintennoji

Tsutenkaku
Tower   Tennoji
Park   Municipal Museum
of Art   Teradacho

Shin-Imamiya

Tennoji

0   1/2 mile
0   1 km

▬ *PRACTICAL INFORMATION*

Telephone area code: 06.

Access

Osaka is located about 27 mi/43 km south of Kyoto and 343 mi/553 km south-west of Tokyo.

From Tokyo, the *Shinkansen* (bullet train) takes 3 hours and 10 minutes and costs about ¥12,000. The plane takes 55 minutes but Shin-Osaka Airport is another half hour at least from the city center (by taxi).

From Kyoto, the Tokaido Line takes 45 minutes, while the *Shinkansen* takes only 17 minutes but costs twice as much.

Accommodation

See p. 217 for hotel classification.

North Osaka

▲▲▲ **Osaka Royal Hotel,** 5-3-68 Nakanoshima, Kita-ku, C1 ☎ 448 1121. 1380 rooms. A shuttle leaves every 15 minutes in the direction of Yodoyabashi Station.

▲▲▲ **Osaka Tokyu Hotel,** 7-20 Chaya machi, Kita-ku, C1 n°6, ☎ 373 2411. Comfortable and well located.

▲▲ **Osaka Tokyu Inn,** 2-1 Doyamacho, Kita-ku, C1 n°7, ☎ 313 3171. Well located and reasonably priced.

South Osaka

▲▲▲ **Nikko Osaka,** 7 Nishi no cho, Daihoji machi, Minami-ku, C3 n°9, ☎ 252 1121. 650 rooms. This ultra-modern hotel is close to Shinsaibashi Station.

▲▲ **Holiday Inn,** 28-1 Kyuzaemon cho, Minami-ku, C3 n°8, ☎ 213 8281. It is difficult to be more central. Here you'll find the usual standards and comfort of this international chain of hotels.

Entertainment

Osaka is the home of *bunraku* (puppet theatre). Every year at the National Bunraku Theater, there are about six different productions offered; each runs for about three weeks. Over the centuries, this form of theatrical expression has gained worldwide recognition. If you are in Osaka when the theatre is open, do not miss the chance to see a performance.

The **National Bunraku Theatre,** C3, is near Kintetsu Nihombashi Station. Tickets range from about ¥3000 to ¥3500. For complete information call, ☎ 212 1122. Information is available at the TIC (see p. 172).

Food

See p. 217 for restaurant classification.

The largest concentration of restaurants in Osaka is found around the principal shopping arcades between Namba and the Dotombori River.

♦♦♦ **Kanidoraku,** C3 n°1, specializing in crab; and **Ebidoraku,** C3 n°2, which serves only shrimp. These two restaurants, both on Dotombori Avenue, are easily recognized by the giant crustaceans that decorate their exteriors.

♦♦♦ **Kawakyu,** B1 n°3 ☎ 346-0770 is just opposite the Central Post Office. This very chic *kaiseki ryori* restaurant, towering over the town, offers a complete meal.

Most of Osaka's stores and restaurants are located on Dotombori Avenue.

♦♦♦ **Sumochaya,** 1-1-7 Namba, Chuo ku, ☎ 211-4158. *Open daily 2-11pm.* A friendly, highly recommended *chanko-nabe* restaurant (sumo wrestlers' cuisine) which serves very copious meals.

♦♦ **Shibato,** 2-1-3 Nakanoshima, Kita-ku, C2, ☎ 231 4810. Not far from Osaka Station. *Open daily 11am-8pm.* Excellent *unagi* (grilled eel).

There are also a number of agreeable Japanese restaurants in the Higashi Umeda district; a good one is **Jan Ken Pon,** C1 n°5, a *yakitoriya* with excellent chicken brochettes.

Useful addresses

Bank of Japan, 23 Nakanoshima 1-chome, Kita-ku, C2.
Central Post Office, Nada machi, Kita-ku, B1, ☎ 235 1321.
Osaka Tourist Information Office, Higashi-guchi, JR Osaka Station, 3-1-1 Umeda, Kita-ku, B2 ☎ 345 2189.

Visiting a Factory

The Osaka Chamber of Commerce and Industry organizes guided tours to a wide choice of Japanese factories. For more information, ☎ 944-6200.

▬ GETTING TO KNOW OSAKA

It is difficult to see everything in a day (particularly as a new museum seems to open up every year). The best plan is to spend one day in the northern part of town (the Umeda district) and another in the southern part (the Namba district).

The north

You can start your day with a visit to Osaka Castle (Osakajo). From there, take the Osaka Aquabus (see below) to Yodoyabashi and visit the Oriental Ceramics Museum. Finish the day in the lively districts around Osaka Station (Osaka Eki).

Osakajo (Osaka Castle)* C2

Open daily 9am-4:30pm.

Access: take the Tanimachi Line from Osaka Station to Tanimachi 4 chome. A 10-minute walk will bring you to Osakajo — a 1931 reproduction of the original castle built by Hideyoshi Toyotomi in 1585. Once the most powerful fortress in Japan, it was destroyed in 1615, again in 1868 and most recently during the bombing raids of World War II. The moats were larger than at present, and of the 20 original towers, only four remain. The ramparts were built of massive masonry of which the largest block weighs 520 tons. From the top storey of the concrete keep, there is a good view of the city. The Municipal Museum of Osaka Castle, which recounts local development from prehistory to the present, is on the grounds.

About 20 minutes on foot to the north of the castle is the **Fujita Museum,** ☎ 351 0582. *Open Tues-Sun 10am-4pm; admission stops at 3:30pm.* Fujita is the name of a celebrated collection of traditional Japanese objets d'art.

The **Aquabus,** a relatively recent initiative on the part of the municipality, is a boat service that runs on the Yodo River. The embarkation point is not far from Temmabashi Station, north of Osaka Castle. There are departures every hour. To visit the Oriental Ceramics Museum, get off at Yodoyabashi Station — which also can be reached from Temmabashi Station via the Keihan Line.

Oriental Ceramics Museum C2

1-1 Nakanoshima, Kita-ku, ☎ 223-0055. *Open Tues-Sun 9:30am-5pm; admission stops at 3:30pm.*

At least two hours should be spent visiting this museum. Inaugurated in 1982, it houses about 1000 rare pieces from various private collections. The items, dating from the 7th to 18th centuries, include 14 National Treasures. Each room of the museum corresponds to an historic period in China and Korea. A tearoom, installed among the greenery, affords a pleasant rest.

Around the Osaka Station

Return to Osaka Eki Station (not to be confused with Shin Osaka where the *Shinkansen* arrives) by taking the Midosuji Line from Yodoyabashi Station. The animated district around the Osaka Eki, named Hankyu Higashi Shotengai, consists of small streets full of good restaurants and shopping arcades. Almost all of them belong to the Hankyu company which owns department stores, hotels and a railway line of the same name. After 10pm, strip-tease joints and peep-shows are abundant.

The south

From Namba Station you can take a circular tour which includes the old market of Tsuruhashi and Tennoji Park (with botanical gardens, zoo and municipal art museum). At night, Namba is totally different and boasts thousands of bars and restaurants — claimed to be the best in all of Japan.

Namba*** C3

Access: take the subway to Namba Station. Take exit n°1 and, once outside, find the Shin Kabukiza theatre or the Takashimaya department store. Cross the street and enter the arcades.

Since Ridley Scott filmed *Black Rain*, this commercial district of Osaka has witnessed an extraordinary boom. Much of the scenery will be familiar to anyone who has seen the film, including the bridge at the intersection of Dotombori and the main shopping gallery. A mixture of tradition, and futurism — in a samurai fashion of the 21st century — this hallucinating intersection is dominated by the Kirin building, which is clad in steel and topped by giant screens.

Namba, crowded night and day, is the commercial and entertainment center of Osaka. For shopping, the prices are better than in Tokyo. With its large department stores, underground arcades, foreign restaurants, cabarets and upmarket bars, it caters to a wide range of tastes. Neon light and *mihon* (realistic plastic or resin food) add to the allure of the district and make Namba the palpitating heart of this active city. The **Asahiza Theater,** the **National Bunraku Theater** and the **Shin Kabuki-za Theater** are also all in this district.

The Old Tsuruhashi Market*

Access: from Namba Station take the Sennichi Line to Tsuruhashi.

This district contains one of the few remaining markets of a type that were established immediately after World War II. Merchants set themselves up at random as space became available, and today venders selling shoes, fish, plastic buckets and spiced cabbage are scattered around without any apparent logic. This very authentic market — one of the most pleasant spots in Osaka — is normally overlooked by tourists.

Tennoji Park

Although not a priority, this park is interesting for nature lovers, as well as for anyone staying in Osaka for a few days. Dobutsuenmae Station, on the JR and Midosuji lines, is the closest to the entrance. The major (paying) attractions of this vast, green, open space are the **Osaka Zoo** (particularly for its old, almost kitsch atmosphere); the **botanical gardens** which has several rare species; and the **Municipal Fine Art Museum** *(open daily 9am-5pm)* with its archaeological collections, calligraphies and traditional paintings.

National Museum of Ethnology (Kokuritsu Minzokugaku Hakubutsukan)**

23-17 Yamadaogawa, Suita, ☎ 876 2151. *Open Thurs-Tues 10am-5pm.*

Access: the museum is rather difficult to get to. From Osaka Station, take the subway to Senri-chuo Station. Then take a bus from platform n°6 marked Expoland (pronounced 'ekishiporando' in Japanese) to the terminus, Ekipso Lando. The museum is on the far side of the amusement park so it is best to avoid going at weekends, when buses are packed solid with families en route to the park.

The museum, on the grounds of the 1970 World's Fair site, was designed by Kurokaura Kusho and is furnished with the latest technical equipment. The collections contain extremely rare objects from the far reaches of the world; musical instruments are particularly well documented. Unfortunately, the explanations are in Japanese only. In order to take full advantage of this museum, it is best to go with a Japanese friend.

TOKYO ADDRESSES

This section includes a selection of hotels, restaurants, cafés, bars and shops classified by neighbourhood (see below).

Telephone area code: 03.

▬ SYMBOLS USED

Hotels

The prices given are for single rooms without tax or service charges, and are correct at the time of printing. The following classification system is used:

▲▲▲▲ Over ¥10,000
▲▲▲ ¥10,000 to ¥8000
▲▲ ¥8000 to ¥4000
▲ under ¥4000

① Central heating
② Air conditioning
③ Bathroom
④ Telephone
⑤ Television

All the hotels of the ▲▲▲▲ and ▲▲▲ categories provide ①, ②, ③, ④ and ⑤. For these establishments, the symbols corresponding to these comforts have been omitted. The symbols are systematically included for hotels of ▲▲ and ▲ categories.

Restaurants

The following classification system is used:

♦♦♦♦ Over ¥10,000
♦♦♦ ¥5000 to ¥10,000
♦♦ ¥3000 to ¥5000
♦ under ¥3000

The restaurants, like the hotels, are arranged alphabetically by price group within each neighbourhood.

▬ CONTENTS

▬ *AKASAKA/KOJIMACHI*

Hotels

▲▲▲▲ **Akasaka Prince Hotel**, 1-2 Koiocho, Chiyoda-ku, VII, C3 ☎ 3234111, telex 232 4028. Four minutes from Akasaka-Mitsuke Station. 760 rooms. Restaurants, bar, café, business center and facilities for banquets. This 40-storey hotel is the work of Kenzo Tange, the architect who designed the Olympic Stadium. There is a Rococo-style French restaurant, the Trianon. The view is one of the best in Tokyo.

▲▲▲▲ **Akasaka Tokyu Hotel**, 2-14-3 Nagatacho, Chiyoda-ku, VII, C2, b, ☎ 3580 2311, telex 222 4310. Opposite Akasaka-Mitsuke Station. 540 rooms. Restaurants, bar, café and facilities for banquets and wedding receptions. Very well located.

▲▲▲▲ **Capital Tokyu Hotel**, 2-10-3 Nagatacho, Chiyoda-ku, VIII, D1, c, ☎ 3581 4511, telex 222 3605 CAPTEL J, cable CAPTEL J 24290. One minute from Kokkai-Gijidomae Station. 458 rooms. Restaurants, swimming pool and facilities for conferences and wedding receptions. Formerly the Hilton Hotel, this establishment has changed its name and its management, but the decor is just as refined as before.

▲▲▲▲ **L'Ermitage**, 6-13-12 Akasaka, Minato-ku, VIII, C2, ☎ 3583 9111. Five minutes from Akasaka Station. Near *Los Pratos* restaurant. A small, expensive and luxurious hotel.

▲▲▲▲ **New Otani**, 4-1 Koiocho, Chiyoda-ku, VII, C3, ☎ 3265 1111, telex J24719, cable HOTELNEWOTANI TOKYO. A four-minute walk from Akasaka-Mitsuke Station and eight minutes from Yotsuya Station. 2 057 rooms. This is the largest hotel in Asia, and most of the important international congresses in Tokyo take place here. Its facilities include just about everything: good restaurants (including La Tour d'Argent), a swimming pool, a Japanese garden and shops. There is a shuttle service to Narita airport.

▲▲ **Akasaka Shanpia Hotel** (business hotel), 7-6-13 Akasaka, Minato-ku, VIII, C1, ☎ 3586 0811. Five minutes from Akasaka Station. 250 rooms. ① ② ③ ④ ⑤. Restaurants, café, bar and facilities for banquets. Very calm.

▲▲ **Diamond Hotel**, 25 Ichibancho, Chiyoda-ku, VII, D2, g, ☎ 3263 2211, telex 232 2764, cable HOTELDIA TOKYO. Two minutes from Hanzomon Station. 478 rooms. ① ② ③ ④ ⑤. Restaurants, hairdresser and facilities for banquets and wedding receptions. Located in a very quiet, verdant neighbourhood. Functional.

▲▲ **Hotel Toshi Center**, 2-4-1 Hirakawacho, Chiyoda-ku, VII, D3, h, ☎ 3265 8211. Two minutes from Kojimachi Station. 197 rooms. ① ② ③ ④ ⑤. Restaurants and café.

▲▲ **Hotel Yoko Akasaka** (business hotel), 6-4-12 Akasaka, Minato-ku, VIII, C2, i, ☎ 3580 4050. Three minutes from Akasaka Station. You can easily walk to Roppongi. 245 rooms. ① ② ③ ④ ⑤. Restaurant, café and facilities for conferences.

▲▲ **Kojimachi Kaikan**, 2-4-3 Hirakawacho, Chiyoda-ku, VII, D3, j, ☎ 3265 5361. Two minutes from Kojimachi Station. 180 rooms. ① ② ④ ⑤. Restaurants, café, bar and facilities for banquets and wedding receptions. Most of the rooms are Japanese-style, without bathrooms.

▲▲ **Ma Road Inn Akasaka** (business hotel), 6-15-17 Akasaka, Minato-ku, VII, C3, k, ☎ 3585 7611. Four minutes from Akasaka Station. Not far from Roppongi. 264 rooms. ① ② ③ ④ ⑤. Restaurants and bar.

Restaurants

◆◆◆◆ **La Granata** (Italian cuisine), TBS Kaikan B1, 5-3-3 Akasaka, Minato-ku, VII, C1, n° 1, ☎ 3582 3241. Open daily 11am-10:30 pm. Very near Akasaka Station. This is where the Italian residents of Tokyo meet. The staff is very friendly. Reservations recommended.

◆◆◆ **Hayashi** (Japanese cuisine), Sanno Kaiban Building 4F, 2-14-1 Akasaka, Minato-ku, VIII, C1, n° 2, ☎ 3582 4078. Open Mon-Sat 11:30am-2pm, 5:30-11pm. An outer door opens on to a gravel path. Behind a 2nd door there is a rustic-style restaurant. *Sumiyaki* (charcoal-grilled food) of fish, meat and vegetables is prepared at your table. At lunch, only *oyako-donburi* (chicken and egg on a bed of rice) is served. Very pleasant.

♦♦♦ **Kaisaki** (Japanese cuisine and seafood), Akasaka New Plaza 1F, 7-6-47 Akasaka, Minato-ku, VIII, C2, n° 3 ☎ 3586 8538. Open Mon-Sat noon-2pm, 5-11pm; Sun and holidays 4-9pm. You cannot find fresher fish and seafood anywhere. You choose your meal from an aquarium at the counter !

♦♦♦ **Los Pratos** (Spanish cuisine), Terrace Akasaka 1F, 6-13-11 Akasaka, Minato-ku, VIII, C2, n° 4, ☎ 3583-4262. Open 11:30-10:30pm. This restaurant has a good reputation in Tokyo.

♦♦♦ **Muryoan** (Buddhist cuisine), 6-9-17 Akasaka, Minato-ku, VIII, C2, n° 5, ☎ 3583 5829. Open Mon-Sat noon-3pm, 5-9pm. Closed holidays. Five minutes from Akasaka Station. The *fucha-ryori* (a type of *shojin-ryori*, or Buddhist cuisine) and the *cha-kaiseki* (tea ceremony cuisine) are served by Buddhist nuns in a traditional Japanese house with a garden. Very good but expensive. Reservations are essential.

♦♦ **Ao Zai** (Vietnamese cuisine), Trade Akasaka Building 1F, 5-4-14 Akasaka, Minato-ku, VIII, C1, n° 6, ☎ 3583 0234. Open Mon-Sat 5-10pm. Closed holidays. Near Akasaka Station.

♦♦ **Mimiu** *(udon)*, 3-12-13 Akasaka, Minato-ku, VIII, C1, n° 7, ☎ 3505 3366. Open daily noon-9pm. Closed the first Sun of every month. Near Akasaka Station. Sumptuous *udon* (wheat noodles). From 1-4pm you can eat *udonsuki* (noodles) for 10% less in this elegant restaurant.

♦♦ **Moti** (Indian cuisine), Kinpa Building 3F, 2-14-31 Akasaka, Minato-ku, VIII, B3, N° 8, ☎ 3584 6640. Akasaka Station. Open Mon-Sat 11:30am-10pm; Sun noon-10pm. Very aromatic food. The curries are particularly good. There is another branch in Roppongi, ☎ 3479 1939. Inexpensive.

♦♦ **Mugyodon** (Korean cuisine), Akasaka Sangyo Building 2F, 2-17-74 Akasaka, Minato-ku, VIII, C1, n° 9, ☎ 3586 6478. Open Mon-Sat 5pm-3am. Closed holidays. The atmosphere is very friendly. Authentic Korean cuisine.

♦♦ **Taji** (Indian cuisine), 3-2-7 Akasaka, Minato-ku, VIII, C1, n° 10, ☎ 3586 6606. Open Mon-Fri 11:30am-2:30pm, 5:30-10:15pm; Sat-Sun and holidays noon-9pm. The lunch menu is reasonably priced.

♦♦ **Tambaya** (eel), 3-2 Kojimachi, Chiyoda-ku, VII, D2, n° 11, ☎ 3261 2633. Open Mon-Sat 11:30am-8pm. Closed holidays. Near Kojimachi and Hanzomon stations. The interior, although modernized, is still very Japanese. There is an excellent eel salad. The menu is in English.

♦♦ **Yotaro** (Japanese cuisine), Akasaka-Kan Arai Building 1F, 3-12-18 Akasaka, Minato-ku, VIII, C1, n° 12, ☎ 3584 7686. Open Mon-Sat noon-1:30pm, 5:30-10:30pm. Near Akasaka and Akasaka-Mitsuke stations. A specialist of *tai* (gilt-head bream). Try the *tai meshi* (bream with rice). Not too crowded at lunch.

♦ **Akimoto** (eel), 3-4 Kojimachi, Chiyoda-ku, VII, C2, n° 13, ☎ 3261 6762. Open Mon-Sat 11:30am-2pm, 5-8pm. Closed holidays. One minute from Kojimachi Station. The eel melts like butter in your mouth. The atmosphere is very Japanese. The inexpensive menu is good.

Shop

Fuso (antiques), Akasaka New Plaza 1F, 7-6-47 Akasaka, Minato-ku, VIII, C2, n° 14, ☎ 3583 5945. Open Mon-Sat 9am-6pm. Between Akasaka and Nogizaka stations, opposite a primary school. A large variety of antiques and exotic curiosities. Quality is guaranteed.

▬ AOYAMA

Hotels

▲▲▲ **The President Hotel Aoyama**, 2-2-3 Minami-Aoyama, Minato-ku, VIII, B1, a, ☎ 3497 0111. One minute from Aoyama-itchome Station. 210 rooms. Restaurants, cafés and facilities for conferences. A pleasant and quiet hotel near the Omiya Gosho (Prince's Palace).

▲▲ **Asia Center of Japan**, 8-10-32 Akasaka, Minato-ku, VII, C3, b, ☎ 3402 6111. Five minutes from Aoyama-itchome Station. ① ② ③ ④. Not far from Roppongi, this hotel is situated in a calm district near the Nogi Jinja, where a flea market is held on the 2nd Sunday of every month.

▲▲ **Nihon Seinenkan**, 15 Kasumigaoka, Shinjuku-ku, XI, D1, C, ☎ 3401 0101. ① ② ③ ④. This hotel is surrounded by greenery. Very peaceful. Well-known musicians sometimes give concerts here.

Restaurants

♦♦♦♦ **Sabatini Aoyama** (Italian cuisine), Aoyama Sun Crest Building B1, 2-13-5 Kita-Aoyama, Minato-ku, VIII, A2, n° 1a, ☎ 3402 3812. Open 11:30am-2:30pm, 5:30-11pm. Near the Aoyama Belle Commons Building. This is the most well known and undoubtedly the best Italian restaurant in Tokyo. Reservations are necessary.

♦♦♦ **Antonio's** (Italian cuisine), nº 22 Daikyo Building 1F, 7-3-6 Minami-Aoyama, Minato-ku, VIII, A3, nº 2a, ☎ 37970388. Open Tues-Sun noon-2:30pm, 6-10pm. Antonio's has been in Tokyo for 40 years. Select clientele.

♦♦♦ **Cay** (Thai cuisine), Spiral B1, 5-6-23 Minami-Aoyama, Minato-ku, XI, D3, nº 3, ☎ 34985790. Open Mon-Sat 6pm-1am. A fashionable restaurant that occasionally hosts concerts.

♦♦♦ **Chez Pierre** (French cuisine), 1-23-10 Minami-Aoyama, Minato-ku, ☎ 34751400. Open daily 11:30am-11:30pm. One minute from Nogizaka Station. Good authentic French cooking. There is also a small bar.

♦♦♦ **Daini's Table** (Chinese cuisine), 6-3-14 Minami-Aoyama, Minato-ku, VIII, A3, nº 5, ☎ 34070363. Open daily 6pm-2am. Chinese *nouvelle cuisine* in a very elegant atmosphere.

♦♦♦ **Isshin** *(shabu shabu),* Sugimoto Building 2, 4F, 4-21-29 Minami-Aoyama, Minato-ku, XI, D2, nº 6a, ☎ 34014611. Open daily 11:30am-3pm, 5-11pm. This rather chic restaurant serves good *sukiyaki* and *shabu shabu* (meat dishes prepared at your table). There is a fixed menu at lunch.

♦♦♦ **Joël** (French cuisine), 5-6-24 Minami-Aoyama, Minato-ku, XI, D2, nº 7, ☎ 34007149. Open daily noon-2:30pm, 6-10pm. On the 2nd floor above Dunkin Donuts. This is where many French residents of Tokyo meet. The wine list is impressive.

♦♦♦ **La Marée** (French cuisine), Maison de la Mia B1, 5-1-25 Minami-Aoyama, Minato-ku, XI, D2, nº 8, ☎ 34990077. Open daily noon-2pm, 5:30-10pm. Near Omote Sando Crossing. Very imaginative family cooking based on fresh (never frozen) fish. Excellent.

♦♦♦ **Le Poisson Rouge** (French cuisine), From 1st Building B1, 5-3-10 Minami-Aoyama, Minato-ku, XI, D3, nº 9, ☎ 34993391. Open Mon-Sat noon-3pm, 6-11:30pm. The chef of this restaurant is well acquainted with French cuisine. Take his suggestions and you will not be disappointed.

♦ **Uomussa** (Japanese cuisine), Takahashi Building 2F, 2-27-13 Minami-Aoyama, Minato-ku, VIII, A2, nº 10a, ☎ 34012216. Open Mon-Sat 11am-2pm, 5pm-7am. Closed holidays. A good fish restaurant.

Cafés and Discotheques

♦♦ **Hippofellow** (discotheque), Akasaka Heights B1, 8-5-28 Akasaka, Minato-ku, VIII, C1, ☎ 34042640. Open daily 7pm-5am. The interior is covered with marble.

♦ **Spiral Garden** (café), Spiral 1F, 5-6-23 Minami-Aoyama, Minato-ku, XI, D3, nº 12, ☎ 34981171. This café almost resembles a museum of modern art.

♦ **Tokio** (discotheque) Aizawa Building B1, 5-9-12 Minami-Aoyama, Minato-ku, XI, D3, nº 13, ☎ 34071085. Open 6pm-5am. In the various rooms, you can watch a video, play electronic games or dance on the dance floor. This spot is frequented by fashion models.

♦ **Yoku Moku** (café), 5-3-3 Minami-Aoyama, XI, D3, nº 14, ☎ 34064121. Open daily 10am-7pm. South of Omotesando Station. Good pastries.

Shops

Japan Traditional Craft Center (arts and crafts), Plaza 246 Building 2 F, 3-1-1 Minami-Aoyama, Minato-ku, VIII, A2, nº 15, ☎ 34032460. Open Fri-Wed 10am-6pm. Exhibits and sells objects from every region of Japan.

Kinokuniya International (supermarket), 3-11-7 Kita-Aoyama, Minato-ku, XI, D3, nº 16, ☎ 34091231. Open daily 9:30am-8pm. From French camembert to Russian caviar; you will find here anything that comes from the West.

Matsushita Gallery (*ukiyo-e*), 6-3-12 Minami-Aoyama, Minato-ku, XI, D3, nº 17, ☎ 34074966. Open Tues-Sat 10:30am-5:30pm. Exhibits and sells *ukiyo-e* (Japanese prints).

West (pastry shop), 1-22-10 Minami-Aoyama, Minato-ku, XI, D3, ☎ 34026901. Open Mon-Sat 9am-11pm; Sun and holidays noon-9pm. A well-known establishment.

Y's (fashion), 5-3-6 Minami-Aoyama, Minato-ku, XI, D3, nº 19, ☎ 34865314. Open 11am-9pm. This is one of Yoji Yamamoto's shops.

▬ *ASAKUSA*

Hotels

▲▲▲▲ **Asakusa View Hotel,** 3-17-1 Nishi-Asakusa, Taito-ku, V, A2, a, ☎ 38422111. Eight minutes from Tawaramachi Station. 342 rooms. Restaurants, café, bar, Japanese garden, Japanese bathrooms, swimming-pool, gymnasium and facilities for conferences and wedding receptions. The most international hotel in Asakusa.

▲▲ **Asakusa Plaza Hotel,** 1-2-1 Asakusa, Taito-ku, V, B2, ☎ 3845 2621. In the heart of this lively district, near Asakusa Station. 69 rooms. Restaurants. ① ② ③ ④. Very handy for visiting Asakusa.

▲▲ **Mikawaya Bekkan** *(ryokan),* 1-31-11 Asakusa, Taito-ku, V, B2, C, ☎ 3843-2345. 12 rooms. Five minutes from Asakusa Station. ① ②. In the center of this animated district. Not expensive.

Restaurants

♦♦♦ **Chinya** 1-3-4 Asakusa, Taito-ku, V, B2, n° 1, ☎ 38410010. Open Thurs-Tues 11:30am-9:30pm. Near Kaminarimon Gate. This is one of the oldest restaurants in Asakusa. Excellent *sukiyaki.*

♦♦♦ **Ichimon** (Japanese cuisine), 3-12-6 Asakusa, Taito-ku, V, A1, n° 2, ☎ 3875 6800. Open Mon-Sat 5-11pm. Closed holidays. There is a large barrel at the entrance. To follow tradition, you pay in *mon* (ancient Japanese money) bought at the door when you arrive. The *take-dofu* (*tofu* served in a bamboo bowl) is the speciality of the house. In the winter, you can order *yose-nabe* (literally, 'odds and ends pot').

♦♦♦ **Imhan Bekkan-Aguratei** *(sukiyaki and shabu shabu),* 2-2-5 Asakusa, Taito-ku, V, AB3, n° 3, ☎ 3841 2690. Open Fri-Wed 11:30am-8:30pm. The atmosphere is interesting. The speciality of the house is *ohmi no gyu-niku* (ohmi beef).

♦♦♦ **Kuremutsu** (Japanese cuisine), 2-2-13 Asakusa, Taito-ku, V, n° 4, ☎ 3842 0906. Open Fri-Wed 4-10pm. The interior is almost a museum, and the cuisine is very refined.

♦♦♦ **Mugitoro** (Japanese cuisine), 2-2-4 Kaminarimon, Taito-ku, V, B3, n° 5, ☎ 3842 1066. Open Mon-Sat 11:30am-9:30pm; Sun and holidays 11am-9:30pm. A yam specialist. There is an inexpensive menu at lunch.

♦♦♦ **Nakasei** *(tempura),* 1-39-13 Asakusa, Taito-ku, V, B2, n° 6, ☎ 3841 4015. Open Wed-Mon noon-8pm. A peaceful restaurant with a Japanese garden.

♦♦ **Aramasa** (Japanese cuisine), 2-12-8 Nishi-Asakusa, Taito-ku, V, n° 7, ☎ 3844 4008. Open Mon-Sat 5pm-1am. Clients dine around an open fire as in the north of Japan. The cuisine is warming and original. Try the *kirotampo-nabe* or the *inaniwa-udon.*

♦♦ **Daikokuya** *(tempura)* 1-38-10 Asakusa, Taito-ku, V, B2 n° 8, ☎ 3844 1111. Open Tues-Sun 11am-3pm, 5-9pm. This restaurant may appear simple and rather banal, but people queue for the copious and inexpensive *ebitendon* (shrimp on a bed of rice).

♦♦ **Iidaya** (Japanese cuisine), 3-3-2 Nishi-Asakusa, Taito-ku, V, A2 n° 9, ☎ 3843 0881. Open Thurs-Tues 11:30am-10pm. A family restaurant with a varied clientele. The loach (a freshwater fish) is excellent.

♦♦ **Miuraya** *(fugu),* 2-19-9 Asakusa, Taito-ku, V, A1 n° 10, ☎ 3841 3151. Open daily noon-10pm. Closed Aug and Wed from Apr to Sept. A *fugu* specialist with efficient service. The owner possesses a fabulous collection of sumo objects.

♦♦ **Tatsumiya** (Japanese cuisine), 1-33-5 Akasaka, Taito-ku, V, B2 n° 11, ☎ 3842 7373. Open Tues-Sat noon-2pm, 5-9pm; Sun noon-4:30pm. A charming restaurant.

♦♦ **Toritako** (chicken), 2-32-2 Asakusa, Taito-ku, V, B2 n° 12, ☎ 3844 2756. Open Tues-Sun 6-9pm. When the kitchen runs out of chicken, the restaurant closes no matter what time it is. Reservations are absolutely essential.

♦♦ **Yakko** (eel), 1-10-2 Asakusa, Taito-ku, V, A2 n° 13, ☎ 3842 1066. Open Wed-Mon 11:30am-10pm. Yakko has served Edo-style eel for over 200 years.

♦ **Futaba** *(kamameshi),* 1-6-4 Asakusa, Taito-ku, V, A2 n° 14, ☎ 3841 5354. Open Fri-Wed 1-10pm. The *kamameshi* (rice stewed in a small pot) is very good.

♦ **Namiki Yabu Soba** *(soba),* 2-11-9 Kaminarimon, Taito-ku, V, B2-3 n° 15, ☎ 3841 3151. Open Fri-Wed 11:30am-8pm. This restaurant serves only *soba* (a noodle dish) but it is always excellent.

♦ **Sometaro** *(okonomiyaki),* 2-2-2 Nishi-Asakusa, Taito-ku, V, A2 n° 16, ☎ 3844 9504. Open Tues-Sat 5-10pm; Sun and holidays noon-9:30pm. This old restaurant, frequented by writers and artists, is the place to taste *okonomiyaki* in a friendly atmosphere.

♦ **Hontosaya** (Korean cuisine), 3-1-9 Asakusa, Taito-ku, V, AB1, n° 17, ☎ 3845 0138. Asakusa Station. Open daily 2:30pm-5am. This is one of the best *yaki-niku* (Korean restaurants) in Tokyo. After you have dined, try a ginseng or garlic liqueur.

Café

♦ **Enzeru** (café), 3-22-12 Asakusa, Taito-ku, V, B1 n° 18, ☎ 3874 0617. Open daily 9am-11pm. A local carpenter has built the café of his dreams; charming decor.

Shops

Asakusa is an ideal neighbourhood for shopping. The **Nakamise Dori**, V, B2 nº 19, is the main shopping street of the district.

Adachiya (costumes), 2-22-12 Asakusa, Taito-ku, V, A1 nº 20, ☎ 3841 4915. Open daily 10am-8:30pm. A large choice of traditional Japanese festival costumes, including *happi* (Japanese T-shirts), *kobi* and *momoshiki*.

Bunsendo (fans), 1-20-2 Asakusa, Taito-ku, V, B2 nº 21, ☎ 3844 9711. Open daily 10:30am-6pm. A specialist of Japanese fans, selling the most exquisite products available anywhere.

Fujiya Tenugui-ten (handkerchiefs), 2-2-15 Asakusa, Taito-ku, V, B2 nº 22, ☎ 3841 2283. Open Fri-Wed 9am-8pm. The Japanese handkerchiefs and napkins sold here make excellent light and inexpensive gifts.

Hanato (lanterns), 2-25-6 Asakusa, Taito-ku, V, A1 nº 23, ☎ 3841 6411. Open daily 10am-9pm. Closed the second and fourth Tues of every month. Here you can order a paper lantern with your name on it.

Hyakusuke (cosmetics), 2-2-14 Asakusa, Taito-ku, V, B2 nº 24, ☎ 3841 7058. Open daily 11am-5pm. This simple shop supplies cosmetics to geishas and Kabuki actors. Good cosmetic brushes also are available.

Noren House 'Bengara' *(noren)*, 2-35-11 Asakusa, Taito-ku, V, B2 nº 25, ☎ 3841 6613. Open Fri-Wed 10am-6pm. *Noren* are pieces of decorated cloth used inside Japanese houses. Printed in traditional or modern patterns, they make very beautiful and practical gifts.

Shimizu Honten (antiques), 2-30-11 Asakusa, Taito-ku, V, B2 nº 26, ☎ 3841 5951. Open daily 10am-9pm. Behind Asakusa Park.

Umenura (Japanese pastry), 3-22-12 Asakusa, Taito-ku, V, B1 nº 27, ☎ 3873 6992. Open Mon-Sat 1-11pm. An unpretentious establishment offering the traditional pastries stuffed with red beans.

Yonoya (combs), 1-37-10 Asakusa, Taito-ku, V, B2 nº 28, ☎ 3844 1755. Open Thurs-Tues 10am-7pm. Since the 18th century, Yonoya has made three handmade boxwood combs a day! These very high quality articles produce no static electricity.

The **Kappabashi district**, V, A2 nº 29, is where the Tokyo restaurateurs come to buy their kitchen equipment. You will certainly be able to sell you a dealer who is willing to sell you a mihon (a wax reproduction of a dish) at retail.

▬ *DAIKANYAMACHO*

Restaurants

♦♦♦ **Daikonya** *(Kaiseki)*, Daikanyama Park Side Village B1, 9-8 Sarugakucho, Shibuya-ku, I, A2, ☎ 3496 6664. Open Mon-Sat 1-3pm, 5:30-10pm. Five minutes from Daikanyama Station. This restaurant instigated the trend for Japanese *nouvelle cuisine*. Reservations are essential.

♦♦ **Chez Lui** (French cuisine), 17-22 Daikanyamacho, Shibuya-ku, I, A2, ☎ 3461 9550. Open daily 11:30am-2:30, 5:30-9:30pm. Three minutes from Daikanyama Station. A little family restaurant with good food.

Shops

Hillside Terrace, 29-6 Sarugakucho, Shibuya-ku, I, A2, is a very chic district with many shops, restaurants and cafés.

Junko Shimada (fashion), Aobadai Terrace, 1-1-4 Aobadai, Meguro-ku, I, A2, ☎ 3463 2346. Open Tues-Sun 11am-8pm.

Tokio Kumagai (shoes), Cederstone Villa B1, 15-5 Hachiyamacho, Shibuya-ku, I, A2, ☎ 3477 2613. Open daily 11am-8pm. Started by Fiorucci's former designer.

▬ *EBISU*

Restaurants

♦♦ **Beer Station** (bistro), 4-20-18 Ebisu, Shibuya-ku, X, A3, ☎ 3447 6811. Six minutes from Ebisu Station. This former Sapporo brewery has been transformed into a 'beer village'. Food (grilled meat, sausages and the like) is served in either a train carriage or a large German-style room. Loud and cheerful. Relatively inexpensive.

♦ **Kagetsu** *(ramen)*. Honma Building 1F, 1-10-8 Ebisu-Nishi, Shibuya-ku, I, A2, ☎ 3496 6885. Open daily 11am-6am. Closed the 3rd Mon of every month. Two minutes from Ebisu Station. Near the Ebisu-Minami Crossing. A good *ramen* (noodle) restaurant for night hawks.

♦ **Phnom Penh** (Cambodian cuisine), Ebisu-Nishi Building 2F, 1-10-14

Ebisu-Nishi, Shibuya-ku, I, A2, ☎ 3461 2769. Open Mon-Sat noon-2pm, 5-11pm. A good little restaurant where half the clientele are foreigners.

▬ FUNAMACHI

Restaurant

♦♦ **Pas à Pas** (French cuisine), 5 Funamachi, Shinjuku-ku, VII, AB2, ☎ 3357 7888. Open daily 11:30am-1:30pm, 6-10pm. Near Yotsuya-Sanchome Station. A typical Parisian bistro, complete with check-ered napkins, posters of artists on the walls and Ricard pitchers and ashtrays. The dishes are copious and very refined. The veal sweetbreads are remarkable. Reasonable.

▬ GINZA

Hotels

▲▲▲▲ **Ginza Daiichi Hotel,** 8-13-1 Ginza, Chou-ku, III, C2, a, ☎ 3542 5311, telex 252 3714. Near Higashi-Ginza Station. 800 rooms. Restaurants, café, bar, hairdresser and facilities for banquets. Very well located.

▲▲▲▲ **Ginza Tobu Hotel,** 6-14-9 Ginza, Chuo-Ku, III, G2, b, ☎ 3546 0111. One minute from Higashi-Ginza Station. 206 rooms. Restaurants, bar, café, florist, travel agency, business center, secretarial services and facilities for banquets. This hotel opened in 1987. The service is good.

▲▲▲▲ **Ginza Tokyu Hotel,** 5-15-9 Ginza, Chuo-ku, III, CD2, c, ☎ 3541 2411, telex 252 2601 THCGIN J, cable GINZATOKYUTEL. One minute from Higashi-Ginza Station. 447 rooms. Restaurants, bar, café and facilities for wedding receptions. This hotel is well located near the most animated area in Ginza.

▲▲▲▲ **Hotel Seiyo Ginza,** 1-1-1 Ginza, Chuo-ku, III, D1, d, ☎ 3535 1111. 80 rooms. Restaurant, bar, theatre and cinema. This is an extremely fashionable hotel owned by Seibu. Each room is decorated differently.

▲▲▲ **Ginza Nikko Hotel,** 8-4-21 Ginza, Chuo-ku, III, C2, ☎ 3571 4911. 136 rooms. Restaurants, bar, café and facilities for banquets. This hotel, owned by Japan AirLines, is in the commercial district of Ginza.

▲▲▲ **Hotel Ginza Daiei,** 3-12-2 Ginza, Chuo-ku, III, D1, f, ☎ 3541 2681. Three minutes from Ginza Station. 102 rooms. Restaurants, café, bar, sauna and facilities for banquets and wedding receptions. Well located.

▲▲▲ **Mitsui Urban Hotel Ginza,** 8-6-15 Ginza, Chuo-ku, III, C2, g, ☎ 3572 4131. One minute from Shimbashi Station. 263 rooms. Restaurants, bars and facilities for banquets. Conveniently located for shopping and transport. The service is friendly and efficient.

Restaurants

♦♦♦♦ **Maxim's de Paris** (French cuisine), Sony Building B3, 5-3-1 Ginza, Chuo-ku, III, C1, n° 1, ☎ 3572 3621. Open Mon-Sat 11:30am-2:30pm, 5:30-11pm. This is one of the best French restaurants in Tokyo. The cuisine is the same as in Paris and so is the art nouveau decor. The list of 270 wines should satisfy the most demanding.

♦♦♦♦ **Sabatini di Firenze** (Italian cuisine), Sony Building 7F, 5-3-1 Ginza, Chuo-ku III, C1, n° 2, ☎ 3573 0013. Near Ginza and Yurakucho stations. Open daily noon-2:30pm, 5:30-10:30pm. Along with Maxim's (located in the same buiding), this is one of the most expensive restaurants in Tokyo. The Italian chef offers excellent Florentine cooking in all its glory. The presentation is particularly refined.

♦♦♦ **Chichibunishiki** (Japanese cuisine), 2-13-14 Ginza, Chuo-ku, III, D1, n° 3, ☎ 3541 4777. Open Mon-Sat 5-10:30pm. Closed holidays. Behind Showa Dori. This old establishment will captivate you as soon as you walk in. It serves fresh mountain vegetables and sake from the country.

♦♦♦ **Izusen** (*shojin ryori,* or Buddhist cuisine), 8-2-3 Ginza, Chuo-ku, I, B2, ☎ 3571 8123. Open Mon-Sat 11am-8pm. Closed holidays. Behind the Kyoto Center Buiding. This cuisine is called *tetsuhachi,* named after the bowl used by the Buddhist bonzes. The food, inspired by Zen, is simple yet refined. There is only one fixed menu.

♦♦♦ **Nenohi-ryo** (Japanese cuisine), Takumi Building B1, 8-4-2 Ginza, Chuo-ku, III, C2, n° 5, ☎ 35730873. Open Mon-Sat 5-10:30pm. Closed holidays. The owner is Mr. Morita, the president of Sony. His family brews sake in the Aichi Prefecture, and the cuisine served at this restaurant is — of course — from his home region.

♦♦♦ **Shabusen,** Ginza Core Building B2 and 2F, 5-8-20 Ginza, Chuo-ku, III, C1, n° 6, ☎ 35723806 and 35711717. Open daily 11am-9:30pm. The *sukiyaki* and the *shabu shabu* are reasonably priced.

♦♦♦ **Suehiro** (steak), 6-11-2 Ginza, Chuo-ku, III, C2, n° 7, ☎ 35719271. Open daily 11am-9:30pm. This is part of a chain of restaurants, but each branch has its own original feature. The steak is inexpensive.

♦♦♦ **Ten'ichi** (tempura), 6-6-5 Ginza, Chuo-ku, III, C1, n° 8, ☎ 35711949. Open daily 11:30am-9:30pm. This is the world's most famous *tempura* restaurant. Supposedly, there is a secret to the frying of the fritters. Excellent but more expensive than other *tempura* restaurants.

♦♦♦ **Yasuko** (udon), 5-4-6 Ginza, Chuo-ku, III, C1, n° 9, ☎ 35710621. Open daily 4-11pm. Closed Sun in July and Aug. Behind the Sony Building. A bit expensive for noodles but well worth trying.

♦♦ **Ashoka** (Indian cuisine), 7-9-18 Ginza, Chuo-ku, III, C2, n° 10, ☎ 3572 2377. Open Mon-Sat 11:30am-9:30pm; Sun noon-7:30pm. Near Ginza Station. Located next door to the Indian Tourist Office, this is one of the most elegant Indian restaurants in Tokyo. *Tikka* (marinated chicken) and *masala* (mutton curry) are among the specialities of the house.

♦♦ **Kanmon-gonendo** (soba, udon), Tshii-Kishuya Building 1 F, 7-6-5-Ginza, Chuo-ku, III, C2, n° 11, ☎ 35716076. Open Mon-Sat 11:30am-2:30pm, 5pm-1am. Closed holidays. The speciality of the house, *inaniwa-udon* (noodles), is from the Akita Prefecture.

♦♦ **Shiruhachi** (Japanese cuisine), n° 12 Togen Building B1, 8-6-4 Ginza, Chuo-ku, III, C1-2, ☎ 35710456. Open Mon-Sat 5:30pm-2am. Closed holidays. About 20 different *miso-shiru* (Japanese soups) are offered, but you can also order rice and other typical Japanese side dishes.

♦♦ **Tsubohan** (Japanese cuisine), 5-3-9 Ginza, Chuo-ku, III, C1, n° 14, ☎ 35713467. Open Mon-Sat 4:30-10:30pm. Closed holidays. Behind the Sony Building. The women who run this restaurant have served family cooking for about 40 years.

♦♦ **Yukun-Sakagura** (Japanese cuisine), Seio Building B 1, 2-2-18 Ginza, Chuo-ku, III, C1, n° 15, ☎ 35616672. Open Mon-Fri 11:30am-1:30pm, 5-10pm; Sat 4-9pm. Closed holidays and the 1st and 3rd Sat of every month. The cuisine is from the Kyushu district. Arrive early because of the crowds. There is another branch at Kyowa Bank B 1, 1-16-4 Shimbashi, Minato-ku.

▲ **Baden Baden** (German cuisine), 2-1-8 Yurakucho, Chiyoda-ku, II, B3, n° 18, ☎ 35082806. Near Yurakucho Station. Open Mon-Sat 11:30am-1:30pm, 4-10:30pm; Sun 11:30am-1:30pm, 4-9pm. A beer hall where you can order sausages and fried potatoes with your beer.

♦ **Omatsuya** (soba), Ginza In Building 2 F, 5-4-18 Ginza, Chuo-ku, III, C1, n° 16, ☎ 35717053. Open Mon-Sat 11:30am-2pm, 5-10:30pm. The interior resembles a samurai's house from northern Japan. This restaurant specializes in handmade *soba* (noodles).

▲ **Steinhaus** (German cuisine), 2-1-8 Yurakucho, Chiyoda-ku, II, B3, n° 19, ☎ 35950417. Near Yurakucho Station. Open daily 11:30am-10pm. Part of the Delicatessen chain, this restaurant offers slightly more elaborate food than does Baden Baden.

♦ **Toraya** (Japanese pastry), 7-8-6 Ginza, Chuo-ku, III, C2, n° 17, ☎ 35713679. This establishment is 450 years old! On the second floor, above the shop, there is a café that serves green teas (gyokuro, macha and sencha) and Japanese pastries.

Bars

♦♦ **Lupin** (bar), Tsukamoto Fudosan Building B 1, 5-5-11 Ginza, Chuo-ku, III, C1, n° 20, ☎ 35710750. Open Mon-Sat 5-11pm. Closed holidays. This bar has been open for 60 years. The decor evokes the 'good old days' of Ginza.

♦♦ **Pilsen** (beer), 6-8-7 Ginza, Chuo-ku, III, C2, n° 21, ☎ 35712236. Open Mon-Sat noon-10pm; Sun and holidays noon-9pm. On the ground floor of the Kojunsha Building. An old bistro that will transport you to a Bavarian village. A beer with sauerkraut and ham will make you forget your trying day.

♦♦ **Sans Souci** (bar), 6-8-7 Ginza, Chuo-ku, III, C2, n° 22, ☎ 35715377. Open Mon-Fri 5-10:30pm. Closed holidays. In the same building as Pilsen but on the opposite side. This very old establishment, frequented by writers and artists, was named the 'sans souci' by the writer Tanizaki. The atmosphere is pleasant.

Shops

Beishu (dolls), 5-9-13 Ginza, Chuo-ku, III, C2, nº 23, ☎ 3572 1397. Open Fri-Wed 1-7pm. Traditional dolls. Beishu Hara was considered a living National Treasure.

Itoya (paper), 2-7-15 Ginza, Chuo-ku, III, C1, nº 24, ☎ 3561 8311. Open Mon-Sat 9:30am-6pm; Sun and holidays 10am-6pm. This is one of the largest stationery shops in Tokyo. Postcards, *washi* (Japanese paper) and modern office equipment can be found here. Bilingual visiting cards also can be ordered.

Kunoya (kimono accessories), 6-9-8 Ginza, Chuo-ku, III, C2, nº 25, ☎ 3571 2546. Open daily 10am-8pm. Opposite Matsuzakaya department store.

Kyo-noren (wares from Kyoto), 8-2-8 Ginza, Chuo-ku, III, B2, nº 26, ☎ 3572 6484. Open Mon-Sat 11am-7pm. Closed holidays. Opposite Ginza Nikko Hotel. Full of interesting gifts.

Kyukyodo (paper), 5-7-4 Ginza, Chuo-ku, III, C1, nº 27, ☎ 3571 4429. Open Mon-Sat 10am-8pm; Sun and holidays 11am-7pm. Lots of handsome paper objects (envelopes and writing paper) but also anything needed for calligraphy (brushes, inks and so forth).

Tachikichi (pottery), 5-6-13 Ginza, Chuo-ku, III, C1, nº 28, ☎ 3571 2924. Open Mon-Sat 11am-7pm. A wide choice of pottery.

Takumi (folklore), 8-4-2 Ginza, Chuo-ku, III, C2, nº 29, ☎ 3571 2017. Open Mon-Sat 11am-7pm; holidays 11am-5pm. Near the Ginza Nikko Hotel.

▬ *HARAJUKU*

Hotels

▲▲ **Coop Inn Shibuya**, 6-24-4 Jingumae, Shibuya-ku, XI, C2, a ☎ 3486 6600. Four minutes from Meiji-Jingumae Station and eight minutes from Harajuku Station. 74 rooms. ① ② ③ ④ ⑤. Restaurant, tennis court and facilities for conferences. Run by a university co-op, this hotel is both luxurious and inexpensive. Comfortable and practical for those who like the Harajuku district.

▲▲ **Hotel Harajuku Trimm** (business hotel), 6-28-6 Jingumae, Shibuya-ku, XI, C2, b, ☎ 3498 2101. Located in the centre of Harajuku, this hotel is part of Trimm, an athletic club.

Restaurants

♦♦♦ **La Patata** (Italian cuisine), Shiobara-Gaien Building 1 F, 2-9-11 Jingumae, Shibuya-ku, XI, D2-3, nº 14, ☎ 3403 9664. Open Tues-Sun noon-2pm, 6-11:30pm. Italian family cooking with ingredients that are always fresh.

▲▲▲ **Ristorante Basta Pasta** (Italian cuisine), Face Building 2-32-5 Jingumae, Shibuya-ku, XI, C1, nº 2, ☎ 3478 3022. Open Mon-Sat noon-2pm, 5-10pm; Sun 5-10pm. Five minutes from Harajuku Station. The kitchen is in the middle of the restaurant, and you can watch dishes being prepared.

▲▲▲ **Sin** (Mediterranean cuisine), Lunar House Part 4 B 1, 3-35-15 Jingumae, Shibuya-ku, XI, D1, nº 3a, ☎ 3470 0400. Open daily 1:45-2:30pm, 6pm-1am. Matsui Masami, a fashionable decorator, has designed the impressively painted interior.

♦ **Genroku-Zushi** *(sushi)*, 5-8-5 Jingumae, Shibuya-ku, XI, C2, nº 4, ☎ 3498 3968. Open daily 11am-8:30pm. This restaurant is part of a chain that can be found throughout Tokyo. The *sushi* is served on a conveyor belt, and the number of plates are counted when you pay. A quick and practical way of eating.

♦ **Issen** *(tonkatsu)*, 4-8-5 Jingumae, Shibuya-ku, XI, D2, nº5, ☎ 3470 0071. Open daily 11am-10pm. The fillet of pork is so tender that you can cut it with chopsticks! At any rate, that is the restaurant's slogan.

♦ **Mominoki House** (macrobiotic cuisine), You Building 1 F, 2-18-5 Jingumae, Shibuya, XI, C1, nº 6, ☎ 3405 9144. Open Mon-Sat 11am-11pm. Health food and jazz in a room decorated entirely in wood. The sorbets and ices are famous throughout Tokyo.

♦ **Ton-Chan** *(nomiya)*, 3-22-11 Jingumae, Shibuya-ku, XI, D2-3, nº 7, ☎ 3401 9288. Open daily 11am-2pm, 5pm-midnight. This restaurant always attracts a crowd. Excellent lunch menus.

Bars and Discotheques

♦♦♦ **Radio** (bar), Villa Gloria B 1, 2-31-7 Jingumae, Shibuya-ku, XI, D1, nº 8a, ☎ 3405 5490. Open Mon-Sat 7pm-2:30am. Closed holidays. There are only nine seats at the bar. This is a very classy place.

♦♦ **Club D** (discotheque), 2-33-12 Jingumae, Shibuya-ku, XI, C1, nº 9, ☎ 3423 1471. Opens at 6pm. On the Meiji Dori. The letter 'D' is written on the façade.

♦ **Café Behen Haus** (café), Vivre 21 1 F, 5-10-1 Jingumae, Shibuya-ku, XI, C2, n° 10, ☎ 3498 2655. Open daily 9am-10:30pm. You might think you were in a café in Paris or Vienna. This is one of the trendiest places in Harajuku.

♦ **Café de Ropé** (café), 6-1-8 Jingumae, Shibuya-ku, XI, C2, n° 11, ☎ 3406 6845. Open daily 10:30am-2am. One of the best-known cafés in Harajuku. Frequented by foreigners.

Shops

Kansai Yamamoto (women's fashion), 3-28-7 Jingumae, Shibuya-ku, XI, D1, n° 12a, ☎ 3478 1958. Open daily 11am-8pm.

Kiddy Land (toys), 6-1-9 Jingumae, Shibuya-ku, XI, C2, ☎ 3409 3431. Open Mon-Fri 10am-7pm; Sat-Sun 10am-8pm; closed the 3rd Tues of every month. Five storeys of toys and electronic games.

On Sundays (modern art), 3-7-6 Jingu Mae, Shibuya-ku, XI, D2-3, ☎ 3478 0809. Open Tues-Sun 11am-10pm. Foreign books on photography, art and so on. A large selection of postcards.

Oriental Bazaar (antiques-souvenirs), 5-9-13 Jingumae, Shibuya-ku, XI, C2, ☎ 3400 3933. Open Fri-Wed 9:30am-6:30pm. A large selection of antiques. There is a complete range of Japanese souvenirs (T-shirts, dolls, fans and so on). Secondhand silk kimonos can be found at reasonable prices.

Quanpow (Chinese medicine), Sun's Building 2 F, 1-7-2 Jingumae, Shibuya-ku, XI, C2, n° 16a, ☎ 3478 4382. Open daily 10am-8pm. On the famous Takeshita Dori. Natural medicines and herbal teas.

▬ IDABACHI/ICHIGAYA

Hotels

▲▲▲▲ **Hotel Edmont**, 3-10-5 Iidabashi, Chiyoda-ku, IX, A3, a, ☎ 3237 1111. Five minutes from Iidabashi Station. 449 rooms. Restaurants, cafés, bar, and facilities for conferences and wedding receptions. New and functional.

▲▲ **Japan YWCA Hostel**, 4-8-8 Kundan-Minami, Chiyoda-ku, VII, D1, b1, ☎ 3264 0661. Four minutes from Ichigaya Station. 9 rooms. ① ② ④. Women only. Communal bathroom.

▲▲ **Seifu-So** (ryokan), 1-12-15 Fujimi, Chiyoda-ku, IX, A3, c, ☎ 3263 0681. Five minutes from Iidabashi Station. ① ② ③ ④ ⑤. Half of the hotel is taken up by a fantastic Japanese garden. Rather expensive, but a room without a bathroom is reasonable. Communal shower.

▲▲ **YWCA Tokyo Sadohara Hostel**, 3-1-1 Ichigaya Sadohara, Shinjuku-ku, VII, C1, d, ☎ 3293 7313. Seven minutes from Ichigaya Station. 23 rooms. Restaurant and facilities for conferences. There are also automatic washing machines and an ironing room. ① ② ③ ④. Single women or married couples only.

▲ **Tokyo International Youth Hostel**, Central Plaza Building 18, 19 F, 21-1 Kagurakashi, Shinjuku-ku, IX, A2, ☎ 3235 1107. Next to Iidabashi Station. ① ② ④. There is a fantastic view, particularly from the communal bathroom!

Restaurants

♦♦ **Iseto** (nomiya), 4-2 Kagurazaka, Shinjuku-ku, ☎ 3260 6363. Open Mon-Sat 5-9pm. Closed holidays. Near Bishamonten. This is an authentic Japanese bistro. The cuisine and service are perfect.

♦♦ **Tawaraya** (Western cuisine), 5-35 Kagurazaka, Shinjuku-ku, ☎ 3269 0979. Open Mon-Sat 11:30am-9:30pm. An old establishment frequented by writers and artists.

♦ **Harunami** (okonomiyaki), 9 Tsukudocho, Shinjuku-ku, ☎ 3260 4729. Open daily 5pm-midnight. Closed the 3rd Sun of every month. There are 25 types of okonomiyaki (a kind of omelette) and 40 types of teppanyaki (meat dish cooked at your table) to choose from. The ingredients are fresh, the atmosphere is friendly and the prices are very low!

Shop

Omeisha (bookstore), 2-3-4 Fujimi, Chiyoda-ku, IX, A3, ☎ 3262 7276. Open Mon-Fri 9:30am-5:50pm; Sat 9:30am-4:30pm. Closed holidays.

▬ IKEBUKURO

Hotels

▲▲▲▲ **Hotel Metropolitan**, 1-6-1 Nishi-Ikebukuro, Toshima-ku, XII, A2, a, ☎ 3980 1111. Three minutes from Ikebukuro (west exit). 818 rooms. Restaurants, cafés, bars, sauna, shopping gallery, swimming pool and travel agency. This modern hotel is located in a rather dreary neighbourhood but is close to the lively center of Ikebukuro.

▲▲▲▲ **Sunshine City Prince Hotel,** 3-1-5 Higashi-Ikebukuro, Toshima-ku, XII, B2, b, ☎ 3988 1111. Ten minutes from Ikebukuro Station and three minutes from Higashi-Ikebukuro Station. 1 166 rooms. Restaurants, bars and facilities for banquets and wedding receptions. Part of the Prince Hotel chain, this hotel is near Sunshine City, Japan's tallest building.

▲▲▲ **Hotel Sunroute Ikebukuro** (business hotel), 1-39-4 Higashi-Ikebukuro, Toshima-ku, XII, B1, ☎ 3980 1911. Two minutes from Ikebukuro Station (east exit). Located in the center of the district. 144 rooms. Restaurants and facilities for banquets.

▲ **Kimi Ryokan** *(ryokan)*, 2-1034 Ikebukuro, Toshima-ku, XII, A1, d, ☎ 3971 3766. Five minutes from Ikebukuro Station (west exit). To get there, ask for a map at the *koban* (police-box) near the west exit of the station. 9 Japanese-style rooms. ① ②. Restaurant. Although recently renovated, this *ryokan* is still very Japanese. It is pleasant and inexpensive.

Restaurants

♦♦♦ **Bouchée** (French cuisine), 1-8-7 Higashi-Ikebukuro, Toshima-ku, VIII, B3, ☎ 3983 2461. Near Ikebukuro Station. Open Mon-Sat noon-2pm, 5-9:30pm; Sun noon-2pm, 5-8pm. Very good traditional French cuisine served in a vaulted cellar.

♦♦ **Bistro Trente-Trois** (French cuisine), Belle Building 1 F, 3-27-1 Nishi-Ikebukuro, Toshima-ku, XII, A1, n° 2, ☎ 3986 7487. Open Mon-Sat 11:30am-2pm, 5-10:30pm; holidays 5-10:30pm. French family cooking at moderately prices.

♦♦ **Niigata Inakaya** (Japanese cuisine), 1-9-24 Minami-Ikebukuro, Toshima-ku, XII, A2, n° 3, ☎ 3984 6437. Open Mon-Sat 11am-2pm, 4-11pm. Six minutes from Ikebukuro Station (east exit). This restaurant specializes in the cuisine from the Niigata region in northern Japan. The decor is rustic. The *wappa-meshi* (rice) and the *noppe-jiru* (soup) are outstanding.

♦♦ **Sango** (Japanese cuisine), 1-4-12 Nishi-Ikebukuro, Toshima-ku, XII, A2, n° 4, ☎ 3982 6435. Open Mon-Sat 5-11 pm; closed holidays. Four minutes from Ikebukuro Station (west exit). Near the Hotel Metropolitan. Specialities from Okinawa. Try the *awamori* (strong alcohol).

Shops

Bic Camera (photographic equipment), 1-11-17 Higashi-Ikebukuro, Toshima-ku, XII, B1, n° 5, ☎ 3988 0002. Open daily 10am-8pm. One of the cheapest stores in Tokyo for computers, cameras, lenses and video equipment.

Camera No Kimura (photographic equipment), 1-18-8 Nishi-Ikebukuro, Toshima-ku, XII, A1, n° 6, ☎ 3981 8437. Open daily 8am-8pm. New and secondhand cameras.

Tokyo Folkcraft and Antiques Hall (antiques), Satomo Building 1 F, 3-9-5 Minami-Ikebukuro, Toshima-ku, XII, A2, n° 7, ☎ 3980 8228. Open Fri-Wed 11am-7pm. Lots of antiques.

Tokyo Hands (hardware, decor), 1-28-10 Higashi-Ikebukuro, Toshima-ku, XII, B1, n° 8, ☎ 3980 6111. Open daily 10am-8pm. Closed the 2nd and 3rd Thurs of every month. Near Sunshine City. A store for artisans and handymen. There is another branch in Shibuya.

IKEJIRI

Restaurant

♦♦♦ **Domani** (French cuisine), 4-37-7 Ikejiri, Setagaya-ku, ☎ 3421 4011. Open daily 5:30-11:30pm. Take the Inokashira Line to Ikenoue Station. Turn left and walk as far as Awashima Dori. Turn left and a little farther down the street you will see the restaurant on the right. In the rooms of an astonishing private house, Domani offers a Mediterranean cuisine based principally on fish. The speciality of the house is *bouillabaisse* from Marseilles. Each dish is carefully prepared and elegantly served.

KUDAN

Hotels

▲▲▲▲ **Hotel Grand Palace,** 1-1-1 Iidabashi, Chiyoda-ku, IX, A3, a1, ☎ 3264 1111, telex 232 2981 GRAPA J. One minute from Kudanshita Station.

491 rooms. Restaurants, café, bar, beauty parlour and facilities for conferences and wedding receptions.

▲▲▲ **Fairmont Hotel,** 2-1-17 Kudan-Minami, Chiyoda-ku, II, AB1, ☎ 3262 1151, telex 232 2883 FAIRHO J. Six minutes from Kudanshita Station. 241 rooms. Restaurants, bar, café, swimming pool and facilities for conferences and wedding receptions. Very well located. In summer, the guests are greeted by a 'tunnel' of flowers. The view is very pleasant.

▲▲▲ **Hotel Kayu Kaikan,** 8-1 Sanbancho, Chiyoda-ku, II, A2, ☎ 3230 1111. Five minutes from Hanzomon Station. Near the British Embassy. 129 rooms. Restaurants, bar and facilities for banquets. This hotel belongs to the same chain as does the Hotel Okura (see p. 233) and offers similar services at a lower price.

▲▲ **Kudan Kaikan Hotel,** 1-6-5 Kudan-Minami, Chiyoda-ku, II, AB1, d, ☎ 3261 5521. One minute from Kudanshita Station. 131 rooms. ① ② ③ ④ ⑤. Restaurants, café, hairdresser and facilities for conferences and wedding receptions. Some rooms of this newly renovated hotel overlook the Imperial Palace.

Restaurant

◆◆◆ **Bistro-Bon Voisin** (French cuisine), 1-3-6 Kudan-Kita, Chiyoda-ku, ☎ 3264 6456. Open Mon-Sat 11:30am-2pm, 5:30-9pm. Closed holidays. Near the Hotel Grand Palace. This is a high-quality family restaurant with reasonable prices. It is best to make reservations.

▬ MARUNOUCHI

Hotels

▲▲▲▲ **Imperial Hotel** ('Teikoku Hotel' in Japanese), 1-1-1 Uchisaiwaicho, Chiyoda-ku, II, B3, ☎ 3504 1111, telex 222 2346, cable IMPHO TOKYO. Near Hibiya Station and Yurakucho Stations. 1300 rooms. Restaurants, beauty parlour, swimming pool, clinic, post office, shopping gallery and facilities for conferences, banquets and wedding receptions. Originally founded in 1890, it was renovated in 1983. It is one of the best hotels in Tokyo.

▲▲▲▲ **Palace Hotel,** 1-1-1 Marunouchi, Chiyoda-ku, II, B2, b, ☎ 3211 5211, telex 222 2580, cable PALACEHOTEL TOKYO. One minute from Otemachi Station and seven minutes from Tokyo Station. 404 rooms. Restaurants, bar and facilities for banquets and wedding receptions. This very calm hotel, overlooking the Imperial Palace, is conveniently located for business people.

▲▲▲ **Hotel Yaesu Ryumeikan** (ryokan), 1-3-22 Yaesu, Chuo-ku, II, C2, c, ☎ 3271 0971. Three minutes north of the Yaesu-guchi exit of Tokyo Station. 35 Japanese-style rooms. Restaurants and facilities for conferences. Quiet and well located.

▲▲▲ **Tokyo Marunouchi Hotel,** 1-6-3 Marunouchi, Chiyoda-ku, II, C2, d1, ☎ 3215 2151, telex 222 4655. Five minutes from Tokyo Station. 194 rooms. Restaurants, bar, beauty parlour and facilities for banquets and wedding receptions. The staff are attentive.

▲▲▲ **Tokyo Station Hotel,** 1-9-1 Marunouchi, Chiyoda-ku, II, C2, e, ☎ 3231 2511. This hotel is in Tokyo Station. 55 rooms. Restaurants, bar, hairdresser and facilities for banquets. The rooms and bathrooms are spacious and the ceilings are high. There is an antique bar.

▲▲▲ **Yaesu Fujiya Hotel,** 2-9-1 Yaesu, Chuo-ku, II, C3, f, ☎ 3273 2111. Three minutes from Yurakucho Station. 377 rooms. Restaurants, bar, café, tea-room and facilities for banquets and wedding receptions. Well located near the business district.

Restaurants

◆◆◆◆ **Apicius** (French cuisine), Sanshi-Kaikan B1, 1-9-4 Yurakucho, Chiyoda-ku, II, B3, ☎ 3214 1361. Open Mon-Sat 11:30am-2:30pm, 5-10pm. Traditional French cuisine. The decor is luxurious, and the service is impeccable.

◆◆◆◆ **Kocho** (kaiseki), Shin-Yurakucho Building B2, 1-12 Yurakucho, Chiyoda-ku, II, C3, n° 2 ☎ 3214 4741. Open Mon-Sat 11:30am-2pm, 5-9pm. Closed holidays. Real kaiseki ryori cuisine (see p. 92) served in a classical Japanese setting. Everything is perfect except the exorbitant price.

◆◆ **Chiengmai** (Thai cuisine), Kaede Building 2, 3F, 1-6-10 Yurakucho, Chiyoda-ku, II, C3, ☎ 3580 0456. Open Sun-Fri 11:30am-11pm. The Thai chef prepares hot dishes.

◆ **Ajiwai** (yakitori), 2-3-1 Yurakucho, Chiyoda-ku, II, C3, ☎ 3573 7084. Open daily 4-11pm. Take an empty seat and order a beer or sake to go with your yakitori (chicken Kebabs). The restaurant is very pleasant. There are several other yakitori restaurants in the neighborhood.

Shop

International Arcade, V, B3, 1-7-23 Uchisaiwaicho, Chiyoda-ku, II, BC3, n° 5, ☎ 3591 2764. Open Mon-Sat 10am-7pm; Sun and holidays

10am-6pm. Kimonos, pearls, electrical appliances and the like. Most tourists buy their souvenirs and gadgets here.

The prices are among the lowest anywhere, and you can buy duty-free if you bring your passport.

MEGURO

Hotels

▲▲▲▲ **Miyako Hotel Tokyo**, 1-1-50 Shimo-Meguro, Minato-ku, I, A2, a, ☎ 3447-3111, telex 2423111 MYKTKY J, cable MIYAKO TRY. Three minutes by car from Takanawadai Station. 488 rooms. Restaurants, café, bar, swimming pool, Japanese garden and facilities for conferences and wedding receptions. There is a shuttle service to Narita airport. The hotel is not very well located but is calm and luxurious.

▲▲▲ **Meguro Gajoen** *(ryokan)*, 1-8-1 Shita-Meguro, Meguro-ku, I, A2, ☎ 34910074. Five minutes from Meguro Station. Walk downhill from the Mitsui bank. This hotel offers only Japanese-style rooms without bathrooms or private toilets. A beautiful Japanese garden compensates for these inconveniences.

▲▲ **Gajoen Kanko Hotel**, 1-8-1 Shimo-Meguro, Meguro-ku, I, A2, ☎ 3491-0111, telex 2466006, cable GAJOENHO TOKYO. Five minutes from

Meguro Station. 77 rooms. ① ② ③ ④ ⑤. Restaurants and facilities for conferences and banquets. There are paintings everywhere and the hotel looks like a museum. It is well worth staying here, if just for the decor.

Restaurants

♦♦ **Shuhoen** (Chinese cuisine), 3-14-2 Shiroganedai, Minato-ku, I, A2, ☎ 34457007. Open Thurs-Tues noon-2:30pm, 5:30-9:30pm. About 15 minutes from Meguro Station, near the NTT building. Excellent.

♦ **Tonki** *(tonkatsu)*, 1-1-2 Shimo-Meguro, Meguro-ku, I, A2, ☎ 3491 9928. Open Wed-Mon 4-11pm. Near the station. This clean and bright restaurant is reputed to serve the best *tonkatsu* (sauteed pork) in Tokyo. Customers eat at a white counter. Go before 6pm if possible, unless you like crowds.

NAKANO

Hotels

▲▲ **Nakano Musashino Hotel**, 5-60-11 Nakano, Nakano-ku, ☎ 33856511. One minute north of Nakano Station, in a very lively district. 44 rooms. ① ② ③ ④ ⑤. All the rooms have refrigerators. In the same building there is a cinema that shows old films.

▲ **Shin Nakano Lodge**, 6-1-1 Honcho, Nakano-ku, ☎ 33814886. Five minutes from Shin-Nakano Station. ① ②.

Restaurants

♦♦♦ **Irori** (Japanese cuisine), 5-56-15 Nakano, Nakano-ku, ☎ 33879177. Open Mon-Sat 5-11pm. This ancient house, imported from the Hida region, is impressive. *Suppon* (turtle), frogs and wild game are among the specialities. There is a choice of 50 fruit alcohols.

♦♦ **Okajoki** *(robata)*, 5-59-3 Nakano, Nakano-ku, ☎ 33883753. Open daily 11:30am-1:30pm, 5-11pm. Opposite the Nakano Musashino Hotel. The restaurant is decorated with railway equipment; *okajoki* is the old Japanese name for the railway. Lots of charm in a country atmosphere.

Café

♦ **Classic** (café), 5-66-8 Nakano, Nakano-ku, ☎ 33870571. Open Tues-Sun noon-9:30pm. Do not hesitate to enter this superb little café. Its pre-war decor has miraculously remained intact. You order and pay when entering. You can choose a record to listen to by writing its name on a chalkboard.

NIHOMBASHI

Restaurants

♦♦♦♦ **Chez Ino** (French cuisine), Daihyaku Seimei Building 1 F, 3-2-11 Kyobashi, Chuo-ku, II, C3, n° 1, ☎ 3274 2020. Open Mon-Sat 11:30am-2pm, 6-9:30pm; Sun 6-9:30pm. French *haute cuisine* (foie gras *truffé*, and so on).

♦♦♦ **Munakata** (Japanese cuisine), Hirose Building B1, 3-1-17 Nihombashi, Chuo-ku, II, CD2, nº 2a, ☎ 3281 3288. Open Mon-Fri 11:30am-2pm, 5-10pm; Sat-Sun 11:30am-9:30pm. The interior is 'modern Japanese'. You can order a menu or eat *a la carte*. Either way, the food is good.

♦♦♦ **Sasaya** *(nomiya)*, 2-10-1 Kyobashi, Chuo-ku, II, D3, nº 3, ☎ 3561 5037. Open Mon-Fri 11:30am-1:30pm, 5-10pm; Sat 11:30am-1:30pm. Closed holidays. Near Kyobashi Station. Located in a wooden house surrounded by concrete buildings. The produce is incredibly fresh, and the sake is delicious.

♦♦♦ **Toriyasu** (duck), 2-11-7 Higashi-Nihombashi, Chuo-ku, ☎ 3862 4008. Open Mon-Sat 4-9pm. Closed holidays. The establishment has existed for over a century. The grilled duck in soy sauce is excellent.

♦♦ **Mimiu** *(udon)*, 3-6-4 Kyobashi, Chuo-ku, II, C3, nº 5, ☎ 3567 6571. Open daily 11:30am-8:30pm. Closed the 3rd Sun of every month. Near the post office. There is an impressive choice of Kansai-style *udon* (wheat noodles).

♦♦ **Isehiro** *(yakitori; chicken kebabs)*, 1-5-4 Kyobashi, Chuo-ku, II, C3, nº 6, ☎ 3281 5864. Open Mon-Sat noon-2pm, 4:30-9pm. Closed holidays. All the ingredients, carefully chosen, are grilled on charcoal. Delicious.

♦♦ **Uogashi** (Japanese cuisine), 2-2-3 Nihombashi, Chuo-ku, II, D2, nº 7, ☎ 3271 8833. Open Mon-Sat 11:30am-2pm, 4-10pm. Closed holidays. Near Takashimaya department store. Inexpensive, delicious fish dishes.

♦ **Taimeiken** (Western cuisine), 1-12-10 Nihombashi, Chuo-ku, II, D2, nº 8, ☎ 3271 2464. Open Mon-Sat 11am-9pm. Closed holidays. Perhaps a little out of fashion but still rather good. There is a kite museum above the restaurant.

Shops

Heiando (lacquerware), 3-10-11 Nihombashi, Chuo-ku, II, D2, nº 9, ☎ 3272 2871. Open Mon-Sat 9am-6pm. Closed holidays.

Ishizuka (folklore), 1-5-20 Yaesu, Chuo-ku, II, C2 nº 10, ☎ 3275 2991. Open Mon-Sat 9:30am-7:30pm. Closed holidays. A good selection of Japanese articles. There is a pleasant café above the shop.

Kamiyama Sudare-Ten (Japanese blinds), 1-8-8 Kyobashi, Chuo-ku, II, D3, nº 11, ☎ 3561 0945. Open daily 8am-8pm. You can chose the colour and shape of your blinds.

Kuroeya (lacquerware), Kuroeya Kokubu Building 2 F, 1-2-6-Nihombashi, Chuo-ku, II, D2, nº 12, ☎ 3272 0948. Open Mon-Fri 9am-5pm. Sat 9am-noon. Closed holidays and the 1st and 3rd Sat of every month.

Maruzen (bookstore), 2-3-10 Nihombashi, Chuo-ku, II, D2 ☎ 3272 7211. Open Mon-Sat 10am-6pm. Foreign books and magazines are on the 4th floor.

Maruyama and Company, Ltd. (antiques), 2-5-9 Kyobashi, Chuo-ku, II, C3, nº 14, ☎ 3561 5146. Open Mon-Sat 9:30am-6pm. Closed holidays.

▬ NINGYOCHO (TOKYO CITY AIR TERMINAL)

Hotels

▲▲▲▲ **Holiday Inn**, 1-13-7 Hatchobori, Chuo-ku, II, D3, a ☎ 3553 6161. One minute from Hatchobori Station and three minutes by taxi from the TCAT (Tokyo City Air Terminal). 120 rooms. Restaurants, bar, swimming pool and facilities for conferences. A typical Holiday Inn.

▲▲ **Kayabacho Pearl Hotel** (business hotel), 1-2-5 Shikawa, Chuo-ku, II, D2-3, ☎ 3553 2211. Two minutes from Kayabacho Station and three minutes from the TCAT. 259 rooms. ① ② ③ ④. Restaurant and facilities for conferences. Very convenient for the stock market and the business district.

▲▲ **Sumisho Hotel** (business hotel), 9-14 Nihombashi-Kobunacho, Chuo-ku, II, D2, ☎ 3661 4603. Three minutes from Ningyocho Station and eight minutes from the TCAT. 63 rooms. ① ② ③ ④ ⑤. Restaurant and facilities for conferences. The decor is a harmonious compromise between Japanese and Western styles.

Restaurants

♦♦ **Tamahide** (chicken), 1-17-10 Nihombashi-Ningyocho, Chuo-ku, I, B1, ☎ 3668 7651. Open Mon-Sat 11:30am-1pm, 2-9pm. Closed holidays. At lunch, there is always a queue for the *oyako-donburi* (chicken and egg on rice). At less than ¥1000, it is famous throughout Tokyo.

♦ **Kiraku** (Western family cooking), 2-6-6 Nihombashi-Ningyocho, Chuo-ku, I, B1, ☎ 3666 6555. Open Wed-Mon 11:30am-8pm. Closed on the 1st and 3rd Wed of every month. Excellent *beef-katsu*.

Shops

Shigemori Eishingo (pastries), 2-1-1 Nihombashi-Ningyocho, Chuo-ku,I, B1, ☎ 36665885. Open Mon-Sat 9am-8pm. Specialist of *ninguo-yaki* (pastries filled with sweet red bean paste).

Twai-Shoten *(tsuzura)*, 2-10-1 Nihombashi-Ningyocho, Chuo-ku,I, B1, ☎ 36686058. Open Mon-Sat 8am-8:30pm. Closed holidays. Cupboards for kimonos.

▬ NISHI-AZABU

Restaurants

♦♦♦ Bistro de la Cité (French cuisine), Tujo Building 1 F, 4-2-10 Nishi-Azabu, Minato-ku,VIII, B3, 1b, ☎ 34065475. Open Tues-Sun noon-2pm, 6-10pm. Try a fish dish. The ingredients are always fresh and savory, and the service is excellent.

♦♦♦ Chez Figaro (French cuisine), 4-4-1 Nishi-Azabu, Minato-ku,VIII, B3, n° 2b, ☎ 34008718. Open Mon-Fri noon-2pm, 6-9:30pm; Sun 6-9:30pm. In an agreeable art nouveau decor, both traditional and *nouvelle cuisine* are served. The lobster and cheese are imported from France. The prices are reasonable considering the quality of the food. Reservations are necessary.

♦♦♦ Hokkaien (Chinese cuisine), 2-12-1 Nishi-Azabu, Minato-ku, VIII, A3, n° 3b, ☎ 34078507. Open daily 11:30am-3pm, 5-10:30pm. Near Kasumicho Crossing. Very good lacquered duck.

♦♦♦ Queen Alice (French cuisine), 3-17-34 Nishi-Azabu, Minato-ku,VIII, B3, n° 4b, ☎ 34059039. Open Tues-Sun noon-3pm, 6-11pm. Located at the end of a dead-end street in a residential area. An inventive cuisine prepared with fresh and carefully chosen ingredients.

♦♦♦ San-Roku-Kyu Hanten (Chinese cuisine), 1-13-14 Nishi-Azabu, Minato-ku, VIII, B3, n° 5b, ☎ 3402 3239. Open Mon-Sat 11:30am-2:30pm, 5-11pm; Sun 10:30am-10pm. Cuisine from Shanghai. The crab in soy sauce is delicious.

♦♦ Arisugawa (Japanese cuisine), Arisugawa National Court Building B1, 2-1-20 Moto-Azabu, Minato-ku, X, B1, n° 6, ☎ 34424177. Open Mon-Sat 6-11pm. Closed holidays. The decor is simple, but the cuisine is copious and excellent.

♦ Kusa no ya (Korean cuisine), 4-6-7 Azabujuban, Minato-ku, X, C1, ☎ 34558356. About 15 minutes on foot from Roppongi Station. Open daily 11am-2pm, 5-10pm. This is practically the 'official' restaurant of the Korean Embassy, which is nearby. The meat is excellent.

♦ Meshi Dokoro (Japanese cuisine), 4-1-4 Nishi-Azabu, Minato-ku, VIII, n° 7b, ☎ 34074556. Open Thurs-Tues 11am-4am. The food is served at the counter and is a real bargain. The *Gohan* and *misoshiru* are cooked as in a Japanese home.

La Palette (ice cream), 3-12-22 Nishi-Azabu, Minato-ku,VIII, B3, n° 9b, ☎ 34082595. Open daily 9am-8pm. A French-style ice-cream parlour. All the flavours are natural — and good!

Bars

Bohemia, TK Building B1 and B2, 3-17-25 Nishi-Azabu, Minato-ku, VIII, B3, n° 10b, ☎ 34018143. Open daily 7pm-2am. The interior, designed by Nigel Coates, resembles an airplane cabin. Jazz.

Kasumi Club, 3-24-17 Nishi-Azabu, Minato-ku, VIII, B3, n° 11, ☎ 3405 1090. Open Mon-Sat 6pm-2am. Victorian bar.

Red Shoes, Azabu Palace Building B1, 2-25-18 Nishi-Azabu, Minato-ku, VIII, A3, n° 12b, ☎ 34994319. Open daily 8pm-6am. A small group has played rock-'n'-roll music here every night since 1981. A little out of fashion, perhaps, but lively.

Turkish Blue, Kasumi Heights B1, 1-7-11 Nishi-Azabu, Minato-ku, VIII, B3, n° 13, ☎ 34233300. Open daily 8pm-4am. The staff's costumes alone are worth the visit.

Shops

Meidiya (supermarket), 5-6-6 Hiro-o, Shibuya-ku, X, B2, n° 14, ☎ 3444 6221. Open daily 10am-9pm. Near Hiro-o Station.

National Azabu Supermarket, 4-5-2 Minami-Azabu, Minato-ku, X, B1, n° 15, ☎ 34423181. Open Mon-Sat 9:30am-6:30pm; Sun 9:30am-4:45pm. Near Arisugawa Park. Large choice of alcoholic drinks. Pharmacy.

Takeo Kikuchi (fashion, hairdresser), TK Building, 3-17-25 Nishi-Azabu, Minato-ku, VIII, B3, n° 16, ☎ 3401 7346. Open Mon-Sat 11am-8pm. An original shop where you can see and buy Takeo Kikuchi's creations and have your hair done as well.

Washi-Kobo (Japanese paper), 1-8-10 Nishi-Azabu, Minato-ku,VIII, B3, n° 17, ☎ 3405 1841. Open Mon-Sat 10am-6pm. Closed holidays.

▬ OCHANOMIZU/KANDA/AKIHABARA/JIMBOCHO

Hotels

▲▲▲▲ **Hilltop Hotel**, 1-1 Kanda-Surugadai, Chiyoda-ku, IX, BC3, a2, ☎ 3293 2311, cable HILTOP TOKYO. Five minutes from Ochanomizu Station. 95 rooms. Restaurants, bar, café, and facilities for banquets and wedding receptions. This old establishment has had a good reputation among artists and writers for a long time, and so has its French restaurant, the À Bientôt.

▲▲ **Akihabara Washington Hotel**, 1-8-3 Kanda-Sakumacho, Chiyoda-ku, IX, D3, b, ☎ 3255 3311. One minute from Akihabara Station, near the electronic equipment district. 311 rooms. ① ② ③ ④ ⑤. Restaurants, café and bar. This red-brick building will catch your eye.

▲▲ **Hotel Juraku**, 2-9 Kanda-Awajicho, Chiyoda-ku, IX, C3, c2, ☎ 3251 7222. Two minutes from Shin-Ochanomizu Station. 232 rooms. ① ② ③ ④ ⑤. Restaurants, bar, café, and facilities for banquets and wedding receptions. Ideal location, efficient service and comfortable atmosphere.

▲▲ **Hotel Kacho** (business hotel), 1-21 Kanda-Sudacho, Chiyoda-ku, IX, D3, ☎ 3255 1711. Two minutes from Shin-Ochanomizu Station. 58 rooms. ① ② ③ ④ ⑤. Not far from Akihabara, from where it is easy to get anywhere in Tokyo.

▲▲ **Tokyo Green Hotel Suidobashi** (business hotel), 1-2-16 Misakicho, Chiyoda-ku, IX, B3, e, ☎ 3295 4161. Three minutes from Suidobashi Station. 324 rooms. ① ② ③ ④ ⑤. Restaurants and facilities for conferences. There is another branch in Awajicho, ☎ 3255 4161.

▲▲ **Tokyo YMCA**, 7-1 Kanda-Mitoshirocho, Chiyoda-ku, II, C1, ☎ 3293 1911. Three minutes from Awajicho, Ogawamachi and Shin-Ochanomizu stations. 80 rooms. ① ② ③ ④ ⑤. Restaurants and facilities for banquets and wedding receptions. A typical inexpensive YMCA.

▲▲ **Tokyo YWCA Hostel**, 1-8 Kanda-Surugadai, Chiyoda-ku, IX, C3, ☎ 3293 5421. Four minutes from Ochanomizu Station. 20 rooms. ① ②. Restaurants, automatic washing machines, public bathrooms on every floor and a swimming pool. Only women are accepted.

▲▲ **YMCA Asia Youth Center**, 2-5-5 Sarugakucho, Chiyoda-ku, IX, B3, ☎ 3233 0611. Five minutes from Suidobashi Station. 55 rooms. ① ② ③ ④. Restaurant, swimming pool and facilities for banquets and conferences. In a very calm neighbourhood.

▲▲ **Yushima Kaikan-Tokyo Garden Palace**, 1-7-5 Yushima, Bunkyo-ku, IX, C2, i, ☎ 3813 6211. Five minutes from Ochanomizu Station. 324 rooms. ① ② ③ ④ ⑤. Restaurant, beauty parlour and facilities for conferences and wedding receptions. Clean and functional.

Restaurants

♦♦♦ **Balalaika** (Russian cuisine), 1-63 Kanda-Jimbocho, Chiyoda-ku, II, B1 and IX, B3, ☎ 3291 8363. Open Mon-Sat 11:30am-11pm; Sun and holidays 5-10pm. Near Jimbocho Station. Real Russian cuisine in a Russian decor. In the evening, there is music. The **Sarafan**, ☎ 3292 0480, in the same neighbourhood, is just as good.

♦♦♦ **Ichinotani** *(chanko-nabe)*, 2-10-2 Soto-Kanda, Chiyoda-ku, IX, CD3, ☎ 3251 8500. Open Mon-Sat 11am-9pm; Sun and holidays 11:30am-8pm. The chef was formerly a sumo wrestler. Excellent food.

♦♦♦ **Isegen** (monkfish), 1-11-1 Kanda-Sudacho, IX, D3, Chiyoda-ku, ☎ 3251 1229. Open Mon-Sat noon-10pm. Closed holidays and Sat in July and Aug. This is the only restaurant in Tokyo specializing in monkfish. During the summer, when monkfish is out of season, eel and other dishes are served. It is necessary to make reservations.

♦♦ **Botan** (chicken), 1-15 Kanda-Sudacho, Chiyoda-ku, IX, D3, ☎ 3251 0577. Open Mon-Sat noon-9pm. Closed holidays. Near Yabu Soba. This old establishment serves chicken grilled on charcoal. The service is irreproachable. It is best to make reservations, particularly for groups of more than four.

♦ **Imoya** (Japanese cuisine). Open daily 11am-8pm. There are many outlets of this chain in this student district. Some serve *tonkatsu* (breaded pork), some serve *tempura* (deep-fried vegetables) and others serve *tendon*. The service is quick, which means that you are supposed to pay and leave as soon as you finish eating.

♦ **Izumo Soba Honke** *(soba)*, 1-51 Kanda-Jimbocho, Chiyoda-ku, IX, B3, ☎ 3291 3005. Open Mon-Sat 11am-8:30pm. Closed holidays. To get here, take the little street opposite the Shogakukan Building. Try the *wariko-soba* (noodles).

♦ **Yabu Soba** (soba), 2-10 Kanda-Awajicho, Chiyoda-ku, IX, CD3, 6a, ☎ 3251 0287. Open Tues-Sun 11:30am-7pm. Near Awajicho, Shin-Ochanomizu, Ochanomizu and Akihabara stations. This restaurant, surrounded by bamboo, was the first of the Yabu chain. It is worth the visit.

Cafés

♦ **Chopin**, 1-19 Kanda-Sudacho, Chiyoda-ku, IX, D3, ☎ 3251 6227. Open Mon-Sat 8am-11pm. Closed holidays. Opposite Yabu Soba. This little café has retained the same charm for over half a century.

♦ **Soba Candle**, 1-35 Kanda-Jimbocho, Chiyoda-ku, IX, B3, ☎ 3291 6303. Open Mon-Sat 10am-1pm, 3-8pm. Closed holidays. Near Izumo Soba Honke. This antiquated yet adorable little café has only five tables. The old couple who run it serve coffee, English or Japanese tea and even *habuji-cha* (seaweed-flavoured tea).

♦ **Rihaku**, 2-24 Kanda-Jimbocho, Chiyoda-ku, IX, B3, ☎ 3264 6292. Open Mon-Sat 10am-8pm. Closed holidays. Hidden in a quiet back street off Hakusan Dori near Jimbocho Crossing, this is a slightly snobbish café decorated with Korean antiques. The cheesecake is a must.

Shops

Takemura (Japanese pastries), 1-19 Kanda-Sudacho, Chiyoda-ku, II, C1,

☎ 3251 2328. Open Mon-Sat 11am-8pm. Closed holidays. Opposite Isegen. The *anmitsu, shiruko* (red bean soup) or *age-manju* (fried cakes) are delicious after a Japanese meal. If you prefer Western pastry, **Ohmiya-Yogashi-Ten** is nearby.

Jimbocho, IX, B3, is the book dealer's district. Antique books in English or French may be found at several shops, including **Kitazawa Shoten** and **Ohya Shobo**. There are some real treasures, but the dealers are aware of the market value and consequently the prices are high.

The most popular district for electronic equipment is **Soto-Kanda**, IX, CD3. Most of the shops are concentrated near the exit of Akihabara Station. All of the large dealers have duty-free departments and offer excellent delivery services. Among them are:

Hirose, Green Cap Building, 1-10-5 Soto-Kanda, Chiyoda-ku, IX, D3, ☎ 3255 2271.

Laox, 1-2-9 Soto-Kanda, Chiyoda-ku, IX, D3, ☎ 3255-9041. Open daily 10am-7pm.

Shintoku, 1-16-9, Soto-Kanda, Chiyoda-ku, IX, D3, ☎ 3255 071.

▬ OKUBO

Hotels

▲ **Okubo House**, 1-11-32 Hyakunincho, Shinjuku-ku, I, A1, ☎ 3361 2348. One minute from Shin-Okubo Station. ① ②. There is a map at the station exit. This inexpensive hotel can easily be recognized by the mass of little flags suspended from its windows.

Restaurants

♦♦ **Namazu-Ya** (catfish), 2-31-16 Okubo, Shinjuku-ku, 1, A1, ☎ 3200 0283. Open Mon-Sat noon-2pm, 5-11pm. Three minutes from Okubo

Station. From the station, turn left and then right when you get to Dunkin Donuts. Namazu-Ya is the only restaurant in Japan that specializes in catfish, a dish supposed to make men more 'efficient' and women more beautiful.

♦ **Hi Lac Nam** (Vietnamese cuisine), 3-9-16 Kita-Shinjuku, Shinjuku-ku, I, A1, ☎ 3369 5431. Open Tues-Sun 11am-2:30pm, 5-10pm. Closed 2nd Tues of every month. Five minutes from Okubo Station. Pleasant and not expensive. Frequented by *gaijin* (foreigners), particularly the French.

▬ ROPPONGI

Hotels

▲▲▲▲ **Ana Hotel Tokyo**, 1-12-33 Akasaka, Minato-ku, VIII, D2, a1, ☎ 3505 1111, 900 rooms. Restaurants, café, bar, secretarial services and facilities for banquets and conferences. A modern (1986) hotel located in the Ark Hills district. Many foreigners live in this area, one of the most expensive in Tokyo.

▲▲▲▲ **Hotel Okura**, 2-10-4 Toranomon, Minato-ku, ☎ 3582 0111, telex J22 790 HTLOKURA, cable HOTEL

OKURA TOKYO. Eight minutes from Kamiyacho and Toranomon stations. 899 rooms. Restaurants, bar, café, beauty parlour, swimming pool, sauna, gymnasium, garden and Japanese tearoom, secretarial services and facilities for banquets and wedding receptions. The Hotel Okura is one of the most prestigious hotels in the world. The service is impeccable, and the restaurants are excellent. The hotel even has its own art museum.

▲▲▲▲ **Roppongi Prince Hotel,** 3-2-7 Roppongi, Minato-ku, VIII, C2, c1, ☎ 3587 1111. Five minutes from Roppongi Station. 222 rooms. Restaurants, café, bar, swimming pool and facilities for banquets. This is a resort hotel. In the center of the building, there is a swimming pool with a glass side that can be seen from a café. The architecture is original and includes an Escher stairway. Well located for anyone who wishes to stay out late at night.

▲▲▲ **Hotel Ibis,** 7-14-4 Roppongi, Minato-ku, VIII, C2-3, d1, ☎ 3405 8158. One minute from Roppongi Station, at the very heart of this animated district. 190 rooms. Restaurants, bar, shops and discotheque. Well located for the night life in Roppongi. The lobby is a good meeting place.

Restaurants

◆◆◆◆ **Takamura** (Japanese cuisine), 3-4-27 Roppongi, Minato-ku, VIII, C2, n° 1, ☎ 3585 6600. Open Mon-Sat noon-3:30pm, 5-10:30pm. This restaurant specializes in wild game and mountain vegetables, and offers a cosy atmosphere and extraordinary country-like charm.

◆◆◆ **AD Coliseum** (French-style Vietnamese cuisine), Ark Towers West 1F, 1-3-40 Roppongi, Minato-ku, VIII, D2, n° 2c, ☎ 3505 4545. Open daily noon-2pm, 6pm-2am. The decor, by Timney and Fowler, is a composition in black and white. The kitchen is managed by the chef of Tan Dinh of Paris.

◆◆◆ **Gonin Byakusho** (Japanese cuisine), Roppongi Square Building 4F, 3-10-3 Roppongi, Minato-ku, VIII, n° 4, ☎ 3470 1675. Open Mon-Sat 11:30am-2pm, 5-11pm; Sun and holidays noon-10pm. The name Gonin Byakusho means 'five peasants', and this restaurant specializes in country cooking. When you arrive, you must take your shoes off and put them in a box. In exchange you are given an enormous key.

◆◆◆ **Hasejin** (sukiyaki), 3-3-15 Azubudai, Minato-ku, VIII, C3, n° 5c, ☎ 3582 7811. Open daily 11:30am-10pm. The meat used for the sukiyaki is of excellent quality and the prices are reasonable.

◆◆◆ **Ile de France** (French cuisine), Comu Building B1, 3-11-5 Roppongi, Minato-ku, VIII, C3, n° 6, ☎ 3404 0384. Open daily 11:30am-2pm, 5:30-10:30pm. The French chef is proud of his provençale cuisine.

◆◆◆ **Inakaya** (robata), 7-8-4 Roppongi, Minato-ku, VIII, B2, n° 7c, ☎ 3405-9866. Open daily 5pm-5am. Opposite the Ministry of Defense. You will get a show as well as a meal here. The waiters shout the orders, while the cooks, in the middle of the room, grill whatever you point to.

◆◆◆ **Koshi** (Japanese cuisine), 4-12-12 Roppongi, Minato-ku, VIII, C2, n° 8c, ☎ 3403 4902. Open Mon-Sat 5pm-5am. This restaurant serves good Japanese food until dawn.

◆◆◆ **La Terre** (French cuisine), 1-9-20 Azabudai, Minato-ku, VIII, D3, n° 11c, ☎ 3583 9682. Open Mon-Sat 11:30am-2pm, 6-9:30pm. Closed holidays. Four minutes from Kamiyacho Station. Located on a quiet street, this restaurant offers authentic French cuisine.

◆◆◆ **Les Choux** (French cuisine), 5-11-28 Roppongi, Minato-ku, VIII, C3, n° 3, ☎ 3470 5511. Open Wed-Mon noon-3pm, 5:30-10:30pm. The terrace resembles a French café. Excellent head chef. Warm welcome and reasonable prices.

◆◆◆ **Marie-Claude** (French cuisine), Ochiai Building 2F, 1-7-28 Roppongi, Minato-ku, VIII, D2, n° 9c, ☎ 3583 9567. Open Mon-Sat 11:30am-2pm, 6-10pm. Closed holidays. The owner is Japanese but he studied cooking in Lyons. Excellent and not too expensive.

◆◆◆ **Metropole** (Chinese cuisine), 6-4-5 Roppongi, Minato-ku, VIII, B2, n° 10c, ☎ 3405 4400. Open daily 11:30am-11:30pm. Frequented by celebrities, Japanese as well as foreign, the Metropole nostalgically recalls Shanghai of the 1930s.

◆◆ **Bangkok** (Thai cuisine), Woo Building 2F, 3-8-8 Roppongi, Minato-ku, VIII, C3, n° 12c, ☎ 3408 8722. Near Roppongi Station. Open Mon-Sat 11:30am-11pm. Authentic Thai cuisine (hot!). The welcome is more than friendly. Go early as the restaurant gets crowded later. There is a menu in English with pictures.

◆◆ **Bengawan Solo** (Indonesian cuisine), Kaneko Building 1F, 7-18-13 Roppongi, Minato-ku, VIII, B3, n° 13c, ☎ 3408 5698. Open daily 11:30am-3pm, 5-11pm. Opposite Wave. This restaurant has been in Roppongi for nearly 30 years. Each island of Indonesia is represented by a special dish. If you wish to taste them all, order a rijsttafel, which consists of eight copious dishes.

◆◆ **Brasserie Bernard** (French cuisine), Kaijimaya Building 7 F, 7-14-3 Roppongi, Minato-ku, VIII, C2, n° 14c, ☎ 3405 7877. Open daily 11:30am-2pm, 5:30pm-0:30am. Chef Bernard offers good food at honest prices.

◆◆ **Ex** (German cuisine), 7-7-6 Roppongi, Minato-ku, VIII, B2, n° 15c, ☎ 3408 5487. Open Mon-Sat

5pm-2am. Near Roppongi Station. Beer and sauerkraut in a pleasant atmosphere.

♦♦ **Gino** (Italian cuisine), 3-10-9 Roppongi, Minato-ku, VIII, B2, ☎ 3402 2227. Near Roppongi Station. Open Mon-Sat 5-11pm. A small pleasant restaurant specializing in seafood.

♦♦ **Kuimonoya Raku** *(nomiya)*, Sansei-Kaikan Hall 1 F, 7-14-2 Roppongi, Minato-ku, VIII, C2, ☎ 3403 0868. Open Mon-Sat 6pm-midnight. Near the Hotel Ibis. There are 25 large plates on the counter. The decor is modern and elegant.

♦♦ **Moti** (Indian cuisine), Hama Building 3 F, 6-2-35 Roppongi, Minato-ku, VIII, B3, nº 18, ☎ 3479 1939. Open Mon-Sat 11:30am-2am; Sun and holidays noon-2am. Near Wave. Decor and cuisine from northern India. The dessert and milk tea help to put out the fire from the very spicy, but reasonably priced, food.

♦♦ **Nambantei** *(yakitori)*, 4-5-6 Roppongi, Minato-ku, VIII, C2, nº 19, ☎ 3402 0606. Open Mon-Sat 5:30-11:30pm; Sun and holidays 5:30-11pm. This is a chain that offers identical kebab menus. All the *nambantei* are excellent.

♦♦ **Sanroku** (Japanese cuisine), Dai-ni, Torikatsu Building B1, 5-2-4 Roppongi, Minato-ku, VIII, C2, nº 20, ☎ 3402 6774. Open Mon-Fri 5:30-midnight. Closed holidays. Excellent family cuisine.

♦♦ **Toricho** *(yakitori)*, 7-8-2 Roppongi, Minato-ku, VIII, B2, nº 21, ☎ 3401 1827. Open Mon-Sat 5-11pm; Sun and holidays 5-8pm. You can satisfy your appetite at a reasonable price in this rather chic *yakitoriya*. Ask for the *chochin-yaki* (egg tube), a dish not frequently found.

♦ **Chu** (Japanese cuisine), 4-5-14 Roppongi, Minato-ku, VIII, C2-3, ☎ 3423 1600. Open daily 5pm-midnight. A small restaurant specializing in delicious *oden* (a type of Japanese noodles) and *koniyaku* (tuber-root cake). In the evening, regulars come to sing *karaoke*.

♦ **Daihachi** *(ramen)*, 7-12-1 Roppongi, Minato-ku, VIII, B2, nº 22, ☎ 3405 0721. Open Mon-Sat 5:30pm-1am. Closed holidays. An ideal place to grab something to eat after the disco.

♦ **Mamiana Soba** *(soba)*, 3-5-6 Azabudai, Minato-ku, VIII, D3, nº 23, ☎ 3583 0545. Open Mon-Sat 11:30am-4pm, 5-8pm. Closed holidays. Next to the Soviet Embassy. An old establishment that serves delicious *soba*.

Bars and Discotheques

♦♦ **EX** (bar), Roppongi Maisonnette 1 F, 7-7-6 Roppongi, Minato-ku, VIII, B2, nº 15c, ☎ 3408 5487. Open Mon-Sat 5pm-4am. Closed holidays. A good choice of beers. Very pleasant.

♦♦ **Harrington Gardens** (bar-discotheque), 7-7-4 Roppongi, Minato-ku, VIII, B2, nº 27, ☎ 3403-6700, 3403-5246 or 3403 5358. A Western-style house with a very distinctive atmosphere. The bar is on the ground floor, and the discotheque is in the basement.

♦♦ **Lexington Queen** (discotheque), Daisan Goto Building B 1, 3-13-14 Roppongi, Minato-ku, VIII, C3, nº 28, ☎ 3401 1661. Opens at 6pm. Foreign musicians frequently come here.

♦♦ **Maggie's Revenge** (bar), Takano Building 1 F, 3-8-12 Roppongi, Minato-ku, VIII, C3, nº 29, ☎ 3479 1096. Open daily 6:30pm-4am. The Australian owner has succeeded in creating a friendly atmosphere. The food is not expensive, and single women need not worry about being bothered.

♦♦ **Néo Japanesque** (discotheque), Roppongi Forum Building B 2, 5-16-5 Roppongi, Minato-ku, VIII, C3, nº 30, ☎ 3581 0050. Open Mon-Sat 7pm-dawn. Closed holidays. It has recently been renovated.

♦ **Berni Inn** (bar), Daisan Goto Building 2 F, 3-13-14 Roppongi, Minato-ku, VIII, C3, Nº 31, ☎ 3405 4928. Open daily 4pm-2am. An English-style pub where foreigners frequently meet.

♦ **Charleston** (bar), 3-8-11 Rappongi, Minato-ku, VIII, C3, nº 32, ☎ 3402 0372. Open daily 6pm-6am. This American-style cocktail bar is always crowded, mostly by foreigners. An ideal place for a drink after the disco.

♦ **Henry's Africa** (bar), Hanatsubaki Building 2F, 3-15-23 Roppongi, Minato-ku, ☎ 3403 9751. Open Sun-Thur 6pm-2am; Fri-Sat 6pm-4am. Tropical drinks and a 'popcorn-and-pinball' atmosphere. A good place to start the evening.

♦ **Kirin City** (bar), Roi Building B1, 5-5-1 Roppongi, Minato-ku, VIII, C3, nº 34, ☎ 3408 6581. Open Sun-Thurs 11:30am-11pm; Fri-Sat 11:30am-2am. A good place to have a beer while waiting for someone either before or after dinner.

♦ **Pidgeon** (bar), Kokubu Building 3 F, 1-4-49 Nishi-Azabu, Minato-ku, VIII, B3, nº 35, ☎ 3403 2962. Open Mon-Sat 7pm-3am. Closed holidays. This is a reggae club. Unfortunately, it is not very close to the centre of the district.

Café

♦♦ **Hard Rock Café** (café restaurant), 5-4-20 Roppongi, Minato-ku, VIII, C3, n° 26, ☎ 3408 7247. Open Mon-Sat 4pm-2am; Sun 4-11:30pm. Behind the Roi Building. You can recognize the Hard Rock thanks to King Kong hanging from the façade. Décor of the 1950s and 1960s. Copious servings.

Shops

Aoyama Book Center (bookstore), 6-1-20 Roppongi, Minato-ku, VIII, C3, n° 36, ☎ 3479 0479. Open Mon-Sat 10am-5:30pm; Sun 10am-10pm. The foreign books are at the back of the shop.

Axis, 5-17-1 Roppongi, Minato-ku, VIII, C3, n° 37. There are restaurants (Kisso, A Tantôt, Perrier and so forth) and shops selling the latest household appliances.

Nuno (cloth). Open Tues-Sun 11am-7pm. This shop sells superb fabrics that are often the works of well-known Japanese artists and designers.

Wave, 6-2-27 Roppongi, Minato-ku, VIII, B3, ☎ 3408 0111. Open daily 11am-9pm. Large choice of records and video cassettes. French films, usually contemporary works (by Godard, Téchiné and so on), are shown in the Ciné Vivant.

▬ SHIBA

Hotels

▲▲▲▲ **Tokyo Prince Hotel,** 3-3-1 Shiba-Koen, Minato-ku, III, A3, ☎ 3432 1111, telex 242 2488. Two minutes from Onarimon Station, near the Tokyo Tower and the Zozo ji Temple. 466 rooms. Restaurant, tearoom, bar, cocktail lounge, beauty parlour, swimming pool, travel agency, shops and facilities for conferences and wedding receptions. There is a shuttle to Narita airport.

▲▲▲ **Shiba Park Hotel,** 1-5-10 Shiba-Koen, Minato-ku, III, B3, d ☎ 3433 4141. Two minutes from Shiba Koen Station. 416 rooms. Restaurants, bar, café and facilities for banquets and conferences. There is a shuttle service to Narita airport. Frequently used by athletes who have come to Tokyo to participate in an event, this hotel is calm, with efficient service.

Restaurants

♦♦♦♦ **Beaux Séjours** (French cuisine),

Tokyo Prince Hotel 1 F, 3-3-1 Shiba-Koen, Minato-ku, III, A3, ☎ 3432 1111. Open daily 11:30am-2:30pm, 5:30-10pm. Authentic French cuisine.

♦♦♦♦ **Crescent** (French cuisine), 1-8-20 Shiba-Koen, Minato-ku, III, A3, ☎ 3436 3211. Open daily 11:30am-2:30pm, 5-10:30pm. Closed Sun in July and Aug. Jackets and ties are mandatory for men if you wish to taste the traditional French cuisine at the Crescent.

♦♦ **Shinta-Hanten** (Chinese cuisine), 2-3-2 Shiba-Daimon, Minato-ku, III, B3, ☎ 3434 0005. Open Mon-Sat 11:30am-10pm; Sun and holidays noon-10pm. Near the McDonald's at the Daimon Crossing.

♦ **Akitaya** (*nomiya*), 2-1-1 Hamamatsucho, Minato-ku, III, BC3. You can smell the kebabs all the way from the Daimon Crossing. Workmen come here and eat *yakitori* with beer or sake. Customers eat standing.

▬ SHIBAURA

Restaurant

♦♦♦ **Tango** (Mediterranean cuisine), 2-2-18 Shibaura, Minato-ku, X, D2-3, ☎ 3798 1311. Open daily 7pm-4am.

Ten minutes by foot from Tamachi Station. A trendy restaurant with tango music.

▬ SHIBUYA

Hotels

▲▲▲▲ **Shibuya Tokyu Inn,** 1-24-10 Shibuya, Shibuya-ku, XI, C3, a1, ☎ 3498 0109. Two minutes from Shibuya Station. 224 rooms. Restaurants, café, bar and facilities for banquets and conferences. The Tokyu Inn chain hotels are usually very good.

▲▲▲ **Aoyama Chanpia Hotel,** 2-14-15 Shibuya, Shibuya-ku, XI, C3, b1, ☎ 3407 2111. Eight minutes from Shibuya Station. 135 rooms. Restaurants, bar and café.

▲▲▲ **Hillport Hotel,** 23-19 Sakuragaokacho, Shibuya-ku, I, A2, ☎ 3461

2074. Three minutes south from Shibuya Station. 61 rooms. Restaurants, bar, café and facilities for conferences. Located on a very quiet street, this little hotel is modern and bright. The clients are greeted with a warm welcome.

▲▲▲ **Hotel IB Flats**, 2-26-2 Dogenzaka, Shibuya-ku, XI, B3, d, ☎ 3770 1122. Five minutes from Shibuya Station. 43 rooms. Restaurant, café and facilities for conferences. A charming hotel, with flowers at the entrance.

▲▲▲ **Shibuya Tobu Hotel**, 3-1 Udagawacho, Shibuya-ku, XI, B3, e, ☎ 3476 0111. Five minutes from Shibuya Station. 199 rooms. Restaurants, café, bar, shops and facilities for banquets and wedding receptions. Just opposite the Tobacco and Salt Museum, this is one of the most practical hotels in Tokyo. It is near several restaurants as well as Yoyogi Park.

▲▲ **B and B Shibuya**, 2-24-4 Ohashi, Meguro-ku, I, A2, ☎ 3795 6600. One minute from Ikejiri-Ohashi Station and 10 minutes from Shibuya Station. ①②③④⑤. B and B stands for 'Bed and Breakfast'. This hotel is very practical and inexpensive.

▲▲ **Komaba Eminence**, 2-19-5 Ohashi, Meguro-ku, I, A2, ☎ 3485 1411. Four minutes from Komaba-Todaimae Station. ①②③④⑤. This hotel is managed by a non-profit organization. The price is very moderate, but guests must be in by 11pm.

Restaurants

♦♦♦ **Brasserie EX** (Alsatian cuisine), Junikagetsu Building B 3, 1-18-7 Jinnan, Shibuya-ku, XI, B3, n° 1, ☎ 3467 8699. Open Mon-Sat 5pm-2am; Sun and holidays 5-11:30pm. The main attraction is the post-modern decor, particularly the impressive concrete ceiling.

♦♦♦ **Champs de Mars** (French cuisine), 1-15-10 Dogenzaka, Shibuya-ku, XI, B3, n° 2b, ☎ 3461 5013. Open Tues-Sun 11:30am-2pm, 5:30-10:30pm. Seven minutes from Shibuya Station. The chef was trained in several French towns. His little brick restaurant offers an inventive cuisine that aims at preserving the natural taste of the ingredients.

♦♦ **Izumiya** (*yakitori*), Casa de Shibuya B 1 F, 16-15 Sakuragaoka, Shibuya-ku, I, A2, ☎ 3461 4962. Open daily 5pm-midnight. One minute south of Shibuya Station. Although not expensive, this restaurant has a certain amount of class.

♦♦ **Jizake** (*nomiya*), 1-15-8 Dogenzaka, Shibuya-ku, XI, B3, n° 4b, ☎ 3464 5876. Open Mon-Sat 5pm-2am. Closed holidays. There are about 40 different sakes that come from every region of Japan. Excellent *sashimi*. You can order from a set menu.

♦♦ **Komagata Dojo** (Japanese cuisine, loach), 32-8 Udagawacho, Shibuya-ku, XI, B3, n° 5b, ☎ 3464 5522. Open Mon-Sat 11:30-2am; Sun and holidays 11:30am-9pm. The main restaurant is in Asakasa but the annex in Shibuya is just as good. If you're feeling courageous, try the *dojo nabe*, a dish of loach (a type of small eel) served alive with grated leeks. Delicious and not expensive.

♦♦ **Orenchi** (*nomiya*), Miyazaki Building 1 F, 42-7 Udagawacho, Shibuya-ku, XI, B3, n° 6b, ☎ 3476 1735. Open daily 5:30pm-1am. Closed on the 1st and 2nd Sun of every month. Behind the NHK Service Center. The name 'Orenchi' means 'my place'. *Hijiki* (seafood) and *okara* (crab in soy sauce) are among the several specialities of the house.

♦♦ **Reikyo** (Taiwanese cuisine), 2-25-18 Dogenzaka, Shibuya-ku, XI, B3, n° 7b, ☎ 3464 8617. Open Mon-Wed noon-2pm, 5pm-1am; Sat-Sun and holidays noon-1am. You might think you were in Taiwan. Excellent and inexpensive, this restaurant is always crowded. There is another Taiwanese restaurant, **Ryu do Hige** ('Dragon's mustache'), XI, B3, n° 8b, behind the *koban* (police-box) that is in the form of an elephant.

♦♦ **Shibuya no Kochan** (Japanese cuisine, fish), Shu Building 3 F, 1-24-2 Shibuya, Shibuya-ku, XI, C3, n° 9b, ☎ 3409 5557. Open Mon-Sat 5pm-midnight. Closed holidays. To find the building, just look up and search for the *optic ogura* sign. The restaurant is on the 3rd floor. It serves some of the freshest fish in Tokyo.

♦♦ **Tentsui** (Chinese cuisine), Shibuya Business Hotel B 1, 1-12-5 Shibuya, Shibuya-ku, XI, C3, n° 10b, ☎ 3409 9323. Open daily noon-2:30pm, 5:30-9:30pm. Not far from Miyamasuzaka. Pekinese cuisine from Taiwan! Reasonably priced, the dishes are good and copious.

♦ **Bengal** (Islamic cuisine), Shibuya Metro Plaza 2 F, 1-16-14 Shibuya, Shibuya-ku, XI, C3, n° 11, ☎ 3498 0916. Open daily 11am-10pm. Closed the 1st and 3rd Tues of every month. Bengali, Indian and Pakistani cuisine served in a pleasant setting.

♦ **Chotoku** (*udon*), 1-10-5 Shibuya, Shibuya-ku, XI, C3, n° 12b, ☎ 3407 8891. Open daily 11am-9:30pm. Closed the 1st and 3rd Sun of every month. The speciality is *sanuki-udon* (*udon* or wheat noodle, from the region of Shikoku). The chef can be seen preparing the meals behind a window. A wide variety of *udon* are attractively presented in bowls.

◆ **I-ro-ha-ni-ho-he-to** (Japanese cuisine), Nihon Seimei Annex Building B 1, 1-19-3 Jinnan, Shibuya-ku, XI, B3, nº 13, ☎ 3476 1682. Open daily 4:30pm-4am. Near Swensen's ice-cream parlour. This spacious restaurant serves a cuisine from Hokkaido (Northern Japan) and is always crowded with students and workers.

◆ **Tamakyu** (Japanese cuisine and fish), 2-30-4 Dogenzaka, Shibuya-ku, XI, B3, nº 1h, ☎ 3461 4803. Open Mon-Sat 4-11pm. Closed holidays. Next door to the '109' building. An old and slightly dilapidated restaurant, it is always full. Serves fish only.

◆ **Tami-e** (Chinese cuisine), 1-17-6 Dogenzaka, Shibuya-ku, XI, B3, ☎ 3464 7544. Shibuya Station. Open daily 11-2am. Excellent, inexpensive cuisine in an extraordinary atmosphere. There is a menu in English with photographs.

◆ **Tenmi** (macrobiotic cuisine and health food), Daiichi Twashita Building 2 F, 1-10-6 Jinnan, Shibuya-ku, XI, B3, nº 15, ☎ 3496 9703. Open Mon-Sat 11:30am-2:30pm, 4:30-7:30pm; Sun and holidays 11:30am-6:30pm. Closed the 3rd Thurs of every month. Delicious macrobiotic food (Japanese style). At lunch, the *teishoku* (set-price menus) are very inexpensive.

Shops

Bunkaya Zakka-ten (souvenirs), 1-9-5 Jinnan, Shibuya-ku, XI, C2, nº 17b, ☎ 3461 0985. Open daily 11am-8pm. Closed on the 20th of every month. Located on Fire Street, near Miyashita Park. Inexpensive dresses and kitsch gadgets. You will certainly be able to find something to bring home as a souvenir.

Parco Part 1, XI, B3; **Parco 2**, XI, B3; **Parco 3**, XI, B3; 15-1 Udagawacho, Shibuya-ku, ☎ 3464 5111. Open 10am-8pm (10pm for the restaurants). Closed on January 1. **'109'** Bldg, **Tokyu Plaza**, XI, B3, nº 18. These are the fashionable department stores in Shibuya. There are numerous shops and restaurants.

Pink Dragon (trinkets and knick knacks), 1-23-23 Shibuya, Shibuya-ku, XI, C2, nº 19b, ☎ 3498 2577. Open daily 10am-8pm. Turn at the corner near the Surplus Company clothes shop. A veritable museum of the 1950s. There is a café on the 2nd floor.

Tokyu Hands (hardware, decoration), 12-18 Udagawacho, Shibuya-ku, XI, B3, nº 20, ☎ 3476 5461. Open daily 10am-8pm. Closed the 2nd and 3rd Wed of every month. A great store for artisans and handymen. You can also find many original gifts.

▬ *SHIMBASHI*

Hotels

▲▲▲▲ **First Hotel Yoshikawa**, 2-9-4 Shimbashi, Minato-ku, III, B2, ☎ 3592 0024. One minute from Shimbashi Station. 70 rooms. Restaurants. One of the newest hotels in Tokyo.

▲▲▲▲ **Shimbashi Daiichi Hotel**, 1-2-6 Shimbashi, Minato-ku, III, B1, b1, ☎ 3501 4411, telex 252-3714. Near Shimbashi Station. 1124 rooms. This hotel has a large foreign clientele.

▲▲ **Bangkok Hotel** (business hotel), 2-8-10 Nishi-Shimbashi, Minato-ku, III, B2, ☎ 3503 0111. Two minutes from Uchisaiwaicho Station and five minutes from Shimbashi Station. 50 rooms. ①②③④. Bar.

▲▲ **Sun Hotel Shimbashi** (business hotel), 3-5-2 Shimbashi, Minato-ku, III, B2, d1, ☎ 3591 3351. Three minutes from Shimbashi Station. 119 rooms. ①②③④. Restaurant and café. Well located, this hotel is frequently used by businesspeople.

Restaurants

◆◆◆ **Misono** (steak), Wataru Building B 1, 2-11 Nishi-Shimbashi, Minato-ku, III, AB2, ☎ 3591 7823. Open daily 11am-2pm, 5-10pm. Very popular with foreigners. Expensive.

◆ **Honjinbo** *(soba)*, 2-14-5 Shimbashi, Minato-ku, III, B2, nº 2a, ☎ 3591 1719. Open Mon-Fri 11:30am-3pm, 5-9:30pm; Sat 11:30am-3pm, 5-7pm. Closed holidays. The service is pleasant. The *shiso-kiri* (in summer) and the *yuzu-kiri* (in winter) are remarkable.

◆ **Komorosoba** *(soba, tendon)*, 1-16-2 Shimbashi, Minato-ku, II, B2. Open Mon-Sat 8am-5pm. Closed holidays. Opposite the Bank of Tokyo. Excellent Japanese fast food. The prices are incredibly low. You eat standing up.

SHINAGAWA/TAKANAWA

Hotels

▲▲▲▲ **Hotel Pacific Méridien**, 3-13-3 Takanawa, Minato-ku, I, A2-3 ☎ 3445 6711, telex: 242-3074. One minute from Shinagawa Station. 952 rooms. Restaurants, café, bar, swimming pool, sauna, shops, bakery, Japanese garden, cable television and facilities for conferences and wedding receptions. There is a shuttle service to Narita airport. This hotel belongs to the Méridien chain.

▲▲▲▲ **New Takanawa Prince Hotel**, 3-13-1 Takanawa, Minato-ku, I, A2-3 ☎ 3442 1111. Three minutes from Takanawadai Station and eight minutes from Shinagawa Station. 1080 rooms. Restaurants, bar, pharmacy, shops, travel agency, swimming pool, Japanese garden, florist, business center and facilities for conferences. There is a shuttle service to Narita airport. All the rooms are large and have balconies.

▲▲▲▲ **Takanawa Prince Hotel**, 3-13-1 Takanawa, Minato-ku, I, A2-3 ☎ 3447 1111. Five minutes from Shinagawa Station. 403 rooms. Restaurants, café, swimming pool, Japanese garden and facilities for conferences, banquets and wedding receptions. There is a shuttle service to Narita airport. A venerable establishment decorated in the old style.

▲▲ **Shinagawa Prince Hotel**, 4-10-30 Takanawa, Minato-ku, I, A2-3 ☎ 3440 1111. One minute from Shinagawa Station. 1016 rooms. ①②③④⑤. Restaurants, café, bar and facilities for conferences. This hotel has a large sports center (tennis court, swimming pool, ice-skating rink and bowling lanes). There are only single rooms in the main building, but an extra bed can always be added. The annex, with 254 rooms, is reserved for couples.

▲▲ **Takanawa Tobu Hotel** (business hotel), 4-7-6 Takanawa, Minato-ku, I, A2-3 ☎ 3447 0111. Five minutes from Shinagawa Station. 42 rooms. ①②③④⑤. Restaurant, bar and facilities for banquets. This calm little hotel is near the New Takanawa Hotel.

SHINJUKU

Hotels

▲▲▲▲ **Century Hyatt Tokyo**, 2-7-2 Nishi-Shinjuku, Shinjuku-ku, VI, A2 ☎ 3349 0111, telex: J29-411. Nine minutes from Shinjuku Station. 800 rooms. There are 23 conference halls, a swimming pool on the 28th floor, 11 restaurants, a discotheque and secretarial services. European atmosphere. Limousine services to Narita airport and the center of Shinjuku.

▲▲▲▲ **Hilton International**, 6-6-2 Nishi-Shinjuku, Shinjuku-ku, VI, A2 ☎ 3344 5111, telex: 232-4515. About 10 minutes from Shinjuku Station. 841 rooms. Restaurants, bars, swimming pool, gym room, travel agency, beauty parlour, hairdresser, business center and facilities for banquets and wedding receptions. Limousine services to Narita airport and the center of Shinjuku. Although the hotel is not particularly close to the center of Shinjuku, the neighbourhood possesses a number of excellent small restaurants, such as Shinagawa.

▲▲▲▲ **Keio Plaza Hotel**, 2-2-1 Nishi-Shinjuku, Shinjuku-ku, VI, A2 ☎ 3344 0111, telex: J26874, cable KEIOPLATEL. Five minutes from Shinjuku Station. 1485 rooms. 25 restaurants and bars, hairdresser, travel agency, sauna, outdoor swimming pool, shops, dental clinic, Japanese tearoom, business center, day nursery and facilities for banquets and wedding receptions. This hotel, which belongs to the Inter-Continental chain, is one of the largest in Asia. The shuttle service to Narita airport stops just in front of the hotel.

▲▲▲▲ **Shinjuku Prince Hotel**, 1-30-1 Kabukicho, Shinjuku-ku, VI, B1 ☎ 3205 1111. Located right next to Shinjuku Station. 571 rooms. Restaurants, café, and shops. Very convenient for the Kabukicho district.

▲▲▲ **Hotel Sunroute Tokyo**, 2-3-1 Yoyogi, Shibuya-ku, VI, B2, e ☎ 3375 3211. Two minutes south of Shinjuku Station. 600 rooms. Restaurants and facilities for banquets and conferences. The hotel is part of the Sunroute chain. You can hire a computer, a typewriter or a video machine.

▲▲ **Hotel Ristel Shinjuku**, 5-3-20 Shinjuku, Shinjuku-ku, VI, D2, f ☎ 3350 0123. Five minutes from Shinjuku-gyoenmae Station. Near Kosei Nenkin Hall. 213 rooms. ①②③④⑤. Restaurants and secretarial services. The rooms are decorated in red and white for a warm atmosphere.

▲▲ **Inabaso** (ryokan), 4-6-13 Shinjuku, Shinjuku-ku, VI, D2, g ☎ 3341 9581. Three minutes from Shinjuku-sanchome

Station, near the center of Shinjuku. 13 rooms. ①②③. All the rooms have their own bathrooms (rare for *ryokan*). Not expensive.

▲▲ **Washington Hotel,** 3-2-9 Nishi-Shinjuku, Shinjuku-ku, VI, A2-3, h, ☎ 33433111. Eight minutes from Shinkuju Station. 1638 rooms. ①②③④⑤. Restaurants, bars, café and facilities for banquets. Magnetic cards replace door keys. The annex is new and more comfortable than the older section. There is a shuttle service to Narita airport.

▲ **Tokyo Yoyogi Youth Hostel** 3-1 Yoyogi-Kamizonocho, Shibuya-ku, XI, AB1, ☎ 34679163. Take the Odakyu Line from Shinjuku Station to Sangubashi Station, then walk for 10 minutes. 150 rooms. ①②.

Restaurants

◆◆◆◆ **Kakiden** *(kaiseki ryori),* Yasuyo Building 8, 9 F, 3-37-11 Shinjuku, Shinjuku-ku, VI, B2, n° 1, ☎ 3352 5121. Open daily 11am-9pm. Real *cha-kaiseki* cuisine. The restaurant is run by a tea-ceremony school *(Omote Senke).* Expensive, as are all *kaiseki* (Japanese *haute cuisine*) restaurants.

◆◆◆ **Kurumaya** (French cuisine), 2-37-1 Kabukicho, Shinjuku-ku, VI, C1, n° 2, ☎ 32320301. Open daily 11:30am-3pm, 5-10pm. At the end of the Koma-gekijo. The cuisine is inspired as much by French cooking as by *kaiseki ryori.* The food is refined and, of course, rather expensive.

◆◆ **Chirinbo** *(nomiya),* Yoshikawa Building 1 F, 3-8-7 Shinjuku, Shinjuku-ku, VI, C2, n° 3, ☎ 33506945. Open Mon-Sat 5pm-5am. Below Yajirobei. This restaurant is always crowded, particularly with people from the cinema and publishing businesses. The menu is varied, and the prices are low.

◆◆ **Kakei** (Japanese cuisine), 3-12-12 Shinjuku, Shinjuku-ku, VI, C2, n° 5, ☎ 33527646. Open Mon-Fri 5pm-midnight; Sat-Sun 5pm-5am. Near Suehiro-tei. The interior is tastefully furnished in a rustic style. The fish dishes are good.

◆◆ **Le Coupechou** (French cuisine), 1-15-7 Shinjuku, Shinjuku-ku, VI, B2, n° 4, ☎ 33481610. Open Mon-Sat 11:30am-2pm, 5:30pm-midnight; Sun and holidays 5:30-midnight. In the camera shop district. A large selection of fish dishes served with light sauces. Warm welcome and low prices.

◆◆ **Mana** (natural cuisine), Kikusui Building B 1, 1-16-5 Nishi-Shinjuku, Shinjuku-ku, VI, B2, n° 6, ☎ 33446606. Open Mon-Thur 11am-9pm; Fri 11am-3pm. Closed holidays. No smoking in this restaurant that has a 1960s atmosphere.

◆◆ **Ran Thai** (Thai cuisine), Daiichi Metro Building 3 F, 1-23-14 Kabukicho, Shinjuku-ku, VI, B1, n° 7, ☎ 32070068. Open Mon-Fri 5pm-1am; Sat-Sun 11:30-1am. Authentic Thai cuisine.

◆◆ **Shinagawa** (Japanese cuisine), at the end of Nishi-Shinjuku, VI, A1. Three excellent and friendly restaurants with the same name, each is run by one of three brothers and with its own speciality. The first, ☎ 33762990, is a *tonkatsu;* the second, ☎ 33781178, is a *kushi-age;* while the third, ☎ 33781033, specializes in chicken.

◆◆ **Tarugen** (Japanese cuisine), Sumitomo Building 49 F, 2-6-1 Nishi-Shinjuku, Shinjuku-ku, VI, A1, n° 9, ☎ 33446496. Open daily 11:30am-10pm. West of Shinjuku Station. The interior of the restaurant resembles a rural home. In striking contrast, the view of Tokyo from the 49th floor is fantastic.

◆◆ **Tokyo Dai Hanten** (Chinese cuisine), 5-17-13 Shinjuku, Shinjuku-ku, VI, C1, n° 10, ☎ 32020121. Near Shinjuku Station. Open daily 11am-10pm. According to the Chinese residents of Tokyo, this restaurant serves one of the most delicious, authentic Cantonese cuisines in Tokyo. Steamed dishes as well as other specialities are served on rotating trays set in the center of the table. Lunch costs ¥2000 to ¥3000. Dinner is more expensive.

◆◆ **Yajirobei** (Japanese cuisine), Shoshikawa Building 2 F, 3-8-7 Shinjuku, Shinjuku-ku, VI, C2, n° 11, ☎ 33505739. Open Mon-Sat 5:45pm-1am. Three minutes from Shinjuku-sanchome Station. The chef proposes an inventive, almost humorous, cuisine. You can also just come for a drink and admire the elegant décor.

◆◆ **Zuien Bekkan** (Chinese cuisine), 1-10-6 Shinjuku, Shinjuku-ku, VI, C2, n° 12, ☎ 33513511. Open daily 11am-10pm. One minute from Shinjuku-gyoenmae Station. The interior resembles a restaurant in Hong Kong or Taiwan. The food is authentic, copious and inexpensive.

◆ **Fureai no Mura** (natural cuisine), 2-45-6 Kabukicho, Shinjuku-ku, VI, B1, n° 13, ☎ 32098622. Open Mon-Sat 11am-11pm. Closed holidays. A good, pleasant restaurant.

◆ **Keiba** *(ramen),* 3-25-6 Shinjuku, Shinjuku-ku, VI, C2, n° 14, ☎ 3352 4836. Open daily 11-12:45am. There are three branches in Shinjuku. The *ramen* soup is remarkable.

◆ **Tsunahachi** *(tempura),* 3-31-8 Shinjuku, Shinjuku-ku, VI, C2, n° 15, ☎ 33521012. Open daily 11:30am-10:30pm. Behind Mitsukoshi. This is a branch of a large chain that serves excellent *tempura* at moderate prices.

Bars and Discotheques

♦♦ **Daisan Soko** (discotheque), Hanazono Building B 1, 5-17-6 Shinjuku, Shinjuku-ku, VI, C1, n° 17, ☎ 3207 6953. Open Sat-Sun from 7pm on. Near Hanazono Jinja. Select and trendy clientele.

♦♦ **Pin Inn** (live house and jazz) YK Building B 1, 3-16-4 Shinjuku, Shinjuku-ku, VI, C2, n° 18, ☎ 3354 2024. Open daily 11:30am-11pm. Concerts at noon, 3pm and 7:30pm. Behind Kinokuniya bookstore. Very well known.

♦♦ **Tsubaki House** (discotheque), Théâtre Building 5 F, 3-14-20 Shinjuku, Shinjuku-ku, VI, C2, n° 19, ☎ 3354 3236. Open daily from 5pm on. This establishment has attracted young people for years. The music changes every day.

♦ **'69'** (bar), Daini Seiko Building B1, 2-18-5 Shinjuku, Shinjuku-ku, VI, C2, n° 20, ☎ 3341 6358. Open daily noon-3am. International atmosphere with a mixed clientele. Drinking and dancing to the sound of reggae.

♦ **Tokachi** (bar), Isetan 1 F, 3-14-1 Shinjuku, Shinjuku-ku, VI, C2, n° 21, ☎ 3356 5946. Open Thurs-Tues noon-9pm. In the middle of Isetan department store, this bar is a convenient meeting place. _

♦ **Volga** *(nomiya)*, 1-4-16 Nishi-Shinjuku, Shinjuku-ku, VI, B1, n° 16, ☎ 3342 4996. Open Mon-Sat 5-11pm. Near the Odakyu Halc Building. This old house, covered with ivy, hides a very popular and inexpensive Japanese bar.

Shops

Bingoya (folk art), 10-6 Wakamatsu-cho, Shinjuku-ku, I, A1, ☎ 3202 8778. Open Tues-Sun 10am-7pm. Take a bus from Odakyu Halk in the direction of Tokyo Joshi Idai and get off at Wakamatsucho. Bingoya is just opposite the bus stop. There is a good selection of traditional arts and crafts.

Kinokuniya (bookstore), 3-17-7 Shinjuku, Shinjuku-ku, VI, B2, n° 23, ☎ 3354 0131. Open daily 10am-7pm. Closed the 1st and 3rd Wed of every month. This bookstore is a well-known meeting place in Shinjuku. On the 6th floor, there is an international section with magazines, guides and literature.

Shinjuku is very well known for its camera shops. The main dealers include:

Camera no Doi, VI, B2, n° 24, ☎ 3344 2310; n° 2, ☎ 3348 2241. Open daily 10am-8pm. Located in the western half of Shinjuku.

Camera no Kimuraya, VI, A31-2, ☎ 3354 2701. Open daily 10am-8pm. In the eastern half of Shinjuku.

Camera no Sakuraya. There are two stores, one in the western half (☎ 3344 2310 or 3352 4711) and the other in the eastern half (☎ 3346 3939). Open daily 10am-8pm.

Yodobashi Camera, ☎ 3346 1010. Open 9:30am-8:30pm. There are two stores. The largest is to the west of the station, VI, B2, n° 27, while the smaller outlet is to the east, VI, B2, n° 28, near *My City*.

All these shops sell duty-free. Do not forget your passport as it will be required when you fill out the customs forms. You can bargain over prices.

▬ *TSUKIJI/TSUKUDAJIMA*

Restaurants

♦♦♦♦ **Tamura** *(kaiseki)*, 2-12-11 Tsukiji, Chuo-ku, III, D2, 1b, ☎ 3541 2591. Open daily 11:30am-10pm. The chef gives lectures at the university on *kaiseki* cuisine. Very sophisticated. The menu changes every month.

♦♦♦ **Kanemasa** (Japanese cuisine), 2-10-13 Tsukuda, Chuo-ku, III, D2, n° 2b, ☎ 3531 6519. Open Mon-Sat 5-11pm. Closed mid-July to mid-Aug. Two minutes from the Shin-Tsukudajima bus stop. In the centre of the popular Tsukudajima district, this restaurant is a treasure. For a reasonable price, you can sample a cuisine that changes with the seasons. By reservation only.

♦♦♦ **Tsukiji Uemura** (Japanese cuisine), 1-13-10 Tsukiji, Chuo-ku, III, D2, n° 3b, ☎ 3541 1351. Open daily 11:30am-3pm, 5-10pm. Less expensive than *kaiseki ryori* cuisine but rather sophisticated nonetheless.

♦♦ **Sushi Sei** *(sushi)*, 4-13-9 Tsukiji, Chuo-ku, III, D2, n° 4, ☎ 3541 7720. Open Mon-Sat 7am-2pm, 5-10pm. Closed holidays. There is usually a half-hour wait. There are other branches in Ginza, Roppongi and Akasaka.

♦♦ **Tsukiji Edogin** *(sushi)*, 4-5-1 Tsukiji, Chuo-ku, III, D2, n° 5b, ☎ 3543 4401. Open Mon-Sat 11am-9:30pm. This restaurant takes advantage of its location near the

Tsukiji fish market to offer excellent and copious *sushi* and very good *tempura*. About 80 cooks await your visit.

Shops

Around the **fish market**, III, D1, there

are many wholesalers, XI, A2, nº 6. It is interesting to look around, even if you do not buy anything.

Kashiwaya (lanterns), 2-3-13 Shintomicho, Chuo-ku, III, D1, ☎ 35511362. Open Mon-Sat 10am-5pm.

▬ *UENO*

Hotels

▲▲ **Hokke Club Ueno-Ikenohata-ten**, 2-1-48 Ikenohata, Taito-ku, IV, A3, a1, ☎ 38223111. Five minutes from Yushima Station. 305 rooms. ①④⑤. Restaurants, bar and facilities for conferences and wedding receptions. On the banks of the Shinobazuno-ike River. Not expensive, even with breakfast. The Japanese-style rooms do not have private bathrooms, but the public bathrooms are large. There is another branch opposite Ueno Station, IV, B3, ☎ 3834-4131.

▲▲ **Hotel New Park**, 2-19-5 Higashi-Ueno, Taito-ku, IV, B3, c1, ☎ 3835 2020. Three minutes from Ueno Station. 49 rooms. ①②③④⑤. This is an ideal hotel for anyone with an interest in this district, which includes Ueno Park, Ueno Zoo, the museums and Ameyoko.

▲▲ **Suigetsu Hotel Ohgai-so**, 3-3-21 Ikenohata, Taito-ku, IV, A2, d, ☎ 38224611. Ten minutes from Ueno Station. ①④. The house and gardens of Mori Ohgai, a Meiji-period writer, are part of the hotel. Demonstrations of *ikebana* and the tea ceremony.

▲ **Sawanoya** (*ryokan*), 2-3-11 Yanaka, Taito-ku, IV, A2, e, ☎ 38222251. Seven minutes from Nezu Station in an old neighborhood. ①.

Restaurants

♦♦♦ **Bon** (Zen cuisine), 4-37-19 Hakusan, Bunkyo-ku, off map IV, AB1, ☎ 39471525. Open Wed-Mon noon-8:30pm. Three minutes from Sengoku Station. Of Chinese origin, *fucha-ryori* is a Buddhist school of cooking heavily influenced by Zen. This cuisine is entirely vegetarian; no meat or fish.

♦♦♦ **Goemon** (*tofu*), 1-1-26 Hon-Komagome, Bunkyo-ku, IV, B3, nº 2a, ☎ 38120900. Open Mon-Sat 5-10pm; Sun and holidays 3-8pm. Three minutes from Hakusan Station. One of the best *tofu* restaurants in Tokyo. The interior resembles a country inn of the Kyoto region. An unforgettable experience.

♦♦♦ **Nibiki** (*fugu*, see **warning** p. 91), 3-3-7 Shitaya, Taito-ku, IV, B1, ☎ 3872 6250. Open Oct-March, daily 5-9pm. Closed July, Aug, and Sun and holidays in Apr, May, June and Sept.

The cheapest *fugu* in Tokyo. An old establishment, it has retained tradition. Start with *fugu sashimi*, followed by *fugu-nabe*. Accompany your meal with *hirezake* (warm sake served with a floating *fugu* fin). Reservations are recommended.

♦♦♦ **Sasanoyuki** (*tofu*), 2-15-10 Negishi, Taito-ku, IV, B1, nº 4a, ☎ 38731145. Open Mon-Sat 11am-9pm. Three minutes from Uguisudani Station, opposite the Negishi primary school. *Tofu* is served in all its forms. The cuisine is very good, but the setting leaves something to be desired. Ask for places near the fountain.

♦♦ **Hantei** (*kushi-age*), 2-12-15 Nezu, Bunkyo-ku, IV, A2, nº 5a, ☎ 38281440. Open Tues-Sat 5-11pm; Sun and holidays 4-10pm. Two minutes from Nezu Station. This restaurant is housed in a three-storey wooden building, which is, needless to say, rare in Tokyo. The interior is extraordinary. Start with a set menu; if you are still hungry, order a few extra sides dishes.

Shops

Ameyoko Arcade, 4-7-8 Ueno, Taito-ku, IV, B3, nº 6a. Most of the shops are open daily 10:30am-7pm. At Ameyoko you might think that you were in Hong Kong. Clothes, cosmetics, alcohol, shoes and so on are sold 30% to 40% cheaper than elsewhere. Toward the New Year's holidays, the crowds are nearly impenetrable.

Isetatsu (Japanese paper), 2-18-9 Yanaka, Taito-ku, IV, A1, nº 72, ☎ 38231453. Open daily 9am-6pm. A charming shop. There is another outlet in Aoyama.

Kikuya Shamisen-ten (*shamisen*), 3-45-11 Yushima, Bunkyo-ku, IV, A3, nº 8a, ☎ 38314733. Open Mon-Sat 9am-7:30pm.

Torindo (pastry), 1-5-7 Ueno-Sakuragi, Taito-ku, IV, A2, nº 9a, ☎ 38289826. Open Tues-Sun 9am-5pm. A well established Japanese pastry shop that specializes in *soba-manju*, a soup made of red beans (*shiruko*).

Tshizuka Shoten (lamps), 3-34-10 Yushima, Bunkyo-ku, IV, A3, nº 10a, ☎ 38310891. Open daily 7am-7pm.

Features Japanese lamp shades made of bamboo. You can order lamps in any imaginable form.

Usagiya (Japanese pastry), 1-10-10 Ueno, Taito-ku, IV, A3, n° 11a, ☎ 3831 6195. Open daily 9am-6pm. Near Matsuzakaya department store. The speciality of the house is *dorayaki*.

▬ YOTSUYA

Restaurants

◆◆◆◆ Hotel de Mikuni (French cuisine), 1-18 Wakaba, Shinjuku-ku, VII, B2, ☎ 3351 3810. Open Tues-Sat noon-2:30pm, 6-9:30pm. The atmosphere is so friendly that you might almost think you were dining at a friend's house. Traditional French and *nouvelle cuisine*.

◆◆◆ Ichoan *(kaiseki)*, 8 Honshiocho, Shinjuku-ku, VII, BC1, ☎ 3359 2636. Open daily noon-2:30pm, 5:30-10pm. This is an annex of Daikonya in Daikanyama, well known for having launched Japanese *nouvelle cuisine*. The decor is simple and high-tech.

◆◆ Kahin (Chinese cuisine), Daison Shikakura Building 2 F, 1-7 Yotsuya, Shinjuku-ku, VII, BC2, ☎ 3358 7912. Open Mon-Sat 11am-2pm, 5-10pm. Closed holidays. Delicious Cantonese cuisine.

◆◆ Shinobu (tongue), 16 San'eicho, Shinjuku-ku, VII, B2, ☎ 3355 6338. Open Mon-Sat 5-11pm; Sun and holidays 5-10pm. Closed the 3rd Sun of every month. This popular old bistro is always crowded. It is best to go early. Beef tongue is served raw, boiled and grilled. Excellent and relatively inexpensive.

Shop

Bonjin-sha (bookstore), Kojimachi Rokuchome Building 6 F, 6-2 Kojimachi, Chiyoda-ku, VII, CD2, ☎ 3265 7782. Open Mon-Sat 9:30am-5:30pm. Closed holidays. Texts on the Japanese language.

GLOSSARY

Abec hoteru: love hotels; establishments catering to the amorous.
Abekura-mochi: type of pastry.
Age-manju: fried cakes.
Amacha: sweet tea (poured over images of Buddha on his anniversary).
Amae: sphere of dependence (Japanese notion of moral obligation).
Amakuchi: sweet sauce served with *tonkatsu* (deep-fried pork).
Amazake: sweet, yogurt-like drink made from sake lees.
Anago: conger or sea eel (frequently served grilled as *kabayaki*).
Arai: toilets.
Awabi: abalone.
Azekura: ancient architectural style of building without nails.

Bakufu: tent government (military dictatorship or shogunate).
Bashi, hashi: bridge.
Basu: bus.
Bento: box lunch, generally a selection of an expensive cuisine.
Bijutsukan: museum.
Biyoin: hospital.
Bodara: edible fish unknown outside of Japan.
Bugaku: posturing dances in which masks were worn.
Bunraku: musical narrative puppetry from Osaka.
Bushi: warrior; the Japanese term for samurai.
Bushido: the way of the warrior, the samurai chivalric code of conduct.
Byobu: folding screens, frequently painted.

Chabana: sparsely arranged bouquets specifically designed for the tearoom.
Cha-kaiseki: tea ceremony cuisine.
Chanko-nabe: sumo wrestlers' food.
Chanoyu: tea ceremony (associated with Zen and landscape gardening).
Cha-seki: tea gardens (developed under the influence of Kobori Enshu).
Chikatetsu: subway.
Cho: small town or city district (administrative division).
Chome: neighbourhood or group of buildings (administrative division).

Dai: Chinese ideogram meaning 'large' or 'great'.
Daikodo: Lecture Hall of a Buddhist temple.
Daikon: enormous Japanese radish, usually served grated or pickled.
Daimyo: landed feudal noble lords (whose retainers were the samurai).
Daishodo: Founder's Hall of a Buddhist temple.
Daki, Taki: waterfall.
Danna-san: geisha patrons, or sponsors, who in the past 'owned' the geishas.
Daruma: rag doll representing the Zen monk Bodhidarma or Daruma.
Den, do: hall; temple building.
Denwa: telephone, colour-coded in Japan according to coin capacity.
Depato: Japanization of 'department store'.
Dera: Buddhist temple.
Dogu: totemistic ceramic figurines of people and animals (Jomon Culture).
Dotaku: decorated bronze bell-shaped objects (Yayoi period).

Ebi: shrimp.
Emakimono: horizontal picture scrolls, developed during the Late Heian period.
En, koen: garden, park.
Endaka: rise of the yen.

A boy dressed up for Children Day (Kodomo No Hi) celebrated at the Meiji Jingu shrine in Tokyo.

Fu: city prefecture.
Fucha ryori: type of *shojin ryori* from China, heavily influenced by Zen.
Fugu: pufferfish or globefish, a poison fish eaten in Japan.
Fusuma: sliding partitions forming walls and doors in Japanese buildings.
Futon: Japanese mattress (put away every day and unrolled at night).

Gaijin: foreigner; anyone who is not Japanese.
Ganjitsu: New Year, the major Shinto holiday (celebrated for several days).
Gawa, kawa: river.
Genkan: vestibule (small, low entrance hall to a Japanese house).
Geta: wooden clogs.
Gidayu: narrator in Kabuki theater.
Gigaku: elegant music; court music and dance of the 7th-9th centuries AD.
Ginbura: to stroll in Ginza; to window shop.
Ginko: bank.
Giyoza: grilled ravioli (generally served with a hot sauce).
Gofun: lime carbonate used to cover earthen statues before gilding.
Gohan: word reserved for plain boiled white rice.
Goraiko: Fuji sunrise (as witnessed only from the summit).
Gu: Shinto shrine.
Gyoretsu: procession or parade.

Hakubutsukan: museum.
Haiden: the oratory of a Shinto shrine.
Haiku: short 17-syllable poem derived from the linking verse in *renga.*
Ha-isha: dentist.
Haitatsu: baggage delivery service.
Hanabi: fireworks display.
Hanamichi: flower path; entrance to the Kabuki stage.
Haniwa: cylindrical clay figurines associated with *kofun* (Yayoi period).
Han-pan: small round breads filled with red bean paste.
Happi: article of clothing.
Hara, nohara: field.
Heya: sumo schools or teams.
Henna-gaijin: strange foreigner; foreigner who likes Japanese ways.
Hibachi: open charcoal braziers.
Higashi, to: east.
Hikari: light train; fast, direct trains on the Tokaido/Sanyo Line.
Hikitechaya: meal with a courtesan before the evening's entertainment.
Hinoki: Japanese cedar *(Cryptomeria japonica).*
Hinoshita kaisan: Universal champion; unbeaten sumo wrestler.
Hiragana: phonetic alphabet used by ladies of the court (10th century).
Hirezake: warm sake served with a *fugu* (pufferfish) fin floating in it.
Hojo: Superior's Quarters in a Buddhist temple.
Hommatsuri: Main feast.
Honden: Main Hall of a Shinto shrine.
Hondo: Main Hall of a Buddhist temple.
Honne: that which is thought but never said (see *Tatemae*).
Hozo: Treasure Hall of a Buddhist temple.

Ichi nin mae: assortment of *sushi.*
Ijikan: American-style houses.
Ika: squid or cuttlefish.
Ike: pond.
Ikebana: flower arranging, heavily influenced by Zen philosophy.

Jima, shima: island.
Jinga, gu, sha: Shinto shrine.

Kabayaki teishoku: grilled eel menu, served with rice in a lacquer box.
Kagura: ritual dances.

Kai: sea.
Kaigan: coast, shore.
Kaisando: Founder's Hall of a Buddhist temple.
Kaiseki ryori: Japanese *haute cuisine.*
Kakemono: vertical scrolls; painting mounted for hanging vertically.
Kakueki teisha: local train that stops at every station (JR Line).
Kamameshi: dish of rice stewed in a small pot.
Kamemona: painted scrolls used to decorate Japanese houses.
Kami: Shinto gods or divinities.
Kamikaze: divine winds; storm that saved Japan from the Mongols.
Kampaku: civil dictator; military, totalitarian dictatorship.
Kani-nabe: crab casserole.
Kanji: Chinese ideograms used to write Japanese (4th century AD onward).
Kano: school of painting that dominated Japanese art for centuries.
Karakuchi: hot sauce served with *tonkatsu* (deep-fried pork).
Karaoke: bars where people get together to sing.
Karayo: Zen-influenced style of Chinese architecture (Kamakura period).
Karesansui: dry landscape; designed without streams or ponds.
Karmon: Chinese Gate.
Katana: Japanese sword.
Katakana: phonetic alphabet of 48 symbols based on Chinese ideograms.
Katashiro: paper dolls launched during the Water Festival.
Katsudon: tonkatsu with grilled onions and eggs mixed with rice and sauce.
Kiku: chrysanthemum.
Kita, hoku: north.
Kimo: eel liver.
Kimono: traditional loose robe or outer garment.
Kimoyaki: grilled eel liver.
Kitte: postage stamp.
Koban: police-box, miniature neighbourhood police stations.
Kodama: local train that stops at every station (Tokaido/Sanyo Line).
Kodo: Lecture Hall of a Buddhist temple.
Koen: garden (public).
Kofun: giant keyhole-shaped burial mounds (Yayoi period).
Koinobori: multicoloured carp-shaped kites (flown on Boys' Day).
Kokoro: Chinese ideogram meaning 'heart', 'mind' or 'spirit'.
Koku: traditional Japanese measure of volume, about 20 US pecks/180 l.
Kokugikan: sumo wrestling center.
Kondo: Main Hall of a Buddhist temple.
Konnyaku: translucent vegetable cake made from the devil's tongue plant.
Koto: two-stringed musical instrument producing a drone.
Koyo: autumn colour of the forests.
Ku: ward (administrative division of a city).
Kumade: small wooden rakes, used to symbolize the money 'to be raked in'.
Kuni: region.
Kun yomi: Japanese sounds used with Chinese ideograms.
Kushi-age: variant of *yakitori* from Osaka (wider range of ingredients).
Kushi-katsu: variant of *yakitori* from Osaka, frequently including pork.
Kusuriya: pharmacy.
Kyoku dome: Poste Restante (General Delivery).
Kyo ningyo: dolls from Kyoto.
Kyo ryori: cuisine of Kyoto, based on *Yusoku, Kaiseki* and *Shojin* cuisines.
Kyuko densha: ordinary express trains with a limited number of stops.

Macha: tea ceremony.
Machi: town (administrative division).
Machiya: courtyard grouping several private houses with a common alley.
Magatama: prehistoric necklaces of curved jewels (Yamato period).
Maguro: bluefin tuna.
Maiko: young apprentice geisha receiving training.

Manga: comic strips (frequently of a dubious moral nature).
Matsuri: religious festival or shrine feast.
Meishi: calling or business card (Japanese form of identification).
Menzei: duty-free.
Mihon: imitation wax or resin food for display in restaurant windows.
Mikoshi: portable shrines used in religious processions.
Minami: south.
Minshuku: lodgings in a private home (often a farmer's or fisherman's house).
Mirin: sweet amber sake used exclusively in cooking.
Miso: fermented soy bean paste, basic staple in Japan.
Misogi: Shinto ritual cleansing before worship.
Miyako: capital (ancient).
Mizu: water.
Mizu-shobai: water commerce; the café and bar trade.
Mochi: rice cakes.
Moku-gyo: wooden gong.
Momoshiki: article of clothing.
Mon: ancient unit of Japanese currency.
Mura: village (administrative district).

Nabe: cooking pot of varying shape for different dishes.
Nama-gashi: red bean pastries.
Namban: barbarians from the south; the Portuguese and other Europeans.
Natto: fermented soy.
Netsuke: ornate toggle used to fasten a kimono or a purse.
Nihon shu: Japanese wine, or sake.
Nihon shu ippon: carafes or small pitchers for sake.
Nishi: west.
Nishijin: indigo cloth.
Niwa: Japanese garden.
Noren: cloth ornament used to decorate Japanese houses.
Nori: purple seaweed served with *sushi* and other dishes.
Nomi no ichi: flea markets.
Nomiya: traditional establishment for consuming alcohol on the premises.

O bento: see *Bento.*
Obi: deep sash worn with a kimono.
O-Bon: festival dedicated to the dead.
Ocha: green Japanese tea.
O hanami: see the flowers; massive outings to the parks in April.
Oiran: courtesan.
Okonomiyaki: beef, vegetables and seafood cooked into an omelet.
Omiyage: souvenirs.
Omote senke: tea ceremony school.
Onsen: natural geothermal hot spring.
Onigiri: rice balls (frequently grilled and wrapped in seaweed).
Onnagata: female impersonators in Kabuki theater.
On yomi: Chinese sounds used for pronouncing composite ideograms.
O shibori: warm towel brought to customers in cafés and restaurants.

Pachinko: Japanese equivalent of pinball.

Raigo: Amidist-influenced school of painting of the Late Heian period.
Raisu: any rice or rice-based dish not served in the Japanese style (see Gohan).
Ramen: Chinese noodles.
Renga: tanka linked verse, developed during the 15th century.
Rikka: school of flower arranging that uses large arrangements.
Robata yaki: grilled seafood and vegetables.
Romaji: roman script used to transliterate Japanese ideograms.
Ronin: masterless samurai or knights who have lost their lord.

Ryokan: Japanese-style hotels.
Ryotei: high-class *Kyo ryori* restaurant where geisha are met.

Saba: mackerel.
Sai: west.
Saka: slope, hill.
Sake: fermented rice wine.
Sakura: cherry trees and by extension, the cherry blossom season.
Sakura no hana: cherry blossoms.
Sammon or *sanmon:* Main Gate to a Buddhist temple.
Samurai: military retainer of a *daimyo* (a chivalric feudal knight).
Sankin-kotai: shogun law obliging *daimyo* to reside periodically in Edo.
Sansho: hot pepper used exclusively with eel dishes.
Sashimi: raw seafood, usually served as an hors d'œuvre with various garnishes.
Satori: a state of enlightenment in Zen Buddhism.
Sei-i-tai-shogun: great generalissimo for the subjugation of barbarians.
Senshu: pure sake, practically impossible to find on the market.
Sento: public baths (more social than functional).
Seppuku: ritual suicide (disembowelment); called *hara-kiri* by Westerners.
Sessho: regents of the Imperial family, who ruled Japan in their name.
Shabu-shabu: dish similar to *sukiyaki* but with a different bouillon.
Shakkei: borrowed landscape; a garden design using the local environment.
Shamisen: three-stringed musical instrument similar to a mandolin.
Shariden: Holy Relics Hall in a Buddhist temple.
Shibumi: Zen school of subtle and refined garden landscaping.
Shi: city (administrative division).
Shin: new.
Shinden: main building of a formal Heian- or Kamakura- period temple.
Shinkansen: high-speed railway line, called the Bullet Train by Westerns.
Shiruko: sweet soup made of red beans and *mochi* (rice cakes).
Shiso: leaves of the beefsteak plant, used as a garnish on many dishes.
Shochu: alcohol made from grain, potatoes or even noodles *(soba shochu).*
Shogatsu: New Year's holiday (generally lasting several days).
Shogitai: partisans of the shogun during the Imperial Restoration.
Shoji: wood-and-paper door.
Shojin ryori: strictly vegetarian cuisine eaten by Buddhist monks.
Shoro: belfry in Buddhist temple complexes.
Shoyu: Japanese soy sauce (dark and amber types).
Shunga: erotic wood-block prints of the Edo period.
Soba: thin, brown buckwheat noodles eaten either hot or cold.
Soto: the outside (other people, foreigners and other nations).
Suiboku: in art, the use of lines to evoke volumes.
Suijo basu: waterbus; ferryboat service on the Sumida River in Tokyo.
Sukiyaki: pseudo-Japanese dish of grilled beef, *tofu* and vegetables.
Sumi-e: China-ink monochrome paintings.
Sumo: a popular form of Japanese wrestling.
Sumotori: sumo wrestlers.
Suppon ryori: cusine based on *suppon* (turtle).
Surippa: slippers worn inside traditional Japanese buildings.
Sushi: raw fish and rice.
Sushiya: sushi restaurant.

Tabi: Japanese socks.
Takenokozoku: bamboo shoots; Japanese punks.
Taki no: torchlight.
Takoyaki: octopus croquettes, frequently sold by street vendors.
Takushi: taxi.
Tamago: sort of Japanese omelette.
Tanka: traditional *choka* poem of 31 (or, 5-7-, 5-7, 7) syllables.
Tatamaki-e: three-dimensional lacquerworks.

Tatami: floor mats made of rice straw.
Tatemae: that which is thought but never said (see Honne).
Teien: Japanese garden.
Teishoku: fixed-price lunch menu (usually a good bargain).
Tempura: fish-and-vegetable fritters, introduced by the Portuguese.
Tempuraya: tempura restaurant.
Tenchijin: sky-man-earth; popular school of flower arranging.
Teppan yaki: iron-fry; grilled meat and shrimp.
Tenno: he who comes from the sky; the emperor of Japan.
Temizuya: ablution basin at a Shinto shrine.
Tetsuhachi: eating bowl used by Buddhist monks.
Tofu: soy bean curd.
Tofu ryori: Buddhist-inspired vegetarian cusine based on *tofu.*
Toire: toilet.
Tokonoma: picture alcove or small niche reserved for a bouquet or a scroll.
Tokkyu: limited express train that stops only at major cities.
Tome oki: Poste Restante (General Delivery).
Tomoe dengaku: tofu brochettes.
Tonkatsu: breaded pork cutlets.
Torii: wooden two-pillared gateway to a Shinto Shrine.
Toro: fatty tuna.
Toruco: Turkish baths; bath-house/brothel (not to be confused with *sento).*
Tosa: school of painting from the Late Heian to the Edo periods.
Toshiya: archery tournament.
Tsuba: metal scabbard for Japanese swords.
Tsubo: surface area equivalent to two tatami, or about 36 sq ft/ 3.3. sq m.
Tsukemono: salted vegetables.
Tsukimochi: moon cakes; that is cakes in the shape of the moon *(tsuki).*
Tsukudani: fish conserved in soy sauce.

Uchi: the inner (family, village and Japan) as opposed to the outside.
Udon: thick, white wheat noodles.
Ugusia: see *Uguisubari.*
Uguisubari: nightingale floors, that is a parquet that 'chirps' when walked on.
Uji: clan.
Ukiyo-e: floating world picture; colour wood-block prints of the Edo period.
Ume: apricot tree.
Umi: sea.
Unagi: eel, generally served grilled *(kabayaki).*
Unagiya: eel restaurant.
Uni: sea urchin or sea chestnut.

Washi: Japanese paper-making; a highly developed art that originated in the 7th century AD.

Yakata: robe worn at public baths.
Yakiniku: Korean restaurants, also called Korean barbecue.
Yakisoba: fried noodles, frequently sold by street vendors.
Yakitori: grilled chicken brochettes.
Yakitori kosu: assorted *yakitori* menu including chicken and vegetables.
Yakitoriya: yakitori restaurant.
Yakuza: gangsters (more prevalent in Japan than is commonly thought).
Yama: mountain.
Yamato-e: Japanese picture; insular style of painting from the Fujiwara period.
Yokozuna: greatly coveted hemp belt worn by unbeaten sumo wrestlers.
Yuba: dried soy paste used by Buddhist monks.

Yudofu: simmered bean curd of Kyoto cuisine.
Yukata: robe similar to a kimono, worn indoors.
Yusoku ryori: Imperial cuisine.

Za: artisans guild.
Zabuton: flat cushions used in Japanese homes instead of chairs.
Zashiki: teahouses renting reception rooms for entertaining with geishas.
Zazen: Zen Buddhist seated meditation.
Zen: disciplined Buddhist school based on *dhyana* (meditation).
Zori: straw sandals.
Zosui: warm rice and egg mixed with *fugu* bouillon.

Buddhas and other Gods

Amida *(Amitabha):* Buddha of Infinite Light. The great protector of humanity, his paradise is open to all. He remains on earth until he has saved all people. Favoured by the Shinshu and Jodo sects, he is commonly shown enthroned in paradise or rising from behind a mountain.

Fugen Bosatsu *(Samantabhadra):* Buddha of Wisdom. He understands the motives of all human action and is usually shown seated on a lotus supported by white elephants at the end of the 'path of wisdom'.

Gautama Buddha: The Historical Buddha or Siddhartha Gautama (563-483 BC), who lived, taught and died in north-east India. The son of the king of the Sakyas, a warrior tribe, he is also known as Sakyamuni. The original teachings of Gautama were rational and agnostic.

Jizo Bosatsu *(Kshitigarbha):* Revered in China as the Judge of Souls, he is worshipped in Japan as the patron of children, pregnant women and travelers. The protector of all humanity, he is frequently portrayed as a merry pilgrim. Jizo has inspired great artists whose masterpieces may be seen in numerous temples; roughly carved images may also be seen along country roads. Usually represented as a Buddhist monk, he is able to redeem the sinful from hell and deliver them into eternal paradise.

Kannon Bosatsu *(Avalokitesvara):* Buddha the Merciful, the most compassionate of the Bodhisattvas. Frequently portrayed in female form, this divinity has seven major manifestations, including Kannon-of-the-Eleven-Heads (Juichimen Kannon), Horse-Headed Kannon (Bato Kannon) and Kannon-of-the-Thousand-Arms (Senju Kannon).

Miroku Bosatsu *(Maitreya):* The Future Buddha, who will reappear on earth 5670 million years after the Buddha enters Nirvana. Statues normally show him seated cross-legged with his head bent.

Shaka Buddha *(Sakyamuni):* The Historical Buddha (see above).

Yakushi Nyorai *(Bhaishajyaguru):* Buddha the Healer, the god of medicine. A popular divinity in Japan from the 8th century onward, he is usually represented holding a flask of medicine in one hand.

USEFUL VOCABULARY

For pronunciation, see pp. 59-60.

Common phrases

Courtesy

Goodbye	*Sayonara*
See you soon	*Dewa mata*
Good morning	*O hayo gozaimasu*
Good afternoon	*Konnichi wa*
Good evening	*Konban wa*
Good night	*O yasumi nasai*
Have a good journey	*O genki de/Itte irasshai*
How are you?	*O genki desu ka?*
I'm fine, thanks	*O akesama de*
How do you do?	*Hajimemashite*
Excuse me, sorry	*Sumimasen/Gomennasai*
You're welcome	*Doitashimashite*
Thank you	*Arigato/Arigato gozaimasu*
No	*Iie*
Yes	*Hai*
Please	*Onegai shimasu/Kudasai*
It was delicious	*Gochisosama deshita*

Introductions

This is Mr (Mrs, Miss) (person's name)	*Kochira wa* (person's name) *san desu*
What is your name?	*Nan to iu namae desu ka?*
My name is (your name)	(Your name) *to iimasu*
I am (your name)	(Your name) *desu*
Do you speak English?	*Eigo a hanasemaku ka?*
I speak a little Japanese	*Nihongo ga sukoshi dekimasu*
Do you understand?	*Wakarimasu ka?*
Yes, I understand	*Hai, wakarimasu*
No, I don't understand	*Iie, wakarimasen*
What is this?	*Kore wa nan desu ka?*
What does that mean?	*Do iu imi desu ka?*
What does this word/sign/symbol mean?	*Kono kotoba/kono kigo/kono shirushi wa do iu imi desu ka?*
How?	*Dono yo ni?*
How do you say this in Japanese?	*Nihongo de nan to iimasu ka?*

Numbers

Zero	*Re*
One	*Ichi*
Two	*Ni*
Three	*San*
Four	*Shi/yon*
Five	*Go*
Six	*Roku*
Seven	*Shichi/nana*
Eight	*Hachi*
Nine	*Kyu/ku*
Ten	*Ju*
Eleven	*Ju ichi*
Twelve	*Ju ni*
Thirteen	*Ju san*
Fourteen	*Ju shi/ju yon*
Fifteen	*Ju go*

Sixteen	*Ju roku*
Seventeen	*Ju shichi / ju nana*
Eighteen	*Ju hachi*
Nineteen	*ju ku*
Twenty	*Ni ju*
Twenty-one	*Ni ju ichi*
Thirty	*San ju*
Forty	*Yon ju*
Fifty	*Go ju*
Sixty	*Roku ju*
Seventy	*Nana ju*
Eighty	*Hachi ju*
Ninety	*Kyu ju*
One hundred	*Hyaku*
Two hundred	*Ni hyaku*
Three hundred	*San hyaku*
Four hundred	*Yon hyaku*
Five hundred	*Go hyaku*
Six hundred	*Roppyaku*
Seven hundred	*Nana hyaku*
Eight hundred	*Happyaku*
Nine hundred	*Kyu hyaku*
One thousand	*Sen / issen*
Two thousand	*Ni sen*
Three thousand	*Sanzen*
Four thousand	*Yon sen*
Five thousand	*Go sen*
Six thousand	*Roku sen*
Seven thousand	*Nana sen*
Eight thousand	*Hassen*
Nine thousand	*Kyu sen*
Ten thousand	*Ichi man*

The Japanese count by units of ten thousand *(man)*. Twenty thousand is two ten thousands *(ni man)* and a million is a hundred ten thousands *(hyaku man)*. A hundred million is *ichi oku*.

Twenty thousand	*Ni man*
Thirty thousand	*San man*
One hundred thousand	*Ju man*
Two hundred thousand	*Ni ju man*
One million	*Hyaku man*
Ten million	*Sen man*

Time

Year	*Nen/toshi*
One year	*Ichi nen*
Two years	*Ni nen*
Years (old)	*Sai*

Month	*Tsuki/getsu/gatsu*
January	*Ichigatsu*
February	*Nigatsu*
March	*Sangatsu*
April	*Shigatsu*
May	*Gogatsu*
June	*Rokugatsu*
July	*Shichigatsu*
August	*Hachigatsu*
September	*Kugatsu*
October	*Jugatsu*
November	*Juichigatsu*
December	*Junigatsu*

Week .... *Shu/shukan*
Day .... *Hi/hiru/jitsu*
Monday .... *Getsuyobi*
Tuesday .... *Kayobi*
Wednesday .... *Suiyobi*
Thursday .... *Monkuyobi*
Friday .... *Kinyobi*
Saturday....................... *Doyobi*
Sunday .... *Nichiyobi*
Public holiday .... *Kyujitsu*

Now .... *Ima*
Today .... *Kyo*
Yesterday...................... *Kino*
Tomorrow .... *Ashita*
Morning .... *Asa*
In the morning................. *Gozenchu*
Afternoon...................... *Gogo*
Evening........................ *Yugata/ban*
Night.......................... *Yoru*
This morning .... *Kesa*
This afternoon................. *Kyo no gogo*
This evening .... *Komban*
Tomorrow evening .... *Myoban*
Tonight....................... *Konya*
Noon.......................... *Ohiru*
Midnight...................... *Mayonaka*

A few expressions
When ? .... *Itsu?*
What time is it?................ *Ima nanji desu ka?*
At what time? .... *Nan ji ni?*
What day (date) is it?.......... *Kyo wa nan nichi desu ka?*
How old are you? .... *O ikutsu desu ka?*
I am (thirty) .... *(san ju) sai desu*

At customs

Alcohol .... *Arukoru*
Consulate...................... *Ryojikan*
Customs....................... *Zeikan*
Embassy....................... *Taishikan*
Export .... *Yushutsu*
Foreigner .... *Gaikokujin*
Frontier....................... *Kokkyo*
Passport...................... *Ryoken*
Quarantine.................... *Ken eki*
Tobacco....................... *Tabako*
Vaccination .... *Shuto*
Visa .... *Biza*

A few expressions
What is the purpose
  of your journey .... *Taizai no mokuteki wa?*
Tourism .... *Kanko desu ka*
How long do you plan
  to stay in Japan?............. *Dono kurai nihon de taizai shimasu ka?*
Three weeks; one month .... *San shukan; ikagetsu*
How much money
  do you have? .... *Okane wa dono kurai omochi desu ka?*
I have £1000
  and $500.................... *Ichimangosen furan to gohyaku ka?*
Do you have anything
  to declare?................... *Shinkoku suru mono ga arimasu ka?*

No, nothing .... *Arimasen*
These are gifts/
  personal items .... *Omiyage (okurimono)/irui desu*

In the street

Bank .... *Ginko*
Barber....................... *Tokoyasan*
Beach (resort) .... *Amabe (kaisuiyokujo)*
Bridge........................ *Hashi, bashi*
Building .... *Tatemono*
Cinema....................... *Eigakan*
Hairdresser .... *Biyoin (not byoin, hospital)*
Here/there/over there .... *Koko/soko/asoko*
Hospital .... *Byoin*
Information office .... *Kanko annaijo*
Museum...................... *Hakubutsukan*
Museum of art .... *Bijutsukan*
Park/gardens .... *Niwam/koen*
Pharmacy..................... *Kusuriya*
Police .... *Keisatsu*
Policeman (officer) .... *Junsa (omawarisan)*
Port .... *Minato*
Store (shop) .... *Omise*
Square .... *Hiroba*
Station (railway) .... *Eki*
Street .... *Dori*
Theatre....................... *Gekijo*
Town hall .... *Shiyakusho*
Exit .... *Deguchi*

A few expressions

Where are you going? .... *Doko e irasshaimasu ka?*
I am going to (place name)....... *(Place name) e ikimasu*
I would like to go
  to (place name).............. *(Place name) e ikitai (desu)*
Where....................... *Doko*
From where.................... *Doko kara*
To where .... *Doko made*
Where is it? .... *Doko desu ka?*
Where is (place name)? .... *(Place name) wa doko desu ka?*
Could you show me   *Kono chizu no naka de (place name)*
  (place name) on this map? ...... *o oshiete kudasai?*
Could you draw me a map? .... *Chizu o kaite kudasai?*
Is there a pharmacy .... *Kono chikaku ni Kusuriya (byoin,*
  (hospital, doctor) nearby?   *oishasan) ga arimasu ka?*

Car and taxi

Car .... *Jidosha*
Driver .... *Untenshu*
Fare......................... *Unchin*
Garage .... *Gareji*
Gasoline (petrol) .... *Gasorin*
Gasoline (petrol) station .... *Gasorin-stando*
Taxi .... *Takushi*

A few expressions

Please ring for a taxi.............. *dozo, denwa de takushi wo yonde kudasai*
Please take me here .... *Koko e tsurete itte kudasai*
Please take me to
  the station .... *eki made tsurete itte kudasai*
Go straight ahead................ *Massugu ni*
On the right .... *Migi e*

On the left .... *Hidari e*
Stop here, please .... *Koko de tomatte kudasai*
Wait here, please .... *Koko de matte kudasai*
I'll be back in a second .... *Sugu ni kaerimasu*

Other forms of transport

Airport .... *Kuko*
Arrival .... *Tochaku*
Boat .... *Boto/fune/kisen*
Booking office .... *Shussatsu guchi*
Bus .... *Basu*
Changing trains................. *Kisha wo norikaeru*
Check room..................... *Nimotsu azukarijo/koin rokka*
Class (1st, 2nd) .... *To (itto, nito)*
Departure...................... *Shuppatsu*
Destination .... *Mokutekichi/yukisaki*
Dining car...................... *Shokudosha*
Disembark (to) .... *Joriku suru*
Embark (to) .... *Josen suru*
Express (train)................. *Kyuko*
Journey .... *Ryoko*
Ferry boat .... *Renrakusen/feri boto*
Left luggage .... *Nimotsu azukarijo/koin rokka*
Local (train) .... *Donko*
Luggage....................... *Nimotsu*
Passenger .... *Jokyaku/senkyaku* (boat)
Plane.......................... *Hikoki*
Platform (station) .... *Homu*
Platform n° 1 .... *Ichiban-sen*
Porter .... *Akabo*
Rapid (train)................... *Tokkyu*
Reservation .... *Yoyaku*
Reserved seat .... *Yoyaku seki/shitei seki*
Seat .... *Seki*
Semi-express (train)............ *Junkyu*
Sleeper....................... *Shindai*
Sleeping car .... *Shindaisha*
Station .... *Eki*
Subway (underground) .... *Chikatetsu*
Ticket .... *Kippu*
Trains, railways .... *Kisha*
Tram.......................... *Densha*

A few expressions

Have a good journey .... *Itte irasshai/o genki de*

Where is the booking
   office?........................ *Shussatsu guchi wa doko desu ka?*

What day are you leaving? .... *Itsu odekake desu ka?*

I leave on (date) .... (Date) *ni dekake masu*

When does the train
  for (place name) leave? .... (Place name) *yuko no kisha wa
    nanji ni demasu ka?*

When does the train
  get to (place name)? .... *Kono kisha wa nan ji ni* (place
    name) *e tsukimasu ka?*

Then I will go to (place name) ..... *Sorekara* (place name) *e ikisasu*

I'd like a first-class
  single to (place name) .... (Place name) *yuki no itto o ichimai
    kudasai*

I'd like a second class
  return to (place name)......... (Place name) *yuki no ofuku no nito
    o ichimai kudasai*

Are there any
  sleeping cars? .... *Shindaisha ga tsuite imasu ka?*

I'd like to reserve two   (Place name) *made, shindai ken*
  sleepers for (place name) .... *ni mai kudasai*

How much will it
  cost to go to (place name) ...... (Place name) *made ikura desu ka?*

Which platform does the   (Place name) *yuki wa nan ban kara*
  (place name) train leave from?... *desu ka?*

Platform n° 3 .... *San ban desu*

Single .... *Katamichi*

Return........................ *Ofuku*

Is this the train for (place name) ... (Place name) *Yuki no densha*
                       desu ka?

Is it necessary to
  change trains?................ *Norikaeru koto ga hitsuyo desu ka?*

Hotels and restaurants

Air conditioned	*Reidanbo*
Bathroom......................	*Furoba/Basu rumu*
Beans	*Mame*
Bed	*Nedoko* (Japanese) ; *betto* (Western)
Beef	*Gyuniku*
Beefsteak.....................	*Bifuteki*
Beer	*Biru*
Bill	*Kanjo*
Blanket/cover	*Kake buton/mofu*
Bread	*Pan*
Breakfast	*Choshoku*
Bottle	*Bin*
Bowl/cup	*Chawan/koppu*
Butter	*Bata*
Café	*Kissaten*
Cake	*O kashi* (Japanese); *keki* (Western)
Cancel	*Torikesu*
Cashier	*Suito gakari*
Central heating	*Danbo*
Chambermaid	*Jochu/meido*
Change.......................	*Kozeni*
Cheese	*Chizu*
Check	*Kogitte*
Chicken	*Niwatori*
Chopsticks....................	*Hashi*
Cigar	*Hamaki*
Cigarette	*Makitabako*
Clean (verb)	*Soji suru*
Coffee........................	*Kohi*
Cook	*Ryori nin* (Japanese); *kokku* (Western)
Crab	*Kani*
Dining room...................	*Shokudo*
Dinner........................	*Yushoku*
Director	*Shihainin/maneja*
Dish..........................	*O sara*
Drink	*Nomimono*
Drinkable	*Nomeru*
Eel	*Unagi*
Eggs	*Tamago*
Elevator	*Erebeta*

Emergency	*Hioji/kyuyo*
Face towel	*Tenugui* (Japanese); *taoru* (Western)
Fish	*Sakana*
Fork	*Hoku*
Fruit	*Kudamono*
Fruit juice	*(Furutsu) jusu*
Full	*Man in desu*
Glass	*Koppu*
Ground floor	*Ikkai*
Hall	*Robi*
Horseradish	*Wasabi*
Hotel	*Ryokan* (Japanese) *hoteru* (Western)
Hot napkin	*O shibori*
Key	*Kagi*
Knife	*Naifu*
Lemon	*Remon*
Lemonade	*Saida*
Luggage	*Nimotsu*
Lunch	*Chushoku*
Massage	*Amma/massaji*
Meal	*Shokuji*
Meat	*Niku*
Menu	*Menyu*
Milk	*Gyunyu/miruku*
Napkin	*Napkin*
Omelette	*Omuretsu*
Pepper	*Kosho*
Pillow	*Makura*
Potatoes	*Jagaimo/poteto*
Radiator	*Sutobu*
Raw	*Nama* (also used for draught beer, *nama biru*)
Receipt	*Ryoshusho*
Refrigerator	*Reizoko*
Reservation	*Yoyaku*
Restaurant	*Ryoriya* (Japanese); *resutoran* (Western)
Rice (cooked)	*Gohan*
Room	*Heya/Shinshitsu*
Salt	*Shio*
Sandwich	*Sandoitchi*
Sheets	*Shitsu*
Shower	*Shawa*
Shrimp	*Ebi*
Spicy	*Togarashi*
Spoon	*Supun*
Storey (2nd/3rd)	*Kai (nikkai/sangai)*
Sugar	*Sato*
Tea	*O cha* (Japanese); *ko cha* (Western)
Telephone	*Denwa*
Television	*Terebi*
Toilet (w.c.)	*Semmenjo/benjo*
Tomato	*Tomato*
Tuna	*Maguro*
Vegetables	*Yasai*
Waiter	*Boisan*
Waitress	*Ojosan*
Water	*Mizu*
Water (hot)	*O yu*
Water (mineral)	*Mineraru uota*

Water (drinking) .... *Nomi mizu*
Wine .... *Budo shu*

A few expressions

With a shower (without) .... *Shawa tsuki (nashi)*
Please come here................ *Kite kudasai*
This isn't clean .... *Kore wa kirei dewa arimasen*
May I sit here?................... *Koko e kakete mo ii desu ka?*
Yes, please .... *Hai, dozo*
No, this place is taken .... *Iie, koko wa fusagatte imasu*
Vacant/occupied .... *Aiteiru/aiteinai*
I am (I am not) hot .... *Atsui/atsukunai*
I am (I am not) cold .... *Samui/samukunai*
I am (I am not) hungry .... *Onakaga suita/onakaga suiteinai*
I am (I am not) thirsty .... *Nodo ga kawaiteimasu/nodoga kawaiteinai*

Post office and telephones

Airmail .... *Kokubin*
Envelope .... *Futo*
For (the USA) .... *(USA) yuki*
Hello .... *Moshi moshi*
Mail .... *Yubin*
Mailbox, postbox .... *Posuto*
Ordinary mail .... *Futsu yubin*
Package .... *Kozutsumi*
Picture postcard .... *Ehagaki*
Postcard....................... *Hagaki*
Post office .... *Yubinkyoku*
Registered .... *Kaki tome*
Special delivery .... *Soku tatsu*
Stamp......................... *Kitte*
Telegram .... *Dempo/denshin*
Telephone .... *Denwa*
Telephone number............... *Denwa bango*

A few expressions

Where is the nearest post office? .. *Yubinkyoku wa doko desu ka?*
Where is the central post office?... *Chuoyubinkyoku wa doko desu ka?*
What is the postage for this *letter?* *Kono tegami no soryo wa ikura desu ka?*
Where is the telegram (Poste Restante) office? .... *Dempokyoku (kyokudomari) wa doko desu ka?*
I would like to send a telegram .... *Dempo o uchitai desu ga*
How much by the word?.......... *Ichigo ikura desu ka?*

In shops

Book .... *Hon*
Camera........................ *Kamera*
Cash .... *Genkin*
Cashier........................ *Kaikei*
Cheap/inexpensive.............. *Yasui*
Cloisonné (enamel work).......... *Shippoyaki*
Computer...................... *Kompiuta*
Doll .... *Ningyo*
Duty-free .... *Muzei*
Expensive..................... *Takai*
Fan .... *Uchiwa/sensu*
Film (roll of) .... *Fuirumu*
Flower......................... *Hana*
Gift .... *Okurimono/omiyage*

Kite	*Tako*
Lacquerware	*Urushi*
Map (road)	*(Doro) chizu*
Medicine	*Kusuri*
Mirror	*Kagami*
Newspaper	*Shimbun*
Pottery/porcelain	*Setomono/yakimono*
Price	*Nedan*
Radio	*Rajio*
Screens (folding)	*Byobu*
Sword (Japanese)	*Katana*

Colours

Black	*Kuroi*
Blue	*Aoi*
Brown	*Chairo*
Green	*Midori*
Grey	*Nezumiiro*
Orange	*Orenjiiroi*
Pink	*Pinku*
Red	*Akai*
Violet	*Murasakiiroi*
White	*Shiroi*
Yellow	*Kiiroi*

A few expressions

I want to do some shopping	*Kaimono o shitai desu*
I would like to buy (item)	*(Item) o kaitai desu ga*
Do you have, is there?	*Arimasu ka?*
Which (item) do you want?	*Dono (item) hoshii desu ka?*
How much? (price)	*Ikura?*
How much? (quantity)	*Dono kurai?*
I like this one	*Kore ga suki desu*
I would like this one	*Kore ga hoshii desu*
All right? Is that OK?	*Ii desu ka?/Daijobu desu ka?*
Yes, it is	*Ii desu yo*
No, it isn't	*Dame desu*
I'll take it	*Kore o itadakimasu*
I don't like that one	*Sore wa kirai desu*
How much is this one?	*Kore wa ikura desu ka?*
It's too expensive	*Takasugimasu*
It's very expensive	*Totemo takai*
Could you lower the price?	*Benkyo shite kudasai?*
I would like a receipt	*Ryoshusho o kudasai*

Emergencies

Fire!	*Kaji da!*
Help!	*Tasuketekure!*
Thief!	*Dorobo da!*

A few kanji to know

Men	男（紳士）
Women	女（婦人）
Exit	出口
Emergency exit	非常口
Entrance.......................	入口
Station	駅
North, south, east, west..........	北、南、東、西
Information	案内所
Trains: rapid, express, local	特急、急行、普通
Danger	注意、危険

Numbers

1	一
2	二
3	三
4	四
5	五
6	六
7	七
8	八
9	九
10	十
100.............................	百
1000	千
10,000	万

SUGGESTED READING

Bayrd, Edwin, *Kyoto: Japan's Ancient Capital* (Newsweek, New York, 1981).

Benedict, Ruth, *The Chrysanthemum and the Sword: Patterns of Japanese Culture* (New American Library, 1967).

Booth, Alan, *The Roads to Sata: a 2000 Mile Walk through Japan* (Viking/Penguin, London, 1985).

Clavell, James, *Shogun* (Dell, 1975).

Collcutt, Martin, Jansen, Marius and Kumakura, Isao, *Cultural Atlas of Japan* (Phaidon Press, Oxford, 1988).

Ekiguchi, Kunio and McCreery, Ruth S., *A Japanese Touch for the Seasons* (Kodansha International, Tokyo/New York, 1987).

Hamlyn All Colour Oriental Cookbook (Hamlyn Publishing Co. Ltd, London, 1989).

Hearn, Lafcadio, *Writing from Japan* (Penguin, 1985).

Keene, Donald, *Anthology of Japanese Litterature* (Grove Press, 1955).

Komoda, Shusui and Pointer, Horst, *Ikebana: Spirit and Technique — The Japanese Art of Flower Arranging* (Blandford Press, Poole, 1980).

Lowe, John, *Into Japan* (John Murray, London, 1985).

McInerney, Jay, *Ransom* (Vintage, 1985).

Macintyre, Michael, *The Shogun Inheritance: Japan and the Legacy of the Samurai* (Collins/BBC, London, 1981).

Marasaki-Shikibu, *The Tale of Genji* (Knopf, 1978).

Morley, John David, *Pictures from the Water Trade: an Englishman in Japan* (Andre Deutsch, London, 1985).

Morris, Ivan, *The Nobility of Failure: Tragic Heroes in the History of Japan (Holt, Rinehart and Winston, New York, 1975).*

Picken, Stuart D. B., *Buddhism: Japan's Cultural Identity* (Kodansha, 1982) and *Shinto: Japan's Spiritual Roots* (Kodansha, 1980).

Reischauer, Edwin O., *Japan: The Story of a Nation* (Knopf, 1974) and *The Japanese* (Harvard University Press, 1977).

Stanley-Baker, Joen, *Japanese Art* (Thames & Hudson, London, 1984).

Tsuji, Shizuo, *Japanese Cooking: a Simple Art (Kodansha, New York, 1981).*

Warner, Langdon, *Enduring Art of Japan* (Grove Press, 1985).

Watson, William, *The Great Japan Exhibition: Art of the Edo Period, 1600-1868* (Royal Academy of Arts/Weidenfeld & Nicolson, London, 1981).

World Travel Series Map of Japan (Bartholomew, Edinburgh, 1987).

For the Jidai Matsuri festival in Kyoto, a participator in the procession dressed in an 18th-century Samurai costume.

INDEX